MILITARY TRIBUNALS AND INTERNATIONAL CRIMES

By

JOHN ALAN APPLEMAN, A.B., M.A., J.D.
of the Illinois Bar

GREENWOOD PRESS, PUBLISHERS
WESTPORT, CONNECTICUT

Originally published in 1954 by The Bobbs-Merrill Company, Inc., Indianapolis, Indiana

Reprinted with the permission of John Appleman

Reprinted in 1971 by Greenwood Press, Inc., 51 Riverside Avenue, Westport, Conn. 06880

Library of Congress catalog card number 76-152589
ISBN 0-8371-6022-7

Printed in the United States of America

10 9 8 7 6 5 4 3 2

The Palace of Justice at Nuremberg, where many of the proceedings were held.

INTRODUCTION

For those having no prior familiarity with the question of the trial of so-called war criminals conducted at the close of World War II, some introductory statement is in order.

It was the intention of the Allied Powers, in these proceedings, to accomplish several things: (1) To punish civilian and military leaders for waging aggressive war and thereby to retard war mongering and to increase the possibilities for a permanent peace; (2) To punish persons responsible for the commission of war crimes; (3) To crystallize certain laws of humanity and thereby to deter the repetition of genocide and other oppressions of minority groups and aliens. There were other objectives as well, but those were the primary purposes. Points 1 and 3 came under particularly bitter attack.

It is the purpose of this work to examine into these various proceedings and to determine, first, the legal right to conduct the proceedings; second, the fairness or unfairness of the procedures employed and sentences handed down. Another objective is to attempt to codify the substantive rules of the international law of war and the rules of procedure and evidence as derived from these proceedings to make them available to prosecutors, defense counsel, and judges in similar proceedings in the future.

It is not a simple task to analyze a number of important trials. The analysis of a single trial is a major task and a hazardous one. In the present instance, there was involved the study of numerous volumes of printed proceedings, several hundred volumes of mimeographed proceedings, several hundred thousands of pages of testimony and documents available only in typed or mimeographed form, a number of analytical and critical books upon this subject, many volumes concerning the past history and accepted rules of international law, and numerous articles in the field of international law or presenting analytical criticisms of these proceedings. There was also involved conversations and correspondence with judges, attorneys, court reporters, and others who participated in these trials.

It is believed that the factual material contained in this work will not be subject to much criticism. It is as accurate as possible within human limitations. There are those who may disagree with certain conclusions, particularly some professors of international law. The author does not pretend to be an expert in that field. While he received his undergraduate and graduate degrees in international law, both prior to and subsequent to receiving his degree of Doctor of Law, he is primarily a trial lawyer. It is as a trial lawyer that this subject has been approached, bearing in mind the fundamental purpose of all law, which is to accomplish substantial justice.

The author might add that in some cases his conclusions came as a surprise to him. He had approached this subject with somewhat of a preconceived notion against the validity of the trials. Any such feelings were, however, laid aside in order to report this material accurately. The author further believes that one should not purport to criticize any of the particular proceedings unless he has actually read the transcripts of evidence and has had some experience as a trial lawyer. These trials can be evaluated only upon the basis of study and not of prejudice.

Whatever one's opinion may be of the propriety or fairness of the trials, they are of the utmost importance historically. This was the first time that those in command of a nation's destinies have been called to general account. True, there have been isolated instances where losing leaders have been exiled or slain, but these were the price of defeat, not lawlessness. Henceforth, no leader can initiate or wage war with impunity. It is no longer his victory if he succeeds and the nation's loss if he loses. He may be called to personal account in future tribunals.

However this may operate, whether to the advantage or disadvantage of this nation, it offers a great opportunity for peace. As a lawyer, the author has little faith in the compromises of statesmen. More wars have been stimulated than have been avoided by these means. The author has great confidence in the processes of justice. Whether a judge is selected from this nation, from continental Europe, or South America makes little difference. Jurists are grounded in the fundamental concepts of justice—of weighing evidence and of making a decision thereon. This has been evident from the decisions of the Permanent Court of International Justice, as well as those of courts handling problems solely of national jurisprudence. The elimination of judgments by passion and prejudice and the substitution of reasoned justice presents a threat to any potential violator of international peace. And if a tribunal may be created where statesmen and nations may be called to account for acts leading to aggressive war, prior to its outbreak, the threat of wars may be reduced. No man, no nation, is above the laws of common decency and morality. No man may stand higher than, or be exempt from, the law.

This result may be overly optimistic in view of the immaturity of our civilization. However, violent death is not pleasant. Violent death in war is no more pleasant than death by accident in time of peace. War itself is an anachronism. If these trials point a way toward reduction or elimination of war through the judicial process, it will be a landmark in the direction of peace greater than any yet discovered. Whether or not this result is achieved, the trials are of tremendous historical significance. It is the first time in history that an effort has been made, through the testimony of military and political leaders, and thousands of official documents, to evaluate the causes of war and the steps leading to its outbreak. Propaganda and pretexts are brushed aside; the remaining material is history in a vivid and accurate form.[1] It is the first time, also, that the rise of political and social beliefs has been given through the lips of a nation's leaders under oath and from writings set down at a time when they spoke freely, with no thought of having later to explain them. It is the first time, as well, that the underlying causes for crimes against humanity have been accurately analyzed.

Now, let us look briefly to the origin of the various proceedings to see what types of cases are discussed in this work.

Most nations were shocked by reports of mass murders in Germany and countries overrun by it of Jews and other races, prior to the outbreak of World War II. However, nothing was done to deter that nation in its actions. Whether non-action was due to disbelief of the atrocity stories or a feeling that no nation could restrain another in its internal actions is not clear. At least, no action was taken at that time. Nor was any real action taken to stop German invasion of other territory, such as the Ruhr, Austria, and Czechoslovakia.

However, after the outbreak of hostilities, official protests were lodged by various Allied governments against German war practices in 1940. The United States protested in 1941. In January of 1942, the St. James Declaration was issued by nine allied powers, pledging as a principal war aim the punishment of those responsible for war crimes. In November, 1943, the United States, Great Britain, and the Soviet Union at the Moscow Conference laid the foundation for the post-war trials.

The Conference at London opened upon June 26, 1945 to consider this problem further. It was readily apparent that a

[1] To the same effect Dr. Hans Ehard, Minister-President of Bavaria, declared: "This task must, if it is to have permanent value, be performed without any preconceived ideas, in the spirit of law and of justice, which cannot be the task of a single people or of individual power groups, but must be the concern of the whole human race." "The Nuremberg Trial Against the Major War Criminals and International Law," 43 *American Journal of International Law*, p. 224, (April 1949).

form of procedure would have to be adopted which would embody the protections afforded under legal principles common to the United States, Great Britain, France, and the Soviet Union. The many differences in legal procedures followed by those nations led to a number of problems and the necessity for compromises.

The Charter of the International Military Tribunal at Nuremberg was established by the Conference at London upon August 8, 1945, detailing the nature of the crimes which would be considered and the procedure which would be followed by that tribunal. The purpose of the Charter was to establish that no man stands above international law or principles of common justice. It was determined to try a cross-section of military leaders, statesmen, administrators, bankers, industrialists, propagandists, and educators upon four blanket offenses: namely, crimes against peace, crimes against humanity, and war crimes, with the concept of conspiracy to commit such acts being recognized as a separate offense, in order to include both leaders and followers who had acted in concert to commit certain offenses. In addition, certain organizations were indicted as criminal groups to establish the principle of collective guilt. It was felt fitting that Nuremberg, which was generally regarded as the seat of the Nazi party, should be the place for its trial.

This trial opened November 14, 1945, and lasted nine months. The members of the Tribunal, who were four in number with four alternates, were selected from the United States, France, Great Britain, and Russia. Those same nations also furnished members of the prosecution, with the work of presentation of the evidence being divided among these prosecutors. Defense counsel in this hearing were exclusively Germans, selected by the defendants themselves, or assigned by the Tribunal where no request was made.

There was a total of 33 witnesses for the Prosecution plus several thousand documents introduced against the individual defendants. For the defense, 61 witnesses appeared plus 19 defendants, in addition to 143 witnesses by way of written interrogatories, together with voluminous documents. As to the indicted organizations, there were 101 witnesses plus 1,809 affidavits and 6 reports for the Prosecution introduced before hearing commissioners who reported to the Tribunal. For the defense, before the commissioners, 38,000 affidavits signed by 155,000 people were introduced for the Political Leaders, 136,213 for the SS, 10,000 for the SA, 7,000 for the SD, 3,000 for the General Staff, and 2,000 for the Gestapo. The Tribunal, in addition, heard 22 witnesses for these organizations. A complete stenographic record and an electrical recording was made of all the proceedings.

The proceedings of this trial were, accordingly, voluminous. The reported evidence comprises twenty-four printed volumes, with an additional seventeen of selected documents. The United States furnished the facilities for translation and interpretation. To illustrate the bulk of the materials used, the documents occupied 703,282,352 mimeographed pages, the paper weighing more than 4,000 tons and, stacked flat, reaching 47.4 miles in height. There were 2,296,958 photostats, 640,000 off-set prints, and 950,000 stencils.

Approximately six months after the start of the International Military Tribunal at Nuremberg and prior to its close, the International Military Tribunal for the Far East opened its hearings at Tokyo. It had a separate history, being preceded by the Cairo Declaration of December 1, 1943, the Potsdam Declaration of July 26, 1945, the Surrender Instrument of September 2, 1945, and the Moscow Conference of December 26, 1945. As a result of these instruments, General Douglas MacArthur was designated as Supreme Commander representing the interested nations, and the Charter was issued by him in that capacity upon January 19, 1946.

The Japanese defendants were arraigned upon May 3, 1946, and the judgment completed upon November 11, 1948, or two years later than that at Nuremberg. Eleven nations, namely, the United States, United Kingdom, China, Soviet Russia, France, Netherlands, Canada, Australia, New Zealand, India, and the Philippines participated in the furnishing of judges and members of the prosecution staff. The defense counsel were composed of both Japanese and American attorneys. The proceedings themselves have not been printed but have been bound, the evidence alone containing more than one hundred bound volumes, with an even greater number of volumes of documents. The indictment was wholly different from that at Nuremberg, being composed of many repetitious counts charging in effect the same general types of offenses. No organizations were indicted as criminal.

In the meantime, to try the secondary leaders of those same classes as had been tried by the International Military Tribunal at Nuremberg, a search was made throughout this country, and civilian judges were selected and brought to Germany for this purpose. Twelve subsequent Nuremberg trials were held, the first of these opening upon October 26, 1946, and the last one closing April 14, 1949. In a very real sense, these were international trials, in that by four-power agreement in the administration of Germany, Council Control Law 10 was adopted providing for these hearings.

Each of these subsequent Nuremberg hearings ran many thousands of pages alone. While there was largely a common type of procedure derived largely from the International Military Tribunal at Nuremberg, there were wide variations in the techniques employed and in the results secured. To illustrate the mere mechanical work involved in those hearings, there were 135,598 pages of transcript; 467 witnesses testified for the prosecution and 888 for the defense. 94 attorneys appeared for the prosecution; 375 for the defense, all but three of the latter being German. The prosecution in these 12 proceedings consumed 347 days and the defense 847. Since all of these proceedings were recorded on sound film, this required 273,800 feet of film. There were over 4,000 tons of paper used and over four million reproductions of legal exhibits for both sides.

In addition to the hearings previously referred to, each of the allied nations, in accordance with the Hague Rules of Land Warfare, set up military tribunals to try persons charged with war crimes. It should be understood immediately that these are not the same as courts-martial, but much of the procedure is quite similar. Exclusive of hearings conducted by Russia, as to which the author has no report, there are 2,116 known military tribunal hearings conducted by the United States, Great Britain, Australia, France, the Netherlands, Poland, Norway, Canada, China, and Greece. Of these, the United States conducted 950, of which 500 were held in Europe and 450 in the Pacific theater. While the author has not studied all of these transcripts, those to which he has had access show that the earliest of such hearings started on June 13, 1945, or approximately five months before the International Military Tribunal at Nuremberg. The last which is recorded herein ended upon January 12, 1949.

Other than these hearings, the only other ones of significance in this connection were those conducted by German courts and those by national courts. The Council Control laws provided for denazification or Spruckhammer courts for the trial of members of criminal organizations and, primarily, Nazis. The jurisdiction of these courts was limited, and the maximum punishment which they could fix was ten years. Those hearings started in 1945 and continued until quite recently. There have also been well publicized trials of traitors, such as that of Tokyo Rose and and Lord Haw Haw. These involved only violations of national and not of international law, and will not be considered.

Reference should only be made to one further class of hearings, and that is to the decisions of the United States Supreme

Court upon this subject. Following many of the trials, and particularly the subsequent Nuremberg hearings and those before military tribunals, hundreds of petitions for habeas corpus flooded our United States Supreme Court. Prior to that time this court had established certain controlling principles in the saboteurs' case of *Ex Parte Quirin.*[1] This was in line with earlier pronouncements of that court. When, however, the petitions for habeas corpus began streaming into Washington, an abrupt four to four split developed. Justice Jackson, because of his participation in the first hearing at Nuremberg, abstained initially from any participation in action upon those petitions. Almost uniformly, when these petitions for habeas corpus were denied, Justices Douglas, Black, Murphy, and Rutledge dissented. The law, however, pertaining to such writs was definitely established in June of 1950 in Johnson v. Eisentrager.[2] Combining this case with other pronouncements by the court, we find that the writ of habeas corpus does not apply in such cases.

In view of the great number of such hearings, it has been necessary to adopt an arbitrary division as to the materials discussed in this work. In general, the proceedings before the International Military Tribunal at Nuremberg established the controlling law and procedure. Therefore, major attention is devoted to that trial. The first half of this book deals with that hearing exclusively, being broken down into two basic categories, namely, the controlling law, and the procedure employed. Each of these subdivisions is broken down into appropriate chapters.

The second half of the book deals with the following hearings, in sequence; (1) The 12 subsequent Nuremberg Trials; (2) The International Military Tribunal for the Far East; (3) Trials befor Military Commissions; (4) Related proceedings; (5) Developments since Nuremberg. To avoid repetition, legal and procedural questions are not discussed except where they deviate from the first and major hearing or where they present a problem not encountered theretofore.

This study would not have been possible in its present form without the complete cooperation of many men. Credit is particularly owing to that eminent authority upon international relations, Dr. Clarence A. Berdahl of the University of Illinois. In addition, the following gentlemen have been of the greatest help: Honorable Robert H. Jackson, Justice of the Supreme Court; Honorable Louis A. Johnson, former Secretary of Defense; Brigadier General Telford Taylor; Colonel Edward H.

---

1 Ex parte Quirin; U. S. Ex Parte Quirin v. Cox, 317 U. S. 1, 63 S. Ct. 2, 87 L. Ed. 3.

2 Johnson v. Eisentrager, 339 U. S. 763, 70 S. Ct. 936, 94 L. Ed. 1255.

Young, Captain James J. Robinson, U. S. N.; Lieutenant Colonel Edward J. Murphy, Jr.; Edward F. Lyons, Jr.; Drexel Sprecher; Richard A. Olbeter; Irving Hayett; George Henry Tyne, and Rawlings Ragland.

TABLE OF CONTENTS

PART III

SUBSEQUENT NUREMBERG PROCEEDINGS

PART IV

INTERNATIONAL MILITARY TRIBUNAL FOR THE FAR EAST

PART V

MILITARY COMMISSIONS AND OTHER TRIBUNALS

PART VI

DEVELOPMENTS SINCE NUREMBERG

PART I

THE INTERNATIONAL MILITARY TRIBUNAL AT NUREMBERG

SUBSTANTIVE LAW

Courtroom scene, International Military Tribunal at Nuremberg. Tribunal in upper right hand corner; prosecution table in foreground; podium in right foreground; defense counsel in center; defendants at upper left, immediately in front of guard.

I

THE ACTORS IN THE DRAMA

It is often said by hawkers of programs that one cannot tell the actors without a program. Since the significant performance at Nuremberg involved many performers, it seems important first to identify them so that the defendants, counsel, and tribunal members can be identified readily. This same procedure will be followed as to all further hearings which are discussed in any detail.

Although a writer of fiction would object strongly to the reader skipping to the end of the story, we feel it advisable also to list the sentences imposed by the Tribunal. It will be seen, at once, that not all defendants—even though these particular persons had been charged as controlling the destiny of Germany during the period in question—were summarily condemned to death as leaders of a warring, but defeated, nation.

With this in mind, we introduce the *dramatis personnae* of this trial.

MEMBERS AND ALTERNATE MEMBERS OF THE TRIBUNAL

Lord Justice Lawrence, Member for the United Kingdom of Great Britain and Northern Ireland, President
Mr. Justice Birkett, Alternate Member
Mr. Francis Biddle, Member for the United States of America
Judge John J. Parker, Alternate Member
M. Le Professeur Donnediue De Vabres, Member for the French Republic
M. Le Conseiller R. Falco, Alternate Member
Major General I. T. Nikitchenko, Member for the Union of Soviet Socialist Republics
Lieutenant Colonel A. F. Volchkov, Alternate Member

Prosecution

United States of America

Chief of Counsel:
Mr. Justice Robert H. Jackson

Executive Trial Counsel:
Colonel Robert G. Storey
Mr. Thomas J. Dodd

Associate Trial Counsel:

Mr. Sidney S. Alderman
Brigadier General Telford Taylor
Colonel John Harlan Amen
Mr. Ralph G. Albrecht

Assistant Trial Counsel:

Colonel Leonard Wheeler, Jr.
Lieutenant Colonel William H. Baldwin
Lieutenant Colonel Smith W. Brockhart, Jr.
Commander James Britt Donovan, U.S.N.R.
Major Frank B. Wallis
Major William F. Walsh
Major Warren F. Farr
Captain Samuel Harris
Captain Drexel A. Sprecher
Lieutenant Commander Whitney R. Harris, U.S.N.R.
Lieutenant Thomas F. Lambert, Jr., U.S.N.R.
Lieutenant Henry K. Atherton
Lieutenant Brady O. Bryson, U.S.N.R.
Lieutenant (j.g.) Bernard D. Meltzer, U.S.N.R.
Dr. Robert M. Kempner
Mr. Walter W. Brudno

United Kingdom of Great Britain and Northern Ireland

Chief Prosecutor:

H. M. Attorney-General, Sir Hartley Shawcross, K.C., M.P.

Deputy Chief Prosecutor:

The Rt. Hon. Sir David Maxwell-Fyfe, P.C., K.C., M.P.

Leading Counsel:

Mr. G. D. Roberts, K.C., O. B.E.

Junior Counsel:

Lieutenant Colonel J. M. G. Griffith-Jones, M.C.
Colonel H. J. Phillimore, O. B.E.
Major F. Elwyn Jones, M.P.
Major J. Harcourt Barrington

French Republic

Chief Prosecutor:

M. Francois de Menthon
M. Auguste Champetier De Ribes

Deputy Chief Prosecutors:

M. Charles Dubost
M. Edgar Faure

Assistant Prosecutors (Chiefs of Sections):

M. Pierre Mounier
M. Charles Gerthoffer
M. Delphin Debenest

Assistant Prosecutors:

M. Jacques B. Herzog
M. Henry Delpech
M. Serge Fuster
M. Constant Quatre
M. Henri Monneray

Union of Soviet Socialist Republics

Chief Prosecutor:

General R. A. Rudenko

Deputy Chief Prosecutor:

Colonel Y. V. Pokrovsky

Assistant Prosecutors:

State Counsellor of Justice of the 2nd Class, L. R. Shenin
State Counsellor of Justice of the 2nd Class, M. Y. Raginsky
State Counsellor of Justice of the 3rd Class, N. D. Zorya
Chief Counsellor of Justice, L. N. Smirnov
Colonel D. S. Karev
Lieutenant Colonel J. A. Ozol
Captain V. V. Kuchin

Individual Defendants	Defense Counsel	Sentence
Hermann Wilhelm Goering	Dr. Otto Stahmer	Death
Joachim von Ribbentrop	Dr. Fritz Sauter (to January 5, 1946) Dr. Martin Horn (from January 5, 1946)	Death
Wilhelm Keitel	Dr. Otto Nelte	Death
Ernst Kaltenbrunner	Dr. Kurt Kauffmann	Death
Hans Frank	Dr. Alfred Seidl	Death
Wilhelm Frick	Dr. Otto Pannenbecker	Death
Alfred Rosenberg	Dr. Alfred Thoma	Death
Julius Streicher	Dr. Hanns Marx	Death
Fritz Sauckel	Dr. Robert Servatius	Death
Alfred Jodl	Professor Dr. Franz Exner, Professor Dr. Hermann Jahrreiss, Associate	Death
Arthur Seyss-Inquart	Dr. Gustav Steinbauer	Death
*Martin Bormann	Dr. Friedrich Bergold	Death
Rudolf Hess	Dr. Gunther von Rohrscheidt (to February 5, 1946), Dr. Alfred Seidl (from February 5, 1946)	Life imprisonment
Walter Funk	Dr. Fritz Sauter	Life imprisonment
Erich Raeder	Dr. Walter Siemers	Life imprisonment
Baldur von Schirach	Dr. Fritz Sauter	20 years
Albert Speer	Dr. Hans Flachsner	20 years
Constantin von Neurath	Dr. Otto Freiherr von Ludinghausen	15 years
Karl Doenitz	Flottenrichter Otto Kranzbuehler	10 years
Hjalmar Schacht	Dr. Rudolf Dix, Professor Dr. Herbert Kraus, Associate	Acquittal
Franz von Papen	Dr. Egon Kubuschok	Acquittal
Hans Fritsche	Dr. Heinz Fritz, Dr. Alfred Schilf, Associate	Acquittal
*Robert Ley		
*Gustav Krupp von Bohlen und Halbach	Dr. Theodor Kleifisch (to November 15, 1945) Dr. Walter Ballas, Associate (to November 15, 1945)	

* All individual defendants named in the Indictment appeared before the Tribunal except: Robert Ley, who committed suicide October 25, 1945; Gustav Krupp von Bohlen und Halbach, owing to serious illness; and Martin Bormann, who was not in custody and whom the Tribunal decided to try in absentia.

Groups and Organizations	Counsel	Sentence†
SS and SD	Ludwig Babel, Counsel for SS and SD (to March 18, 1946), Counsel for SS (to June 1, 1946), Co-counsel for SS (to August 27, 1946)	
	Horst Pelckmann, Co-counsel for SS (from March 2, 1946), Counsel for SS (from June 1, 1946)	
	Dr. Carl Haensel, Associate to Dr. H. Pelckmann (from April 1, 1946)	
	Dr. Hans Gawlik, Counsel for SD (from March 18, 1946)	Criminal organization
SA	Georg Boehm	
	Dr. Martin Loeffler	Criminal organization
Gestapo	Dr. Rudolf Merkel	Criminal organization
Leadership Corps of Nazi Party	Dr. Robert Servatius	Criminal organization
Reich Cabinet	Dr. Egon Kubuschok	Acquittal
General Staff and High Command of the German Armed Forces	Dr. Hans Laternser (from January 27, 1946)	Acquittal

Now, bearing in mind the persons accused, let us look to the general principles of international law and of criminal jurisprudence bearing upon the charges presented and the defenses asserted.

† The Russian member dissented from the judgments to the extent that he felt that the Reich Cabinet and the General Staff and High Command should have been declared criminal organizations. He also felt that Schacht, von Papen, and Fritsche should not have been acquitted, and that Hess should have been sentenced to death instead of to life imprisonment.

II

WHAT IS CRIMINAL LAW?

Criminal law is generally considered to be that field of jurisprudence which is concerned with wrongs against society. Such a wrong may arise by reason of an act directed against an isolated individual, but it is the tort against the social structure, resulting from such act, which is punishable. The trial of the wrongdoer is not for the purpose of furnishing redress to the person or persons injured—that is left to the processes of the civil law. The purposes of the criminal law are rather to punish the wrongdoer for his offense against the mores of society and to deter others from acting likewise.

It is, of course, recognized that a particular crime may cause such emotional reaction that it is difficult, if not impossible, for the one charged with its commission to receive a fair and impartial trial. To some extent that may have been true at Nuremberg. Passions were still inflamed, and tempers not upon an even level. The writings of some prominent persons in both the fields of international law[1] and of criminal law reflect this approach.[2] If one expects to conduct a trial and to administer

---

[1] "Retribution for the shocking crimes and atrocities committed by the enemy during World War II was made imperative by the overwhelming demands emanating from the public conscience throughout the world." Finch, "The Nuremberg Trials and International Law," 41 *American Journal of International Law*, p. 20 *et seq.*

In the first place, an accused is no longer an "enemy," but a defendant entitled to fair trial. The "demands of public conscience" are not the test, but, rather, the requirements of the law. "Crimes and atrocities" prejudge guilt, and "retribution" is a different thing from "punishment." The writer scarcely displays a judicial attitude.

[2] "It is doubtful whether there is one among those noble-hearted religionists and moralists who has himself suffered torture at the hands of the Nazis or whose loved ones have undergone the foul indignities, brutalities or anguished death in the concentration camps, ghettos, charnel-houses or 'murder-autos' of the Third Reich. To be sure, the 'thirst for vengeance' is a low sentiment, but it ought not to be confused with the legitimate, commendable, and morally virtuous desire of the survivors of Axis brutality to see that mankind's law and justice speak out, at long last, on their behalf." Glueck, *War Criminals—Their Prosecution & Punishment*, p. 7, 1944, Knopf. At pages 3 and 4 Mr. Glueck uses terms leading one to suspect he does not approach such a trial judicially—e.g., "atrocities," "countless acts of torture, rapine and murder," "mad bid for world-dominance," "even more barbarous," "abominable deeds against the laws of God and man," "self styled superior race has coldbloodedly tortured and slaughtered," "criminalistic and gratuitously cruel practices."

justice, it should be a different thing from that of the famous judge, Roy Bean, who used to apprise an accused that he would "give him a fa'r and squar' trial, and then hang him." Punishment should not be considered until guilt is established, nor should an offense be termed a crime before criminality is established. And one approaching such a matter while embroiled in passion is scarcely apt to give an accused a fair trial, or, if he actually does do so, few will believe it. The cry then seems to be for vengeance, rather than for punishment.

Punishment should be conceived as a vastly different thing than vengeance. It is not approached with a mental state of hostility or of wrath, however righteous; it is approached judicially, even as Jehovah must have acted when, with sorrow in his heart, he condemned his children of Sodom and Gomorrah.

The second purpose of criminal justice is that of deterrence of others from like conduct. Here we strongly suspect that international penal justice may fail. One who bids for great power in his own nation does so, frequently, because of an insatiable ambition which places other factors—including his own safety—at a minimum. The risk of assassination, in some countries, is present, yet that has proved no deterrent in the case of a dictator or revolutionist. In international affairs, if one has the acclaim of his countrymen, the possible self-assumed armor of patriotism, and the possibility of leaving his imprint upon history, the danger of defeat, trial, and death will likely prove no deterrent.[3] A lust for power is greater than the fear of death. Too often, also, such persons are opportunists who line their pockets well and believe they can disappear, under assumed names, into obscurity and leave others to bear the punishment, as do criminals of other types.

But whether the processes of criminal law prove to be deterrent or not, legal sanctions must continue or civilization must perish. The trust of people is in the law and in justice. Such faith cannot long continue if the petty criminal alone is punished and the major malefactor escapes. For that reason, the trial of war criminals, in principle, seems sound.

---

[3] Schick considers that law abiding citizens are always more impressed with legal sanctions than are law violators. "The Nuremberg Trial and the International Law of the Future," 41 *American Journal of International Law*, p. 770 *et seq.* (October, 1947).

III

POWERS OF MILITARY TRIBUNALS

The argument has been advanced that the individual defendants were not taken prisoner during actual hostilities, and for that reason a military government would have no jurisdiction over them.[1] This argument seems spurious, for several reasons. In the first place it has long been established that a victorious power may establish military tribunals to try offenders against the laws of war.[2] It may take considerable time to ferret out such persons and to arrest them. Some may have fled and have to be retaken. Again, hostilities were still going on in parts of Germany through the "Werewolf" organizations. Third, there had been no treaty of peace signed and the war had not ended.

It has been argued also that there was no consent by the German government to the holding of such a trial, thus rendering it invalid.[3] As previously pointed out, the victorious nation has the right to hold such hearings without such consent. Second, the government of Germany, in its prior form, had fallen and there was no one to give consent. In a dictatorship the dictator is the government—or at least it was so argued by the defendants. The dictator was dead and could not consent. Third, there was a consent actually given by the then existing government of Germany to such trials, acting through the occupying powers. Germany was still in existence, being a "dependent state," in the position of a protectorate.[4] Fourth, admittedly, a victorious state may impose any conditions it chooses upon the vanquished, including such a trial as was here conducted.[5] Kelsen also argues that the four powers were not acting as sovereigns of the territory, but in view of the actual participation of such powers in the administration of Germany and the accepted rules of

---

1 Schick, "The Nuremberg Trial and the International Law of the Future," 41 *American Journal of International Law*, p. 770 *et seq.* (October 1947).

2 See discussion post, page 12, notes 6, 7.

3 See Schick, above; also Kelsen, "Will the Judgment in the Nuremberg Trial Constitute a Precedent?", I *International Law Quarterly*, pp. 167-9 (Summer, 1947).

4 Rheinstein, "The Legal Status of Occupied Germany," 47 *Michigan Law Review*, p. 23 *et seq.* (November, 1948).

5 Glueck, *War Criminals—Their Prosecution and Punishment*, 1944, Knopf, pp. 11-12. The ineffectiveness of leaving punishment purely to the courts of the vanquished state was demonstrated after the first World War.

international law regarding the power to conduct military hearings, this reasoning seems somewhat attenuated.

It is no objection, also, to say that these particular defendants should have been tried by a military tribunal. The Nuremberg Tribunal was a military court, and under accepted rules of international law the warring nations could join together in such a trial instead of each proceeding separately.[6] The occupying nations may apply martial law toward the guilty and even employ their own judicial systems, although local tribunals are preferred where feasible. This has been accepted for decades.[7] Of course, in this particular case the law had been defined in the Charter so that arguments to the jurisdiction were not considered.[8]

Kelsen has condemned the Tribunal as being composed of captors who, as a legislative body, create the law; as an active agency, prepare the indictments, bring forward the evidence, and conduct the prosecution; and, lastly, as a judicial body, sit in judgment upon the defendants.[9] Yet is this not true, and necessarily so, in all criminal law? The State of Illinois, for example, enacts a penal statute. Its representative, the state's attorney, investigates the offense and prepares the indictment which is returned by the grand jury. He presents the evidence and prosecutes the defendant either before the court, who represents the State, or before a jury whose compensation is paid by the State and which is instructed by the State's officer, the judge, as to the law. Sentence is passed by the judge. It is literally "The People of the State of Illinois against John Jones," and he stands alone to meet the accusation. That is true of all na-

[6] Glueck, *War Criminals—Their Prosecution and Punishment*, 1944, Knopf, at 86 quoting Elihu Root in the *Proceedings of the American Society of International Law*, pp. 9-10, 1915.

[7] Merignhac, *Les Lois et Coutumes de la Guerre sur Terre*, 1903, Chevalier-Marescq & Cie., pp. 252-4; Holland, *The Laws of War on Land*, 1908, Clarendon Press, pp. 14-17, 59-60; Finch, "The Nuremberg Trial and International Law," 41 *American Journal of International Law*, p. 21 (January, 1947) declaring: "It is accepted international law, conventional as well as customary, that a belligerent has authority to try and punish individuals for crimes which constitute violations of the laws and customs of war, as well as of the laws of humanity, when such persons fall within his power." See also Biddle, "The Nurnberg Trial," 33 *Virginia Law Review*, No. 6, p. 679 *et seq.* (November, 1947).

[8] Seidl, for Hess, at IX *Proceedings* 642-5 challenged jurisdiction of the Tribunal to try other than war crimes. At 693 the objection was overruled.

[9] Kelsen, "Will the Judgment in the Nuremberg Trial Constitute a Precedent in International Law?", I *International Law Quarterly*, pp. 167-171 (Summer, 1947). See also Ehard, "The Nuremberg Trial Against the Major War Criminals and International Law," 43 *American Journal of International Law*, p. 243 (April, 1949).

tional law, and since international law has no superstate to designate the manner of presenting charges, the law has been accepted that the victor nation or nations may try offenders in military courts. Kelsen's objection would not seem valid as an objection to jurisdiction. It will be reexamined later to see whether any injustice was worked by such procedure.

IV

STATE SOVEREIGNTY

Perhaps the objection to jurisdiction which should be regarded with the greatest care, since it has provoked much misunderstanding prior to Nuremberg and will be hotly contested in the future, is that of state sovereignty. It is based upon the doctrine that a State, being sovereign, is subject to no restraint but its own. This argument is, therefore, the very antithesis of international law, since if no state is subject to restraint there can be no such thing as international law. But since all states, including Germany, have freely admitted that there are some concepts of international law which are binding, then admittedly there is no such thing as absolute sovereignty.

Nor does the existence of international law necessarily mean that every State retains absolute sovereignty except where it has yielded it to the common good. Ordinarily the extent of sovereignty is not tested except where it comes into conflict with the concept of sovereignty of some other State. In those relationships, matters may be settled amicably by negotiation. Unless in a treaty of that type some general principle applicable to other and different situations arises, international law is not created. The situation rests upon "comity" and not law. If general treaties are created between states establishing general principles of international conduct, they may amount to law. If such treaties reflect the thinking of a majority of civilized nations they are an expression of acceptance of certain standards of conduct which may be enforced even as to non-signatories. But expressions of such understanding may arise in manners other than by treaties, and where they express the mores of international thought and belief, they become what is known as "customary" law.

The fundamental basis of all law is not a constitution, nor a statute, whether it be municipal, state or international law. It is Justice—the underlying moral concept of right and wrong which is strangely similar in right thinking people. It is the function of law, where there is no codification of the principle involved, to examine into the facts, to determine the equities, and to arrive at a just decision. If it is proper to say that a State can act as it desires with impunity because it, as a sovereign, is controlled by no whim but its own and none can question its acts, then it is equally logical to say that another State can, in the exercise of *its* sovereignty, punish the first State for its acts and none can gainsay it.

Sir Hartley Shawcross, in summing up for the Prosecution, challenged this mystical term "sovereignty." He pointed out that sanctions had always been provided for the breach of international obligations which situation could not be true if the State were supreme. Such sovereignty would be inconsistent with the binding force of any treaty. And, if the defendants did not respect the sovereignty of other nations, how could they claim, he asked, a different or special type of sovereignty for themselves?[1]

One writer questioned the power to apply the national law of one state to the acts of another state.[2] Since the acts charged were all either violations of international law or of the law of Germany itself, this would not seem pertinent. But that writer forgets that an occupying power, under international law of long standing, may establish tribunals and the law applicable for such trials; and that further, those concepts of national law which are common to all nations become customary international law. And certainly, the application of such national law is not prohibited by any edict of international law. If the doctrine of sovereignty is cried for the vanquished, it may be cried for the victors, and their sovereignty to employ such law cannot be questioned. For the same reason, a belligerent may punish a war criminal in one place for a crime committed elsewhere.[3] This view also receives support from adjudicated cases in international law.[4]

---

1 XIX *Proceedings* 462-3.

2 Kelsen, "Will the Judgment in the Nuremberg Trial Constitute a Precedent in International Law?", I *International Law Quarterly*, p. 759 (Summer, 1947).

3 Cowles, "Universality of Jurisdiction over War Crimes," 33 *California Law Review*, p. 177 *et seq.* (June, 1945).

4 *Lotus v. Boz-Kourt*, September 7, 1927, Permanent Court of International Justice, Judgment No. 9, Series A, No. 10; II Hudson World Court Reports 23 *et seq.* This case involved a criminal prosecution in Turkey against the commander of a French vessel for a collision occuring upon the high seas, resulting in the deaths of eight Turkish sailors and passengers. The opinion, by a divided court, reviews the facts extensively, refers to other precedents, and declares: "International law governs relations between independent States. * * * Restrictions upon the independence of States cannot * * * be presumed. * * * Far from laying down a general prohibition to the effect that States may not extend the applications of their laws and the jurisdiction of their courts to persons, property and acts outside their territory, it leaves them in this respect a wide measure of discretion which is only limited in certain cases by prohibitive rules; as regards other cases, every State remains free to adopt the principles which it regards as best and most suitable * * *.

"No argument has come to the knowledge of the Court from which it

The ingenious argument was raised by the defense that after Germany had occupied other nations, it could change the relationship between them and the rules applicable. It was argued that if this be considered duress, then all treaties between victor and vanquished were in the same category.[5] The Tribunal, in its judgment, answered this argument by stating that Germany could not deal with occupied territory as its own when not actually incorporated within its boundaries, nor so long as there was an army in the field attempting to restore the occupied countries to their true owners.[6] A simpler answer would seem to be that if Germany asserted the right to deal with conquered France as it chose, then the Allied powers could deal with conquered Germany as they elected.

---

could be deduced that States recognize themselves to be under an obligation towards each other only to have regard to the place where the author of the offence happens to be at the time of the offence. On the contrary, it is certain that the courts of many countries * * * interpret criminal law in the sense that offences, the authors of which at the moment of commission are in the territory of another State, are nevertheless to be regarded as having been committed in the national territory, if one of the constituent elements of the offence, and more especially its effects, have taken place there * * * Consequently, once it is admitted that the effects of the offence were produced in the Turkish vessel, it becomes impossible to hold from prosecuting Lieutenant Demons because of the fact that the author of the offence was on board the French ship. * * *

"If, therefore, a guilty act committed on the high seas produces its effects on a vessel flying another flag or in foreign territory, the same principles must be applied as if the territories of two different States were concerned, and the conclusion must therefore be drawn that there is no rule of international law prohibiting the State to which the ship on which the effects of the offence have taken place belongs, from regarding the offence as having been committed in its territory and prosecuting, accordingly, the delinquent."

[5] See argument by Flachsner, for Speer, XIX *Proceedings* 180-1.

[6] I *Proceedings* 253-4.

V

RECOGNITION BY DEFENDANTS OF INTERNATIONAL LAW

One of the perplexing questions any student of the Nuremberg Trials must ask, after reading the Indictment and the mass of evidence in support of the charges brought, concerns the mental attitude of the defendants at the time the acts were committed. One possible mental justification which always may exist is—did the defendants consider their acts to be illegal? In short, the National Socialist regime introduced many new philosophical principles into government. Whether these principles are good or bad is beside the point. In formulating this philosophy, did these leaders adopt a concept, at the same time, that there was no such thing as international law? In other words, imbued as they were with the idea of State supremacy and sovereignty, did they honestly believe that there were no reciprocal rights and obligations to other nations, which would mean a non-recognition of theretofore accepted principles of international law?

Strangely enough, this was not the case. While some defendants felt that crystallized rules of international law theretofore recognized were partially obsolete, or inadequate, and felt that some modifications should be made, or different constructions adopted, not a single defendant denied the controlling force of international law. The majority of them were familiar with the doctrines of the Geneva Convention and with the Hague Rules of Land Warfare. This familiarity appears repeatedly throughout the trial.

It was brought out, for example, that the German White Book contained charges against Russia for violations of international law in 1941. The German Foreign Office collected a large number of alleged offenses on the part of this enemy, bound it in book form entitled *Russian Crimes Against Laws of War and Humanity, 1941,* and turned it over to the Red Cross at Geneva.[1] The significance of this is not the accusation against Russia, which will be discussed elsewhere, but the fact that by the making of such charges Germany and its government recognized the binding force of international law.

Goering testified that he had read the Hague Rules of Land Warfare immediately before the Polish War. He regretted not

[1] IX *Proceedings* 684-8.

having read them sooner as he would have informed Hitler "a modern war could not be waged under any circumstances."[2] Von Ribbentrop admitted that he knew that the League of Nations, while Germany was still a member, was against aggressive war, and that he was also familiar with the Kellogg-Briand Pact.[3] He later admitted that the Czechoslovakian agreement was obtained under pressure.[4] And the same defendant spoke of changing concepts of international law between the signing of the Treaty of Versailles and the present time.[5]

Von Neurath claimed that no means were used while he was in office which were "not internationally customary and permissible."[6] Fritsche pointed out that international law has no regulation against the use of propaganda.[7] Speer claimed that all violations of international law had already occurred when he came into power;[8] and later declared that he had not wanted any international crimes committed which might be held against the German people if they lost.[9] And when Sauckel was asked by Biddle if he had ever been advised it was in accordance with international law to force citizens of other countries to come to Germany to work, he answered that he was not.[10]

Jodl's testimony, bearing upon the questions primarily of war crimes, contains many references to international law. He declared, for example, that he had told Hitler he did not see how the Commando decree could be justified under international law.[11] However, he felt there was a question whether soldiers who acted like bandits, meaning the Commandos, placed themselves out of the protection of the Geneva Convention.[12] Opinions upon legal questions, he stated, could differ, and this was true in interpreting international law.[13] Prior to May, 1944, Canaris had been responsible for opinions on such matters, but after the dissolution of his organization on that date, Jodl assumed this function and felt himself responsible for interpretations thereafter.[14] He resolved immediately not to tolerate or participate

---

2 IX *Proceedings* 362. He defined a modern war as entailing (1) A war of weapons on land, sea, and air; (2) Economic war; (3) Propaganda war. See Goering's comments also in XXII 366-8.

3 X *Proceedings* 323.

4 X *Proceedings* 348.

5 XXII *Proceedings* 373-5.

6 XVI *Proceedings* 606.

7 XVII *Proceedings* 155.

8 XVI *Proceedings* 521.

9 XVI *Proceedings* 528.

10 XV *Proceedings* 205.

11 XV *Proceedings* 181.

12 XV *Proceedings* 320.

13 XV *Proceedings* 323.

14 XV *Proceedings* 336.

in any violations of international law. Upon that day he declared that partisans were to be treated as regular troops, and reduced the collective measures decreed by Hitler to things permitted by Article 50 of the Hague Convention. He prohibited collective punishment and took measures to protect civilian populations.[15] He disagreed with the idea of killing low flying enemy airmen as in violation of international law.[16]

About that time Jodl prepared a table listing the stipulations of international law and consulted experts to get their reactions to all acts which might constitute possible violations.[17] "I recognized," he stated, "and valued international law with which I was well acquainted, as a prerequisite for the decent and humane conduct of war. Copies of the Hague Rules of Land Warfare and the Geneva Convention were always lying on my desk."[18] Other references were made by him repeatedly to the application of international law.[19]

Upon cross-examination by Roberts who scoffed at Jodl being a stickler for international law, Jodl replied, "The concept of an aggressive war was not found in any regulation."[20] He engaged in a quite interesting debate with Roberts as to the position of hostages in international law.[21] And in another place he explained his much quoted memorandum to the effect that it was a mistake "to repudiate openly the obligations of international law which we have accepted."[22] But in his final statement to the Tribunal, he declared that the harsh measures adopted, though questionable from the point of view of international law, were justified by the acts of the enemy.[23]

Seyss-Inquart stated that he believed the laws of land warfare were obsolete.[24] Raeder, while not using such strong language, referred to the ethics of warfare and adherence to international law and stated that deviation from existing law might be required from military necessity, which would mean that a new international law would have to be developed.[25] He found it necessary to intensify the submarine warfare, "so as to meet the measures introduced by the British, which also

---

15 XV *Proceedings* 336, 338.
16 XV *Proceedings* 339-40.
17 XV *Proceedings* 341-2.
18 XV *Proceedings* 342.
19 XV *Proceedings* 343-4, 536.
20 XV *Proceedings* 468.
21 XV *Proceedings* 499-50.
22 XV *Proceedings* 506-7.
23 XXII *Proceedings* 400.
24 XVI *Proceedings* 109, 110.
25 XIV *Proceedings* 130.

violated international law."[26] He admitted elsewhere that an all-out war could not be justified on the basis of the hitherto generally accepted principles of international law, but that this followed the improper action of the British in arming merchant vessels.[27] The old rules of warfare, he believed, became obsolete when submarine warfare was changed by arming merchantmen and the advent of radio. One could no longer stop and examine such a vessel without it radioing for planes.[28]

International law, Raeder said, should not be thrown overboard but should be "limited and changed."[29] Since international law was not coordinated with submarine or air warfare, it was necessary to create a new code of naval warfare based upon actual developments. He declared that the use by German vessels of British colors at Norway was justified as a "ruse de guerre," since removed before they went into action.[30] A memorandum of Raeder's was used in evidence against him, where, in speaking of the murders at Bordeaux, he declared, "This is something new in international law, since the soldiers were in uniform."[31]

In referring to charges of firing upon shipwrecked survivors, Doenitz stated, "Firing upon these men is a matter concerned with the ethics of war and should be rejected under any and all circumstances."[32] He admitted that under the Geneva Convention one must take care of survivors if he could do so without imperiling his ship.[33] The London Agreement (by which he apparently meant The Declaration of London, 1909, which was never ratified) was in front of him and in his mind when he prepared the naval orders which were attacked by the Prosecution,[34] and he wanted to fight in accordance with the London Agreement as long as possible.[35] He referred also to the footnotes in the Prize Ordinance, Conference of 1923,[36] which might be deemed a recognition of international law. However, he declared, it was not up to him to start an investigation as to international law, particularly when the enemy had placed itself out of bounds by murdering prisoners and other acts.[37]

[26] XIV *Proceedings* 186.
[27] XIV *Proceedings* 197-8.
[28] XIV *Proceedings* 204.
[29] XIV *Proceedings* 205.
[30] XV *Proceedings* 194.
[31] XV *Proceedings* 339.
[32] XIII *Proceedings* 272.
[33] XIII *Proceedings* 368.
[34] XIII *Proceedings* 370.
[35] XIII *Proceedings* 353.
[36] XIII *Proceedings* 353.
[37] XIII *Proceedings* 329.

Witnesses for the defendants also referred to and recognized the existence of international law, and certain violations. Wagner, for example, stated that from the beginning of the war they had decided to adhere strictly to the London Agreement.[38] However, Hitler instructed them upon February 17 or 18, 1945 that Germany was no longer bound by the Geneva Convention in view of the Allied attacks upon cities.[39] Another witness declared, "The rules of warfare and of international law as set down in the Geneva Convention and the Hague Rules of Land Warfare were always binding for us older leaders, and violations were punished."[40] Hauser declared, "Even in peacetime, as part of their training, the officers and men were instructed on the rules of the Geneva Convention and the Hague Rules of Land Warfare."[41] Witness Reinecke, testifying for the SS, stated, "Not only was the law, including international law, taught in the Junker schools of the SS, but legal proceedings were held openly before the entire units."[42]

Kesselring stated that the German soldiers were instructed as to international law.[43] Witness Milch, for Goering, testified that the "ten commandments" for soldiers were posted in their pay books where they would see them constantly.[44] These Commandments, set out in full in the proceedings, show an adoption, in substance, of the Hague Rules.[45] Milch stated that the recognized rules of international law were known both to the soldiers and to their commanders,[46] and admitted that the forced labor of prisoners was a violation of international law.[47]

---

38 XIII *Proceedings* 469.
39 XIII *Proceedings* 469.
40 XXI *Proceedings* 31.
41 XX *Proceedings* 362.
42 XX *Proceedings* 429.
43 IX *Proceedings* 190.
44 IX *Proceedings* 57.
45 IX *Proceedings* 86.
46 IX *Proceedings* 86, 87.
47 IX *Proceedings* 88, 133.

VI

AGGRESSIVE WAR

So far as the specific violations of the Rules of Land Warfare were concerned, there was adequate authority for the trial of the defendants. Likewise, so far as the crimes against humanity were concerned, there was adequate authority under the national laws of the places where the acts were committed, including Germany, for punishment to be meted out by some appropriate tribunal. There were several phases of the Indictment, however, which were not as well crystallized, and of them the chief charge was that of "planning, preparing, initiating, and waging aggressive war." This, as a crime, was the chief concept which the Tribunal was called upon to establish. True, ever since primitive times and up to and including the defeat of Bonaparte, victorious nations have, through use of exile or the death penalty, punished the leaders of the vanquished state; but such penalty was dependent upon defeat, and not upon the question of aggression. This was the first time that any court was assembled to pass upon the question of guilt because of the planning and waging of aggressive war.

True, that factor alone would not invalidate the trials. There must be a first time for the trial of any offense. The question is, rather, whether there was a sufficient groundwork in international law to make these acts criminal, to make them punishable, which is a different thing, and to create a tribunal to receive evidence and to render judgment.

The Prosecution apparently took the position that the plans for aggression were first formulated in 1921,[1] or around the time that efforts were first made to strike off the shackles of the Treaty of Versailles. It is apparent also that the individual defendants and their counsel took the position that Versailles was an unfair treaty which they had a right to attempt to alter—also contending that the Treaty was signed under duress.[2] Justice Biddle seemed to feel that if other powers had agreed to disarm, evidence concerning Versailles might be pertinent.[3] However, the Tribunal refused repeatedly to permit any reference in evidence or arguments to unfairness of the Treaty,[4] and

---

[1] VIII *Proceedings* 218.
[2] X *Proceedings* 79-90, 102-3, 230-2, 243.
[3] X *Proceedings* 79-90.
[4] X *Proceedings* 90, 102-3, 230.

several times stopped one of defense counsel and required him to rewrite his closing argument twice because of such repeated references.[5] The Prosecution had previously admitted that loyal Germans had a right to strive to change that Treaty.[6] Robert Jackson declared, "We have no charge against Dr. Schacht because he opposed the Treaty of Versailles; we concede it was the right of any German citizen to do that by any means short of war."[7] The distinction is probably crystallized by the defendant Schacht's own statement, "The desire to modify the Versailles Treaty by means of a new war was a crime."[8]

We can gain some insight from the proceedings as to whether or not the plans for altering the Treaty of Versailles contemplated the necessity of war. Goering admitted that the Fuhrer wanted Crimea, the three Baltic states, and a strong economic domination of the Caucasus.[9] Raeder stated that he believed Hitler's acts were clever moves which would be solved peacefully,[10] so that he must have known and approved of their purpose and of the contingency, however remote, of war. And, as one of the prosecutors stated in his summation, after reiterating the statements of the defendants that none of them wanted war. "But they wanted things which they knew they could not get without war. They wanted their neighbor's lands and goods. Their philosophy seems to be that if the neighbors would not acquiesce, then they are the aggressors and are to blame for the war."[11]

Actually, there is much truth in this statement, when one considers the entire record. The fundamental philosophies and desires of the defendants were such as would inevitably lead to war. But, in a judicial trial, it is generally unwise and inexpedient to judge upon the basis of the evidence presented by one side alone. Sir Hartley Shawcross, in summing up for the Prosecution, declared: "It would appear, therefore, that the only way in which the accused can escape liability is to show to the satisfaction of the Tribunal that their wars were not wars of aggression or in violation of treaties. They have not done that."[12]

They were not permitted to do that. It is the major failing of the trials, even though a just result probably was reached,

---

5 XVII *Proceedings* 550-5 (Seidl).
6 XII *Proceedings* 426.
7 XII *Proceedings* 426.
8 XII *Proceedings* 485.
9 IX *Proceedings* 626.
10 XIV *Proceedings* 48.
11 XIX *Proceedings* 420 (Jackson).
12 XIX *Proceedings* 459.

that the defendants were not permitted fully to develop the acts of other nations which may have justified the Nazi actions. It is clear that a seemingly aggressive war may actually be a defensive war, such as when enemy troops mass upon one's border without cause.[13] Furthermore, each nation prepares plans of attack upon every other nation, and mobilization plans for an emergency, without necessarily contemplating a war. It would be surprising if both the United States and Russia, two of the prosecuting nations, do not now have in their war dossiers plans of attack upon each other. The existence of mobilization plans in Germany, however secret, was of itself very weak evidence of a desire for aggression.[14] General Jodl pointed out acts upon the part of the Allied Nations which, had they been supported by evidence, might have been powerful defensive material.[15] It was also pointed out by the German leaders that no subordinate would disagree with the leader at a time when unity was required; that it was not the place of military leaders, but only of political leaders, to determine the necessity of war.[16] For the same reason, Admiral Doenitz stated he would not have entered a Putsch against Hitler as it would have destroyed Germany's unity as a nation.[17] However, other statements do indicate a recognition that aggressive war, if aggressive war was actually committed, was a crime.[18]

In reply to the argument that aggressive war and its correlative steps do not constitute a crime, the Tribunal pointed out that international law is not static, but by continued adaptation follows the needs of a changing world. Therefore, the governing laws are found not only in treaties but in the customs and practices of States and in the general principles of justice applied by jurists and practiced by military courts. It was not,

---

13 Merignhac, *Les Lois et Coutumes de la Guerre sur Terre*, 1903, Chevalier-Marescq & Cie., p. 14.

14 IX *Proceedings* 506-12.

15 Jodl declared in his testimony that the Czechs had first mobilized and marched to the German border. Belgium and Holland had massed troops and the British flew over the low countries constantly with impunity. Russia prepared for war and massed on the German border. Jodl's entire testimony is worth reading in XIV *Proceedings*, 1-44; XV *Proceedings* at 344-398.

16 IX *Proceedings* 311 (Goering).

17 XIII *Proceedings* 304-8.

18 XIII *Proceedings* at 618 deals with a speech of Raeder's, delivered prior to the Kellogg Pact, where in speaking of wars of aggression, he stated "to strive after that would certainly in the general opinion of all Germans be a crime." He stated that he was of the same opinion thereafter. And one of his witnesses, Admiral Schulte-Monting, when questioned about the war on Russia, stated in XIV *Proceedings* at 328: "The invasion of Russia was a brutal aggression on the part of Nazi Germany."

accordingly, necessary for such documents as the Pact of Paris to outline administrative rules of procedure but merely to lay down and enunciate general principles of law recognized as just in the community of nations.[19]

Certainly there would seem to be ample evidence that the community of nations had decided to outlaw aggressive war. International cooperation had, long prior to the Kellogg-Briand Pact, been recognized in many ways other than in trade treaties, treaties of mutual alliance and the like. Long prior to the taking of steps to outlaw aggressive war, nations had acted cooperatively to prevent crimes against humanity and to humanize the waging of war. The first real step in the direction of establishing recognized standards for civilized nations probably was taken in 1827 when intervention occurred to prevent crimes against humanity in Turkey.[20] The next steps possibly were the Convention at Geneva in 1864, the St. Petersburg Declaration of 1868, and Brussels Conference of 1874, where each nation was to adopt certain rules as part of its own military law.[21] There was an intervention in the Balkan states in 1878,[22] in Armenia in 1891[23] and in Crete in 1896.[24] Prior to the last intervention, in 1895 rules were drafted by the Institut de Droit Internationale as to the Geneva Convention.[25] The Hague Convention of 1899 agreed "before an appeal to arms * * * to have recourse, as far as circumstances allow, to the good offices or mediation of one or more friendly powers."[26] There was the Geneva Convention of 1906 and The Hague Convention of 1907 which adopted the Rules of Land Warfare.[27]

During all of this time, statesmen and public spirited writers and jurists were gravely concerned about elimination of the causes of war, rather than merely its attendant evils. Article 227 of the Treaty of Versailles provided for a tribunal to try the German emperor for the commission of war crimes and by

---

[19] I *Proceedings* 221 (Judgment). This is almost the same language as was used by Jackson in his opening statement in II *Proceedings* at 147.

[20] XXII *Proceedings* 37.

[21] Holland, *The Laws of War on Land,* 1908, Clarendon Press, pp. 2, 3; Merignhac, *Les Lois et Coutumes de la Guerre sur Terre,* 1903, Chevalier-Marescq & Cie., pp. 21, 22, 210; I *Proceedings* 116; Brunet, *La Garantie Internationale Des Droits de l'Homme,* 1947, Grasset, pp. 342-4.

[22] XXII *Proceedings* 37.

[23] XXII *Proceedings* 37; Brunet *op cit.*

[24] XXII *Proceedings* 37.

[25] Holland, *op cit.*, pp. 2, 3; Merignhac, *op. cit.*, pp. 21, 22, 210; I *Proceedings* 216.

[26] Holland, *op. cit.*, pp. 2, 3; Merignhac, *op. cit.*, pp. 21, 22, 210; I *Proceedings* 216.

[27] Holland, *op cit.*, pp. 2, 3; Merignhac, *op cit.*, pp. 21, 22, 210; I *Proceedings* 216.

Article 228 the German government recognized the right of the Allied Powers "to bring before military tribunals persons accused of having committed acts in violation of the laws and customs of war."[27A] This, however, while recognizing a right to try a former sovereign for violating the rules of war did not purport to lay down a general principle.

In 1920 the idea developed for an international penal code and various international law groups made studies of the subject.[28] The Advisory Committee of Jurists prepared plans in February 1920 for a High Court of International Justice to deal with international crimes but met opposition, and the recommendations were rejected by the League of Nations on December 17, 1920.[29] In 1923, a draft of a "Treaty of Mutual Assistance," prepared by the League, contained these words "aggressive war is an international crime." It was submitted to 29 states, of which about half were in favor of its adoption.[30] The Preamble to the League 1924 Protocol for the Pacific Settlement of International Disputes, commonly called The Geneva Protocol, declares "war of aggression * * * is an international crime," and was recommended to its members by a unanimous vote of the 48 members.[31] Germany was not then a member, nor was the Protocol ratified, but it was signed by many leading statesmen of the world. The Assembly of the League on September 24, 1927, with all delegates present, unanimously adopted a declaration including "war of aggression * * * is * * * an international crime."[32] A unanimous resolution was also adopted on February 18, 1928 by the 21 American Republics at the 6th (Havana) Pan-American Conference as follows: "war of aggression constitutes an international crime."[33]

All of these declarations and recognition of the feeling of nations occurred prior to the signing of the Briand-Kellogg Pact. That document outlawing war was signed upon August 27, 1928

27A I *Proceedings* 216 (Judgment).

28 Brunet, *op cit.*, pp. 342-4.

29 Schick, "International Criminal Law; Facts and Illusions," II *Modern Law Review*, p. 290 et seq. (July, 1948); Ehard, "The Nuremberg Trial Against the Major War Criminals and International Law," 43 *American Journal of International Law*, p. 238 (April, 1949). The League Committee refers to the proposal as a "Court of International Justice." See the interesting comments in League of Nations, *Records of Committee Meetings*, 1920, p. 598, also pp. 463-4.

30 I *Proceedings* 216 (Judgment).

31 I *Proceedings* 216 (Judgment); II *Proceedings* 145 (Jackson). The Protocol also contained an excellent definition of aggressive war.

32 I *Proceedings* 216 (Judgment); II *Proceedings* 145 (Jackson).

33 I *Proceedings* 216 (Judgment); II *Proceedings* 145 (Jackson).

and Germany was a signatory.[34] In that same year, the International Association for Penal Law adopted a project to create a criminal branch in the Permanent Court of International Justice.[35] In 1926 the International Congress of Penal Law had previously recommended conferring such powers directly upon the Permanent Court.[36] On July 3, 1933, a Conference for the Definition of Aggression met in London.[37] In 1935 several leading international law societies under the general charge of Professor Pella, of Bucharest, cooperated in the general preparation of an international penal code.[38] And finally there were, of course, the declarations of the Allied leaders that the Nazi war criminals would be punished, the Potsdam conference, the Treaty of London, and the establishment of the Nuremberg Tribunal.[39]

When one takes these various steps and considers them, as one must if sitting in the place of the Tribunal, together with the declarations of statesmen, the opinions of public lawyers and of jurists, he can come to only one conclusion. That conclusion is that aggressive war was contrary to the mores of the community of nations, and that under both the positive law, concurred in by Germany, and the customary law, aggressive war was a crime. There is some dissent to this view, but it does not seem to be well taken.[40] Of course, there was considerable dis-

---

[34] I *Proceedings* 216 (Judgment); II *Proceedings* 145 (Jackson); VII *Proceedings* 146 et seq. (Rudenko).

[35] Brunet, *op cit.*, pp. 342-4.

[36] U.N. A/CN.4/7/Rev. 1, pp. 74, 75.

[37] II *Proceedings* 148 (Jackson).

[38] Brunet, *op cit.*, pp. 342-4.

[39] Brunet, *op cit.*, pp. 342-4. Lauterpacht refers to 23 states, 10 of which agreed to the creation of an International Criminal Court. I *Oppenheim's International Law*, 1948, p. 649, n. 2. See also League of Nations Document C. 222. M. 162. 1937. V.

[40] Schick, "International Criminal Law; Facts & Illusions," II *Modern Law Review*, p. 290 *et seq.* (July, 1948); Schick, "The Nuremberg Trial and the International Law of the Future," 41 *American Journal of International Law*, p. 770 *et seq.* (October, 1947). One of this author's chief complaints is that nothing has been done since Nuremberg to demonstrate acceptance of these principles. This would not alter the question of legality in any event, but the objection has been met, in part, by actions since taken.

Kelsen, "Will the Judgment in the Nuremberg Trial Constitute a Precedent in International Law?", I *International Law Quarterly*, p. 155 (Summer, 1947), takes the position that the Briand-Kellogg Pact and non-aggression pacts forbade only resort to war, and not planning, preparation, initiation, or conspiracy to wage war. Certainly if it is illegal to wage a war, it is illegal to initiate one. And the planning and preparation of an illegal act, such as the jimmying open of a window in order to burglarize a house, would render one subject to punishment. If it is purely in the thinking stage, one will agree with Mr. Kelsen; if it has passed into the stage of action, one must disagree.

Glueck, who felt in 1944 that aggressive war was no crime, changed

sent from the defense counsel. Dr. Horn, counsel for Von Ribbentrop, took the position that the various declarations and covenants were expressions of a wish, and that all concrete plans remained only in the form of drafts.[41] There was also the problem, he added, of definition—no one has ever defined the term "aggressive war," which statement is open to question. And, he asked, "who shall designate the aggressor?"[42] Many of the other counsel advanced similar arguments.[43]

Dr. Horn's question would not seem too difficult to answer. As to defining "aggression," each individual leader of each nation is at liberty to define the term as he sees fit in the first instance. He does so, if he desires to test the extent of the law, at his own risk, as the ultimate definition may be made by a judicial tribunal which may see fit to take a different view.[44] We do not find it necessary, in national or municipal law, to define every element of an offense. There is, for example, no detailed definition of an assault and battery—detailing the elements of provocation, initial attack, defense, aggravated defense, undue force, or the like, nor are such things capable of minute refinement. Yet triers of fact experience little real difficulty in establishing who is the aggressor. Reckless driving, malicious mischief, and disorderly conduct are other examples of offenses designated only by title, but in which the offenses themselves may consist of a hundred different things which must be scrutinized by the court for a factual determination. Thus, the lack of a statutory definition, alone, would not preclude the judicial determination of "aggression."

---

his mind in 1946. Glueck, *War Criminals—Their Prosecution and Punishment*, 1944, Knopf, p. 38; Glueck, *The Nuremberg Trial and Aggressive War*, 1946, Knopf, pp. 1-8.

[41] XVII *Proceedings* 567 et seq. See also Dr. Ehard's comments, *ante*, note 29.

[42] XVII *Proceedings* 571.

[43] XVIII *Proceedings* 36-40; XIX *Proceedings* 24-5; XIX *Proceedings* 380.

[44] Sir Hartley Shawcross made a similar observation, plus the fact that one proceeding to use his own judgment runs the further risk of abusing such discretion as he possesses. XIX *Proceedings* 461-2. Also definitions of aggression may be found in the Geneva Protocol, 1924, and, other places.

VII

VIOLATIONS OF LAWS OF WAR AND HUMANITY

It has been charged frequently that the acts with which the defendants in the Nuremberg, and the other war crimes, proceedings were charged had not been previously recognized as crimes. The making of this charge is partially due to the fact that new terminology was, in some cases, applied. Actually, many of the acts charged, disregarding for the moment the weight of the evidence, were violations of the German penal code. Many other acts were violations of the Hague Rules of Land Warfare and of the German Military Code.*

In analyzing the specific charges as to their international character, it is well to look first to the recognized rules of Land Warfare to see how closely those provisions would apply to the charges made. Those rules, as set forth by Holland, will be used in view of the fact they were published more than four decades ago and cannot, therefore, be accused of novelty or of passage merely for the purpose of these trials. For this purpose, these matters will be numbered chronologically and not in the order assigned by Holland.

> "1. These laws and usages prohibit all needless cruelty, and even needless destruction of human life, or of property.[1]
>
> "2. Peaceful inhabitants are to be spared in person and property during hostilities, so far as military necessity and the conduct of such inhabitants will permit. Especial care is to be taken of women and children, the sick and the aged, and protection must be given to the diplomatic representatives and counsels of neutral powers in belligerent territory.[2]
>
> "3. It is especially prohibited. . . . to destroy or seize the enemy's property, unless its destruction or seizure be imperatively demanded by the necessities of war.[3]

---

* This is strongly pointed out by Hans Ehard, Minister-President of Bavaria. "The Nuremberg Trials Against the Major War Criminals and International Law," 43 *American Journal of International Law*, pp. 239-41 (April, 1949).

In subsequent notes, references are to Holland, *The Laws of War on Land*, 1908, Clarendon Press, instead of the Hague Convention, because of the helpful discussion in Holland's book following many of these rules. The text of the Rules as contained in the Convention are set forth in the Appendix to Holland.

[1] Holland, *The Laws of War on Land*, 1908, Clarendon Press, p. 13.

[2] Holland, *op cit.*, p. 17.

[3] Holland, *op cit.*, 43.

"4. In sieges and bombardments all necessary steps should be taken to spare, as far as possible, edifices devoted to religion, art, science, and charity, historical monuments, hospitals, and places where the sick and wounded are collected, provided they are not used at the same time for military purposes.[4]

"5. The giving up to pillage of a town or places, even when taken by assault, is prohibited.[5]

"6. Private property cannot be confiscated.[6]

"7. Pillage is formally prohibited.[7]

"8. Neither requisitions in kind, nor services, can be demanded from localities or inhabitants except for the needs of the army of occupation.[8]

"9. An army of occupation can only take possession of cash, funds, and realizable securities, which are strictly State property . . . .[9]

"10. The occupying state shall regard itself as being only administrator and usufructuary of the public buildings, immovable property, forests and agricultural undertakings belonging to the hostile State, and situated in the occupied country. It must protect the substance of these properties, and administer them according to the rules of usufruct.[10]

"11. The property of localities (communes), as also that of institutions devoted to religion, charity, and education, and to the arts and sciences, even when State property, shall be treated as private property is treated. All seizure, destruction, or intentional injury of such institutions, of historical monuments, or of works of art or science, is prohibited, *and should be made the subject of proceedings.*"[11] (Italics author's.)

These are sufficient to indicate that civilian populations are to be treated with due consideration, as well as their properties and those of religious, charitable, educational and historical organizations or when possessed of such a character, even if belonging to an occupied State. Much of the documentary material, including photographs and motion pictures, dealt with such things as the harsh treatment of civilians, the furnishing of inadequate food and clothing to such persons, the looting of their homes, the removal of food supplies and clothing for export

4 Holland, *op cit.*, 46.
5 Holland, *op cit.*, 46.
6 Holland, *op cit.*, 54.
7 Holland, *op cit.*, 54.
8 Holland, *op cit.*, 56.
9 Holland, *op cit.*, 57.
10 Holland, *op cit.*, 59.
11 Holland, *op cit.*, 59.

to Germany, the destruction of crops, animals, and agricultural machinery, and the wrongful arrest and imprisonment of conquered peoples, including needless slaughter, particularly of Russians, Poles, and Jews. Much additional testimony dealt with the suppression of churches and imprisonment of priests and ministers, the closing of institutions of education, the looting of art galleries, destruction of objects of historical and artistic significance, and the needless destruction of private homes. The defendants admitted the confiscation of all properties belonging to such groups as the Freemasons and Jehovah's Witnesses. Upon most of the other matters, questions of fact were presented for the determination of the Tribunal and there was ample evidence to support the judgments.

Again, with reference to the rights of individuals in occupied countries, Holland declares:

> "12. Family honour and rights, the lives of individuals, and private property, as also religious beliefs and liberty of public worship, must be respected.[12]
>
> "13. It is especially prohibited . . . . to declare extinguished, suspended, or unenforceable the rights and rights of action of the subjects of the adverse party.[13]
>
> "14. Any compulsion by a belligerent or the population of occupied territory to give information as to the army of the other belligerent, or as to his means of defence, is prohibited.[14]
>
> "15. Any compulsion on the population of occupied territory to take the oath to the hostile Power is prohibited."[15]

It was claimed by the Prosecution that the Nazis had suspended freedom of worship and civil rights in occupied territories. It was not denied that special criminal courts were established from which there was no appeal, and in which the course of justice was a mockery. Actions of the Gestapo were likewise subject to no checkrein. There were definite attempts made to Germanize certain of the areas captured, including the requirement of taking an oath of loyalty. And the general orders issued by the occupying nation required partisans to be interrogated extensively, prior to being shot. There might be a defensive issue in this regard as to whether partisans were civilians and subject to this rule.

The question of collective punishment is more moot. The relative provisions are:

---

[12] Holland, *op cit.*, 54.
[13] Holland, *op cit.*, 44.
[14] Holland, *op cit.*, 53.
[15] Holland, *op cit.*, 53.

"16. No general penalty, pecuniary or otherwise, can be inflicted on the population on account of isolated acts for which it cannot be regarded as collectively responsible.[16]

"17. If, besides the taxes contemplated in the preceding article, the occupant levies other money contributions in the occupied territory, this can only be for the needs of the army, or of the administration of such territory.[17]

"18. Reprisals must be exercised only subject to the following restrictions:

"(a) The offense in question must have been carefully inquired into.

"(b) Redress for the wrong, or punishment of the real offender, must be unattainable.

"(c) The Reprisals must be authorized, unless under very special circumstances, by the Commander-in-chief.

"(d) They must not be disproportioned to the offence, and must in no case be of a barbarous character."[18]

There was no question that severe financial exactions were made upon occupied territory, the reasonableness thereof being a question of fact for the Tribunal. As to reprisals, all defendants admitted the barbarous nature of those acts but placed the responsibility upon Hitler who, they claimed, changed the ratio from 5 to 1 or 10 to 1 to 50 to 1 or 100 to 1 merely by adding a zero. Nor, admittedly, was any hearing ever given as required by the Rules of War.

As to the question of forced labor of civilian populations, it is provided:

"19. Neither requisitions in kind, *nor services,* can be demanded from localities or inhabitants except for the needs of the army of occupation. They must be in proportion to the resources of the country, and of such a nature as not to imply any obligation upon the population to take part in operations of war against their country.[19]

"20. It is also prohibited to a belligerent to compel the subjects of the adverse party to take part in operations of war directed against their own country, . . ."[20]

These would not, alone, seem to prohibit forced labor except in armament factories, if there was a necessity for labor generally. However, there was considerable evidence of such persons being compelled to work in armament plants and even of the compulsion of Russians to handle artillery in the field.

[16] Holland, *op cit.*, 55.
[17] Holland, *op cit.*, 55.
[18] Holland, *op cit.*, 61.
[19] Holland, *op. cit.*, 56.
[20] Holland, *op cit.*, 44.

As to commencement of a war and the rights of neutrals, it is provided:

> "21. The contracting Powers recognize that hostilities between them ought not to commence without a warning, previously given and unequivocal, which shall take the form either of a declaration of war, accompanied by reasons, or of an ultimatum, with a conditional declaration of war.[21]
>
> "22. The territory of neutral powers is inviolable.[22]
>
> "23. Belligerents are forbidden to send across the territory of a neutral power either troops, or convoys, whether of munitions of war or of provisions.[23]
>
> "24. Belligerents are also forbidden:
>
> "(a) To install on the territory of a neutral power a radio-telegraphic station, or any apparatus intended to serve as a means of communication with belligerent forces on land and at sea.[24]
>
> "25. Bodies of combatants cannot be formed, nor can recruiting offices be opened, in the interests of the belligerents, on the territory of a neutral power."[25]

There is little question that Germany failed to use an open declaration of war prior to an invasion where it was to its interest to act with secrecy. Nor did that nation recognize the rights of neutrals, under the Prosecution's theory, in Holland, Belgium, Luxembourg, Denmark, and Norway.

As to means of waging war in general, it has been provided:

> "26. The attack or bombardment, by whatsoever means, of towns, villages, habitations, or buildings, which are not defended, is prohibited.[26]
>
> "27. The Commander of an attacking force, before commencing a bombardment, except in the case of an assault, should do all he can to warn the authorities of what is about to happen."[27]

While the defendants took the position that the Allies first commenced the bombing of open cities, they had a rather difficult time explaining the early bombings of Polish villages, Rotterdam, and of English cities. In none of these cases, other than Rotterdam, can a definite warning be found, and in that case a message of capitulation had been given by the neutral authori-

---

[21] Holland, *op cit.*, 18.
[22] Holland, *op cit.*, 62.
[23] Holland, *op cit.*, 62.
[24] Holland, *op cit.*, 62.
[25] Holland, *op cit.*, 63.
[26] Holland, *op cit.*, 46.
[27] Holland, *op cit.*, 62.

ties. The Nazis responsible for the air operations claimed the ground forces gave the wrong signal or that it was "misunderstood"—hence the ruthless bombing.[27A]

As to action against enemy soldiers, it is stated:

> "28. It is especially prohibited:
>
> "(a) To kill or wound treacherously individuals belonging to the hostile nation or army.
>
> "(b) To wound or kill an enemy who, having laid down his arms, or having no longer means of defence, has surrendered at discretion.
>
> "(c) To declare that no quarter will be given."[28]

There was considerable evidence, of a very unsatisfactory character, upon the question of the shooting of shipwrecked seamen. The failure of this proof is evidenced in the Tribunal's actions toward Doenitz and Raeder. On the other hand, the evidence as to slaughtering soldiers who had surrendered, refusal to give quarter, killing of commissars and Commandos, and the like, was well established. This was true, also, as regards the treatment of partisans, who, it was contended, were entitled to be treated as soldiers.

Thus it is provided:

> "29. The laws, rights, and duties of war apply not only to the army, but also to militia and to corps of volunteers, which satisfy the following requirements:
>
> "(a) That of being commanded by a person responsible for his subordinates;
>
> "(b) That of having a distinctive mark, fixed and recognizable at a distance;
>
> "(c) That of carrying their arms openly; and
>
> "(d) That of conducting their operations in accordance with the laws and customs of war."[29]

Other provisions contain similar requirements. It could be contended, with considerable logic, that since partisans did their best to keep from having a distinctive mark, carried their weapons secretly, and themselves disrespected the rules of war, they were not entitled to the status of belligerents.

Much evidence appeared concerning the violations of rules concerning prisoners of war.

> "30. They must be humanely treated.[30]
>
> "31. The State may utilize the labour of prisoners of war, other than officers, according to their rank and capa-

---

27A IX *Proceedings* 174-188.

28 Holland, *op cit.*, 43.

29 Holland, *op cit.*, p. 20.

30 Holland, *op cit.*, p. 21.

bilities. Such labour shall not be excessive, and shall have nothing to do with the operations of war.[31]

"32. Failing a special agreement between the belligerents, prisoners of war shall be treated as regards food, quarters and clothing, on the same footing as the troops of the Government which captured them.[32]

"33. Escaped prisoners recaptured before they have succeeded in rejoining the army, or before quitting the territory occupied by the army that captured them are liable to disciplinary punishment. Prisoners who, after succeeding in escaping, are again taken prisoners, are not liable to any punishment for their previous flight."[33]

There are, of course, many related provisions. The major complaints as to prisoners were that they were ill treated and poorly fed and clothed; they were compelled to work at arduous labor, even in the armament business or work related directly to the war effort; they were beaten, tortured, physically abused and often shot without cause. Captured aviators were permitted to be lynched by the populace, and escaping prisoners were frequently shot upon recapture.

These are, in substance, the majority of long accepted rules of land warfare which it was claimed, and which claim was supported by considerable evidence, were violated. It must be remembered, also, that if the war were an illegal one, the excuse of war would not avail as a defense—and these particular acts would be judged by the penal laws of the state where committed. Thus pillage would be burglary, theft, illegal entry, etc., dependent upon the circumstances; destruction of property could be arson or malicious mischief; acts toward individuals might include assault, as well as the various combinations with specific intent crimes, mayhem, murder, rape, kidnapping, false arrest, and abduction. Thus, the Rules of Land Warfare are not the sole test.

It will be observed that many of these acts, committed in time of war, could also constitute crimes against humanity. However, the killings and imprisonments during time of peace, the confiscations of property, and like matters the Tribunal felt to be outside the scope of its examinations, and left for others to determine.[34] However, there can be no question that these various acts were in violation of the German Penal Code and the Weimar Constitution, and those guilty would be subject to trial either in the German courts or those of the occupying nation

[31] Holland, *op cit.*, p. 21.
[32] Holland, *op cit.*, p. 22.
[33] Holland, *op cit.*, pp. 22-3.
[34] I *Proceedings* 254-5.

administering justice in the place of the regular courts. Thus, the general term "crime against humanity" should not be regarded as an innovation in the law but as including a number of crimes well recognized in all penal codes.

The fact that civilized nations have an interest in the protection of minorities and the prevention of atrocities shocking the conscience of mankind was brought out by one of the defense counsel who referred to the intervention in Turkey in 1827, the Balkan States in 1878, Armenia in 1891 and Crete in 1896.[35] The Commission on the Responsibility of the Authors of the War and on Enforcement of Penalties to the Preliminary Peace Conference after the First World War attempted to fix punishment for "offenses against the laws and customs of war or the laws against humanity," but the American members dissented from the report.[36] It is difficult to see why the representatives of a cultured nation should be so hesitant to recognize the laws of common decency. One cannot reconcile a system which purports to guarantee the rights of man with a failure to punish an invasion of those rights.[37]

The Prosecution referred to ample law to sustain its position. Sir Hartley Shawcross referred extensively to the Hague Rules of Land Warfare and traced their repeated violation.[38] Francois de Menthon pointed out that the acts charged were all admittedly illegal, and that the excuse of war was no defense if the particular acts were condemned under the rules of warfare.[39] Pokrovsky referred to the Hague and Geneva Conventions, the

---

[35] Gawlik, XXII *Proceedings* 37. See also Schick's reference thereto in "The Nuremberg Trial and the International Law of the Future," 41 *American Journal of International Law*, p. 770 *et seq.* (October, 1947).

[36] 14 *American Journal of International Law*, 1920, p. 95.

[37] Brunet, *La Garantie Internationale Des Droits de l'Homme*, 1947, Grasset, p. 341.

[38] XIX *Proceedings* 464 *et seq.*

[39] V *Proceedings* 368-427, he declared: "A crime of common law, the war crime is, nevertheless, not an ordinary infraction. It has a character peculiarly intrinsic—it is a crime committed on the occasion or under the pretext of war. It must be punished because, even in time of war, attacks on the integrity of the physical person and or property are crimes if they are not justified by the laws and customs of war. The soldier who in the battlefield kills an enemy combatant commits a crime, but this crime is justified by the law of war. International crime therefore intervenes in the definition of a war crime, not in order to give it essential qualification but in order to fix its outer limits. In other words, every infraction committed on the occasion or under the pretext of hostilities is criminal unless justified by the laws and customs of war—if this justifying fact is taken away the infraction, whether ordinary crime or war crime, remains in its entirety." To the same effect, see Garner, "Punishment of Offenders Against the Laws and Customs of War," 14 *American Journal of International Law*, pp. 70-94 (1920).

instructions issued by the German General Staff recognizing the rules of war, and the German Law of August 17, 1938, which referred to the Geneva Convention.[40] Justice Jackson gave an excellent analysis of the ineptness of the defenses raised.[41] And writers upon the subject have agreed that there is extensive precedent for the punishment of war crimes.[42]

It was the contention of counsel for Goering that there were no Hague Rules as to air warfare, economic warfare, or psychological warfare. The failure to have limitations in these directions altered the conditions of defense, he argued, and justified the deportation of labor.[43] Other counsel discussed this question also,[44] Servatius, counsel for Sauckel and for the corps of Political Leaders, taking the view that the mobilization of labor was no offense unless coupled with murder or ill treatment.[45] It was even argued that the Hague Rules were obsolete,[46] although counsel admitted, upon inquiry by the Tribunal, that no suggestion had ever been made between States to this effect since the time of the First World War.[47] With more justification, it was argued that the Hague Rules applied only where all belligerents were signatories, and therefore had no application to the present situation, the Soviet Union not being a signatory.[48]

Other counsel discussed other aspects of the charges,[49] Horn contending that in the past only members of the armed forces were considered war criminals, and that civilians should not be so considered.[50] This argument received scant attention from the Tribunal. It did hold, however, that the Hague Convention was not made to apply to noncontracting parties, and applied only if *all* belligerents were parties. But it went on to state that

---

[40] VII *Proceedings* 345.

[41] XIX *Proceedings* 421 *et seq.*

[42] Cowles, "Trials of War Criminals (Non-Nuremberg)," 42 *American Journal of International Law*, p. 299 *et seq.* (April, 1948); Green, "The Military Commission," 42 *American Journal of International Law*, p. 832 *et seq.* (October, 1948).

[43] VIII *Proceedings* 522, 526 (Stahmer, counsel for Goering).

[44] XVIII *Proceedings* 89-93 (Thoma, counsel for Rosenberg).

[45] VIII *Proceedings* 478.

[46] XIX *Proceedings* 182 (Flachsner, counsel for Speer). Also see XVI 109-113 to same effect (Seyss-Inquart).

[47] XIX *Proceedings* 183.

[48] XIX *Proceedings* 180 (Flachsner). However, Russia was a signatory, two of the conventions being executed with reservations. Scott, *Reports to the Hague Conferences of 1899 & 1907*, 1917 Oxford University Press, pp. 900-1.

[49] XVIII *Proceedings* 1-36 (Nelte, counsel for Keitel, on hostages and reprisals); XVIII *Proceedings* 312-372 (Kranzbuehler, counsel for Doenitz, upon charges against his client).

[50] XVII *Proceedings* p. 580-6.

the Hague Rules declared general principles of international law which by 1939 had been recognized by all civilized nations.[51]

In view of the fact that there are 44 presently published volumes of evidence bearing upon the various charges, it is obviously impossible to weigh all of the facts or to condense such testimony and documents into a few pages. Much of the evidence was susceptible of documentary proof, such as the orders to kill Commandos[52] and guerillas.[53] The same is true as to orders not to feed prisoners refusing to work.[54] There were, in addition, admissions by certain defendants, a few examples of which might be noted. Goering, for example, speaking of escaping Allied aviators admitted: "Those who were captured by the police were shot without exception."[55] Jodl, referring to the killing of fifty airmen, termed it "sheer murder."[56] Many of the acts were, of course, blamed upon Himmler, and his "great secrecy" was often referred to.[57] And Dr. Exner argued that the war was humanely fought in the beginning, later increasing in bitterness, with violations and reprisals on both sides.[58]

One of the very interesting aspects of the trials, however, was the complete support given to Admiral Doenitz's testimony by one of the leading American naval warriors, Admiral Nimitz. In his deposition, he pointed out that he put in blockades, sank merchantmen without warning after the outbreak of the war, and did not rescue enemy survivors if it created an undue hazard to the rescuing vessel or prevented it from completing its mission.[59] Other phases of his testimony, as well, pointed up the fact that the German navy probably did nothing not common to all navies of the world.

The defendants explained the reasons for certain acts, such as the killing of partisans, by showing the nature of the conduct of such persons.[60] The murder of peasants by low flying Allied airmen was referred to repeatedly.[61] Goering pointed out that German rescue craft was shot down even when marked with a Red Cross.[62] Other violations by Allied soldiers appeared re-

---

51 I *Proceedings* 253-4.

52 IV *Proceedings* 441.

53 IV *Proceedings* 454. See Jodl's admission in XV *Proceedings* 534.

54 IV *Proceedings* 460.

55 IX *Proceedings* 592.

56 XV *Proceedings* 469.

57 E.g., XI *Proceedings* 398-401.

58 VIII *Proceedings* 182.

59 XVII *Proceedings* 378-84.

60 IX *Proceedings* 322-5 (Goering).

61 E.g., IX *Proceedings* 136-7 (Von Brauchitsch).

62 IX *Proceedings* 387.

peatedly in the testimony,[63] but the Tribunal, on the whole, refused to consider the question of Allied violations as a defense.[64]

Speaking succinctly, as to violations of the laws of war and offenses against humanity, a crime is still a crime, whether committed in time of peace or war. Offenses in violation of the generally accepted rules of warfare and international offenses remain crimes even if the war is justified. The act of being at war is no legal excuse for violation of these rules. An illegal war is, furthermore, no longer to be recognized as an excuse for that which would be criminal in time of peace. It is barbarous to contend that one can violate ordinary penal laws with impunity or slay his neighbor if he should so desire simply by saying "a state of war exists," when there is no reasonable justification or excuse of self defense. In time of peace, one cannot load his fellow citizens, who have not been tried nor condemned by a court of justice, into tank cars or rooms and empty poison gases into the atmosphere merely because he does not approve of the shape of their noses, their economic status, or racial backgrounds. Whether he be the one who actually produces the death, or orders it, or creates the conditions from which that result inevitably arises, he is equally guilty. Exalted rank should be no defense. The same is true of torture, imprisonment without cause, medical experimentation, and other acts condemned by all penal codes. No person can, if civilization is to endure, set aside all penal restrictions of his nation by his own decrees and create a personal immunity for himself and his confederates. There is a higher law which cannot be claimed to be *ex post facto* as to those violating its provisions.

Those charged with such violations in the Nuremberg Trials were treated with great fairness by the Tribunal with respect to those particular matters. As to the persons actually performing the acts of crime, and constituting the instruments of action, one must look to other military trials to see what results obtained.

---

[63] Chap. 13, note 26. E.g., XV *Proceedings* 298-322.

[64] VIII *Proceedings* 181, 628; IX *Proceedings* 190, 688; XIII *Proceedings* 521.

VIII

CONSPIRACY; COLLECTIVE RESPONSIBILITY

One of the much mooted questions raised in the trials arose out of the charges in the Indictment against the individual defendants as conspirators to perform the acts charged in Counts II, III, and IV which detailed the separate offenses. Another mooted question arose from the charges against the various organizations alleged to be criminal. In either case, they involve collective responsibility and so will be discussed together.

Jahrreiss, co-counsel for Goering, analyzing the legal views of the defense, claimed that it is impossible to guide a great nation through the means of a conspiracy of a few dozen individuals.[1] Nor, under the leadership principle, was there even a predictable course of conduct. Therefore, he argued, one embarking on a venture could not know, in advance, of its criminality. The doctrine of conspiracy, he stated further, was one of Anglo-Saxon law only and not even employed in England. In order to have a conspiracy, one must have a common, voluntary agreement, which is impossible in a dictatorship. The leader does not conspire with his followers—he dictates. Also, to have a conspiracy, there must be knowledge of a common plan and this was not established by the evidence.[2]

These general arguments were followed and reargued by others of the defense counsel.[3] As usual, Dr. Exner, counsel for Jodl, brought forth some powerful illustrations to bolster his arguments. The fact of joining a group at a time when its intentions may have been innocent, he said, did not mean that one subscribed to illegal acts at a far future time when he was no longer actively associated. "If I buy a book which draws my attention to another one, and I then buy the latter as well, does it follow that at the time of the first purchase I already had the intention of getting the second one as well?" he asked.[4]

---

1 XVII *Proceedings* 481 *et seq.*

2 XVII *Proceedings* 505-14.

3 XVII *Proceedings* 592 (Horn); XVIII *Proceedings* 164-9 (Pannenbecker, counsel for Frick); XVIII *Proceedings* 304 (Dix); XIX *Proceedings* 381-2 (Seidl, counsel for Hess and for Franks); XXII *Proceedings* 128-131 (Boehm, counsel for SA). And, to a similar effect, the reasoning of a German leader since the trials. Ehard "The Nuremberg Trial Against the Major War Criminals and International Law," 43 *American Journal of International Law*, pp. 226-7 (April, 1949).

4 XIX *Proceedings* 23.

Again, he attacked the Prosecution's argument that the military was an integral part of the conspiracy. It was his argument that political leaders make wars, which military leaders, such as Jodl, merely carried out. It was true, he said, that if "the generals do not do their job, there is no war. But we must add: If the infantryman does not march, if his rifle does not fire, if he had nothing to clothe himself with and nothing to eat, there is no war. Is therefore the soldier, the gunsmith, the shoemaker, the farmer guilty of complicity in the war?"[5]

To evaluate the force of Professor Exner's arguments, we must look to ourselves and see how we would react to similar charges. Let us say that war occurred with Russia, and that preceding it our President had ordered our destroyers to sink Russian submarines on sight, as had been done in the case of Germany. Assume further that charges were presented in a similar trial against the leaders of this nation. Who, then, would be the conspirators? If accused upon the same basis as the charges brought at Nuremberg, we might expect the President, his cabinet, and the leaders of the two houses of Congress to be indicted—or perhaps the Congress would be indicted as a criminal organization. The heads of the army, navy, and air force would certainly be selected for individual distinction. Our leading ambassadors, the head of the Federal Reserve System, and the DuPonts and Henry Kaiser, if the latter were again active in war plants, would become war criminals. Certainly Walter Winchell and Arthur Godfrey, who have been crusading against the Russian threat, would be so considered—possibly even Mr. Kaltenborn. And if Bob Hope again participated in war bond drives, he would, perhaps, find himself in the dock. Martyrs? Perhaps, but probably conspirators in the same sense.

Dr. Stahmer bitterly criticized the Prosecution for adopting the theory of "ratification" which, he claimed, was drawn from civil, and not criminal, law. If one did not engage in a common plan but was drawn into it late, because of a war or other emergency, he could not be rightly considered a conspirator. Mere approval, he declared, did not make one a participant.[6] There is logic also in this argument. One should not, of course, be punished merely for condoning or sympathizing with a "fait accompli," if he has not previously incited the act or aided in its commission. The doctrine of ratification is hardly susceptible

[5] XIX *Proceedings* 23.

[6] XVII *Proceedings* 513. Also see Flachsner's argument in XIX *Proceedings* 178. Justice Biddle interrogated Sir David Maxwell-Fyfe as to the date the conspiracy started. The Prosecutor fumbled for a moment and then replied, "1921," but that one joining later might be liable for acts previously committed. VIII *Proceedings* 218.

of such a construction, nor of an extension to criminal law. If it were, many persons would be guilty of attempted murder by approving the attempted assassination of Hitler—or even murder in sympathizing with the slayer of Huey Long.

The question of "class guilt," as related to the indicted organizations, met with equally bitter denunciation by defense counsel.[7] An American writer, Hans Kelsen, has also condemned the theory of collective guilt in the case of the indicted organizations as being primitive.[8] Whether something is primitive or advanced depends upon the point of view. Is it not truly a judicial, rather than a legislative function, to determine this question upon evidence presented impartially into court? In the United States, we would be reluctant to pass a statute pointing to a specific organization as criminal—yet, if our municipal law were as flexible as international law, it might be a mark of civilization to denote such organizations as the Capone gang, the Ku Klux Klan, and Murder, Inc., as criminal and throw the burden upon any member thereof to prove his innocence of wrongdoing.

The Germans also claimed immunity for the organizations charged with guilt upon the ground that "only the individual has the faculty to recognize and to form a will, and, therefore, to have a concept of guilt."[9] Yet they argued elsewhere that no individual, but only the State, which is an organization in an even larger sense, should bear a penal responsibility. The two views seem strangely inconsistent and evolved largely from a sense of expediency.

Other defense counsel raised still different objections. Dr. Kubuschok argued as follows: (1) it would be unjust to impose severe penalties upon an individual member of an organization irrespective of his act; (2) the term "criminal organization" is not defined in the Charter; (3) if the original purpose was not criminal, persons who become involved innocently should not be condemned; (4) in penal codes, any test of joint criminality always involves the element of knowledge.[10]

Dr. Babel, counsel for the SS, argued (1) that the Tribunal had no jurisdiction over criminal organizations; (2) there were

---

[7] XIX *Proceedings* 386-7 (Seidl); XXI *Proceedings* 495 (Merkel, counsel for Gestapo); XXI *Proceedings* 618 *et seq.* (Gawlik, citing Garner, *International Law & the World War*, Vol. I, p. 154); XXII *Proceedings* 4 (Gawlik); XXII *Proceedings* 128-131 (Boehm); XXII *Proceedings* 92-9 (Kubuschok, counsel for Von Papen and for Reich Cabinet).

[8] Kelsen, "Will the Judgment in the Nuremberg Trial Constitute a Precedent in International Law?", I *International Law Quarterly*, No. 2, pp. 165-6 (Summer, 1947). XXII *Proceedings* 93.

[9] XXII *Proceedings* 93.

[10] VIII *Proceedings* 390-7.

many branches of each organization, and not all were liable for acts committed in a separate branch; (3) the organizations had now been dissolved, and could not be tried.[11]

Dr. Laternser, counsel for the General Staff and High Command, pointed out (1) that the Tribunal had the discretion to declare such organizations not be criminal; (2) that the Prosecution failed to take into account the element of duress in joining; (3) that one may have joined without full knowledge of the criminal aims and methods; (4) that under German penal law, Articles 128 and 129, as well as French law, only individuals and not organizations are punishable; (5) that the Charter invokes new law.[12]

These cover, in substance, probably every defense which could have been invoked. If the Germans had contended that they had never acted against organizations, instead of against individuals, this would, of course, have been untrue. Not only was the property of the Jews, as a race, confiscated, but the properties of hostile political parties were seized,[13] in addition to causing the arrest, imprisonment, and death of persons belonging to such organizations. And it will be pointed out that Justice Biddle elicited upon examination of Seyss-Inquart the confiscations of the property of Free Masons, Jehovah's Witnesses, and other groups in occupied countries.[14] It should be remembered also that the Germans were quick to enforce collective punishment in conquered lands.[15] And returning for a moment to the liability of the conspirator or member of an organization who takes a single step in the direction toward guilt, it should be remembered that under German law, the taking of this first step, however legal in itself, would render him punishable.[16]

After counsel for the defense had made their objections to the jurisdiction of the Tribunal upon these varied grounds and had expressed fear that they would not receive a fair trial, Robert Jackson made an impassioned reply. He stated that the Allied Powers had not run out of ammunition and would not have created a judicial tribunal if they had intended simply to

---

[11] VIII *Proceedings* 422-30.

[12] VIII *Proceedings* 431-8.

[13] IX *Proceedings* 264 (Goering).

[14] XVI *Proceedings* 109-113.

[15] Freeman, "War Crimes by Enemy Nationals Administering Justice in Occupied Territory," 41 *American Journal of International Law*, p. 579 *et seq.* (July, 1947).

[16] Bennett, "Notes on the German Legal and Penal System," 37 *Journal of Criminal Law & Criminology*, pp. 368-76 (January-February, 1947). This was admitted also by Dr. Jahrreiss, in referring to Article 49b of the German Penal Code. XVII *Proceedings* 510.

execute the members of such organizations.[17] A fair trial would, instead, be afforded.[18] However, he claimed, the defendants and the members of such organizations could not have failed to have knowledge of their aims and purposes.[19] He explained also a thing which defense counsel seemed to have confused. The Tribunal had no power to pass sentence upon any member of an organization because of his membership.[20] Its sole purpose was to determine whether such an organization was criminal in character, and the trials of individual members would be heard fully by the direction of the Control Council under law No. 10.[21] He also discussed the liability, with Justice Biddle of the Tribunal, of mere clerical and administrative employees of such organizations.[22]

Maxwell-Fyfe, for the United Kingdom, pointed out that the fact of dissolution of such organizations was no defense. Nor was the determination of the Tribunal limited to the professed aims of the constitution or charter of such organizations, the test being its acts and conduct, coupled with the publications and declarations of its leaders. Nor was the question of knowledge of the members important. Rather, it was the existence of a reasonable opportunity to know of such criminal aims.[23]

Rudenko pointed out that while the Tribunal had no legislative power, it had great judicial power. He argued that all members participated in the acts of the organizations. Justice Biddle asked him whether, if the Tribunal declared such acts were so open and notorious that all members must have had knowledge, the national tribunals could hold otherwise. Rudenko refused to alter his position.[24]

Shifting his interrogation to defense counsel, Justice Biddle asked each of them, during their presentations, to give their definitions of criminality. He met only with evasion.[25]

In meeting the challenge of defense counsel that such charges were unknown in penal law, De Ribes, for France, called attention to Article 265 of the French Penal Code dealing with associations existing against public peace.[26] Rudenko declared, "In Russia and other lands, membership in an organization which

[17] VIII *Proceedings* 443-4.
[18] VIII *Proceedings* 438-43.
[19] VIII *Proceedings* 438-43, 449.
[20] VIII *Proceedings* 455.
[21] VIII *Proceedings* 452.
[22] VIII *Proceedings* 446-7.
[23] VIII *Proceedings* 455-66.
[24] VIII *Proceedings* 468-73.
[25] VIII *Proceedings* 476-86.
[26] VIII *Proceedings* 384-7.

has criminal aims makes an individual liable."[27] And, in international law, common liability is far from unknown: "When a whole corps systematically disregards the laws of war, e.g., by refusal of quarter, any individuals belonging to it, who are taken prisoners, may be treated as implicated in the offense."[28]

The final result of the trials against the organizations was to find three of the indicted organizations, the Gestapo, SD and SS (in part), guilty, and four, the SA, Reich Cabinet, the General Staff, and High Command, not guilty.[29] As to the questions of conspiracy, while a number of defendants were found not guilty upon that count, the Tribunal accepted the meaning of the Indictment. It declared that Hitler "had to have the cooperation of statesmen, military leaders, diplomats, and business men. When they, with knowledge of his aims, gave him their cooperation, they made themselves parties to the plan he had initiated."[30]

The far reaching effect of the holdings has already been analyzed. The legal justification is a different matter, and justification can be found at least for the conspiracy theory. In municipal criminal law, if one decides to engage in holding up a filling station and learns that the leader plans to shoot the station operator, but continues to follow him, he is unquestionably guilty of murder if the victim is slain. Likewise, if he participates in the robbery with no knowledge of his leader's intention, he will still be guilty of murder.

It is also no defense to say that under the leadership principle there can be no clearly defined course of conduct or predictable act for which the follower should be charged. One joining the Capone gang would not necessarily know whether one week he would assist in the white slave trade, work in a gambling house, aid in a kidnapping, or commit a murder. He would know, however, that the general course of action was one contrary to ordinary decency and in violation of positive law. This, also, a Nazi must have known from the multitude of beatings, tortures, kidnappings, and murders which occurred. It is not the predictability of a specific crime which is relevant, but the assistance in a continuing course of illegality which could result only in the commission of other, and even more unpredictable, crimes.

---

[27] VIII *Proceedings* 387-90.

[28] Holland, *The Laws of War on Land*, 1908, Clarendon Press, p. 60.

[29] I *Proceedings* 255-279.

[30] I *Proceedings* 226.

IX

EX POST FACTO

Many articles have been written in law reviews by attorneys unfamiliar either with the Nuremberg trials or with the doctrines of international law, raising the cry of "ex post facto"—i.e., there was no crime at the time the act was committed—you cannot now make it a crime and punish its commission. This same position has been taken by some authorities upon international law. Certainly it was bandied about considerably by defense counsel in the Nuremberg proceedings.

The doctrine is commonly called "ex post facto" or "nullum crimen sine lege" or "nulla poena sine lege previa" referring variously to the assertion that there is no crime without established law or no punishment without preexisting law. This argument is predicated upon the belief that there was no precedent to warrant a punishment for planning, initiating, or waging aggressive war or conspiracy to do so, or for crimes against humanity in time of peace so far as this particular tribunal was concerned. It could, of course, hardly be contended that punishment could not be administered under German law for kidnappings, torture, or murder—but those were not invoked in the Charter as the law of the Tribunal. Nor could the defense of *ex post facto* be invoked so far as the offenses against the Rules of Land Warfare are concerned. Ample precedent exists as to those offenses. But, as to these newer concepts, the argument must be weighed with great seriousness.

How important is the matter of precedent? We know, in the law of equity, that there is "no wrong without a remedy" and this concept is carried into the Constitution of our nation and our several states so far as civil law is concerned. From our religious training, we have learned the demands of "an eye for an eye." We have already determined that aggressive war was a crime against international law. But assuming it was not, would the defendants still have been punishable in view of the defense of *ex post facto?*

The concept of Justice occasionally needs reassertion in order that it may be kept constantly in sight. When the rules of the common law became restricted and channelled into narrow boundaries, the ecclesiastical, or church, court came into being to grant justice where no other remedy existed. It required no statutes; it required no precedents. True, its decisions became precedents—but in each new situation some wrongdoer was forced to compensate his victim, and was subjected, actually, to civil justice *ex post facto.* The law of equity has become somewhat formalized, but it remains the master of its maxims and not the servant of them—and, in the eyes of the law, to do equity means to do justice. If justice can be secured only through the enforcement of new principles, then new principles must be established.

If two men are alone upon a desert island where there is no established law and one assaults and robs the other, the victim may justly kill the aggressor. His act is both a punishment and a deterrent which is conclusive in character. Yet his action is definitely a precedent and there is no law, other than the law of survival or of common justice, to condone his act. When there was no law in the days of our frontier, each man carried his court of last resort in his holster. In early gold mining days, vigilantes enforced the laws established by the mores of their surroundings, but with no written law and no precedents, other than those which they then established, to guide them. Each time our higher courts overthrow a previously well established precedent in the law, they have altered the law and the individual adversely affected by such reversal may be gravely damaged—yet he cannot complain.

One may not have visualized the act for which he may be punished under a new law, yet his punishment is not deemed retroactive in character. The Mann Act was passed to eliminate the white slave trade. The first man prosecuted for transporting his secretary across a state line to a hotel room may have been completely unaware of the implications which would be read into it by the federal courts. That did not get him out of the penitentiary. Similarly, the Illinois statute which punishes the "odious crime against nature" gives little warning to an offender. Is it "an odious crime against nature" to fill our lungs with tobacco smoke, to wear tight collars, or to drink ourselves into insensibility? Perhaps, but not according to the Illinois courts. Again, the persons first tried for sodomy, bestiality, cunnilingus, or fellation may not have contemplated the application of this law, but the construction of the court made it law.

The first case tried in any situation is necessarily a case of first impression. It has no precedents to follow. It may become a precedent provided (1) the law construed is not thereafter changed; (2) the tribunal continues to exist, or similar tribunals are thereafter created; (3) the decision is deemed a proper one. In the United States there are many situations in the civil law not aided by the existence of specific provisions in the federal or state constitutions or statutes—nor case law to assist, even by way of analogy. In such instances, the court must strike out unaided except by what it deems to be sound principles of justice. So it is in international law. There is no Constitution, no Magna Charta, no Rights of Man either to aid or to limit its development. It draws upon the laws and customs common to all nations and, when these cease to assist, it must go forward upon common principles of justice as to which nations in general must agree.

It may sound strange to lawyers to speak of a "common law" or "customary law" of crime and punishment—but do we not know right from wrong by the training of parents, rather than by statute? Do we not respect the Ten Commandments even when we violate them? The nations have adopted the laws and customs of war as international law—the adoption being merely a codification or recognition of that which those nations recognized as inherently right or inherently wrong. It is the underlying concept of that which is proper and that which is improper which has helped to develop the underlying strata of international law, whether civil or penal.

In this light, it is no objection to declare that one cannot be punished under international law *ex post facto*. If the above definition is followed, one cannot be punished unjustly under international law—for that which is not recognized as just in the community of nations cannot become and is not international law. But if it is just that one be punished for an offense against the common conscience of nations, then it is immaterial whether such offense has been codified in penal law or reduced to treaty form. For in international law there is no restriction as to *ex post facto* law—the question can be only the enforcement of law which is found in the common conscience and which is not subject to quick mutation.

This defense was the rallying point for most of the defense counsel, whether representing individual defendants or indicted organizations.[1] The British Prosecutor met this defense with the argument that the doctrines of international law which were violated have long existed, the only innovation being to provide machinery for carrying out the punishment of the offenders.[2]

---

[1] XVII *Proceedings* 481 *et seq.* (Jahrreiss); 501 (Stahmer); XIX *Proceedings* 52 (Steinbauer, counsel for Seyss-Inquart); 312-331 (Fritz, counsel for Fritzsche); 382-6 (Seidl); XXI *Proceedings* 495 *et seq.* (Merkel, referring to the Declaration of Human Rights, France, March 14, 1946, Article 10, and the declarations of the Control Counsel); XXII *Proceedings* 4 (Gawlik, referring to Fenwick on *International Law*, 1924, p. 578, which would seem to be against his position). See also Ehard, *op cit.*, pp. 231-9.

[2] XIX *Proceedings* 464 (Sir Hartley Shawcross). In some ways, the same might be said of vigilantes.

Other writers have felt that the principle of *ex post facto* is not a limitation upon sovereignty of the prosecuting nations but a principle of justice—and, if no injustice were worked, there was no violation.[3] This was the view taken by the Tribunal:

> "In the first place it is to be observed that the maxim *nullem crimen sine lege* is not a limitation of sovereignty, but is in general a principle of justice. To assert that it is unjust to punish those who in defiance of treaties and assurances have attacked neighboring states without warning is obviously untrue, for in such circumstances the attacker must know that he is doing wrong, and so far from it being unjust to punish him, it would be unjust if his wrong were allowed to go unpunished."[4]

One writer, endorsing the view taken by the Tribunal,[5] points out also that a retroactive law which provides punishment for acts which were illegal when committed is an exception to the doctrine of *ex post facto*.[6] He points out also that the doctrine does not exist in international law, and is valid within national law only with important exceptions.[7] Another writer makes the point that there is no written constitution in international law, which could raise such an inhibition.[8] Thus, English law, which has no constitution, has no prohibition against *ex post facto* punishment,[9] although in practice the restriction is generally observed. And it has been pointed out that the American rule against *ex post facto* is, historically, a pure accident.[10]

The doctrine of *ex post facto* was argued with particular vigor in connection with the efforts of the Prosecution to fasten personal liability upon the defendants. The defense claimed that this was new and unusual in international law—that, while the vanquished state might be punished, individuals were immune.

---

[3] Mignone, "After Nuremburg, Tokyo," 25 *Texas Law Review*, pp. 475-90 (May, 1947); Biddle, "The Nurnberg Trial," 33 *Virginia Law Review*, p. 679 *et seq.* (November, 1947).

[4] I *Proceedings* 219 (Judgment).

[5] Kelsen, "Will the Judgment in the Nuremberg Trial Constitute a Precedent in International Law?", I *International Law Quarterly*, No. 2, p. 165 (Summer, 1947).

[6] Kelsen, *supra*, p. 165.

[7] Kelsen, *supra*, p. 164, referring to his discussion in *The Judge Advocate Journal*, Vol. II, No. 3, p. 8ff and 46 (1945).

[8] Glueck, *The Nuremberg Trial and Aggressive War*, 1946, Knopf, p. 40 *et seq.* This view is denied by a German writer, citing from a decision of the Permanent Court of International Justice in 1934. See Ehard, *op cit.*, p. 231.

[9] Ireland, "Ex Post Facto from Rome to Toyko," 21 *Temple Law Quarterly*, p. 27-61 (July, 1947).

[10] Glueck, *supra* note 8, pp. 39-40, referring to *U. S. v. Hudson*, 1812, 7 Cranch 32, 2 Curtis 445, 3 L. ed. 259.

This is not, of course, true as to war crimes or violations of a national law, but, assuming that the charges were novel and new, it is important to examine the logic of that rule and its significance in international law.

If it is claimed that one should never punish the individual but only the governmental unit, in this particular instance a nation, what would be the result if the same reasoning were applied in municipal law? If one saw a bully beating a child, he could not restrain him nor strike him, but could only bring an action against the government having jurisdiction over that individual for punitive damages. Yet a nation is only a larger governmental unit than a local body, and occasionally even smaller in both size and population. One writer denies individual responsibility for either an aggressive or illegal war, and says that only the State is punishable, and elsewhere declares that punishment of an individual for an act of a State means that such State is being acted upon.[11] The inconsistency is apparent.

While the counsel for defendants claimed that liability of the individual has never been recognized in international law,[12] certain writers have taken direct issue with this stand.[13] Such acts as piracy,[14] sabotage,[15] breach of blockade,[16] the torpedoeing of boats and machine gunning of survivors,[17] espionage,[18] harboring of fugitives,[19] brigandage,[20] guerilla warfare,[21] and other acts have resulted in trials of the individuals concerned,

---

11 Kelsen, "Will the Judgment in the Nuremberg Trial Constitute a Precedent?", I *International Law Quarterly*, pp. 156, 159 (Summer, 1947).

12 XVII *Proceedings* 478-479 (Jahrreiss); 507 (Stahmer); XVIII *Proceedings* 143 (Seidl).

13 Cowles, "Trial of War Criminals (Non-Nuremberg)," 42 *American Journal of International Law*, p. 299 *et seq.* (April, 1948). Green, "The Military Commission," 42 *American Journal of International Law*, p. 832 *et seq.* (October, 1948).

14 Glueck, *War Criminals, Their Prosecution and Punishment*, 1944, Knopf, pp. 100-4; Glueck, *The Nuremberg Trial and Aggressive War*, 1946, Knopf, pp. 60-71; Cowles, "Universality of Jurisdiction Over War Criminals," 33 *California Law Review*, p. 177 *et seq.* (June, 1945); Shawcross, *Proceedings* XIX, p. 464. Also League of Nations, 1926, December C 196. M. 70, 1927 v. pp. 204-5.

15 Glueck, *op cit.*, (n. 14); Biddle, "The Nurnberg Trial," 33 *Virginia Law Review*, No. 6, p. 679 *et seq.* (November, 1947); *Ex Parte Quirin*, 317 U. S. 1.

16 Glueck, *op cit.*, (n. 14); Biddle, *op cit.*, p. 679 *et seq.*

17 Glueck, *op cit.*, (see n. 14 *supra)*, referring to Leipzig trials.

18 Biddle, *op cit.*, p. 697 *et seq.;* XIX *Proceedings* 464 (Shawcross).

19 Biddle, *op. cit.* (see n. 15 *supra*).

20 Cowles, *op. cit.*, p. 299 *et seq.*, referring to Grotius 794 n. 39; Pufendorf 94.

21 Cowles, *op cit.*, p. 299 *et seq.*, referring to Winfield Scott's General Orders No. 372, Dec. 12, 1847 as to Mexican guerillas.

wholly excluding the common trials by military courts of offenses against the laws of war. Historically, the trials of individuals for international offenses are of long standing. Some of those commonly referred to are the Breisach War Crime Trial of 1474 by Sir Peter of Hagenbach,[22] the trial conducted by the English courts in 1796 for the furnishing of unwholesome food to French prisoners to the discredit of the King,[23] the holding by England that scurrilous reflections upon those of rank and influence in foreign States constituted criminal libel,[24] the making of similar decisions upon libelous matters in the United States,[25] the exile of Bonaparte and final declaration of him to be an "outlaw,"[26] the Leipzig Trials after World War I,[27] and the saboteurs case in the United States.[28]

It was aptly pointed out by Sir Hartley Shawcross that the German Reich had by Article 4 of the Weimar Constitution made the recognized rules of international law a part of the national law of the Reich. Since national law operates only against individuals, this must be deemed a recognition of individual liability for international offenses.[29] Robert Jackson referred to the German military code rendering a soldier guilty if he exceeded orders or carried orders that were, within his knowledge, violations of law.[30] But it should also be pointed out that the function of international law is not to establish tribunals or administrative details. It is, rather, to establish the broad general principles of law and justice recognized by nations. Thus it has long been recognized that individuals may be punished for violations of the Hague Rules of Land Warfare,[31] yet nowhere does that treaty establish what such punishment shall be.

As indicative of the general feeling and conscience of nations upon the subject of individual responsibility, other steps which have been taken to establish some uniformity of application, whether reduced to a final treaty or not, are of interest.

Article 228 of the Treaty of Versailles contained a recognition by Germany of the right of the Allied powers to try and

---

22 Finch, "The Nuremberg Trial and International Law," 41 *American Journal of International Law*, p. 20 *et seq.*, note 32 (January, 1947).

23 Glueck, *op cit.* (see n. 14 *supra*).

24 Glueck, *op cit.* (see n. 14 *supra*).

25 Glueck, *op cit.* (see n. 14 *supra*).

26 Finch, *op cit.*, p. 20 *et seq.;* Glueck, *op cit.*, 1944, p. 127, 1946, pp. 9-10.

27 Glueck, *op cit.* (see note 14, *supra*).

28 Glueck, *op cit.* (see note 14 *supra*), 1942; *Ex Parte Quirin*, 1942, 317 U. S. 1, 63 S. Ct. 2, 87 L. Ed. 3; I *Proceedings* 222-3.

29 XIX *Proceedings* 464.

30 II *Proceedings* 150-1.

31 I *Proceedings* 220-1 (Judgment of the Tribunal); Holland, *The Laws of War on Land*, 1908, Clarendon Press, pp. 14-17, 59-60.

punish war criminals, referring in that case to the Kaiser.[32] The Commission to the Preliminary Peace Conference also had recommended a special body to deal with the "authors" of the acts made illegal and wanted penal sanctions imposed.[33] Article 29 of the 1929 Geneva Convention required the governments of the contracting parties to recommend to their legislatures necessary means to suppress acts in violation of the agreement.[34] This would necessarily contemplate individual punishment, since the independent State, by its laws, contemplates action only against its citizens. And Article 3 of the Treaty Relating to the Use of Submarines and Noxious Gases in Warfare adopted in the Washington Conference for the Reductions of Armaments and for the Pacific and Far Eastern Problems declares that any person in the service of any power who violates a rule, whether subordinate to an official personality or not, will be a transgressor and liable to trial.[35]

One writer points out, however, that the failure of the civilized nations to ratify such expressions is indicative of the non-acceptance of that principle,[36] which is further illustrated by the failure of the same nations to adopt, up to that time, by any international agreement, the same principles since the Nuremberg Trial.[37] However, even opponents of the trial must admit that violations of international law have long been punishable, even in the absence of legislative material fixing the punishments. Clearly the concept of aggressive war was, long prior to 1939, one of illegality. Crimes against humanity have been both offenses against civilization and violations of national laws for many years. And certainly, a defendant who is a national of any State cannot complain when the offenses charged are common to his own law and the tribunal is one competent to pass upon his case.

But, with reference to the concept of individual punishment, it seems that many writers who have quibbled over technicalities in the establishment of the Nuremberg Tribunal, have lost sight of one major factor. It is a crime, *per se,* for one indivi-

[32] I *Proceedings* 222-3 (Judgment of the Tribunal).

[33] Glueck, *The Nuremberg Trial & Aggressive War,* 1946, Knopf, p. 14-16.

[34] VIII *Proceedings* 149-50 (Opening address of Rudenko).

[35] VII *Proceedings* 149-50. See the Conference Proceedings, Government Printing Office, 1922, p. 1608.

[36] Schick, "International Criminal Law; Facts & Illusions," *Modern Law Review,* p. 290 *et seq.* (July, 1948). Ehard, *op cit.,* p. 230.

[37] Schick, "International Criminal Law; Facts & Illusions," II *Modern Law Review,* p. 290 *et seq.* (July, 1948); Schick, "The Nuremberg Trial and the International Law of the Future," 41 *American Journal of International Law,* p. 770 *et seq.* (October, 1947).

dual to kill another. It is a crime to restrain another against his will, or to assault or beat him. These things, occurring in time of war, are legalized, we say, under the doctrine of necessity, justified by the abnormal occasion. But suppose the war, which is relied upon as a defense, is itself illegal? What happens to the defense or excuse upon which the wrongdoer relies?

It may be excusable for a police officer to kill a felon fleeing capture or engaged in robbery. It is not legal, however, for the robber to slay his victim who resists. One who defends against the felonious entry of a burglar is justified even in the slaying of the intruder, but the burglar has no such defense. Aggressive war has, it is believed, by the acceptance of nations and their pacts and assurances, been outlawed. The effect of outlawing aggressive war is to remove the legal excuse or justification for the instigation or commission of acts otherwise condemned by all penal codes, and to render the offenders liable to answer for the crime of murder, mayhem, arson, theft, kidnapping, or whatever it may be. That is the impact of international law upon national law, and the punishments commonly accepted in national law may, themselves, help to constitute international law.

This view was urged also by the American prosecutor,[38] and has been postulated by writers in the field of international law.[39] It is deserving of serious consideration.

---

[38] Jackson in II *Proceedings* 146-7.

[39] Renault, "L'Application du Droit Penal aux faits de Guerre," 25 *Revue Generale du Droit International Publique*, p. 25 et seq.; Garner, *International Law and the World War*, 1920, Longmark, Green & Co., Vol. II, pp. 478-80; Schick, "The Nuremberg Trial and the International Law of the Future," 41 *American Journal of International Law*, pp. 770 *et seq.* (October, 1947).

X

ACT OF STATE; RESPONDEAT SUPERIOR

Defense counsel frequently brought out by testimony or in their arguments that the individual defendants had no choice but to perform the acts charged against them. Particularly in a dictatorship, it was the argument, there was but one leader—all others were mere followers.[1] This raised the question, with reference to subordinates, of the legal defense of *respondeat superior*—or, let the master answer, rather than the servant; and, in the case of those in command, of the doctrine of Act of State—or, in other words, the act of the leader is the act of the sovereign, and the State should answer instead of the individual. These defenses are allied, if not identical, in the eyes of the law. In army parlance they would be termed "passing the buck." Whether the defenses are valid as to violations of international law must be determined.

It is clear that individuals have obligations which transcend those of a purely national character.[2] A killing by a soldier is ordinarily deemed lawful only if he is acting under orders and if his act is in accordance with international law.[3] He can defend neither upon the ground of *respondeat superior* nor of Act of State if the deed is a clear violation of international

---

1 In closing arguments XVII *Proceedings* 482-494, Jahrreiss argued that in a dictatorship the final decision rests with a single individual and his orders are absolutely binding—'legibus solutus.' The subordinates could not question such orders. Horn uses a similar argument in XVII *Proceedings* 595-603. Nelte in XVII *Proceedings* 638 points out that anyone accepting the leadership principle would be bound to obey. Exner gives an excellent discussion in XIX *Proceedings* at 21. Flachsner in XIX *Proceedings* at 210, after pointing out the single supremacy, declares: "All others are only led." In XXI *Proceedings* at 537 Merkel pointed out that every German civil servant is trained in the strictest obedience, while Laternser in XXII *Proceedings* at 45-63 points out the duty of obedience.

The defendant military men repeatedly pointed out that it was their duty to follow out and execute the orders given them. The witness Milch in IX *Proceedings* at 118 pointed out, however, that it was the duty of a soldier to object in matters within his province and where he had a say as a soldier. Speer in XVI *Proceedings* at 558 believed the leaders were responsible for basic principles. But a definite attempt was made in the evidence to show that all orders emanated from Hitler. E.g., Nelte's cross-examination of Paulus in VII *Proceedings* 279-283.

2 Mignone, "After Nuremberg, Toyko," 25 *Texas Law Review*, pp. 475-90 (May, 1947).

3 Glueck, *War Criminals—Their Prosecution and Punishment*, 1944, Knopf, at 43.

law.[4] Thus the soldier may be in a most painful position, that of being punished if he disobeys and of being prosecuted if he obeys.[5]

The question of obedience of a military order may raise a very peculiar situation. Suppose a bombardier should say to his commanding officer, "I will not drop that atom bomb; I consider it contrary to international law." He will be shot if he refuses and he may be hanged if some later tribunal decides that his act has shocked the common conscience of nations. And what of his commanding officer who is instructed by the President: "Mass your troops along the Mexican border." Is he to say, "Now wait a minute. The mobilization of troops along the border would give Mexico the right to declare war upon us as an aggressor nation. Now give me a complete history of all the incidents leading up to your order so that my attorney and I can judge whether to act or whether to refuse to obey your orders."

Professor Exner, representing General Jodl, propounded just such a riddle to the Tribunal.[6] Suppose, he says, the Security Council has set up a World Police to protect the world against aggression. "Now let us imagine that the Security Council decides on a punitive war and the Chief of the General Staff replies that in his opinion there is no aggression." Again, in speaking of general military duties, he declares, "The general will only seldom be in a position to judge whether the state to be attacked by him has broken its neutrality or whether it threatens to attack or not."

It is not always a simple task to draw the dividing line. One must look, necessarily, to the knowledge possessed, the discretion to act or to decline to act, and the motives of the individual. In ordinary criminal law, for example, loyalty to a leader, or a mistaken belief in duty, has never been recognized as a defense to criminal responsibility. In international relations, some line of demarcation between legality and illegality must be drawn.

---

[4] Glueck, *op cit.*, pp. 133-9; Mignone, *op cit.;* Finch, "The Nuremberg Trial and International Law," 41 *American Journal of International Law*, p. 20 *et seq.* (January, 1947); Schick, "The Nuremberg Trial and the International Law of the Future," 41 *American Journal of International Law*, p. 770 *et seq.* (October, 1947) (referring also to 1944 amendment to American Basic Field Manual); II *Proceedings* 150-1 (Jackson referring also to German Military Code making soldier liable if he obeys an order he knows is in violation of law); XIX *Proceedings* 465-6 (Sir Hartley Shawcross).

[5] Baty & Morgan, *War, Its Conduct and Legal Results*, 1915, Dutton & Co., at 148, quoting Dicey; Glueck, *War Criminals—Their Prosecution and Punishment*, 1944, Knopf, pp. 140-160. Glueck points out, however, that knowledge of illegality, or reasonable means for knowing thereof, is usually required.

[6] XIX *Proceedings* p. 21.

An example given by Sir Hartley Shawcross is excellent.[7] Suppose, he says, a State sent a group of individuals into another state to murder and to rob. Could they plead immunity from punishment under the national law of the second state because they acted under orders? The British Prosecutor considered that such a defense would be absurd. The Tribunal, in its opinion, pointed out that the law established by its Charter did not recognize the doctrines of *respondeat superior* or Act of State as absolute defenses, but only in mitigation of the offenses. This, it stated, represented the actual existing doctrines of international law, orders to a soldier not being a defense where the act commanded was in violation of international law. The true test, it held, was "whether moral choice was in fact possible."[8] Although several defendants had stated it was impossible for anyone to withdraw except with great danger, Jackson brought out that General Von Brauchitsch's father had been able to disassociate himself from the Nazis and retire in 1941.[9] Raeder admitted that he could have resigned.[10] And it appeared throughout the evidence that Von Neurath, Von Papen, and Schacht had resigned offices from time to time or given up certain duties.

It has been pointed out also that even a sovereign, or an ex-sovereign, who could more justifiably rely upon the doctrine of Act of State than could a subordinate, may be amenable to punishment.[11]

The doctrine of "Act of State" as a defense to individual criminal responsibility can be carried to absurd lengths. In America, we are prone to speak blithely of a "government of the people, by the people, and for the people." If that were true, the State would be the people and each common citizen would be punishable as the supreme authority. But let us look to a totalitarian state, such as Germany, to determine responsibility for, let us say, the shooting of a prisoner of war.

The soldier says, "I shot this man upon the sergeant's orders." The sergeant says, "The lieutenant ordered it." The lieutenant says, "Captain Hirsch issued a general order covering this situation." Captain Hirsch refers to Major Blank, Major Blank to Colonel Jacobs, Colonel Jacobs to Lieutenant Colonel General Abrams, and Abrams refers to a directive of Goering. Goering says, "Ah yes, but the Fuhrer ordered it." Hitler says,

---

[7] XIX *Proceedings* p. 465.

[8] I *Proceedings* 223-4.

[9] IX *Proceedings* 145-47.

[10] XIV *Proceedings* 220. And see Biddle's discussion in 33 *Virginia Law Review*, p. 679 *et seq.* (November, 1947).

[11] Glueck, *War Criminals—Their Prosecution and Punishment*, 1944, Knopf, pp. 122-7. But compare Ehard's discussion, *op cit.*, p. 240.

"I have communed with God and followed his directives."[12] Are all immune except the Almighty for the folly of his children?

What is a state? Is it some metaphysical being, abstract and personalized only in a spiritual sense—is it territory surrounded by natural and artificial boundaries—is it industry and an economic system operated as an impersonal unit? Actually, there would seem to be no single cogent unit which is the State. A State or nation is merely an aggregate of people having certain elements in common living in more or less defined boundaries. In a dictatorship, the State is often considered as the functioning governmental agency, or, in other words, those involved in making the decisions. That is the leadership principle.[13] But the cry is raised "You cannot punish the individual, you can punish only the State." So you take land or colonies—who is punished? Generally the persons living within the boundaries taken. You impose the payment of reparations. The person punished is the laborer, the white collar worker, the persons either who did not know what was occurring or were powerless to prevent it under the leadership principle. It might well be asked if this is Justice. Yet that is the type of punishment when you punish the State, and the criminal mind directing the punishable acts has already lined his bank account, ready to flee the nation, and so might escape with impunity.

Taking all these factors into consideration, it would seem that the test adopted by the Tribunal was a fair one.

---

[12] In case the reader thinks I am resorting to a "reductio ad absurdum," let him read General Winter's testimony in XV *Proceedings* 604-9. After testifying that one could not resign, he referred to Hitler who told him that others should not resign as he, Hitler, could not go to God and resign. Also remember the divine directives of Jeanne d'Arc.

[13] See Jackson's cross-examination of Goering. IX *Proceedings* 418.

IMT defendants in the dock. Left to right, first row: Goering, Hess, Ribbentrop, Keitel, Kaltenbrunner, Rosenberg, Frank, Frick, Streicher, Funk, Schacht; second row: Doenitz, Raeder, Schirach, Sauckel, Jodl, Von Papen, Seyss-Inquart, Speer, Neurath, and Fritzsche.

XI

MENS REA; RECOGNITION OF GUILT

While some crimes may be committed which are punishable in the absence of criminal intent, most are in the nature of "specific intent" offenses. This does not mean that one needs must know the law and have intended to violate it. It is immaterial that the accused may have tried to walk a legal tightrope, so long as he failed to keep his balance. Indeed, ignorance of the law's existence or application will not excuse him. In the case of a general intent crime, such as manslaughter, the offender need not have intended wrong or injury. If he runs amuck with an automobile, while intoxicated, the occurrence of the result is traced to general culpable conduct and serves as a basis for punishment. In a specific intent crime such as assault with intent to kill, burglary, or murder, the wrongdoer must have intended the consequences of his act. If he intended to do the thing which he did, then no further proof of his mental state is required.

The defense of "mens rea" does not, therefore, require the Prosecution to prove a sense of guilt in the wrongdoer. Whether one had a conscious sense of guilt at the time of commission of the offense, or was conscious of the fact that he might be punished for his act, is immaterial. Certain criminals are proud, rather than ashamed, of their misdeeds and keep scrapbooks of their press clippings. One may have a sense of righteousness in killing his neighbor, but the law will call it murder. The reasonable man test runs through the bulk of criminal jurisprudence, and if reasonable men, such as a jury of one's peers, agree that an act is evil and without justification, that becomes law in action. The will of the errant philosopher must bow to the mores of the majority, where the penal law is concerned.

The defense counsel, however, relied heavily upon this doctrine and it becomes rather impressive in the hands of men with the skill shown by those attorneys. Jahrreiss claimed that one could not be accused of guilt if he felt, at the time of his act, that he was merely performing his duty.[1] Nelte pointed out forcefully how many different concepts of conduct can exist, dependent upon the perspective—*e.g.* "soldierly" versus "militaristic," "natural obedience" versus "blind subservience," "deep love of country" versus "chauvinism" *et cetera.* He declared also

[1] XVII *Proceedings* 484.

that one's interpretation will vary depending upon tradition, education, and point of view.[2] Seidl claimed that "only in primitive law did there exist criminal responsibility without guilt."[3] The other counsel also stressed the defense of "mens rea."[4] The very forceful Professor Exner, who was not even a professional lawyer, came up with another of his excellent illustrations in defending General Jodl. "Someone," he said, "who takes someone else's watch in the belief that it is his own is no thief. * * * So if Jodl believed that facts existed which, had they been true, would have made the war a legally admissible one, no sentence for breach of the peace can be imposed."[5]

The view accepted by the Tribunal was later excellently discussed by Justice Francis Biddle who pointed out that certain German leaders who had demurred had retired and taken no further part in the Nazi program. One could have expected, he said, at least the resistance of decent men.[6] And another eminent writer felt that the defense of lack of moral wrongdoing has no foundation in any national law.[7]

The question also then arises "Did the defendants believe they had any guilt?" By this is not meant responsibility with reference to specific charges. That discussion involves a consideration of the nature of those charges, the legal responsibility of each defendant in that connection, the law applicable, and the specific defense, if any, raised, which questions are discussed elsewhere in more detail. In general, however, the totalitarian state of Germany, with its expanded concept of state sovereignty, its lebensraum, Aryan supremacy and ruthless subordination of the interests of all individuals and all races in the struggle toward that goal, produced a certain unity of purpose and effort which was largely recognized by the defendants in this trial. If this feeling persisted throughout the trial, then those sentenced to death must have conceived themselves to be martyrs; if, however, their philosophies had altered prior to or during the trial, they may have felt punishment to be merited.

In considering this question it is not necessary to consider whether the defendants had particular knowledge of each step performed in the common plan. Not one defendant admitted

---

[2] XVII *Proceedings* 604.

[3] XIX *Proceedings* 387.

[4] XXI *Proceedings* 489 (Servatius); 625-32 (Gawlik); XXII *Proceedings* 128-131 (Bohm).

[5] XIX *Proceedings* 24.

[6] Biddle, "The Nurnberg Trial," 33 *Virginia Law Review*, p. 679 *et seq.* (November, 1947).

[7] Schick, "The Nuremberg Trial and the International Law of the Future," 41 *American Journal of International Law*, p. 770 *et seq.* (October, 1947).

personal knowledge of the slaughter of the Jews. That, apparently, came as a shock to all—although not to Americans who had been reading magazine articles upon the subject since 1935. None of them admitted prior knowledge of Hitler's plans for aggressive war. They all agreed that Hitler apparently knew only two days beforehand what he was going to do, and they merely followed orders. Since they had pledged their undivided allegiance to Hitler and had followed him with blind loyalty, their feelings after the defeat of Germany may be somewhat tested by observing their reactions at the time of trial.

Goering stated calmly that Hitler was the leader and he the follower, that he believed in loyalty in bad times as well as good,[8] and spoke of Hitler with undiminished admiration.[9] Seyss-Inquart one must admire also for his consistency. He declared: "To me he remains the man who made Greater Germany a fact in German history. I served this man. And now? I cannot today cry, 'Crucify him,' since yesterday I cried, 'Hosanna.' "[10]

Hess, in speaking of Hitler, said that the Fuhrer had a tendency to madness in later years.[11] Keitel, in his testimony, placed the blame for every act upon Hitler's doorstep.[12] Schacht termed Hitler a "liar and a deceiver" and a "hundredfold perjurer."[13] Rosenberg claimed that Hitler did not practice National Socialism, but abused it.[14] Von Papen termed Hitler a "great crook."[15] Frank termed the way of Hitler "the way without God."[16] Funk claimed he was deceived and imposed upon.[17] Von Schirach stated that he had supported Hitler out of "erroneous loyalty."[18]

This shows some deviation in the theretofore loyal adherence given to the man. What of the system which he represented? All had formerly been intense in their unity behind the "leadership" principle.

Speer, an intelligent architect and engineer, told in detail the dangers of the dictatorship system which he described as most efficient in war and most prone to engage in war. He pointed out that the advent of radio had deprived people of independent thought. The more technical the world becomes, the

8 IX *Proceedings* 428, 432, 652.
9 IX *Proceedings* 236-9, 427, 428, 438-9.
10 XXII *Proceedings* 405.
11 XXII *Proceedings* 370.
12 X *Proceedings* 473, 477, 478, 482-7, 496, 497, 503-7, 543-9, 565-7.
13 XII *Proceedings* 454, 519.
14 XXII *Proceedings* 382.
15 XVI *Proceedings* 338.
16 XXII *Proceedings* 384.
17 XXII *Proceedings* 387-8.
18 XIV *Proceedings* 514.

greater the danger of conquest by a single State. He described the advancing techniques of war through rockets, atomic power, pestilence and chemistry, declaring that one more war will destroy human culture and civilization. He was obviously much concerned over the system and its threat to the world.[19] Von Ribbentrop expressed great concern over the threat to civilization presented by Soviet Russia.[20]

Goering found no fault with the Nazi system.[21] Doenitz claimed that the Fuhrer principle was the best for military leadership, but, in view of the result, "then this principle as such must be wrong, wrong because apparently human nature is not in a position to use the power of this principle for good, without falling victim to the temptations of this power."[22] Fritzsche claimed it was time to call a halt in the sowing of hatreds.[23]

Frank, in his statement to the Tribunal following the close of the individual cases, expressed himself dramatically. "At the beginning of our way," he said, "we did not suspect that our turning away from God could have such disastrous deadly consequences that we would necessarily become more and more deeply involved in guilt. * * * Thus, by turning away from God, we were overthrown and had to perish. * * * * * * Before all, God pronounced and executed judgment on Hitler and the system which we served with minds far from God. Therefore, may our people, too, be called back from the road on which Hitler—and we with him—have led them. I beg of our people not to continue in this direction, be it even a single step, because Hitler's road was the way without God, the way of turning from Christ, and, in the last analysis, the way of political foolishness, the way of disaster, and the way of death."[24]

Equally dramatic was the testimony of witness Von Dem Bach-Zelewski, in his examination by Dr. Thoma.[25]

Dr. Thoma: Do you believe that Himmler's speech, in which he demanded the extermination of thirty million Slavs, expressed only his personal opinion, or do you consider that it corresponded to the National Socialist ideology?

Von Dem Bach-Zelewski: Today I believe it was the logical consequence of our ideology.

Dr. Thoma: Today?

Von Dem Bach-Zelewski: Today.

---

19 XXII *Proceedings* 405-7.
20 XXII *Proceedings* 373-5.
21 XXII *Proceedings* 366-8.
22 XXII *Proceedings* 390-1.
23 XXII *Proceedings* 410.
24 XXII *Proceedings* 383-5.
25 IV *Proceedings* 494.

Dr. Thoma: What was your opinion at that time?

Von Dem Bach-Zelewski: It is difficult for a German to fight through to this conviction. It took me a long time.

Dr. Thoma: Then how is it that a few days ago a witness, namely, the witness Ohlendorf, appeared here and admitted that through the Einsatzgruppen he had killed 90,000 people, but told the Tribunal that this did not harmonize with the National Socialist ideology.

Von Dem Bach-Zelewski: I am of a different opinion. If for years, for decades, a doctrine is preached to the effect that the Slav is an inferior race, that the Jews are not even human beings, then an explosion of this sort is inevitable.

This, the patient groping of the witness for the truth in his own heart, is more dramatic actually than the protestations of guilt or innocence of individual defendants. But we must see whether these individuals believed they had any general guilt and, in so doing, see whether or not they believed they had received fair trials from the Tribunal.

Goering, upon taking the witness stand, calmly accepted responsibility for any of his acts or decrees.[26] When asked about responsibility of the other defendants, although Jackson on cross-examination elicited much damaging information concerning the other parties, Goering claimed that only he and Hitler could be considered conspirators, none of the others.[27] In his final statement to the Tribunal he claimed that he had never wanted war and had no ulterior motive in any act he had done. He claimed also that the Prosecution had relied on statements when to its interest, and otherwise had termed them falsehoods. Also, he said, international law should work two ways—if the prosecuting nations have the powers they claim as victors of Germany, then Germany had the power to act as it did in occupied nations. German industry was now being dismantled and taken to other nations, the property of Germans confiscated, and serious infringements placed on their freedom. Germany, during the rise of Hitlerism, he added, was treated by other nations as a sovereign state, with none of its actions protested by the prosecuting nations.[28] We may summarize his attitude in his testimony and address to the effect that while he accepted official responsibility, he felt no guilt and believed the acts of the prosecuting nations and the conduct of the trial to be unfair.

Hess had early, upon admitting the feigning of amnesia, accepted official responsibility and stated that he did not want

---

26 IX *Proceedings* 235-6.

27 IX *Proceedings* 401.

28 XXII *Proceedings* 365-68.

to be defended as to those charges.[29] In his address to the Tribunal, he stated that he regretted nothing he had done. He spoke also of the fact that he had predicted false testimony and shameless utterances and that his predictions had come true. He spoke of the Russian situation in 1936-8 when defendants repeatedly accused themselves of crime. They showed, he said, an abnormal state of mind, some influence which made them act according to orders given them. He spoke of people with "strange eyes" who first surrounded him after his flight—persons with "glazed and dreamy eyes" who would be replaced after regaining normality. He believed the personnel of the concentration camps must have been influenced the same way. He spoke also of British concentration camps during the Boer war and the great number of deaths therein.[30] One may conclude that Hess had no feeling of guilt.

Von Ribbentrop felt that the Tribunal had been unfair in rejecting documents and precluding the showing of the attitude of other nations while the acts alleged were being committed. He declared, "This Trial will go down in history as a model example of how, while appealing to hitherto unknown legal formulas and the spirit of fairness, one can evade the cardinal problems of twenty-five years of the gravest human history." He spoke of the injustice of the Treaty of Versailles, the recognition by other nations of Germany's acts, the joinder of Russia in the partition of Poland and of his personal conversations with Stalin, and the threat which Russia represented to Europe and to civilization. He hoped only that the western powers would have more success in checking Russia than had Germany. His only guilt, he declared, was "that my aspirations in foreign policy remained without success."[31]

Keitel denied that he was either a willing tool, or responsible for the acts of branches of the Wehrmacht. In case of a victory, he said, he would have been proud of it; however, if placed in the same position again, he would choose death before he would be drawn into the net of such pernicious methods. He believed, but he erred, and he was not in a position to prevent that which ought to have been prevented. He did not "see that there is a limit set even for a soldier's performance of his duty." His only hope was a new future for the German people.[32]

Kaltenbrunner, who had, in his testimony, accepted full responsibility for his acts and directives since 1943 when he became chief of the RuSHA,[33] denied responsibility for atrocities

[29] II *Proceedings* 496, also IX *Proceedings* 692-3.
[30] XXII *Proceedings* 368-73.
[31] XXII *Proceedings* 373-5.
[32] XXII *Proceedings* 375-8.

and placed the blame upon Himmler. He spoke of his attempts to rectify the conditions he discovered. He acted as a soldier, and in this he may have made mistakes through a "false conception of obedience."[34]

Rosenberg, who had also accepted responsibility earlier, coupled with a statement that he had tried to prevent excesses,[35] spoke of his opposition to all measures of violence, and of the true aims of National Socialism. He welcomed the idea of outlawing genocide by international law with severest penalties.[36]

Frank had testified earlier that he had a deep sense of guilt after having gained a full insight during the five months of trial into the atrocities committed.[37] Much of his statement following the close of the individual cases has already been quoted. However, while admitting personal guilt, he claimed that the guilt of the German nation had been wiped out by the mass crimes now being committed by Russians, Poles, and Czechs. "Who shall ever judge these crimes against the German people?" he asked.[38]

Frick stated that he felt no guilt—he had acted in the service of his fatherland and as a patriotic citizen.[39] Streicher had earlier claimed great unfairness in the Tribunal in refusing to admit documents or to consider all of the defenses made, which required judging the acts of other nations.[40] He apparently now had no feeling of personal guilt.[41]

Funk claimed that he had been deceived and imposed upon; that he had not been aware of the nature of SS deposits in the Reichsbank nor aware of the Jewish massacres. Had he known of these crimes, he would have acted though it cost him his life. He conceded that he had been too gullible, but stated that he felt no criminal guilt.[42]

Schacht described his violent opposition to Hitler and obviously felt himself to be a loyal German and misjudged man.[43] Von Papen spoke of the purpose of his diplomatic actions and evaded all other issues.[44] The statements of Speer and Seyss-Inquart have been discussed at length previously. Sauckel por-

---

33 XI *Proceedings* 232.
34 XXII *Proceedings* 378-81.
35 XI *Proceedings* 536.
36 XXII *Proceedings* 381-3.
37 XII *Proceedings* 8.
38 XXII *Proceedings* 385.
39 XXII *Proceedings* 385.
40 XII *Proceedings* 305-7.
41 XXII *Proceedings* 385-7.
42 XXII *Proceedings* 387-8.
43 XXII *Proceedings* 388-90.
44 XXII *Proceedings* 400-2.

trayed himself as a mere workman lost in the realms of higher intrigue, and while assuming responsibility for importing foreign labor denied that it had been ill-treated.[45] Von Neurath stated he had a clear conscience.[46] Fritzsche stated that his only guilt was that he believed the German denials of the atrocities.[47]

Doenitz considered the submarine warfare justified, stating, "I would do exactly the same all over again."[48] Raeder believed the trial beneficial as proving the German people knew nothing of the atrocities and as proving the cleanness and decency of the German Navy in battle.[49] Jodl spoke with bitterness of the killing of women and children by the Allies through bombing raids and machine gunning and believed even harsh measures were justified under those conditions. He believed his duty "toward his people and fatherland stands above every other."[50] And apparently he believed in the principle of post-war trials. When cross-examined by Roberts who asked, "But should we have heard anything about these convictions and this conscience if Germany had not lost the war?" He replied, "No, but then we might have heard of the strangled at Dieppe in a similar trial."[51]

And Von Schirach denied corruption of the youth of Germany and told of the innocence of the young. He asked the judges to help remove the distorted picture the world had of German youth.[52]

As to the opinion German witnesses had of the guilt of these defendants, Gisevius, of course, excluded none from his condemnations, except Schacht in part.[53] Severing discussed the various defendants in detail,[54] as did Von Steengracht.[55] Many of the defendants passed blame to those now dead, although occasionally to living defendants, while Schacht, when asked by Jackson to name those he would consider criminals, named Hitler, Himmler, Bormann, Goering, Heydrich, and possibly Von Ribbentrop. He stated he regretted also that some of them were dead—he would have preferred to see them die some other way.[56]

---

[45] XXII *Proceedings* 396-9.

[46] XXII *Proceedings* 408.

[47] XXII *Proceedings* 408-10.

[48] XXII *Proceedings* 390-1.

[49] XXII *Proceedings* 391-2.

[50] XXII *Proceedings* 400.

[51] XV *Proceedings* 487.

[52] XXII *Proceedings* 392-4.

[53] XII *Proceedings* 264-8.

[54] XIV *Proceedings* 271-4.

[55] X *Proceedings* 135-8. The witness named Rosenberg, Frank, Hess, Von Schirach, and Streicher as typical Nazis, Goering as an unusual type.

[56] XII *Proceedings* 562-3.

Kauffmann, for Kaltenbrunner, argued that it was too soon after the war to conduct such a trial, when people were still embroiled emotionally. He claimed also that the Tribunal could not truly try Germans because it was impossible to appreciate the turmoil, the psychosis of fear, and the impossibility of changing the regime.[57] Von Ludinghausen, for Von Neurath, praised the Tribunal warmly for the conduct of the trial and spoke of its duty to the defendants and to mankind.[58] And since the trials have closed, the guilt of certain defendants has been recognized by leading Germans.[59]

---

57 XVIII *Proceedings* 40.

58 XIX *Proceedings* at 220. "An extraordinary responsibility is thus placed upon your shoulders, so great as has never before been placed on the shoulders of any court in the world * * * * it is your task, your Honors, to lay the first cornerstone for the temple of peace of the nations of the earth * * * * Coming generations are to continue to build on your judgment. You are to give the directives according to which those who come after us must continue to aspire to this high goal. It is not a precedent you are to establish, not an individual case you are to judge and to punish the guilty men according to your judgment, but you are to lay down the fundamental principles of a new international law which is to govern the world in the future. This alone, this task assigned to you, establishes the meaning of this Tribunal, its justification, and its high ethical inspiration, to which we yield."

59 See the very stirring address of Dr. Hans Ehard, Minister-President of Bavaria, *op cit.*, pp. 223-245.

XII

ACQUIESCENCE OF OTHER NATIONS

The very title of this portion of the discussion will sound strange to any lawyer versed in municipal law. A "blue law" may have been passed a century before and not enforced for several generations, yet, if not repealed, it may be used against some luckless individual tomorrow. A state's attorney may permit slot machines to operate openly in a social club for years, and then conduct a raid without warning. There is no such thing as acquiescence in crime. Metals may rust with age, material things may disintegrate, but a law, unrepealed, remains a vital and sometimes dangerous thing, however much it may be outmoded by changing customs and social mores.

One may wonder, then, at this particular defense. The reaction of the individual defendants to the refusal of the Tribunal to permit them to discuss violations of international law by the prosecuting nations has already been discussed upon the question of fairness of the trials.[1] As a defense, however, it was invoked for different reasons, apparently as follows: (1) if the other nations had recognized Germany as a validly existing State at the time Hitler assumed power and thereafter, they could not claim that such government was, *ipso facto,* illegal; (2) if Germany, and with it the National Socialist government, was recognized until the very end of hostilities, it could not now be claimed that the individuals in power were acting illegally as banditti or as pirates; (3) if such powers, by their acts, ratified the departures from the Versailles Treaty, the Anschluss, the ceding of the Sudentenland and other acts, they were estopped to urge their illegality; (4) if such nations participated in the fruits of conquest, they were now "in particeps criminis" and could not bring charges against a fellow criminal; (5) if such nations were guilty of violations of international law which precipitated the conduct complained of on the part of Germany, then these were a legal defense to the charges brought; (6) if such nations had engaged in violations of international law similar to those charged against the Ger-

---

[1] E.g., VIII *Proceedings* 181, 628; IX *Proceedings* 135-9, 190, 387, 684-8; XIII *Proceedings* 284, 521; XIV *Proceedings* 284, 520; XV *Proceedings* 298, 320-2, 444, 477, 482, 511; XVI *Proceedings* 521; XVII *Proceedings* 218, 466, 474-6, 580-6; XIX *Proceedings* 69; XXII *Proceedings* 332, 366-8, 368-73, 373-5, 385, 400.

man leaders, it demonstrated either that the former existing rules of war had been abandoned and altered, or that there was no such common understanding as would create "customary" law.

These are powerful arguments stated, perhaps, with more precision than was employed in the proceedings. Goering, as a witness, pointed out that the government was recognized by foreign powers until the end, so could not have been considered wholly illegal.[2] He pointed out also that Poland had gotten by with the Lithuanian incident.[3] He brought out in defense of the partisan atrocities the nature of the partisan activities which demanded such reprisals.[4] Others brought out the machine gunning of peasants,[5] the sinking of rescue craft,[6] the acts of merchantmen,[7] the bombing by the Allies of open cities,[8] and the sinking of submarines by American destroyers when this nation was supposed to be observing a state of neutrality.[9] The Russian cooperation in and approval of the Polish invasion was disclosed.[10]

Jahrreiss in his closing address[11] spoke of the Russian partnership in the Polish invasion and its aggressive war against Finland, which no one had dared to question. He pointed out that the President of the United States on September 5, 1939, instead of declaring Germany an aggressor nation, declared a state of neutrality. Jahrreiss pointed out the standing by of all nations when Japan invaded Manchuria and Italy invaded Abyssina, the holding of the Munich conference which approved German acts to that time, and the joinder by all nations in the Olympic games as the guests of that criminal nation, Germany. Other defense counsel alluded to like acts.[12] And Dr. Horn brought out the ultimatums issued by France and Great Britain, which he declared might have been considered causes for war by Germany upon them as a defensive measure; the orders given by the President of the United States, in violation of the doc-

---

[2] IX *Proceedings* 264.

[3] IX *Proceedings* 278.

[4] IX *Proceedings* 322-5.

[5] IX *Proceedings* 135-9; XXII *Proceedings* 400.

[6] IX *Proceedings* 387; XIII *Proceedings* 284-6.

[7] XIII *Proceedings* 253-8; XIV *Proceedings* 204.

[8] IX *Proceedings* 688; XV *Proceedings* 511; XXII *Proceedings* 400.

[9] XIII *Proceedings* 266.

[10] XVII *Proceedings* 218; XXII *Proceedings* 373-5.

[11] XVII *Proceedings* 466 *et seq.* See also the proclamation of May 11, 1940, 54 *United States Statutes at Large*, Part 2, p. 2704. The earlier proclamation is at p. 2704.

[12] XVIII *Proceedings* 277, 280-2, 307 (Dix, counsel for Schacht); XIX *Proceedings* 69 (Steinbauer).

trines of neutrality and all rules of warfare, to fire upon German submarines on sight, and the occupation of Greenland and Iceland by American troops which he claimed constituted acts of overt hostility.[13] The same attorney asked also, how, after the Allies had violated the Geneva Convention by bombing open cities and strafing civilians, the Convention could bind anyone.[14]

Certainly, bearing in mind limitations necessarily imposed by time and relevancy, much of the evidence offered should have been received—however red the victors' faces may have been. International law does not, as previously pointed out, depend upon written law. It is determined by that which nations accept as right and proper, and any evidence which helps to prove the general acceptance or approval of a particular course of conduct aids in establishing what constitutes international law. The doctrine of "particeps criminis" would be no defense, though it would reflect no credit upon the abettor. Upon two other aspects, however, this evidence was clearly admissable, relevant, and necessary. They are upon the questions of (1) provocation and self-defense; (2) reprisal.

If the President of the United States had given orders, however unknown to the citizens of the United States, for our warships to fire on sight upon German submarines, under circumstances where self-defense was not involved, he would have been a violator of the Hague Rules of Land Warfare, the United States would have been an aggressor nation, and a charge of aggressive war by Germany against the United States could have been sustained. If he had believed there was reasonable cause to fear aggression by Germany, or that Germany had made itself a criminal nation by the invasion of Poland, there was a method of properly declaring war against that nation and any other nation engaged in similar crime. The United States was, according to the German charges, guilty of every breach of neutrality conceivable, in addition to arming bases in readiness to attack Germany. It was the argument of German counsel that the United States, and not Germany, was the aggressor.

Poland had massed troops on the Czechoslovakian border in readiness to take its cut when that small nation was invaded by Germany. It invaded Lithuania as a large boy might knock down a small boy to pick up a dime he claimed he had seen first. Whether it had mobilized upon the German borders or not, as claimed, one cannot work up much sympathy for downtrodden Poland. Certainly, at least, any evidence bearing upon this subject should have been received. Russia, whose Stalin prior

---

13 XVII *Proceedings* 585-6.

14 XVII *Proceedings* 592.

to the attack on Poland had not discussed peace but the share of the vanquished nation he would receive, who sent Von Ribbentrop a telegram of congratulations upon the successful completion of the campaign, whose indulgences in like acts against humanity paralleled those of Nazi Germany, must have adopted a strange double standard for judicial purposes.[14A]

If one is charged, under municipal law, with assault and battery, it is not only proper, but necessary, to determine who was the aggressor and whether there was sufficient provocation for the assault. How one can weigh the evidence and determine the charge of aggression without hearing the evidence of the defense upon this subject, I cannot conceive. The very nature of such a charge demands an adequate opportunity to reply.

Similarly, when Germany complained of breaches of the rules of war by the Allies, provoking retaliation, such evidence was admissible, if not in total exoneration, at least in mitigation of the offenses charged. Possibly the Tribunal was correct in stating that it was not assembled to try the victor nations, but the true course of Justice would demand either that they be tried in some court for such violations properly charged by another nation, including Germany, or that such evidence be received either to explain what actually constituted customary law or as evidence of legitimate reprisal. The doctrine of reprisal has been recognized for decades.[15] It was upon this ground that Britain justified its bombing of open cities, that the United States sent avalanches of bombing planes over Berlin and dropped its atom bombs upon Japan. Who was the first offender we shall probably never know, because the evidence upon one side was not fully developed and the Tribunal had no question of fact to determine.

It was doubtless embarrassing to the Prosecution to have to meet such evidence. When nations had watched, with uneasiness but without going to war to prevent, the rape of Abyssinia, the invasion of Manchuria, the butchery of Finland, the attack upon Lithuania; when they had continued diplomatic relations with a nation which had systematically violated each provision of the Treaty of Versailles and sanctioned its acts in a solemn Treaty at Munich; when they had shared in its plunder or themselves been guilty of violations of international law, it is uncomfortable to appear in the role of prosecutors of such nation. But however uncomfortable it might have been, if Justice could have been accomplished in no other manner, then such evidence should have

---

[14A] See the extensive charges made against the Allied Powers in Belgion, *Victor's Justice*, 1949, Regnery Co.

[15] Holland, *The Laws of War on Land*, 1908, Clarendon Press, pp. 60, 61.

been heard.[16] Otherwise defense counsel will say, with some reason, that "no criminal court will threaten a victorious government."[17]

---

16 The views are similar of Finch, "The Nuremberg Trial and International Law," 41 *American Journal of International Law*, p. 20 *et seq.*, (January, 1947); Schick, "Crimes Against Peace," 38 *Journal of Criminal Law & Criminology*, p. 445 *et seq.*, (January-February, 1948).

17 Jahrreiss in XVII *Proceedings*, p. 481. Also Stahmer at p. 505 and Horn at p. 555. Laternser in XXII *Proceedings* pp. 45, 46.

XIII

GUILT OF OTHER NATIONS

In discussing the question of the reactions of the defendants as to the fairness of the trials, and their feeling as to the presence or absence of guilt, these factors involved a certain defense which they were not permitted to make. The defendants, on the whole, believed that the Tribunal acted unfairly in refusing to permit them to show the violations of law committed by the victor nations and occupied countries partly in explanation or extenuation of their own conduct, and to show equal guilt on the part of those preferring the charges. These have been examined in more detail previously in discussing the defenses made.

Ordinarily if one is charged with assault, he may defend by showing that the complainant was the aggressor. If charged with murder, he may demonstrate that he acted in self-defense. If charged with theft, he may show that he merely retook his own property. The British, we know, condoned their bombings of German cities upon the ground that the Germans had first committed such acts, and proceeded upon the basis of reprisal. Only upon such a basis could the United States justify its bombing of German cities and the use of atomic power in Japan. The defendants claimed that each act charged against them was actually provoked by some external act of the enemy—and, in some instances, evidence slipped into the record, indirectly, in corroboration of their claims. Yet, although the very nature of the acts charged required a determination by the Tribunal of the term "aggression," and a proper evaluation of such defenses prior to determining the question of guilt, such evidence was, in most instances, excluded. For that reason, the defendants felt the trials were not fair, and history may judge the Tribunal harshly upon that account alone, if for no other. Several of the tribunals in the subsequent Nuremberg proceedings, and particularly in the Ministries Case, No. 11, permitted such evidence despite the contrary provisions of Council Control Law No. 10.

Statements of the Prosecutors and of the Tribunal repeatedly show that they had no intention of weighing the legality of acts of the Allied nations. In replying to a statement of Stahmer, for Goering, Sir David Maxwell-Fyfe declared: ". . . . if it is necessary to investigate whether other belligerents have committed breaches of conventions, then I join issue with him in toto."[1]

[1] VIII *Proceedings* 181.

Subsequently, Servatius wanted the Tribunal to require production of deportation orders issued by Russia, and asked to have a master investigate this matter and make a report; thus to show that Russia's acts in regard evidenced a belief that the Hague Rules of Land Warfare were obsolete in this respect.[2] This request the Tribunal refused, just as it refused to permit Laternser to interrogate witness Kesselring concerning violations of international law by the enemy.[3] The Tribunal sustained objections by Russia to the German White Book,[4] and also denied evidence upon the question of reprisal.[5] Von Ribbentrop was interrupted several times when telling of British treaties or general conduct, which he considered clearly evidenced hostility to Germany.[6]

The Tribunal later reaffirmed the fact that it would not consider the legality of acts of other nations,[7] and refused to permit testimony as to the foreign policy of other States.[8] Certainly the defendants felt that international crimes were being committed by the victor nations while the trial itself was in progress. Goering pointed out that German industry was even then being dismantled and its assets being shipped to other States.[9] He asked whether international law did not operate equally. Frank referred to the massacre of German people by Russians, Poles, and Czechs. He asked, "Who shall ever judge these crimes against the German people?"[10] Dr. Laternser offered to prove that one of the Allied nations had developed bacterial warfare as a weapon and had 4,000 people occupied with it, but his offer was refused by the Tribunal.[11]

Von Ribbentrop pointed out his visit to Stalin in Moscow in 1939, at which time Stalin was not interested in peace for

---

2 VIII *Proceedings* 628.

3 IX *Proceedings* 190.

4 IX *Proceedings* 684. Objection by Rudenko to book entitled *Crimes by Russia Against War & Humanity*, 1941, turned over to the Red Cross at Geneva, after compilation by the German Foreign Office. Stahmer argued the evidence was pertinent upon motive and upon reprisal, but at 688 the Tribunal held the evidence irrelevant.

5 IX *Proceedings* 688. Maxwell-Fyfe objected to a statement that Germany started attacks upon open cities only after Great Britain had done so. Objection was sustained.

6 X *Proceedings* 240, 258, 260.

7 XIII *Proceedings* 521. "We are not trying whether any other powers have committed breaches of international law, or crimes against humanity, or war crimes; we are trying whether these defendants have."

8 XIV *Proceedings* 284. Witness Von Weizacker. Objection by Rudenko sustained that they were examining crimes of major German war criminals and not the foreign policy of other states.

9 XXII *Proceedings* 366-8.

10 XXII *Proceedings* 385.

11 XIII *Proceedings* 385-6.

Poland, but wanted one half of that nation plus the Baltic countries, Lithuania, and the harbor of Libau. After the Polish campaign a congratulatory telegram was received from Stalin.[12] Fritsche declared that after the capitulation of Poland ". . . . . it was a matter of great satisfaction to me in the weeks that followed. I could see from the Soviet Press that Soviet Russia and its Government shared the German opinion of the question of war guilt in this case."[13]

Jodl spoke with great bitterness of the annihilation of women and children by layers of bombs and by the machine guns of low flying aviators.[14] He spoke of the violences of partisans,[15] the acts of soldiers who landed for demolition purposes with civilian clothes underneath their uniforms and armpit pistols which fired when their arms were raised.[16] He described the stranglings of old people by Canadian forces at Dieppe[17] and the British violation of Norwegian neutrality by the Altmark incident.[18] He described other violations by the Allies.[19]

Goering described the illegality of partisan activities,[20] as well as the shooting down of German rescue craft, though marked with a Red Cross.[21] Doenitz spoke of the illegal shooting war commenced by Roosevelt long before America was in the war, and at a time when German ships were instructed not to fire back.[22] He described the illegal acts of British and American merchantmen.[23] Von Brauchitsch told of the machine gunning of peasants by Allied airmen.[24] And Von Schirach pointed out that the German program of training youth for war was far behind that of Russia.[25] These are only a few of the many references to such matters.[26]

---

[12] XII *Proceedings* 373-5.

[13] XVIII *Proceedings* 218.

[14] XV *Proceedings* 407, 511; XXII *Proceedings* 400.

[15] XXII *Proceedings* 400.

[16] XV *Proceedings* 482.

[17] XV *Proceedings* 320-1, 487.

[18] XV *Proceedings* 444.

[19] XV *Proceedings* 298.

[20] IX *Proceedings* 322-5, over objection by Jackson. Held admissible.

[21] IX *Proceedings* 387.

[22] XIII *Proceedings* 266.

[23] XIII *Proceedings* 253-8; XIV *Proceedings* 204.

[24] IX *Proceedings* 135-9.

[25] XIV *Proceedings* 520,

"Von Schirach: May I say that I think the military training of the youth of Germany falls much behind that of the Soviet Union.

"General Alexandrov: This is an irrelevant comparison."

[26] The alleged guilt of the victor nations as to nearly every offense charged against the defendants is excellently portrayed in Belgion, *Victors' Justice*, 1949, Regnery Co. The author is not exact upon his statements as to law, but his factual data is well authenticated, and, as a matter of fact,

It must be admitted that it would have been most difficult for the Tribunal, appointed by the victorious powers, to have received evidence of the illegal activities of the leaders of their nations and to have rendered an impartial verdict upon such questions as aggression and the legality of acts committed. However, the judicial process is usually considered to transcend any and all ties of nationality, allegiance, and bias—except the single allegiance to the cause of Justice, which is a precious, imperishable thing in the hearts of men. If the Tribunal did not feel itself qualified to act in such an unprejudiced capacity, then impartial judges could have been secured. Certainly, under no pretext or excuse should the defendants have been prevented from presenting any defense relevant to the charges brought, however embarrassing it may have been to the prosecutors. In this respect the claims of unfairness on the part of the defendants may have been justified. History may deal unkindly with this episode if the leaders of the victors, as well as of the vanquished, are not called to account for their acts as well—and finally to establish whether these defenses would have had validity, if aired.

does not disclose the whole story. One cannot agree that the guilt of a victor nation precludes validity of a trial as to guilt of a vanquished, but one can agree that if the victor can commit crimes without punishment, the inequity will shock the civilized world and breed disrespect for international tribunals. The Allied Powers and their leaders must be called to account, as well. See Jackson's comment, II *Proceedings* 154; Ehard, *op cit.*, pp. 238-44.

XIV

THE GERMAN LAW

Defense counsel, throughout the proceedings, kept insisting that the defendants should be judged upon the basis of German law. This is a rather strange position when one considers that many of the charges were predicated upon accepted principles of international law, and particularly strange when one remembers that the crimes were committed in many different lands. It would be a peculiar extension of the doctrine of state sovereignty to insist that one may go into another nation and commit a crime and yet be judged solely by the standards of his native land. One in a position of command could thus, by his own act, create a practical immunity for his every deed, however vile, merely by shaping the law in that direction.

Nor is this a merely academic problem. In a totalitarian state such as Germany, though possessed of a constitution, laws, and court procedure, the highest law was the decree of the Fuhrer. For all practical purposes, the constitutional guarantees to German citizens were set aside when he assumed power. He permitted one set of courts to exist, but largely replaced its personnel; in the meantime, he set up a different set of courts not controlled by nor subject to usual processes. As Fuhrer, his decrees and directives became law. Since he issued the orders directly, or sanctioned them, which led to every act which the Prosecution charged as crimes, then, if those be considered as the law of the German Reich, no defendant was guilty. He merely obeyed this law.

This, obviously, could reach a point of absurdity. It is of interest, however, in view of the claims of defense counsel, to examine the constitution and penal statutes of Germany to discover whether the charges brought could have been sustained in a German court, assuming adequate evidence and an unbiased hearing.

It is the thought of certain writers that international law must, to be effective, be embodied in national law.[1] Others feel that a victorious nation can impose any terms it desires upon

---

[1] Finch, "The Nuremberg Trial and International Law," 41 *American Journal of International Law*, p. 20 *et seq.* (January, 1947); Schick, "The Nuremberg Trial and the International Law of the Future," 41 *American Journal of International Law*, p. 770 *et seq.*, (October, 1947).

the vanquished;[2] or, at least, that one may look to the common law or customs of nations in the absence of a prior penal code.[3] International law, as such, draws from any sources which show a common recognition of the demands of nations;[4] and in view of the marked similarity of penal codes in all civilized nations, those common characteristics may be considered the expression of an international code of criminal justice.[5]

But we do not have to go that far afield in considering German law. Just as the United States, in its Constitution, gives Congress the power to define offenses against the law of nations,[6] the Weimar Constitution, Article 4, provides that generally accepted rules of international law are an integral part of the law of the German Reich.[7] Thus, if the Weimar Constitution was the law of Germany at the time of the Nuremberg Trials, it could not be contended successfully that those rules admittedly constituting international law a part of the national law should be disregarded.

If one insisted that only the law of the vanquished nation could be used to judge its erring citizens, that nation could easily declare all war crimes to be Acts of State and thus give a practical immunity.[8] Amnesty decrees would serve a like purpose. And legalization of organizations such as the Mafia, Molly Maguires, or the SS could preclude examination by other nations, however much the offenses committed overlapped the boundaries of that State, or violated the common dictates of humanity.

---

2 Glueck, *War Criminals—Their Prosecution and Punishment*, 1944, Knopf, pp. 11-12; Glueck, *The Nuremberg Trial and Aggressive War*, 1946, Knopf, pp. 8-10.

3 Glueck, *War Criminals—Their Prosecution and Punishment*, 1944, Knopf, pp. 98-9, citing the German scholars and Schatzel, *Bestrafungen nach Kriegsbrauch, Archiv fur Militarrecht Achter Band*, 1920, pp. 13-24, *and Verdoss, Die Volkerrecht-seidrige Kriegshandlung und das Strafanspruch der Staaten*, 1920, pp. 30-2.

4 Article 38 of the Statute of the Permanent Court of International Justice sets up, in substance, the following sources of international law: (a) International conventions, whether general or particular, establishing rules expressly recognized by the contesting state; (b) International custom; (c) The general principles of law recognized by the civilized nations; (d) Judicial decisions and the teachings of qualified public lawyers.

5 Radin, "International Crimes," 32 *Iowa Law Review*, p. 33 *et seq.* (November, 1946). This author is of the opinion that the acts which shock the sensibilities in one State are substantially the same in another. Therefore, international criminal law exists, and merely needs formulation and expression.

6 *Constitution of the United States*, Article I, Section 8.

7 Schick, "Crimes Against Peace," 38 *Journal of Criminal Law & Criminology*, No. 5, p. 445 *et seq.* (January-February, 1948); II *Proceedings* 146 (Jackson).

8 Glueck, *The Nuremberg Trial and Aggressive War*, 1946, Knopf, pp. 56-7.

The construction of international law, however, does not permit the concept of sovereignty of one state to extend into the sovereignty of another state or to be paramount thereto. This acceptance is confirmed by the Weimar Constitution. And since a national constitution pertains to the government of individuals, it is apparent that Germany intended to accept those aspects of international law which provided for individual, as well as State, responsibility. As pointed out heretofore, an accused cannot defend upon the ground that his act was legal under the law of his state where such law is counter to all recognized rules of international law and morality.[9]

The Weimar Constitution also contained guarantees of basic rights to its citizens which were similar to those guaranteed by the Bill of Rights in the United States, the Magna Charta in England, and the Rights of Man in France.[10] These were suspended by Von Hindenburg when Hitler took power and were thereafter violated constantly—even to the enforcement of *ex post facto* laws,[11] the alleged enforcement of which by the Allied Powers was a cause for complaint by the defendants in the Nuremberg trials. The rights of citizens were violated in the courts, both in substance and in procedure, with excessive punishments being imposed.[12] Judges were selected in occupied countries who were reliable party men, and special criminal courts were set up, the "sondergerichte," to which more and more cases were transferred.[13] The Gestapo, both in Germany and in occupied territory, had power to arrest without warrant, imprison without sentence, and rearrest after acquittal, and their acts were not subject to court review.[14] There is a serious legal question whether a Constitution can ever be set aside by edict of a governing agent—and if the Weimar Constitution was still in force when the rights of German citizens were violated, those violations were illegal and subject to punishment. If those guarantees were permanently suspended, then it would seem that

---

[9] Glueck, *War Criminals—Their Prosecution and Punishment*, 1944, Knopf, pp. 106-7.

[10] Bennett, "Notes on the German Legal and Penal System," 37 *Journal of Criminal Law and Criminology*, pp. 368-76 (January-February, 1947); II *Proceedings* 111, 112 (Jackson).

[11] Glueck, *The Nuremberg Trial and Aggressive War*, 1946, Knopf, pp. 73-7; II *Proceedings* 111, 112 (Jackson).

[12] Freeman, "War Crimes by Enemy Nationals Administrating Justice in Occupied Territory," 41 *American Journal of International Law*, p. 579 *et seq.* (July, 1947).

[13] Marsh, "Some Aspects of the German Legal System Under National Socialism," 62 *Law Quarterly Review*, pp. 366-74 (October, 1946).

[14] Marsh, *op cit.* The author points out that there was no possibility of appeal and that the prosecutor could even set aside an acquittal or increase a sentence.

the defendants would have had no right to complain if they had been judged upon the same basis and as summarily as they had imposed punishment upon their fellow citizens.

The German defense counsel, while admitting that the system of justice during the National Socialist regime was inadequate, claimed that *ex post facto* laws were never employed.[15] This statement could easily be proved untrue,[16] but is of no great consequence as such counsel admitted that *punishments* were increased retroactively.[17] The phase of *ex post facto* which is of primary concern is not the abstract question of guilt, but of punishment—and if the defendants deemed it proper to increase the punishment of a misdemeanor committed by one of their citizens from a simple fine to the death penalty, no complaint should be made of defining the punishment for violations of international law which had long before been declared illegal. At any rate, the doctrine of "precedent" has never been followed literally in the continental courts.[18]

If the defendants had wanted to be judged wholly by German law, then the defenses raised by them of *ex post facto,* non-conspiracy, and the like, upon which they relied so firmly, would have been nullities. During the National Socialist regime, there were three doctrines of law which would have given a complete and total basis for punishment in an appropriate tribunal under which these defenses would have been abrogated. They are as follows:

1. Punishment by analogy. Under an Act dated June 28, 1935, Article 2 of the German Criminal Code, if the act committed was analogous to any other act which was punishable by law, like punishment could be adjudged though the specific act was prohibited by no existing law.[19] The defense counsel

---

[15] XVIII *Proceedings* 504 (Stahmer).

[16] Certainly the penalties imposed for being a non-Aryan must be considered *ex post facto,* since this cannot be changed after birth. Other examples are numerous. Pannebecker in XVIII *Proceedings* at 164 states that the retroactive enforcement of penal laws by the Nazi regime shocked the civilized world, and the Tribunal should not fall into the same error.

[17] XVIII *Proceedings* (Stahmer).

[18] Lipstein points out that French and German jurisprudence followed only statutory law and customary law. If the matter was not covered expressly by statute, then the court would take the law most similar and reason by analogy, or rely upon the reports and debates of the commission drafting the law. If nothing seemed applicable, it would rely on sound discretion and justice. "The Doctrine of Precedent in Continental Law with Special Reference to French and German Law," 28 *Journal of Society of Comparative Legislation,* 3rd Series, pp. 34-44 (November, 1946).

[19] Bennett, "Notes on the German Legal and Penal System," 37 *Journal of Criminal Law and Criminology,* pp. 368-76 (January-February, 1947); Freeman, "War Crimes by Enemy Nationals Administering Justice in Oc-

argued vigorously that this law was vicious and condemned by the civilized world, and should not be used by the Tribunal.[20] They pointed out further that the first step of the Control Council had been to restore civil guarantees and to abolish this vicious law and it was, therefore, no longer in force.[21]

2. Sound instinct. The German law permitted punishment of anyone where it was deemed necessary "according to the principles of the criminal law and to the sound feelings of the people."[22] This, then, required no law at all to justify punishment, but merely a feeling that an unjust act has been committed which should be punished. If the doctrine of estoppel were effective in criminal law, as it is in civil law, how appropriate this would have been in the present proceedings! One would not suppose that defense counsel would urge too vigorously the right of their clients to be tried under German law.

3. The first step doctrine. The defense counsel, as has been discussed previously in more detail as to the specific charge of conspiracy, claimed that one who joined a conspiracy and then retired therefrom should not be found guilty. Under German law, if a person took the first step which might lead to the commission of an offense, even though such step was not unlawful, he might be punished upon the theory that he had completed all of the steps.[23]

Of course, one of the major sources of misunderstanding by the defendants as to the charges brought by the Prosecution, and particularly concerning violations of the Rules of Land Warfare, and the waging of aggressive war based upon the violations of treaties, is based upon the varying concepts of the sanctity of one's oath and obligation. Not only in past generations, but in this generation, the German attitude has been to regard a treaty as merely a scrap of paper. While they pay lip service to the doctrines of international law, they do not feel, fundamentally, that they are bound thereby if it is to the national interest to forget such obligations. For example, Goering testified that around the time of the Munich Conference, when he gave his "word of honor," that those words applied only at that particular time.[24] Von Ribbentrop, when questioned about

---

cupied Territories," 41 *American Journal of International Law*, at 598 *et seq.* (July, 1947). (Citing 2 articles by Pruess).

[20] XVII *Proceedings* 504, 602-3; XIX *Proceedings* 52-3; XXI *Proceedings* 499.

[21] XVII *Proceedings* 504 (Stahmer); XXI *Proceedings* 499 (Merkel).

[22] Bennett, *op cit.*, p. 368 *et seq.*; Glueck, *The Nuremberg Trial and Aggressive War*, 1946, Knopf, p. 73.

[23] Bennett, *op cit.*, p. 368 *et seq.*

[24] IX *Proceedings* 300-301.

certain assurances he had given, stated, "It is perfectly conceivable that I said something like that. * * * * * It is quite clear that that is nothing but diplomatic talk."[25] This sounds strangely reminiscent of a certain Presidential candidate and his statement, "just a little campaign oratory."

One must go to the German philosophy of war to determine its attitude in this regard. That attitude is definitely that there is only one supreme law—and that is the law of necessity. The observance of the laws of war is subordinate to the attainment of the object of the war, and may be abrogated where the object is not otherwise attainable.[26] If one carried over this reasoning to civil life, it would seem justifiable for one losing a tennis match to shoot his opponent and thus not to sustain defeat. And the German rules of war have defined the sanctity of a treaty as consisting only of a "reciprocity of mutual agreement, a limitation of arbitrary action, which usage and convention, good-nature, and a calculating egoism have erected, but for whose observance no express sanction exists except a deciding 'fear of Reprisals.' "[27]

It must be remembered, of course, that the Tribunal sat in judgment upon the defendants for the acts committed by them, not for the philosophies or ideas held by them, however evil they might have been. The mere fact that the Nazi philosophy, or even its philosophy of war, differed from that of other nations was not material until some act was committed creating a direct conflict of philosophies which resulted in a violation of law. We do not condemn nor execute for philosophical differences. Much anti-Semitism exists in other lands, for example, which is not punishable. But when any philosophy is translated into action designed to exterminate the object of one's derision, or into a conduct which is contrary to accepted international law, it becomes criminal and is subject to punishment. It is thought, transformed into action, which provides the offense. It is for that reason that we have examined into the charges brought to determine whether there was any legal foundation for indict-

---

[25] X *Proceedings* 360.

[26] Bordwell, *The Law of War Between Belligerents,* 1908, Callaghan & Co., p. 5. Also see the very enlightening and extensive discussion in Holland, *The Laws of War on Land,* 1908, Clarendon Press, p. 12, citing various German authorities.

[27] Baty and Morgan, *War, Its Conduct and Legal Results,* 1915, Dutton & Co. at 166-7, quoting from *Kriegsbrauch im Landkriege,* p. 2. The authors refer to the doctrine of necessity, and quote Clausewitz to the effect that "War is an act of violence which in its application knows no bounds." They refer also to John Murray's translation of *The German War Book* as a terribly cynical document.

ment, and any factual basis for conviction. It seems without question that there was such a foundation in law, if one deems that the Tribunal acted properly in refusing to hear evidence upon certain defenses. It is important, therefore, to see whether the proceedings were conducted in an orderly manner, with due attention given to evidence presented by all parties.

PART II

THE INTERNATIONAL MILITARY TRIBUNAL AT NUREMBERG

PROCEDURE

Tribunal of IMT at Nuremberg. Left to right are: Lt. Col. A. F. Volchkov, Maj. Gen. Nikitchenko (Russian); Judge Birkett, Judge Lawrence (British); Judge Francis Biddle, Judge John J. Parker (U. S. A.); Prof. de Vabres, and Conseiller R. Falco (French).

XV

INTRODUCTION

One cannot discuss the question of fairness of the trials accorded the defendants as an abstract proposition. Assuming there was jurisdiction of some character in the Tribunal to hear any of the charges filed against the defendants, it then becomes necessary to examine the record of the proceedings in detail to see whether: (1) charges were properly filed and due notice given to all defendants; (2) defendants were represented by counsel; (3) counsel for defendants were competent; (4) opportunity was given to present defensive witnesses and documents in reply; (5) rulings by the Tribunal were fair and proper; (7) sufficient opportunity was given to explain defensive theories and supporting law; (8) presentation by the Prosecution was impartial; (9) the opinion and judgments were supported by the law and evidence. This last point has been treated separately as it dealt with a twofold problem—first, the controlling law, and, second, the weight of the evidence when weighed in the light of the applicable law. And, in examining the procedure used in the trial, attention will be called to matters of unusual interest, or which are outstanding from a historical point of view.

The order of procedure in the trials should first be explained. Omitting for the moment variations caused by special motions or rulings, this was as follows. The charges under the Indictment were read and pleas taken. This was followed by the opening statement for the American Prosecutor as to Count I, and the introduction of his evidence. Following the close of the American case, Great Britain, France, and Russia followed as to Counts II, III, and IV of the Indictment although, quite naturally, evidence introduced as to any Count was considered with reference to any other Count to which it was relevant. Both documentary and oral evidence was presented by the Prosecution, witnesses being called as their testimony became pertinent.

At the close of the case for the Prosecution, counsel for the individual defendants introduced their evidence in the order previously assigned by the Tribunal. Each such unit involved both documentary and oral testimony, the defendant testifying prior to his supporting witnesses. Other defense counsel had a right to examine witnesses called by another defendant, followed by cross-examination by the Prosecution. Each of the four prosecutors had a right to cross-examine a defendant, but only one cross-examination on behalf of all was permitted of a defense witness. Rebuttal examination was permitted, with the Tribunal frequently interrogating a witness or party directly. Rebuttal evidence was also allowed for each side with great liberality, even after the close of arguments. At the conclusion of the individual cases, final arguments were made for those defendants, followed by the closing arguments for the Prosecution.

As to the indicted organizations, it had been ruled finally that their counsel could not cross-examine witnesses nor object to testimony, but that those trials would be conducted following the close of the individual cases. During the latter part of the hearings on the individual cases, evidence for and against the organizations was being heard before commissioners. The findings of the commissioners, supporting evidence, and additional oral and documentary evidence was then presented to the Tribunal in a manner similar to that of the prior hearings. Closing arguments were then made by the defense counsel, followed by the Prosecution. The individual defendants were then permitted to make brief statements on their own behalf.

The Tribunal recessed for thirty days, and then announced its opinion as to both the individual defendants and the organizations, passing sentence upon the individuals convicted.

XVI

RELATIONSHIP OF TRIBUNAL TO PARTIES AND COUNSEL

It will be recalled that the Indictment was filed in four Counts setting out the general nature of the acts charged, with some particularization as to the types of conduct alleged to be criminal in nature. The defendants were at that time in custody. Each of them, other than Bormann, was served with a copy of the Indictment more than thirty days prior to the commencement of the trial. Each defendant was permitted to select his own attorney. In cases where such defendant had no idea of whom he desired for counsel, he was furnished with a list of available attorneys. If no specification was made, counsel was assigned by the Tribunal. The majority of counsel were voluntarily selected, and, on the whole, the caliber of defense counsel was excellent.*

Upon the convening of the Tribunal, a plea to the jurisdiction of the court was filed immediately by Dr. Stahmer,[1] which was adopted by all other counsel. The motion was promptly overruled by the Tribunal as in violation of Article 3 of the Charter, which defined the jurisdiction over the parties and over the acts charged. An announcement was made of the medical examination of Julius Streicher, who was found by the examining physicians to be sane, and his counsel's request for a continuance as to Streicher's case was overruled.[2]

The report of the French and Russian examiners as to Hess was announced to the effect that the defendant was "not insane."[3] A very interesting development arose in this connection subsequently, when counsel for Hess pointed out that the reports of all medical commissioners tended to show that Hess was suffering from amnesia as to all acts occurring prior to his flight to England, which made it impossible for Hess or his attorney to prepare an adequate defense to the acts charged as to which Hess had no recollection.[4] The Tribunal listened attentively to this argument and then called upon Hess personally, who ex-

* See Streicher's comment as to manner of selections. XII *Proceedings* 306. A German writer recently commented upon the high standards of defense counsel. Ehard, *op cit.*, pp. 224, 229.

1 I *Proceedings* 168.

2 I *Proceedings* 154.

3 I *Proceedings* 157, 167.

4 II *Proceedings* 478, 496.

ploded his counsel's argument by confessing he had been feigning amnesia:

> "Henceforth my memory will again respond to the outside world. The reasons for simulating loss of memory were of a tactical nature. * * * I also simulated loss of memory in consultations with my officially appointed defense counsel. He has, therefore, represented me in good faith."[5]

A motion was also made by counsel for Von Krupp for dismissal of the charges as to him, upon the ground that the medical examinations showed Von Krupp to be physically incapacitated and hopelessly insane.[6] This motion was vigorously opposed by Robert Jackson and the other prosecutors upon the ground that Von Krupp was an indispensable party representing, in effect, the industrialists of Germany without whose active assistance the entire plan for aggressive war must have failed.[7] The prosecution argued further that Von Krupp was represented by able counsel and that his defense would not be impaired substantially by his absence. The Prosecution's argument seems strangely opposed to established principles of criminal jurisprudence which refuses to try a person insane at the time of the trial. The Tribunal, after considering the arguments, granted the motion for Von Krupp in part, holding that he should not be tried at that time, but retained the case upon the docket in the event he should subsequently regain competency.[8]

The American chief prosecutor had apparently realized that the Tribunal might so rule and had previously suggested that if the Tribunal saw fit to dismiss as to Krupp, the father, that Alfried, his son, be joined as a defendant. He pointed out that defense counsel were already chosen and prepared to defend, and would use the same material in defense of one as the other. He therefore urged that the Tribunal immediately add Alfried Von Krupp as a party so that all cases could be tried together.[9] Counsel for the other prosecutors had refrained from urging this motion for fear of producing a delay in the pending cases, but now joined their support and insisted that the Tribunal act in accordance with the motion.[10] The Tribunal called attention to the thirty-day notice provision as to service of the Indictment and refused to add a new party defendant at that stage of the proceedings.[11] M. Dubost, quivering with indignation, dis-

---

[5] II *Proceedings* 496.

[6] I *Proceedings* 124, 133; II *Proceedings* 1-5.

[7] I *Proceedings* 134; II *Proceedings* 5, 6.

[8] I *Proceedings* 143; II *Proceedings* 1-17.

[9] I *Proceedings* 134-8, 145; II *Proceedings* 5-17.

[10] I *Proceedings* 141-2, 145; II *Proceedings* 6-17.

[11] I *Proceedings* 146; II *Proceedings* 28.

patched a memorandum to the Tribunal that it could not prevent the Prosecution from indicting Alfried Von Krupp and that the four prosecutors had now done so, the proceedings to be handled at a later date.[12] Actually, Alfried was later tried before a regular military tribunal and convicted, being sentenced to twelve years imprisonment and deprived of all his property by forfeiture.[12A]

Other matters arose, at that time and subsequently, upon matters of illness of the defendants, motions for severance and for continuances. Nearly every day, it was announced by the officers of the Tribunal that certain defendants would be absent that day because of illness. Dr. Ley, having committed suicide while in custody, was, of course, not tried. Dr. Kauffmann, for Kaltenbrunner, at one stage of the proceedings requested a postponement because of his client's continuing illness.[13] The Tribunal ruled that the evidence against him individually would be postponed until the end of the individual cases; if he was at that time still ill, the evidence would then be heard.[14] This did not, however, preclude the Prosecution from introducing evidence bearing upon Kaltenbrunner's guilt, in the course of presenting its general documents, over the objection of Dr. Kauffmann.[15] Dr. Horn, on behalf of Von Ribbentrop, pointed out that the extreme nervousness of his client had produced a severe impediment in his speech which was becoming worse, and requested a continuance or leave to read his client's testimony, which Von Ribbentrop could confirm later, which motions were overruled.[16]

Counsel for Bormann was in a most peculiar position, his client being absent and presumably dead. His motion attacking jurisdiction of the Tribunal to try Bormann was overruled,[17] but his application that such case be tried at the end of all cases against other defendants was allowed.[18] However, his later motion at the close of all evidence for a further continuance was denied.[19]

It was pointed out to the Tribunal during the course of the proceedings by defense counsel that a tremendous job had been

---

[12] I *Proceedings* 147.

[12A] Telford Taylor, "Nuremberg Trials," *International Conciliation*, No. 450, p. 312 (April, 1949).

[13] IV *Proceedings* 284-5.

[14] IV *Proceedings* 286.

[15] IV *Proceedings* 291.

[16] X *Proceedings* 93-4.

[17] XIV *Proceedings* 568.

[18] VIII *Proceedings* 543.

[19] XVII *Proceedings* 244-250.

placed upon their shoulders. These attorneys were required to be in court by day and to confer with their clients at night—which, with the necessary tasks of locating witnesses, procuring evidence, and reading documents introduced by the Prosecution was an exhausting process greatly taxing their strength. A written motion was made for a recess.[20] Sir David Maxwell-Fyfe pointed out that the indictment had been filed four months previously with more particulars than any indictment in the history of jurisprudence.[21] The motion was taken under advisement and finally overruled by the Tribunal, with the statement that no further recess would be granted.[22] However, the Tribunal had previously adjourned over the Christmas period, despite Jackson's vigorous protests.[23]

To go back to the chronological development of the trial itself, the charges were first read as against the various defendants.[24] Pleas were then taken as to the individual defendants, some of those pleas being simply "not guilty," others being elaborated, in substance, as "not guilty to the particular acts charged," or with other variations.[25] Because of Kaltenbrunner's illness, his plea was received late.[26] Subsequently, it appeared that the statement of charges contained in the Indictment was dangerously general in character and the Tribunal required the Prosecution to file a more specific statement of charges.[27] Dr. Seidl, representing the defendant Frank, protested that the indictment against Frank had been general in character and that upon January 9, for the first time, a thirty page document had been served upon him pertaining to the "individual responsibility" of that defendant.[28] The Tribunal refused to consider his motion to strike said document until the motion was placed in writing.[29] As a matter of fact, no unfairness was worked by the Prosecution in filing that document at any time. It did not constitute evidence in itself, except where supported by data which could have been introduced in any event. It was, rather, of benefit in aiding the defendant Frank in preparing his defense.

The question then arose as to the relationship of the defendants to their counsel. Certain defendants wished personally

20 VII *Proceedings* 516-24; also V *Proceedings* 19-26.
21 VII *Proceedings* 519-524.
22 VII *Proceedings* 562.
23 III *Proceedings* 209.
24 II *Proceedings* 30-94.
25 II *Proceedings* 97-8.
26 III *Proceedings* 367.
27 V *Proceedings* 228-9.
28 V *Proceedings* 19-21.
29 V *Proceedings* 21.

to cross-examine witnesses for the Prosecution, but it was properly ruled by the Tribunal that such an examination by counsel for any defendant precluded a further examination by his client.[30] Rudolf Hess was the most troublesome defendant in regard to his representation. He caused an announcement to be made, for example, that Dr. Von Rohrscheidt had broken his ankle and that Hess intended to defend himself.[31] The case against Hess was then postponed in order that his counsel might be present when the evidence was heard.[32] The Tribunal a short time later announced receipt of a letter from Hess that he was not satisfied with his original counsel and wished to represent himself. The Tribunal declared that Hess having elected to be represented by counsel, his election was conclusive, and appointed Dr. Stahmer to act further. It pointed out that such representation was in Hess' own best interests and those of the Tribunal.[33] Julius Streicher also at one time stated that his counsel had been intimidated and that he had not, for that and other reasons, received an opportunity for a proper defense.[34] Dr. Marx, the able attorney representing him, denied such intimidation, but stated that if his client had no confidence in him he would withdraw. The Tribunal graciously urged him to continue, which he did.[35]

The question previously referred to (*ante*, notes 20-2) as to the extreme demands upon the stamina of defense counsel was pointed up in other ways. Defense counsel were finally forced to forego attending previews of motion pictures to be introduced in evidence, because of the necessity of nightly conferences with their clients.[36] Dr. Sauter, counsel for Von Schirach, pointed out the difficulties caused by receiving documents of the Prosecution tardily and untranslated, requiring a great deal of time to secure translations and to study those documents during times when conferences with clients were essential.[37] And, because of the physical difficulties involved, the Tribunal consistently ruled that counsel could confer with their clients prior to under-

---

[30] III *Proceedings* 32-5.

[31] VI *Proceedings* 84.

[32] VI *Proceedings* 84, 344.

[33] VI *Proceedings* 344. Actually it appears that Dr. Seidl took over for Hess a few days later, substituting for Von Rohrscheidt upon February 5 although no formal announcement was found to that effect.

[34] XII *Proceedings* 305-7.

[35] XII *Proceedings* 307. Streicher's claim actually had some slight basis in fact. See VIII *Proceedings* 532-3. This has been discussed fully in relation to the Press, post, p. 137, note 27.

[36] III *Proceedings* 241.

[37] V *Proceedings* 19-26, particularly pages 23, 24.

taking cross-examination of a witness for the Prosecution.[38] These rulings later led to some controversy as to the right of defense counsel to talk to a witness for the Prosecution prior to cross-examination.[39]

Following the reading of the charges, the chief Prosecutor for the United States, Robert Jackson, made his opening address.[40] History has pointed to great addresses of counsel in the past—the masterly orations of Cicero, Burke, Erskine, and others. Unquestionably the history of the future will point to passages in this masterly oration as among the greatest of all time. For example:

> MR. ROBERT JACKSON: "May it please Your Honors:
>
> "The privilege of opening the first trial in history for crimes against the peace of the world imposes a grave responsibility. The wrongs which we seek to condemn and punish have been so calculated, so malignant, and so devastating, that civilization cannot tolerate their being ignored, because it cannot survive their being repeated. That four great nations, flushed with victory and stung with injury stay the hand of vengeance and voluntarily submit their captive enemies to the judgment of the law is one of the most significant tributes that Power has ever paid to Reason. * * *
>
> "The common sense of mankind demands that law shall not stop with the punishment of petty crimes by little people. It must also reach men who possess themselves of great power and make deliberate and concerted use of it to set in motion evils which leave no home in the world untouched. It is a cause of that magnitude that the United Nations will lay before Your Honors.
>
> "In the prisoners' dock sit twenty-odd broken men. Reproached by the humiliation of those they have led almost as bitterly as by the desolation of those they have attacked, their personal capacity for evil is forever past. It is hard now to perceive in these men as captives the power by which as Nazi leaders they once dominated much of the world and terrified most of it. Merely as individuals their fate is of little consequence to the world.
>
> "What makes this inquest significant is that these prisoners represent sinister influences that will lurk in the world long after their bodies have returned to dust. We will show them to be living symbols of racial hatreds, of terrorism and violence, and of the arrogance and cruelty of power. They are symbols of fierce nationalisms and of militarism, of intrigue and war-making which embroiled

---

[38] II *Proceedings* 95; II *Proceedings* 439, 475-8; IV *Proceedings* 287-8; VI *Proceedings* 461.

[39] VIII *Proceedings* 495-504.

[40] II *Proceedings* 98-155.

Europe generation after generation, crushing its manhood, destroying its homes, and impoverishing its life. They have so identified themselves with the philosophies they conceived and with the forces they directed that any tenderness to them is a victory and an encouragement to all the evils which are attached to their names. Civilization can afford no compromise with the social forces which would gain renewed strength if we deal ambiguously or indecisively with the men in whom those forces now precariously survive. * * * * * *

"Unfortunately, the nature of these crimes is such that both prosecution and judgment must be by victor nations over vanquished foes. The worldwide scope of the aggressions carried out by these men has left but few real neutrals. Either the victors must judge vanquished or we must leave the defeated to judge themselves. After the first World War, we learned the futility of the latter course. The former high station of these defendants, the notoriety of their acts, and the adaptability of their conduct to provoke retaliation make it hard to distinguish between the demand for a just and measured retribution, and the unthinking cry for vengeance which arises from the anguish of war. It is our task, so far as humanly possible, to draw the line between the two. We must never forget that the record on which we judge these defendants today is the record on which history will judge us tomorrow. To pass these defendants a poisoned chalice is to put it to our own lips as well. We must summon such detachment and intellectual integrity to our task that this Trial will commend itself to posterity as fulfiling humanity's aspirations to do justice. * * * * * *

"No charity can disguise the fact that the forces which these defendants represent, the forces that would advantage and delight in their acquittal, are the darkest and most sinister forces in society—dictatorship and oppression, malevolence and passion, militarism and lawlessness. By their fruits we best know them. Their acts have bathed the world in blood and set civilization back a century. They have subjected their European neighbors to every outrage and torture, every spoilation and deprivation that insolence, cruelty, and greed could inflict. They have brought the German people to the lowest pitch of wretchedness, from which they can entertain no hope of early deliverance. They have stirred hatreds and incited domestic violence on every continent. These are the things that stand in the dock shoulder to shoulder with these prisoners.

"The real complaining party at your bar is Civilization. In all our countries it is still a struggling and imperfect thing. It does not plead that the United States or any other country, has been blameless of the conditions which made the German people easy victims to the blandishments and intimidations of the Nazi conspirators.

"But it points to the dreadful sequence of aggressions and crimes I have recited, it points to the weariness of flesh, the exhaustion of resources, and the destruction of all that was beautiful or useful in so much of the world, and to greater potentialities for destruction in the days to come. It is not necessary among the ruins of this ancient and beautiful city with untold members of its civilian inhabitants still buried in its rubble, to argue the proposition that to start or wage an aggressive war has the moral qualities of the worst of crimes. The refuge of the defendants can be only their hope that international law will lag so far behind the moral sense of mankind that conduct which is crime in the moral sense must be regarded as innocent in law.

"Civilization asks whether law is so laggard as to be utterly helpless to deal with crimes of this magnitude by criminals of this order of importance. It does not expect that you can make war impossible. It does expect that your juridical action will put the forces of international law, its precepts, its prohibitions and, most of all, its sanctions, on the side of peace, so that men and women of good will, in all countries, may have 'leave to live by no man's leave, underneath the law.' "[41]

Jackson's address was followed by the presentation of the evidence on behalf of the United States, primarily upon Count I of the Indictment but having a direct bearing upon the other charges as well. This was followed by the opening address by Sir Hartley Shawcross, for Great Britain,[42] and the evidence by that Prosecutor; then the skilled and persuasive address of De Menthon for France,[43] followed by his evidence; and finally the fiery and pointed speech of Rudenko, for Russia,[44] and his evidence. Attention should also be called to the masterly address of Robert Jackson dealing with the indicted organizations, delivered at a later date.[45]

In view of the fact that it was necessary for the Tribunal to secure documents for the defendants, have them translated, printed and bound, and also to locate witnesses and secure their attendance, it became necessary in the early stages of the proceedings to determine what evidence each defendant would require. Only in this way could enormous duplication of work be avoided, evidence be limited to relevant matters, and the attendance of witnesses be assured. Thus the defendants' counsel were instructed early to prepare themselves to give such infor-

---

[41] II *Proceedings* 98-155.
[42] III *Proceedings* 91-145.
[43] V *Proceedings* 368-427.
[44] VII *Proceedings* 146-194.
[45] VIII *Proceedings* 438-55.

mation to the Tribunal. Prior to the close of the evidence offered for Great Britain, defense counsel were directed to submit to the Tribunal at the close of the Prosecution's case the evidence they intended to use, confining such statement to the names of witnesses and the matters to which they would be relevant, without making a speech about it.[46] When this time approached, the Tribunal ordered the counsel to confine their evidence to that necessary to meet the charges brought, to file written statements giving the names of witnesses and the particulars of documents they intended to employ, and arguments were set for hearing thereon.[47] At a later date extensive orders were entered as to the calling of witnesses, the sequence of witnesses called, the use of documentary evidence, document books, use of co-counsel, and closing arguments.[48] Dr. Horn objected that the defense counsel should be allowed to proceed in the same manner as the Prosecution.[49] The Tribunal pointed out that substantially the same method was being employed but that different problems were presented by the necessity of locating defense witnesses and securing the translation of documents.[50]

In view of the fact that affidavits and written interrogations were often used instead of oral testimony, discussions were frequently held between the Tribunal, Prosecution, and defense counsel as to the material to be used.[51] On the whole, the rulings of the Tribunal as to such evidence seemed to be quite fair, and there was little animosity between counsel on that score. Applications were frequently made after the close of evidence for a particular defendant as to the introduction of additional testimony and documents, and these were allowed with great liberality,[52] even after the close of arguments upon the individual cases and commencement of the hearings as to the indicted organizations.[53] Although no rulings had been made in the beginning of the hearings as to the order in which defense witnesses should be called, the Tribunal finally required the individual defendants to be called prior to supporting witnesses for such defendant.[54]

Dr. Kubuschok objected to the order in which the defendants were to be heard, but without avail.[55] Dr. Servatius, who had

---

46 III *Proceedings* 335.
47 VII *Proceedings* 516.
48 VIII *Proceedings* 159-165.
49 VIII *Proceedings* 161.
50 VIII *Proceedings* 163.
51 E.g., see VIII *Proceedings* 495-504.
52 XVII *Proceedings* 386-432; XXI *Proceedings* 272-6.
53 Repeated examples are found in Vol. XX and XXI of *Proceedings*.
54 XII *Proceedings* 2.
55 VIII *Proceedings* 390-7.

the double task of representing an individual defendant, Dr. Sauckel, and an indicted organization, suggested a severance of the trials of criminal organizations so that counsel could reorganize their defenses.[56] The Tribunal, after deliberation, overruled this motion;[57] but later on its own accord adopted this form of procedure.[58]

As to arguments for the defense, the Tribunal early in the proceedings established the rule that counsel would be permitted one argument only, and that at the close of all the evidence.[59] Also, arguments on behalf of the individual defendants would be heard prior to taking evidence as to the organizations, but no decision would be announced until all evidence and arguments had been heard as to all cases—with defense counsel speaking first, and the Prosecution last.[60] Some controversy arose as to the length of time to be permitted for these arguments. The Tribunal announced that the Prosecution would be given three days for summation and that defense counsel would have fourteen days, which they could divide as they saw fit. Objection was immediately made by the defense counsel that this was too restrictive, affording each counsel only a half day, in which he would have to speak very slowly because of the translators.[61] This matter was discussed subsequently by counsel[62] and finally the Tribunal requested counsel voluntarily to limit themselves to half a day and to eliminate needless repetition.[63] It indicated at that time that a longer discussion might be permitted counsel for certain defendants, and requested the attorneys to hand in their arguments three days in advance for translation and printing. Defense counsel objected upon the basis of not wanting the Prosecution to have this material, whereupon the Tribunal stated that the material would be kept secret. Other discussions were held as to the length of speeches to be made for the indicted organizations.[64]

As to the speeches for the individual defendants, Dr. Jahrreiss delivered the first address, limiting himself to a discussion of the principles of international law involved.[65] Other counsel discussed primarily the questions of fact relating to the

[56] VIII *Proceedings* 397-405.

[57] VIII *Proceedings* 543.

[58] The individual trials end at XX *Proceedings* p. 14. The trial of organizations takes to XXII *Proceedings* p. 365.

[59] III *Proceedings* 335.

[60] XV *Proceedings* 211.

[61] XVI *Proceedings* 141-6.

[62] XVI *Proceedings* 551-6.

[63] XVII *Proceedings* 1, 2.

[64] XXI *Proceedings* 358-362.

[65] XVII *Proceedings* 458-494.

guilt or innocence of their particular clients, but touching upon the legal issues where necessary as to the individual charges.[66] The defense arguments were, on the whole, outstanding, with certain of them approaching brilliance.[67] Poor Dr. Seidl, however, representing Hess, was apparently so imbued with his client's philosophy that he was unable to avoid repeated discussion of the justice of the Treaty of Versailles, was required to rewrite his speech twice, and then required to delete much of his material.[68] Other counsel were told to shorten their arguments and get to the point.[69] Dr. Servatius, in final argument for the organizations, was commended for keeping his talk within a half day, the Tribunal pointing out that it expected other counsel to follow his excellent example.[70] At the close of the entire proceedings, the Tribunal warmly thanked the attorneys for both the defense and Prosecution for the able performance of their duties as officers of the Court.[71]

With these observations upon the organization of the trials in mind, it is important to look to the evidence introduced, both oral and documentary, and the rulings of the Tribunal thereon. Several things must be remembered in this connection, however. 1. The Tribunal was a military, not a civil, tribunal, with its practice in many respects following that of military commissions, rather than that of civilian courts. 2. By the Charter, it was not restricted to ordinary rules of evidence or procedure.[72] 3. Because of the fact that the Prosecution and Tribunal were both composed of representatives of four nations, speaking three languages, with the defendants and their counsel speaking a fourth language, and witnesses from still other nations speaking

[66] XVII *Proceedings* 497-661; XVIII *Proceedings* 1-510; XIX *Proceedings* 1-396. See ruling at XVII *Proceedings* 572.

[67] E.g., Kranzbuehler for Doenitz XVIII *Proceedings* 312-372; Exner for Jodl XVIII *Proceedings* 506-10; XIX *Proceedings* 1-46; Von Ludinghausen for Von Neurath XIX *Proceedings* 216-312.

[68] XVII *Proceedings* 550-5; XIX *Proceedings* 331; XIX *Proceedings* 353-396.

[69] E.g., XVIII *Proceedings* 43.

[70] XXI *Proceedings* 493.

[71] XXII *Proceedings* 410.

[72] Charter, "Article 19. The Tribunal shall not be bound by technical rules of evidence. It shall adopt and apply to the greatest possible extent expeditious and nontechnical procedure, and shall admit any evidence which it deems to have probative value.

"Article 21. The Tribunal shall not require proof of facts of common knowledge but shall take judicial notice thereof. It shall also take judicial notice of official government documents and reports of the United Nations, including the acts and documents of the committees set up in the various Allied countries for the investigation of war crimes, and the records and findings of military or other Tribunals of any of the United Nations." I *Proceedings* 15.

other tongues, all documents had to be translated by interpreters into the four chief languages. These matters raised certain technical difficulties which had to be overcome, and which were largely overcome during the course of the trial.

XVII

DOCUMENTARY EVIDENCE

One thing which is profoundly impressive to the student of the Nuremberg proceedings is the mass of documentary material available and introduced into evidence. Many of these documents are found in the Reports, Volumes 25 to 44, but these represent only a small percentage of the materials used. Such materials included orders and directives of the defendants themselves and of their associates, copies of speeches, diaries, record books, photographs, motion pictures, depositions, popular books, and affidavits of persons having knowledge of relevant facts. It has been said that this wealth of material fell into Allied hands because of the unexpectedly quick capitulation of Germany, before these documents could be destroyed. From the testimony of the defendants, however, it appeared that certain of defendants, with typical German fondness for detail, deliberately preserved these records and voluntarily delivered them to their captors.[1] Other documents were definitely of a captured character, some being found in secret hiding places, and others being taken from the bodies of dead soldiers. Much of the material was in the nature of reports of investigating commissions, charges preferred by occupied countries and by the Vatican, or material in support of such charges.

Considerable confusion arose immediately as to the manner in which such documents were rendered admissable into evidence. The first ruling of the Tribunal was that only the portion of the documents read in open court by the Prosecution would be deemed a part of the Record, this partially for the reason that defense counsel would thus hear such evidence in court as it was read.[2] It next made a general ruling that all documents presented might be filed, but only those would be admitted which were read in open court or cited in court with translated copies furnished to the defense counsel, this requirement not to apply, however, to those documents of which the Tribunal would take judicial notice.[3] Some difference of opinion seemed to obtain between one of the four members of the Tribunal, Justice Francis Biddle, and the President as to the appli-

[1] E.g. Speer's testimony, XVI *Proceedings* 481. Also Ehard, *op cit.* p. 223 *et seq.*

[2] II *Proceedings* 255.

[3] IV *Proceedings* I; VI *Proceedings* 21, 29.

cation of these rulings,[4] and a later clarification was made requiring documents of which the Tribunal could not take judicial notice to be read if they were to be offered.[5] Justice Biddle also obviously did not like the fact that any evidence collected and sent in by the government of the four prosecuting powers was considered, *ipso facto,* official evidence.[6] Sir David Maxwell-Fyfe, for the United Kingdom, pointed out that under the Charter the Tribunal had no choice but to admit such documents,[7] which is strangely reminiscent of M. Dubost's earlier statement to the Tribunal of its partial subordination to the Prosecution.

The Tribunal required proof of the authenticity of documents prior to their admission into evidence,[8] although admission was permitted where a promise was made to furnish further proof thereof.[9] In this connection the Tribunal ran into repeated difficulties with the Russian prosecution which had retained the original documents in its headquarters and forwarded photostatic copies only to the Tribunal. The Tribunal declared that all originals must be deposited with the Secretary, finally relenting and agreeing to accept photostatic copies if a certificate was furnished showing that it was impossible or highly inconvenient to produce the originals.[10] The same Russian was also instructed not to read documents previously read into evidence.[11]

As to documents offered by the defendants, the Tribunal ruled that documents translated into the four languages could be introduced without being read, with the right in counsel to summarize or direct the Tribunal's attention to relevant and non-cumulative portions, but abstaining from long quotations and arguments thereon.[12] Mr. Dodd of the American prosecution objected to the defense counsel reading any portion of their documents, although the Prosecution had done so at great length, stating:

> "At that time it was physically impossible for the Prosecution to have its material all translated into the four languages, or the three languages in addition to the one in

---

[4] V *Proceedings,* compare pp. 308 and 339.

[5] V *Proceedings* 525.

[6] VIII *Proceedings* 285-6.

[7] VIII *Proceedings* 301.

[8] VII *Proceedings* 67-8; Also VI *Proceedings* 335; but upon further showing by Dubost and Maxwell-Fyfe at 361-3 as to the authentic character of the documents, they were admitted.

[9] VII *Proceedings* 30 (lack of identifying mark to show it was a captured document).

[10] VII *Proceedings* 199, 202-5.

[11] VII *Proceedings* 368.

[12] X *Proceedings* 181-3.

which the original was written. Now the defendants do have those facilities. Had we been able to have our papers all translated, we would have submitted them and we would not have commented."[13]

In view of the extended and frequently argumentative remarks of counsel for the Prosecution in introducing their documents, to which attention will be called later, the statement seems flagrantly untrue. Mr. Dodd's objection was overruled by the Tribunal.

The Tribunal did, however, to avoid excessive translation, require defense counsel to indicate what passages were to be introduced so that objections could be made and passed upon before translation.[14] Copies of documents were introduced where personally certified by defense counsel, if shown to be by agreement of the Prosecution.[15] The Tribunal rejected an unsolicited telegram offered by Dr. Stahmer,[16] and an affidavit offered by Dr. Boehm based upon a newspaper story,[17] but admitted letters offered by another counsel although not under oath, where it considered the evidence not to be of great importance.[18]

It will be remembered from the prior discussion that complaints were made by defendant's counsel as to the labor thrust upon them by receiving untranslated documents at a late date, adding much to their ardous duties.[19] Most of the Prosecution's documents were kept in the Allied Documentary Room. Notices were posted as to the order of proceedings in the Defendant's Information Center, together with copies of the Prosecution's documents books, while documents were generally delivered at a later date to individual counsel in the Defendant's Counsel Room. Much of the controversy, and perhaps some unfairness in the proceedings, arose from the noncompliance with the Tribunal's orders as to the posting of notices and delivery of copies of these documents.

The Tribunal early ruled that a copy of any document sought to be used by the Prosecution must be placed in the Defendant's Counsel Room at the same time it was listed in a document

---

[13] XI *Proceedings* 207, also see a similar comment of Jackson at IX *Proceedings* 657-74. Dr. Stahmer and Dr. Dix objected that the Prosecution had brought out the material by public reading and the defense wanted the same right, since the whole world was interested in the contents. The Tribunal ruled at p. 673 that the documents could be introduced without reading, but that counsel could summarize the contents briefly.

[14] IX *Proceedings* I.

[15] X *Proceedings* 98-9.

[16] IX *Proceedings* 690.

[17] XXI *Proceedings* 431-2.

[18] XIV *Proceedings* 354.

[19] n. 37, *ante* p. 95.

book.[20] It is apparent that twenty-five counsel could not conveniently study a single document simultaneously. The defense attorneys appealed to the Tribunal to enter an order for one copy to be served upon each counsel for the defense.[21] Robert Jackson explained that the presses were working night and day, and that it was impossible for the Prosecution to do more than it had done. The defense attorneys promptly pointed out that, since the Prosecution had printed and delivered two hundred and fifty copies to the Press, certainly it should not complain of delivering ten to the defense attorneys. At a later date, the distinguished associate prosecutor for Great Britain, Sir David Maxwell-Fyfe, was careful to point out that copies had been promptly given to all defense counsel.[22]

As to the translation, the Tribunal reprimanded Mr. Storey for the Prosecution for delivering a document to defense counsel in English, instead of in German,[23] when defense counsel complained of the extra work thus imposed upon them.[24] Defense counsel, on the other hand, it was held, should indicate the exact passage desired by them for introduction from any document prior to its translation,[25] and documents were not to be discussed prior to such translation for which the Prosecution would furnish the facilities.[26] When objection was made that there was no translation of Russian material, however, the objection was overruled where it appeared that the material had been turned in in ample time.[27] And where documents had not been speedily translated, the defendants were permitted to refer to documents in German in their arguments.[28] But the Tribunal was forced to reprimand defense counsel for not getting in their document books two weeks prior to their use, as originally ordered.[29]

The first impression of one reading the record of the Proceedings and observing the frequent protests made by defense attorneys upon the various failures of the Prosecution to furnish or to list documents, and the rulings thereon, is that the proceedings were somewhat confused in the beginning, that the Prosecution was making no great effort at fairness, and that the Tribunal was doing its best to follow a consistent procedure. The later volumes of the reports, also, show an ever increasing

20 II *Proceedings* 255.
21 II *Proceedings* 292.
22 III *Proceedings* 173.
23 V *Proceedings* 21. See also IX *Proceedings* 648.
24 V *Proceedings* 23, 24.
25 IX *Proceedings* 674.
26 X *Proceedings* 9.
27 X *Proceedings* 158.
28 XXII *Proceedings* 170.
29 X *Proceedings* 415.

sharpness in the attitude of the Tribunal toward the Prosecution and a growing recognition of the technique to be followed. It appeared very frequently in the early portions of the trial, for example, that the Prosecution repeatedly attempted to use documents which it had not previously listed in its document books, in violation of the Tribunal's instructions; and the Tribunal seemed to be quite critical of such conduct.[30] The same situation appeared with reference to serving copies of the documents proposed to be used upon counsel for the defense, and, after several such occurrences, the Tribunal began to investigate the conduct of the Prosecution and to enforce compliance with the rules theretofore laid down.[31] However, this requirement as

---

[30] II *Proceedings* 214-216; II *Proceedings* 250-2; II *Proceedings* 292; III *Proceedings* 410-414, where documents neither on list nor certified. However, the Tribunal commented at 414, "It is inconvenient to the Tribunal to have many interruptions of this sort."

In V *Proceedings* 19, after Seidl had complained of late additions to the Indictment, Sauter at 22 pointed out that a big volume of documents had been delivered only the evening before in English, when he had to spend hours talking to his client. The Tribunal at 23 stated that nearly every document referred to in recent days was an old document, the fresh ones being very few, and that counsel could hear these over the microphone. Sauter stated this was untrue, and that the time required to translate and examine the documents overtaxed his strength. Sauter was actively supported by Boehm who stated at p. 25 that it required weeks to secure documents requested, and then only after repeated requests. The Tribunal asked to have the complaints specified in writing.

Again, in VI *Proceedings* 356-7, Exner protested that he was never given any notice of the following day's program. At page 375, Stahmer stated that documents allegedly served three days ago were not received until the night before and then were not numbered.

[31] E.g., II *Proceedings* 250-2. At page 437 of that volume, defense counsel pointed out that one document had been received just that morning, and then not in translation. In III *Proceedings* 410-415, it was objected that the last three documents had not been made available. Dodd (U.S.) claimed that a copy had been placed in the Defendant's Information Center. This did not mean, however, that counsel had been served with copies.

In III *Proceedings* at 415 Seidl, for Frank, pointed out that he had applied six weeks ago to see the forty-two volumes of Frank's diary—that he had made four different requests and the material was still not available. Also, although the Tribunal had ruled on December 4 that Frank's speeches be made available, it was now December 12 and they had not yet been furnished. The Tribunal promised to investigate.

In III *Proceedings* at 424 an objection was made by Thoma, for Rosenberg, that Rosenberg's complete interrogatory was not offered in evidence and had not been shown to defense counsel. At 426, Dodd (U.S.) admitted that fact, and was rebuked by the Tribunal. It ordered that if the Prosecution proposed to put in part of a document or interrogatory, the entire document must be shown to that defendant's counsel and must be furnished in German.

In V *Proceedings* at 25 Boehm pointed out that it still took weeks to get any documents and then only after repeated requests. In VI *Proceedings*

to the furnishing of copies did not give defense counsel any right to conduct a fishing expedition through the documents of the Prosecution;[32] nor did it mean that the Prosecution was forced to expose documents used solely for purposes of impeachment upon cross-examination.[33] To do so would, of course, remove any element of surprise and destroy the effectiveness of much cross-examination. But where a cross-interrogation had been taken only the day before, a defendant was given an opportunity to read the document before completing his testimony.[34]

A somewhat similar situation occurred later in the proceedings which points up the disadvantage of defense counsel having to reveal their evidence in advance of its use. Dr. Sauter had submitted interrogatories to be asked of a witness, Ida Vasseau, but had never received them back. Upon cross-examination, the Russian prosecutor endeavored to introduce an affidavit from that witness. Upon questioning by the Tribunal, he stated that the witness had just been located, and that Dr. Sauter's inter-

---

430, Stahmer pointed out that he still had not received certain documents. At 431 the Tribunal proposed to investigate to find out if its rules were being carried out. Thereupon Fauré, for France, said that the documents had not yet been distributed but were in the Defense Room. With that explanation, the Tribunal permitted Fauré to continue his talk.

In VII *Proceedings* at 244, Laternser pointed out that the Russian Prosecution was not distributing enough copies for each defense counsel to have a separate copy, although the United States, Great Britain, and France had done so following the Tribunal's prior ruling. (II *Proceedings* 292). The Tribunal passed over the matter.

32 XX *Proceedings* 278-281. Controversy between Pelckmann and Dodd about former being refused permission to look through Allied Documentary Room. The Tribunal denied the right to any such fishing expedition, although it would require the Prosecution to produce any document for inspection specified by Pelckmann. It also intimated that it expected the Prosecution voluntarily to produce material of assistance to the defense.

Actually this controversy arose over what defense counsel conceived to be the duty of the Prosecution under German law and what these particular prosecutors believed the limit of their duty. This is discussed in greater detail, *post*, p. 131.

33 IX *Proceedings* 500. Objection by Siemers to cross-examination on documents not first submitted to the defense. Jackson refused to disclose the documents at 501-2 for the reasons given above. Dix protested Jackson's attitude, and at 503 the Tribunal ruled it sufficient to furnish one copy to counsel whose witness was being cross-examined and later to other counsel.

In XIII *Proceedings* at 164 an objection was made to the use of an untranslated document upon cross-examination. The Tribunal pointed out that defense counsel would have a chance to recall the witness for further testimony on rebuttal, but requested Dodd to furnish a copy of the document in German. Dodd refused to do so at that time, stating that he intended to use the document the next day and did not want to spoil the element of surprise.

34 XI *Proceedings* 227, with reference to defendant Kaltenbrunner.

rogatories could now be issued. The Tribunal thereupon refused to permit further interrogation based upon the affidavit until Dr. Sauter's interrogatories had been returned.[35]

Other objections made to documents were varied, such as lack of proper authentication,[36] prejudice on the part of the witness,[37] irrelevancy,[38] lack of genuineness,[39] inaccuracy,[40] and lack of official character.[41] Strangely enough, only two defendants

---

[35] XIV *Proceedings*. Objection by Dr. Sauter at 529. Ruling of Tribunal at 533.

[36] VII *Proceedings* 243. Objection by Nelte that Russian documents were uncertified. Overruled by Tribunal as premature. Similar objections at pp. 250-2 and 264-6. The Tribunal stated its willingness to locate the affiants if possible and produce them for cross-examination, but that its facilities were not unlimited.

VII *Proceedings* 462-3. Kauffmann objected that the investigation report offered by Russia failed to disclose the source of the material, so that it was impossible to cross-examine upon it. The Tribunal ruled that it was compelled under the Charter to take judicial notice of such documents.

VIII *Proceedings* 285. Objection by Nelte as to identification; also at p. 290 by Kubuschok, with document admitted at 291 subject to right to call witness in rebuttal.

XII *Proceedings* 165. An unsolicited letter from a Catholic priest was refused admission, but with the privilege in counsel to apply for an affidavit or to call the witness personally.

XVIII *Proceedings* 87-8. Objections were made that the affidavit was uncertified; also that the witness was dead and not subject to cross-examination.

XXI *Proceedings* 434-442. Objection to a rebuttal document because sworn to before a notary and not an officer. Overruled.

[37] XV *Proceedings* 106. Marx's objection that the report was one from a witness who was an enemy of Streicher was properly overruled.

[38] V *Proceedings* 112. A certain book written by Frick was objected to by Marx upon the case against Streicher, but it appeared that the introduction was written by Streicher who had approved the contents. Objection overruled. But in V *Proceedings* at 366, where it was objected by Frick's attorney that a document offered against him showed no evidence of guilt, the objection was sustained. Similarly, in XIV *Proceedings* 556-8, the Tribunal refused documents offered to discredit a witness by showing he had ordered prisoners killed where not relevant for purposes of impeachment.

[39] VII *Proceedings* 443-4. Objection by Nelte to document offered by Smirnov was withdrawn, after Nelte personally verified the signatures. IX *Proceedings* 610, objections by Stahmer for Goering to document as not genuine. Document of Raeder at IX *Proceedings* 615-17 excluded by Tribunal.

[40] XV *Proceedings* 531-3. The Tribunal excluded document which was poorly translated unless translated in its entirety and shown to Jodl.

[41] IV *Proceedings* 503. Objection by Seidl to data furnished by Vatican. He asked whether Vatican was a signatory to Charter or a co-prosecutor. Objection overruled at 504 as irrelevant. In XI *Proceedings* 375-8 an

claimed that their interrogatories used for purposes of impeachment were procured under duress,[42] although Goering claimed that false representations had been made to him at the time of taking his deposition and it was withdrawn.[43] Jodl's interrogation was refused by the Tribunal when his counsel pointed out that the impeaching document was in English, and that his client could speak and read only German.[44]

It was not a proper ground for objection that an attorney for the Prosecution read only part of a document, instead of its entirety, in view of the practice of summarizing documents to shorten the proceedings.[45] But an American attorney was severely reprimanded by the Tribunal for misstating the purpose of a document when asked to summarize its contents.[46] Even then the Tribunal placed other safeguards around such testimony for the benefit of the defense, and its rulings are of considerable interest.

---

argument developed over a copy of a letter from Dr. Kauffmann and the reply thereto sent direct to the Prosecution and offered by the Prosecution. The Tribunal sustained Kauffmann's objection and held the documents inadmissible as unofficial in character.

[42] XV *Proceedings* 64. Sauckel claimed his statements were procured under duress. The Tribunal permitted the Prosecution to cross-examine on it, but at 68 refused admission of the document.

XVII *Proceedings.* Fritsche on cross-examination by Rudenko, at 203, was shown a confession signed in Moscow. He claimed both the questions and answers were untrue and stated he would give his reasons for signing the document if Rudenko insisted. Rudenko dropped the matter, but the Tribunal, at 204, demanded an explanation. Fritsche claimed he was kept in solitary confinement for several months and wanted to terminate it. He also claimed the questions and answers were placed before him in a complete form and they indicated he sign in that form, although he wanted to make twenty or thirty changes. However, see the discussion in Heiden, "Why They Confess," *Reader's Digest,* pp. 22-6 (September, 1949).

[43] IX *Proceedings* 551-2. This is discussed more fully *post,* p. 135, note 21.

[44] XV *Proceedings* 454. On objection by Exner. This gentleman, who was a university professor and not a trial lawyer, did a surprisingly good job for his old friend Jodl. One is inclined to believe that Jodl convicted himself by his statement to the Tribunal at the close of all the evidence, XXI *Proceedings* 400.

[45] V *Proceedings* 63. Thoma objected that Brudno, for Russia, read only a part of a paragraph with an intent to mislead. In V *Proceedings* 80, Seidl made similar objection to a document and stated he would read it in its entirety when his turn came. And in VI *Proceedings* 182-3, Nelte objected that the portion read indicated Keitel had approved certain orders which was not true in the light of the entire document. Such objections were properly overruled. They were premature, and such matters can always be shown as part of the defendant's case.

[46] V *Proceedings* 81. Mr. Baldwin. This was an unfortunate incident, since Mr. Baldwin gave an otherwise very clear and unbiased presentation,

With reference to the first affidavits introduced, those of George Messersmith, a former American diplomatic representative in the Central European area, considerable controversy arose. In view of the fact the witness was then in Mexico City, aged and ill, it was held that written cross-interrogatories must be submitted and the witness would not be required to attend.[47] An affidavit was then admitted of another witness though the witness was actually in Nuremberg.[48] The Tribunal reversed its position upon this subject and rejected successive affidavits where the witness was available.[49] Upon the next tender of an affidavit, Jackson locked horns with the Tribunal and compelled the adoption of the prior rule requiring the defendant's counsel to make a motion in writing for the attendance of such a witness for cross-examination, giving the reasons therefor,[50] and that rule obtained thereafter.[51] This did not, of course, change the usual rule that reports of an examining commission were *per se,*

---

which was a far different situation from that of some of the American Prosecutors.

[47] II *Proceedings* 341-364. Ruling at 364.

[48] II *Proceedings* 369.

[49] II *Proceedings* 384-5, Von Schussnig affidavit; III *Proceedings* 80-1, Berger affidavit. Naujoks affidavit obtained under like circumstances not offered.

[50] III *Proceedings* 542. Objection by Kauffmann to Pfaffenberger affidavit that witness could appear personally. Jackson replied that he had no intention of participating in a Warren Hastings' Trial which would last 7 years. Only two requirements, pointed out, were set up in the Charter for the admissibility of evidence: 1. that it be relevant; 2. that it have probative value. Common law proof was not involved in this case. There was no jury and no need to apply jury rules. This was a military tribunal and not an ordinary court of law. The Tribunal at 545-7 asked Jackson how a defendant's counsel can possibly cross-examine an affidavit. Jackson replied that he would have that right only if the Prosecution calls the witness personally; otherwise it would be up to the defendant to call such witness. No such right existed where an affidavit is used. There was also a provision to take deposition by commission. The Tribunal did not agree that the defense could be wholly precluded from cross-examination but adopted the equitable rule discussed in the text.

[51] III *Proceedings* 571. Kauffmann objected to Hoettl's testimony, since he was still at Nuremberg. The Tribunal at 572 ruled he might make a motion in writing for the attendance of the witness for cross-examination. In IV *Proceedings* 297, Kauffmann made like objection, with a similar ruling at 298. In VI *Proceedings* 81, an objection by Kubuschok to Schroder's affidavit provoked renewed discussion at 81-4, but with a like ruling coupled with a demand by the Tribunal that the witness be arranged for immediately. In VII *Proceedings* 116-19, a like objection and a like ruling. In VII *Proceedings* 359-360, 361-2, 419-23, similar objections by Nelte persuaded the Russian prosecutor not to use the material unless he could locate the witness for cross-examination by the defense. The usual rule was again followed in IX *Proceedings* 589.

admissible,[52] nor, on the other hand, did it render admissible documents not conforming to the rules of evidence adopted.[53]

Reference has been made several times to the question of judicial notice, the application of which doctrine doubtless saved considerable time in the trial but which also permitted the introduction of much evidence which otherwise would not have been competent. Ordinarily the doctrine of judicial notice is used sparingly in the legal process and refers only to those truths which are so universally known that no man can dispute them, or to public acts and records which import verity from their face. The Charter, it will be recalled, greatly increased the scope of judicial notice, and made it applicable to many other things.[54]

The Tribunal, of course, took judicial notice of the articles of the Hague Convention upon the Rules of Land Warfare,[55] and of the amnesty decree issued by the German government following the National Socialist revolution to the persons involved therein.[56] It was repeatedly called upon to admit the results of investigating commissions, although not under oath,[57] and of the records and findings of military tribunals.[58] Justice Biddle was definitely disturbed by the fact that the Tribunal was required to admit, without further proof, any and all evidence collected and sent in by any of the signatory powers to the Charter as official evidence.[59] And the Tribunal flatly refused to take judicial notice of facts of which it was ignorant.[60]

Memoranda were admissible if possessing any relevancy to the questions at issue.[61] Quotations were made by both sides

---

[52] VI *Proceedings* 160-4. Objection to an affidavit as not in proper form or under oath. Admitted 164. (One is prompted to ask, as did the Tribunal: How can one cross-examine an affidavit? Also, a further question: How can one interrogate an investigating commission submitting such a report?)

[53] VII *Proceedings* 116. See the excellent objections of Nelte to the introduction of a summarized report for six concise reasons. These objections were sustained.

[54] *Ante*, p. 101, note 72. And it should be remembered that where judicial notice was taken, reading of the documents in evidence was not required. E.g., IV *Proceedings* 1; V *Proceedings* 525; VI *Proceedings* 21, 29.

[55] V *Proceedings* 534.

[56] VI *Proceedings* 85.

[57] E.g., VI *Proceedings*. Discussion at 161-2. Ruling of Tribunal at 164.

[58] E.g., VII *Proceedings* 462-3. Kauffmann pointed out the impossibility of cross-examination in such instances, since such reports did not show the sources of the materials relied upon.

[59] VIII *Proceedings* 255-8. At 301 Maxwell-Fyfe pointed out the Tribunal had no choice under the Charter but to admit such document.

[60] VI *Proceedings* 159.

[61] E.g., memoranda of Bullitt's conversations with Schacht and Goering. II *Proceedings* 401-2.

from speeches, letters, and statements of famous men;[62] and since many prominent persons are prone to reduce their observations and sagacity to book form, excerpts from such volumes were quoted by the defendants, witnesses, and counsel for both Prosecution and defense as actual evidence in the cause.[63] This was one of the most radical departures from the conventional methods of trial familiar to American lawyers.

As additional documentary material, there were introduced copies of posters which the Nazis had posted in occupied countries,[64] still photographs,[65] and motion pictures,[66] many of

---

[62] E.g., IX *Proceedings* 674-84, quotations from correspondence of Neville Henderson and Lord Halifax by Stahmer. On the other hand, statements of Borah, Lord Rothermere (XI *Proceedings* 444) and Winston Churchill were not considered particularly relevant. See IX *Proceedings* 364, 369, where the presiding officer seemed to take a backhanded slap at Mr. Churchill. Many more quotations of prominent persons were made in closing arguments. And the Prosecution repeatedly referred to speeches and writings of the defendants as affirmative evidence of their guilt.

[63] *Mein Kampf* was one of the principal documents for the Prosecution, to show the Nazi goal and awareness by all defendants of the common design—e.g., IV *Proceedings* 519-527. Ambassador Dodd's Diary was quoted by both sides—e.g., II *Proceedings* 357. Other examples of books to which reference was made include John Gunther's *Inside Europe*, XII *Proceedings* 166; Dahlerus, *Last Attempt*, IX *Proceedings* 457-491; Martin Luther, *The Jews and Their Lies*, XII *Proceedings* 305-44; Henry Ford, *The International Jew*, XIV *Proceedings* 361; and works of Neville Henderson and Sumner Welles (see rulings at XI *Proceedings* 444). The Tribunal refused, however, to permit extensive reference to books of philosophy sought by Rosenberg, Streicher and other defendants, holding that a man's personal philosophy is immaterial—it is only the use which he makes of such philosophy which is material. VIII *Proceedings* 505-15, XI *Proceedings* 73-87, 386-395. And books expressing purely the individual opinion of the author were deemed incompetent. IX *Proceedings* 673-4.

Of course, in closing arguments counsel referred to many authorities upon international law in support of their respective positions such as Garner, Oppenheim, Schussler, and Scherff.

[64] VII *Proceedings* 16-22. Also see reproduction of posters and of Anti-Semitic cartoons and stories XXVIII *Proceedings* 304-345; XXXIV *Proceedings* 98-102.

[65] III *Proceedings* 558; VIII *Proceedings* 293. And see reproductions of photographs as to weapons of torture at Mauthausen, XXIX *Proceedings* 308-14; at Essen, XXXI *Proceedings* 71; undernourished prisoners, XXX *Proceedings* 381-7; atrocities, XXX *Proceedings* 389-93, 403-457; XXXII *Proceedings* 259-271; executions XXX *Proceedings* 399-401; XXXVI *Proceedings* 669-71; German leaders, XXX *Proceedings* 395-7, XXXI *Proceedings* 525-75.

[66] Titles of such pictures were somewhat as follows: "Rise of NSDAP, 1921-33," "Acquiring Totalitarian Control of Germany 1933-5," "Preparation for War of Aggression 1935-9," "Wars of Aggression 1939-44," "Persecution of the Jews," "Crimes in Concentration Camps," "Atrocities by German Fascist Invaders in U.S.S.R.," "Destruction of Art Museums of National Culture, etc.," and the like. References to the introduction or showing of such films are contained in I *Proceedings* 147-68; II *Proceedings*

which were in the nature of captured documents. These constituted powerful visual evidence both as pertaining to the crimes against humanity and offenses in violation of the rules of war.

340, 431-4; III *Proceedings* 241, 400-2, 536; VII *Proceedings* 15-16, 601; VIII *Proceedings* 100, 124; XIII *Proceedings* 190-6.

XVIII

WITNESSES; OBJECTIONS TO EVIDENCE

It must be remembered that the witnesses at the trial were from many lands, each having a slightly different form of jurisprudence. Accordingly, the record of the proceedings shows the administration of a different form of oath to the witnesses of different nations. And in one instance a priest was permitted to testify without being sworn at all.[1]

Only one witness claimed that he had been abused in any way. Witness Erhard Milch, testifying for Goering, stated that his memory was impaired "through heavy blows on the head received at the time of my capture."[2] Counsel for one of the defendant organizations charged that prisoners in the Russian zone were kept in ignorance of the charges against them and were not given the hearing to which they were entitled. Upon questioning by the Tribunal, he based his statement upon information given him by Dr. Servatius, who pointed out that this was incorrect. Counsel was rebuked by the Tribunal and apologized.[3] Servatius had previously, however, claimed that his visits to the camps were restricted,[4] and both he and another counsel pointed out the failure to receive back replies to letters and interrogatories.[5]

The Tribunal early laid down the rule that it would summon witnesses for the defense, but only if their testimony was relevant and noncumulative.[6] It pointed out later, however, that while it was willing to ascertain the whereabouts of witnesses and bring them forward, if possible, its facilities were not unlimited.[7] And where definite requests were made for the calling of witnesses whose interrogatories had been used in chief by the

---

[1] VIII *Proceedings* 334.

[2] IX *Proceedings* 108. However, in Case 2 of the Subsequent Nuremberg Trials, Milch claimed such mental instability existed long before.

[3] XXII *Proceedings* 132.

[4] VIII *Proceedings* 404.

[5] VIII *Proceedings* 404. Servatius stated that he had taken affidavits which were turned over to the camp commanders, but not returned to him. VIII *Proceedings* 405-8, Merkel stated that he had sent letters to various camps five to seven weeks previously and had as yet received no replies. He, also, charged that individual members of indicted groups did not know they were being represented.

[6] IV *Proceedings* 1-2.

[7] VII *Proceedings* 264-6.

Proscution, they were granted.[8] Although an argument had developed as to the right of defense counsel to talk to a witness prior to cross-examination,[9] it was definitely held that where a request for a witness was granted, the defense attorney could talk to such witness without the Prosecution being present.[10]

As to the calling of parties, it was held that any defendant could cause any other defendant or witness to be interrogated while upon the stand, and that counsel for indicted organizations could call a defendant as a witness but not as a party to those charges.[11] A counsel was permitted tô examine a witness upon the motives or credibility of another witness, although the Tribunal stated it did not intend thereby to establish such action as a precedent.[12] It was ruled also that written application could be made for recall of a witness for further examination, with no assurance as to the ruling,[13] although such recall was certain where so stipulated by counsel.[14]

Although the giving of notice as to the names of witnesses to be used by the Prosecution did not seem to be mandatory,[15] the Tribunal required the Prosecution to so state,[16] and that procedure was generally followed thereafter. The defendants were permitted to use notes to refresh their recollections;[17] and, after it was directed to the Tribunal's attention that a witness not a party defendant was using notes, it was ruled that he might do so for the purpose of refreshing his recollection but not for the purpose of reading therefrom.[18] And it was ruled also that where a witness for one defendant was called to testify in person, other counsel would have to examine him orally rather than to rely upon an interrogatory or affidavit of that witness.[19]

The Tribunal, throughout, imposed limitations upon all counsel as to the calling of oral witnesses, in order to expedite the

---

[8] VIII *Proceedings* 282, as to Halder and Warlimont. Previously, Nelte had objected to use of their interrogatories and asked production of the witnesses. VII *Proceedings* 359-60, 361-2. And at VII *Proceedings* 419-23 the same objection was made as to Wengler, Pokrovsky deciding not to use the interrogatory unless he could locate the witness.

[9] VIII *Proceedings* 495-504. See Maxwell-Fyfe's prior objections at VIII *Proceedings* 190-1.

[10] VIII *Proceedings* 513.

[11] IV *Proceedings* 2, 3.

[12] XIII *Proceedings* 458-60.

[13] IX *Proceedings* 234-5.

[14] IX *Proceedings* 364-5, as to recall of Goering.

[15] II *Proceedings* 435-9.

[16] V *Proceedings* 157.

[17] IX *Proceedings* 1.

[18] IX *Proceedings* 13.

[19] IX *Proceedings* 1.

proceedings.[20] Nor was it deemed material that both Prosecution and defense were willing for additional testimony to be introduced.[21] Counsel had no right to interrogate a witness as to matters which could have no bearing upon the guilt or innocence of his particular client.[22] And cross-examination on behalf of the organizations was denied, since interrogation would be permitted before the commissioner.[23] The Tribunal also refused to permit testimony as to personal philosophies,[24] or as to isolated incidents having no particular bearing upon a general course of conduct.[25] But interrogatories of the defendants themselves were admissible against them, though their attorneys were not present at the time of taking them.[26]

It was originally stipulated by Jackson that defense counsel need not make objections during the introduction of prosecution evidence, but might be deemed to have reserved such objections until the end of the case.[27] The Tribunal at one point lost sight of this stipulation,[28] but later corrected its ruling.[29] It was also held that documents might be presented without reading, objections to be heard when formal offer was made.[30] And this pro-

---

[20] This will be observed throughout the reports. The Tribunal determined the relative importance of the witnesses to the defendants' cases, and permitted only major, noncumulative, witnesses to be called.

[21] XVII *Proceedings* 371. The Tribunal limited witnesses in the Katyn Wood incident to three upon a side and refused both Stahmer's and the Russian prosecutor's request for additional evidence.

[22] XVII *Proceedings* 286. Siemers for Raeder on Katyn Wood incident. At 302 it refused permission to Kranzbuehler to ask questions, but suggested he have Stahmer ask them.

[23] XV *Proceedings* 593-4, by Laternser. Also at XII *Proceedings* 300-305 the Tribunal refused to let Laternser bring out by Gisevius that the generals were ready for a Putsch against Hitler.

[24] XI *Proceedings* 449, 451, 515, 516 (Rosenberg); XII *Proceedings* 318, 319 (Streicher).

[25] XI *Proceedings* 427. Neubacher was not permitted to testify that Kaltenbrunner used his power to liberate two church dignitaries, although he was accused of oppressing the churches. This ruling is, to say the least, questionable.

[26] II *Proceedings* 321-2; III *Proceedings* 246. But see IX *Proceedings* 551-2.

[27] III *Proceedings* 597. For some reason Boehm, one of defense counsel, objected. The Tribunal also referred to this right in V *Proceedings* 23.

[28] VIII *Proceedings* 164. Stahmer pointed out that all objections had been reserved. He was contradicted by the Tribunal, which stated that any objection had to be made at the time of admission. This was clearly erroneous.

[29] VIII *Proceedings* 169. The Tribunal held that a written motion could be made at any time to strike a document from the record.

[30] IX *Proceedings* 673.

cedure was voluntarily suggested by the Prosecution at another stage of the proceedings.[31]

It was, of course, proper to cross-examine a defendant's witness on the basis of a document introduced by the defense,[32] and statements of a defendant which were clearly improper were, at one stage, stricken from the record by the agreement of counsel.[33]

As to the ordinary objections raised in courts of law, a somewhat different rule applied. As has already been seen, the Tribunal was required to take judicial notice of reports of investigating commissions. A member of such a commission, testifying as to documents which he has seen or as to information given to him by others, would be violating both the "best evidence" rule and the rule against "hearsay evidence." These objections were raised as to the testimony of Van den Essen, of the Dutch Commission. M. Fauré, for the French prosecution, pointed out that the Tribunal expressly was not bound by formal rules of evidence and offered evidence of affidavits in support of the witness's statements. The Tribunal refused to strike the evidence, stating that it would consider these objections in determining the weight of the evidence. However, it declared also that if a member of a governmental investigating commission were called as a witness, the report of the commission must be introduced.[34] At another place it admitted a document containing a clear conclusion of a witness, holding the objection as to such "conclusion" went only to the weight of the evidence;[35] but it did refuse to take notice of statements not supported by the evidence.[36]

To condense the proceedings it was necessary, of course, to avoid cumulative evidence when possible, and objections were made upon this ground,[37] such an objection not being sustained,

---

31 X *Proceedings* 8, 9. Sir David Maxwell-Fyfe suggested that Seidl's documents be offered first and received "de bene esse" with objections to be made later as to admissions. The suggestion was accepted by the Tribunal with the restriction that the documents not be discussed until translated, which would be the task of the Prosecution.

32 XIII *Proceedings* 376. Kranzbuehler objected to cross-examination of Doenitz.

33 XII *Proceedings* 398. Agreement of Marx and Jackson.

34 VII *Proceedings* 1.

35 XIV *Proceedings* 239-41. At 241 the Tribunal stated, "The passage contains an opinion only. . . .," which goes to its probative value.

36 VII *Proceedings* 59.

37 VII *Proceedings* 50. Objection by defense counsel as to pillaging of works of art. VIII *Proceedings* 117-8, objection by defense counsel to interrogatories of Von dem Bach-Zelewski, as cumulative, since witnesses testified personally. Sustained by Tribunal.

however, where the evidence was clearly relevant.[38] Objections were frequently made upon other grounds, however, which were premature and overruled for that reason.[39]

One of the great faults to be observed in the technique of trial counsel was due to the unfamiliarity of many of the attorneys with the procedure of direct questioning and cross-examination of a witness by trial counsel. The practice in many continental courts is for the presiding judge to conduct the interrogation of witnesses, in contrast to the American system.[40] Consequently it will be observed throughout the proceedings that counsel on both sides continually asked leading questions, without objection, the questions often running a printed page in length and consisting of testimony of the counsel as to the documents, activities of the witness, and mental attitudes, and requiring a simple assent on his part. The Tribunal pointed out that, while it was not bound by ordinary rules of evidence, the use of such questions did affect the probative value of the testimony.[41]

The Tribunal, to reduce the number of oral interruptions to a minimum, was early forced to rule that objections to documents[42] or motions to strike documents[43] be placed in writing. It subsequently adopted the same requirement as to applications for rebuttal or further evidence.[44]

---

[38] XXII *Proceedings* 330. Objections by Prosecution to Seyss-Inquart affidavit.

[39] III *Proceedings* 540, objections by Thoma that document was not one of his defendant's, as he would show by his evidence. IV *Proceedings* 132, Sauter objected that Von Schirach was never a member of the Reich Cabinet and testimony was incompetent as to him. IV *Proceedings* 528-9, Thoma that there was no evidence against Rosenberg though accused by name as to church activities. X *Proceedings* 175-8, objection by Russia to slanderous documents, which had not yet been admitted.

[40] Telford Taylor, "The Nuremberg Trials," *International Conciliation*, No. 450, p. 262 *et seq.* (April, 1949).

[41] See, for example, Von Ludinghausen's objections, with long speeches, attempting to lead a witness who was being cross-examined by the Prosecution, X *Proceedings* 63, 66-8. At XV *Proceedings* 309, the Tribunal commented, "You have heard me say on several occasions that when counsel ask leading questions, which put the answer in the mouth of the witness, it carries very little weight with the Tribunal."

A little levity appeared at another point where the Tribunal asked Dr. Jahrreiss, cross-examining a witness, the reason for his question. Dr. Jahrreiss stated, XV *Proceedings* 568: "Mr. President, if I am to give the reason for that, then I will have to tell the witness what I want him to tell me. Then my question will become a leading one." The President retorted, "Well, that is not an unusual thing in this court."

[42] V *Proceedings* 20-1, as to late addition to Indictment. V *Proceedings* 26 as to documents being furnished late and in an untranslated form.

[43] VIII *Proceedings* 169.

[44] VIII *Proceedings* 281.

In view of the fact that this was an international tribunal, required to be conducted in many languages simultaneously, certain physical problems somewhat hindered the progress of the hearing. It has already been observed that all documents were required to be translated into four different languages for the benefit of the various members of the Tribunal. This necessarily resulted in a tremendous strain upon both the translating and printing facilities of the Tribunal, and occasional errors in the translation of documents arose,[45] although certainly they were minor in comparison with the amount of material handled. To understand some of the other problems, one must visualize the courtroom itself. The person addressing the court advanced to the rostrum and spoke into the microphone. Another microphone was in front of the witness chair. The remarks went to the interpreters—who, in turn, translated the statements into the four chief languages employed, or three, if the witness or speaker employed one of the major languages. Each defendant, attorney, witness and judge wore earphones, and the language most common to him would be the only language other than the original one which he would hear. It was necessary for counsel and witnesses to speak slowly in order for the interpreters to operate properly, and they were constantly warned by the Tribunal to pause for the interpretations.[46] A yellow warning light was placed before them also, and the flashing of it was a signal to proceed more slowly—the Tribunal constantly reminding counsel to "look out for the light" or "don't you see the light?". Frequently technical difficulties developed in the speaker mechanism requiring a temporary suspension of the proceedings.[47] And occasional objections were made to the accuracy of translation by the interpreters.[48]

As to cross-examination of witnesses, in addition to the rules heretofore discussed, the Tribunal ruled that only one counsel for the entire Prosecution might cross-examine any witness

[45] III *Proceedings* 465-74, objections by Flachsner, for Speer, as to inaccuracy of translation. Overruled. VI *Proceedings* 373-5, numbers upon documents were incorrectly translated and were corrected. VI *Proceedings* 400, Servatius, for Sauckel, pointed out an error in translation which was acknowledged by Dubost for Prosecution. XV *Proceedings* 531, Jodl upon cross-examination by Russian prosecutor points out that a certain order was poorly translated, making it "pure unadulterated nonsense." The Tribunal demanded the original and at 532-3 refused admission unless first translated into German and submitted in its entirety to the defendant.

[46] E.g., see comments in IV *Proceedings* 475-95.

[47] E.g., see X *Proceedings* 184-5.

[48] E.g., IX *Proceedings*, Goering pointed out throughout his testimony many inaccuracies of the interpreters and the substitution of much stronger expressions than used in his testimony. See p. 632, for example. Servatius made like observations in IX *Proceedings* 647.

other than a defendant.[49] However, leave was granted in a particular instance to cross-examine as to special matters.[50]

Upon the question of skill displayed in cross-examination, one would conclude that the continental attorneys, who were less familiar with the technique than Anglo-Saxon attorneys, would display less ability than their experienced adversaries. This was largely true. Of course, upon many occasions, witnesses were not cross-examined at all.[51] Also, occasional fine examples of cross-examination were displayed by the Germans[52] and by the Russian member of the Tribunal, General Nikitchenko.[53] But on the whole, the more able cross-examinations were conducted by the British[54] and by the American Prosecutors. In this last regard, Jackson, who was a rough and ready trial lawyer in his approach throughout the proceedings, handled himself with particular brilliance.

For example, witness Bodenschatz, testifying for Goering, had stated that Goering did not know that any persons were wrongfully sent to concentration camps, and also had testified as to Goering's great heart in securing the release of persons from that place. Jackson posed a masterly question which left the witness squarely on the horns of a dilemna.[55]

> "Jackson: Now were the persons that you intervened for innocent of crime or were you helping those who were guilty of crime?"

What could the witness answer? In one case, Goering was an accessory to criminals. Otherwise, Goering knew that innocent persons were being sent to concentration camps. He actually replied.

> "Those I helped were innocent people.
>
> "Jackson: So it came to your notice that innocent people were being put in concentration camps."

---

[49] X *Proceedings* 154 where Russian prosecutor was precluded from interrogation. Also at XI *Proceedings* 419.

[50] XI *Proceedings* 315-6.

[51] E.g., VI *Proceedings* 183-194 (Lampe); VIII *Proceedings* 257-61 (Grigoriev); VIII *Proceedings* 302-8 (Suzkever); VIII *Proceedings* 324-9 (Rajsinan); VIII *Proceedings* 334-44 (Lomakin); VII *Proceedings* 317-22 (Shmazlevskaya).

[52] V *Proceedings* 187-199 of Dr. Franz Blaha, casting serious doubt on his identification of various defendants visiting Dachau, and upon their ability to learn what was going on. XVII *Proceedings* 321-33 by Stahmer of witness Bazilevsky on Katyn Wood incident.

[53] XVII *Proceedings* 102-7 of Von Neurath.

[54] X *Proceedings* 18-39 of witness Bohle for Hess. X *Proceedings* 123-55 of witness Von Steensgracht. In the latter instance, additional and very damaging evidence was elicited against certain defendants.

[55] IX *Proceedings* 17.

He followed this up very shortly after the witness had stated that Jews were arrested under a general order.

> "Jackson: It came to your attention that Jews were being thrown into concentration camps merely because they were Jews."[56]

Questions of this character were, of course, unanswerable consistent with the witness's prior testimony, and helped largely to destroy the witness's evidence. The cross-examination by Jackson of Goering himself was one of the greatest of all time and actually proved the Prosecution's case without the need of other evidence.[57] The famous cross-examination of Oscar Wilde

---

[56] IX *Proceedings* 19.

[57] IX *Proceedings* 417-56. For example:

MR. JUSTICE JACKSON: You are perhaps aware that you are the only living man who can expound to us the true purposes of the Nazi Party and the inner workings of its leadership?

GOERING: I am perfectly aware of that.

MR. JUSTICE JACKSON: You, from the very beginning, together with those who were associated with you, intended to overthrow, and later did overthrow, the Weimar Republic?

GOERING: That was, as far as I am concerned, my firm intention.

MR. JUSTICE JACKSON: And, upon coming to power, you immediately abolished parliamentary government in Germany?

GOERING: We found it to be no longer necessary. Also I should like to emphasize the fact that we were moreover the strongest parliamentary party, and had the majority. But you are correct, when you say that parliamentary procedure was done away with, because the various parties were disbanded and forbidden.

MR. JUSTICE JACKSON: You established the Leadership Principle, which you have described as a system under which authority existed only at the tip, and is passed downwards and is imposed on the people below; is that correct?

GOERING: In order to avoid any misunderstanding, I should like once more to explain the idea briefly, as I understand it. In German parliamentary procedure in the past responsibility rested with the highest officials, who were responsible for carrying out the anonymous wishes of the majorities, and it was they who exercised the authority. In the Leadership Principle we sought to reverse the direction, that is, the authority existed at the top and passed downwards, while the responsibility began at the bottom and passed upwards. * * *

MR. JUSTICE JACKSON: But you did not permit the election of those who should act with authority by the people, but they were designated from the top downward continuously, were they not?

GOERING: Quite right. The people were merely to acknowledge the authority of the Fuhrer, or, let us say, to declare themselves in agreement with the Fuhrer. If they gave the Fuhrer their confidence, then it was their concern to exercise the other functions. Thus, not the individual persons were to be selected according to the will of the people, but solely the leadership itself. * * *

MR. JUSTICE JACKSON: The principles of the authoritarian government which you set up required, as I understand you, that there be

pales by comparison, as does the much overrated cross-examination of William Jennings Bryan by Clarence Darrow in the

---

tolerated no opposition by political parties which might defeat or obstruct the policy of the Nazi Party?

GOERING: You have understood this quite correctly. By that time we had lived long enough with opposition and we had had enough of it. Through opposition we had been completley ruined. It was now time to have done with it and to start building up.

Mr. JUSTICE JACKSON: After you came to power, you regarded it necessary, in order to maintain power, to suppress all opposition parties?

GOERING: We found it necessary not to permit any more opposition, yes. * * *

MR. JUSTICE JACKSON: But you are explaining, as the high authority of this system, to men who do not understand it very well, and I want to know what was necessary to run the kind of system that you set up in Germany. The concentration camp was one of the things you found immediately necessary upon coming into power, was it not? And you set them up as a matter of necessity as you saw it?

GOERING: That was faultily translated—it went too fast. But I believe I have understood the sense of your remarks. You asked me if I considered it necessary to establish concentration camps immediately in order to eliminate opposition. Is that correct?

MR. JUSTICE JACKSON: Your answer is "Yes," I take it?

GOERING: Yes. * * *

MR. JUSTICE JACKSON: Protective custody meant that you were taking people into custody who had not committed any crimes but who, you thought, might possibly commit a crime?

GOERING: Yes. People were arrested and taken into protective custody who had not yet committed any crime, but who could be expected to do so if they remained free, just as extensive protective measures are being taken in Germany today on a tremendous scale. * * *

MR. JUSTICE JACKSON: Well, you had to have organizations to carry out orders and to carry your propaganda in that kind of state, didn't you?

GOERING: Of coure, we carried on propaganda, and for this we had a propaganda organization.

MR. JUSTICE JACKSON: But when it was State necessity to kill somebody, you had to have somebody to do it, didn't you?

GOERING: Yes, just as in other countries, whether it is called secret service or something else, I do not know. * * *

MR. JUSTICE JACKSON: Well, the SS carried out arrests and carried out the transportation of people to concentration camps, didn't they? You were arrested by the SS weren't you?

GOERING: Yes, I say, yes; but later.

MR. JUSTICE JACKSON: At what time did the SS perform this function of acting as the executioner of the Nazi Party?

GOERING: After the seizure of power, when the police came to be more and more in the hands of Himmler. It is difficult for me to explain to an outsider where the SS or where the Gestapo was active. I have already said that the two of them worked very closely together. It is known that the SS guarded the camps and later carried out police functions.

MR. JUSTICE JACKSON: And carried out other functions in the camps?

GOERING: To what functions do you refer?

Scopes trial.[58] And again, Jackson's examination of witness Milch, who had testified that Germany had not prepared for an aggressive war, and was far less prepared than her neighbors, reduced that testimony to insignificance.[59]

MR. JUSTICE JACKSON: They carried out all of the functions of the camps, didn't they?

GOERING: If an SS unit was guarding a camp and an SS leader happened to be the camp commander, then this unit carried out all the functions.

MR. JUSTICE JACKSON: Now, this system was not a secret system. This entire system was openly avowed, its merits were publicly advocated by yourself and others, and every person entering into the Nazi Party was enabled to know the kind of system of government you were going to set up, wasn't he?

GOERING: Every person who entered the Party knew that we embraced the Leadership Principle and knew the fundamental measures we wanted to carry out, so far as they were stated in the program. But not everyone who joined the Party knew down to the last detail what was going to happen later.

MR. JUSTICE JACKSON: But this system was set up openly and was well known, was it not, in every one of its details? As to organization, everybody knew what the Gestapo was, did they not?

GOERING: Yes, everyone knew what the Gestapo was. * * *

MR. JUSTICE JACKSON: And there was nothing secret about the establishment of a Gestapo as a political police, about the fact that people were taken into protective custody, about the fact that these were concentration camps? Nothing secret about those things, was there?

GOERING: There was at first nothing secret about it at all.

MR. JUSTICE JACKSON: As a matter of fact, part of the effectiveness of a secret police and part of the effectiveness of concentration camp penalties is that the people do know that there are such agencies, isn't it?

GOERING: It is true that everyone knows that if he acts against the state he will end up in a concentration camp or will be accused of high treason before a court, according to the degree of his crime. But the original reason for creating the concentration camps was to keep there such people whom we rightfully considered enemies of the State.

[58] Few attorneys and fewer laymen realize the skill required for an able cross-examination. A reading of the actual record of the Scopes trial discloses it to be the futile swinging of senile opponents armed with powderpuffs. The most able counsel in that case, from reading the record, appears to have been a practically unknown local prosecutor.

[59] IX *Proceedings* 77, 79. MR. JUSTICE JACKSON: Do you know of any occasion when any one of the defendants in the box ever took a public position against going to war?

MILCH: Publicly, no; I cannot remember any occasion. But I rather think that also to the gentlemen who now stand accused the whole question of the war came as a great surprise.

MR. JUSTICE JACKSON: You would like to believe that?

MILCH: I do believe it, yes.

MR. JUSTICE JACKSON: You do believe it. How long did it take the German Armed Forces to conquer Poland?

MILCH: To conquer Poland—18 days, I believe.

MR. JUSTICE JACKSON: Eighteen days. How long did it take to drive England off the Continent, including the disaster of Dunkirk?

Of all the men who participated in the hearings, one who was particularly outstanding was the American representative upon the Tribunal. Francis Biddle's persistent seeking of the issues frequently forced the Tribunal to the adoption of fair and uniformly administered rules; certain of his observations as to defenses, which have been discussed fully elsewhere, were later adopted by the defense as the basis of cogent arguments. And his adroit questioning, concise in nature, was usually more successful than fifty pages of interrogation by the Prosecution in getting to the heart of a problem or exposing the weakness of a witness' position.[60]

MILCH: I believe 6 weeks.

MR. JUSTICE JACKSON: How long did it take to overrun Holland and Belgium?

MILCH: A few days.

MR. JUSTICE JACKSON: And how long did it take to overrun Denmark and take possession of Norway?

MILCH: Also a short time. Denmark took a very short time, because Denmark gave in immediately, and Norway gave in in a few weeks.

[60] XV *Proceedings* 550-61, 186-207, particularly 205; XVI *Proceedings* 109-113, 587-8.

(As to Anschluss)

THE TRIBUNAL (Mr. Biddle): All right; now there are two short questions. You said that you told the Fuhrer that you would not act as a Trojan Horse; it that right?

SEYSS-INQUART: Yes, of course.

THE TRIBUNAL (Mr. Biddle): Well, had he suggested to you that you should act as a Trojan Horse?

SEYSS-INQUART: No, not that, but I was fully aware of my difficult position. It was quite obvious to me that I could be misused for such purposes, that behind the back of my ministerial post a situation could be prepared so that Austria would be overrun.

THE TRIBUNAL (Mr. Biddle): Well, you used that expression after you had been talking to the Fuhrer for some time, did you?

SEYSS-INQUART: In the course of the discussion, but the thought itself had come to me previously; I only brought it up during the discussion.

THE TRIBUNAL (Mr. Biddle): Yet, you had had this thought for some time?

SEYSS-INQUART: Yes.

THE TRIBUNAL (Mr. Biddle): Ever since you had gotten into this Austrian matter actively you had had the thought I suppose?

SEYSS-INQUART: The possibility of dissension and of a difference of opinion about this situation was quite clear to me.

THE TRIBUNAL (Mr. Biddle): That your actions might be misconstrued?

SEYSS-INQUART: First of all; and secondly, that the fact of my activity could be exploited in a way that I did not intend.

THE TRIBUNAL (Mr. Biddle): Of course, because you represented both sides at the same time and that was always a difficult position, was it not?

Of course, the repartee between the Prosecution and defendants was not wholly one-sided. The defendants were not stupid men. They were, on the whole, intelligent and learned men, with considerable facility of expression. Jackson, for example, in interrogating Goering upon the secrecy of Germany's mobili-

---

SEYSS-INQUART: That is correct.

(As to Confiscations of Property)

THE TRIBUNAL (Mr. Biddle): Now, the property of the Freemasons was confiscated under that decree. What other property, of what other groups, was confiscated in the Netherlands under that direction of the Fuhrer? I do not mean individuals; I mean groups.

SEYSS-INQUART: At the moment I cannot think of any others, although there were a few other groups.

THE TRIBUNAL (Mr. Biddle): But, in effect—see if I state the practice correctly—the Police would decide that an individual or group of individuals, on account of their words or their actions, were enemies of the Reich, and then their property would be confiscated; is that right?

SEYSS-INQUART: Yes. And the decisive office at the time was that of Heydrich. * * *

THE TRIBUNAL (Mr. Biddle): And you carried through Heydrich's decisions; right?

SEYSS-INQUART: I carried through Heydrich's decisions when it came to property rights. The association of Jehovah's Witnesses belonged to those groups. * * *

THE TRIBUNAL (Mr. Biddle): And the property of Jehovah's Witnesses was confiscated also, since they were enemies of the Reich?

SEYSS-INQUART: They probably did not have very much, but what they had was confiscated because of their attitude in refusing to serve in the war effort.

THE TRIBUNAL (Mr. Biddle): They refused—let me get this straight. This is interesting. Jehovah's Witnesses refused to fight or to serve in the German war effort and therefore their property was confiscated. Is that right?

SEYSS-INQUART: Not quite. Jehovah's Witnesses in Germany refused to serve in the German Army. So first of all they were prohibited there and then this prohibition was expanded for all other regions.

THE TRIBUNAL (Mr. Biddle): Wait a minute. I am not talking about that. I am talking about the Netherlands. Was that true in the Netherlands?

SEYSS-INQUART: Yes; but Jehovah's Witnesses in the Netherlands were not prohibited because they refused to serve in the German Army, but rather because we were against this group on principle.

THE TRIBUNAL (Mr. Biddle): Oh, I see, on general principles. As pacifists, you were against them, so you confiscated their property; right?

SEYSS-INQUART: Yes.

(Upon Use of Prisoners in Armament Plants)

THE TRIBUNAL (Mr. Biddle): Defendant, you spoke of not using the western prisoners in war industry and in the making of munitions, do you remember?

SPEER: Yes.

THE TRIBUNAL (Mr. Biddle): Were there regulations to that effect?

SPEER: Yes.

THE TRIBUNAL (Mr. Biddle): You never saw any regulation which made that distinction, did you?

zation plans was countered with the comment that the defendant did not remember readily the publication of mobilization plans

---

SPEER: No.

(As to Responsibility of Leaders)

THE TRIBUNAL (Mr. Biddle): Only one other question. I was interested in what you said at the end about all of the leaders being responsible for certain general principles, certain great things. Can you say any one of those things? What did you mean? What principles? Did you mean going on with the war, for instance?

SPEER: I think that, for example, the beginning of the war or the end of the war are such basic principles. I think * * *

THE TRIBUNAL (Mr. Biddle): You deem the beginning of the war and the end of the war basic principles for which the leaders were responsible?

SPEER: Yes.

THE TRIBUNAL (Mr. Biddle): Thank you.

(As to Atrocities)

THE TRIBUNAL (Mr. Biddle): Defendant, if you would listen to the question and try to answer it, I think we would get along much faster. You used the expression "catastrophic nature," those were your words. Did you get any reports of a catastrophic nature?

SAUCKEL: I learned through Field Marshal Kluge, and through reports, which have been mentioned here, from Rosenberg, about a few cases which I considered catastrophic and tried to correct.

THE TRIBUNAL (Mr. Biddle): These were what you call catastrophic cases?

SAUCKEL: Yes.

THE TRIBUNAL (Mr. Biddle): What were they?

SAUCKEL: There was the case in the East which Field Marshal Kluge reported to me, where motion picture houses were surrounded by recruiting agents. I considered that catastrophic. The second case was the case of the returning transport, where according to one report—it is called the later report, but I do not remember the number of the document —children are said to have died on the way and been placed outside the train. I considered that catastrophic. But there could * * *

THE TRIBUNAL (Mr. Biddle): You have answered.

SAUCKEL: But * * *

THE TRIBUNAL (Mr. Biddle): You have answered that now. Did you get any complaints about Koch?

SAUCKEL: I received complaints about Koch at times from the Minister for the Occupied Eastern Territories, Rosenberg, and also from another source. Koch, of course, always defended himself very vehemently.

THE TRIBUNAL (Mr. Biddle): Then you had complaints from several people about Koch?

SAUCKEL: Yes I could * * *

THE TRIBUNAL (Mr. Biddle): And the complaints said what Koch was doing, did they?

SAUCKEL: I did not received complaints from many sides about Koch, but rather from one side * * *

THE TRIBUNAL (Mr. Biddle): Now wait * * *

SAUCKEL: But from several people * * *

THE TRIBUNAL (Mr. Biddle): Wait. Won't you answer the question? I did not ask you if you have received many complaints. I said, "The complaints said what Koch was doing." Is that right?

of the United States. The Prosecutor exploded and asked the Tribunal to require the witness to answer "yes" or "no." He

---

SAUCKEL: Yes, in some cases.

THE TRIBUNAL (Mr. Biddle): And what did you do with those complaints?

SAUCKEL: As far as my field of work was concerned, when I received complaints such as have been discussed here, I called a conference in my office. That was the case immediately after the complaints from Rosenberg and on that occasion I adopted the attitude which my defense counsel cited and pointed out with respect to the conference of 6 January, 1943.

THE TRIBUNAL (Mr. Biddle): And the Koch matter ended after the conference, I take it? That was all you did?

(There was no response.)

(As to Forced Labor)

THE TRIBUNAL (Mr. Biddle): I did not ask you that. I am not interested for the moment in your convictions. I said: Was it contrary to German law? It was, wasn't it, against law?

SAUCKEL: It was in general contrary to the German labor laws.

THE TRIBUNAL (Mr. Biddle): That is right. Now I am going to come to another subject for a moment. I simply want to understand your defense and what your point of view is. Now see if this is correct. You did no recruiting yourself. The Police did no recruiting. Your main job was, in the first place, to see that everything was done lawfully and legally. Was not that right, that was your important function?

SAUCKEL: That was my endeavor.

THE TRIBUNAL (Mr. Biddle): In order to do that you had to arrange to have the proper laws passed so as to have the recruiting done under the law; that is right, isn't it? That was your job?

SAUCKEL: Yes.

THE TRIBUNAL (Mr. Biddle): Yes. And very often those laws—by the way, those laws were simply decrees, of course. They were just orders that were signed by the Fuhrer, or by you, or by some of the ministers. When you say laws, you mean, of course, decrees?

SAUCKEL: The laws in the occupied territories for the recruitment of manpower had to be decreed by the Fuhrer and issued by the chiefs in the territories. * * *

THE TRIBUNAL (Mr. Biddle): I understand that. I did not say you signed them. I understand that. You have explained that in great detail. Now let us see where the Police came in. They had nothing to do with the recruiting. Once a decree was signed, it became law, did it not? When a decree was signed, it was law?

SAUCKEL: Yes.

THE TRIBUNAL (Mr. Biddle): And if any man resisted being brought in as a workman, or did not register, or did not live up to his contract, he became a criminal. That is right, isn't it?

SAUCKEL: In this case he violated the law. We did not call it a crime, but rather an offense.

THE TRIBUNAL (Mr. Biddle): But he broke the law?

SAUCKEL: Yes. * * *

THE TRIBUNAL (Mr. Biddle): Good. Or after the men—let us say in Paris—were rounded up, if they offered physical resistance, then the Police had to be called in, had they not? If there was physical resistance you had to call in the Police, had you not?

SAUCKEL: Yes, but I can say that that was hardly ever reported to me. In most cases the men were then released. It can be clearly seen

was promptly overruled.[61] Again Goering upon interrogation as to plans for dividing Russia in the event of victory commented that he did not want to divide the bear's skin before shooting the bear.[62] The defendant Jodl more than held his own upon cross-examination,[63] and in referring to witness Gisevius who had spoken of a plot by loyal Germans against Hitler commented, "The witness spoke of revolts as casually as of washing his hands."[64] Streicher referred to Gisevius more bitterly as a traitor, stating that all decent people had adopted the slogan, "Freedom from Versailles."[65]

Nor was the trial wholly free from humor. Dr. Nelte, for Keitel, pointed out how Gisevius, when cornered, had always given the source of his information as some person who was now deceased and, therefore, could not be cross-examined. "Dead

---

from the lists of the workers' transports—for instance, in the year 1944—that of a large program not even 10 percent came to Germany. Then there was nothing else for us to do but to shanghai, * * *.

THE TRIBUNAL (Mr. Biddle): I mean, every German had to work, had he not, under the law? Right?

SAUCKEL: Yes, that is right.

THE TRIBUNAL (Mr. Biddle): And that law was finally applied to foreign workers as well, as you just said. Right?

SAUCKEL: That law was also introduced into the occupied territories.

THE TRIBUNAL (Mr. Biddle): Wait, wait, Defendant. Don't let us fool over this. It is quite simple. If there was a law which made it necessary for men to work when their quotas had been called up, they had to work, had they not? Right?

SAUCKEL: Yes, they had to work, in their own countries first of all, but they also could volunteer to work in Germany instead of working in their own country. And we attached great importance to this.

THE TRIBUNAL (Mr. Biddle): In other words, a man had a choice of forced labor in an industry in France or in Germany, so in that sense it was voluntary; is that right?

SAUCKEL: Yes.

THE TRIBUNAL (Mr. Biddle): You did not know about that before? Did anyone advise you that it was in accordance with international law to force people in occupied countries to come to Germany to work?

SAUCKEL: I was expressly urged by the Fuhrer to take that measure, and it was described to me as admissible. No office raised any objections to or had any misgivings about this measure; rather, it met with the requirements of all offices.

THE TRIBUNAL (Mr. Biddle): I did not ask you that. I asked you whether anybody advised you that it was in accordance with international law.

SAUCKEL: No.

[61] IX *Proceedings* 506, ruling of Tribunal at 512.

[62] IX *Proceedings* 628.

[63] XV *Proceedings* 444 *et seq.*

[64] XV *Proceedings* 299.

[65] XII *Proceedings* 311. In view of Jackson's statement at XII *Proceedings* 426 that it was the right of every German citizen to use all means short of war, Streicher's statement is of enlarged importance.

witnesses," Nelte commented, "are the best witnesses."[66] He also pointed out the inconsistencies in the positions assumed toward his client—the British and American prosecutors called Keitel "a powerful officer with great influence," the French "a willing tool," and the German witnesses a "yes man."[67]

In another situation, Dr. Babel was interrogating witness Van den Essen, a professor of history of the University of Lourain. The witness spoke of the horrors of the war and as evidence of his mental anguish caused by the war stated that he had lost fifteen kilos in weight. Babel immediately retorted that he had lost thirty five kilos during the war without being ill. "What conclusion do you draw from that?"[68] The comment drew laughter and a rebuke from the Tribunal.

Rudenko, for the Russian Prosecution, in summarizing the testimony as to the General Staff, declared, "And so we saw the peculiar spectacle of wolves turning into sheep."[69]

Again it was Justice Jackson who, although engrossed in the progress of the trial, was able to wring a little grim humor from it. In discussing with the Tribunal the vagueness of the provisions relating to punishments to be imposed, he agreed with the Tribunal's dissatisfaction. Like the Mikado, he stated, he preferred to "let the punishment fit the crime."[70] At another point, the defendant Schacht stated that while he had lost practically all his properties, he still received his pension, adding "how else should I pay my expenses?" Jackson, bearing in mind a possible death penalty, grimly replied, "Well, they may not be very heavy, Doctor."[71] And when bored by the lengthy answers from the witness stand, he declared, "Well, let's go on with the interrogation. The interrogations are always so much briefer than the answers made in court where the press is present, if I may say so."[72] His associate, Major Jones, was met with a statement of witness Lammers to the effect that Frick had little responsibility for the acts charged, and was primarily a "decorative" figure. Jones retorted, "You may say he was a decorative figure. That is a matter of taste."[73]

And the defendant Goering pointedly requested Sir David Maxwell-Fyfe not to refer to Himmler as "my friend Himmler."[74]

---

[66] XVII *Proceedings* 644.
[67] XVII *Proceedings* 645.
[68] VI *Proceedings* 553-4.
[69] XII *Proceedings* 351.
[70] VIII *Proceedings* 451.
[71] XIII *Proceedings* 28.
[72] XII *Proceedings* 590.
[73] XI *Proceedings* 125.
[74] IX *Proceedings* 612.

XIX

CONTROVERSIES BETWEEN COUNSEL

The amount of humor in a trial of this sort is, of course, at a minimum. Counsel for all parties were deadly serious in their approach to the problems involved, and the charges were grave ones, with possible death penalties involved. There also was a definite feeling of hostility on the part of the members of the Prosecution toward the individual defendants, coupled perhaps with some fear of disclosures which might prove, at the least, embarrassing to their respective governments, which produced an attitude of non-cooperation, at certain times. It is necessary to see how far this attitude persisted in determining the fairness of the proceedings.

It must be remembered also that this was a military tribunal. Ordinarily in court martial proceedings the prosecutor does not act solely as the government's representative, but acts also as an investigator of the truth—which at times requires him to bring forward evidence favorable to a defendant. This role, it is also true, is occupied by a German prosecutor under the laws of the German Reich, and the defendants' counsel expected some slight cooperation in the procurement and presentation of their evidence.[1] Robert Jackson early announced a different view which was thereafter followed by the Prosecution. He stated. . . . "under the Charter our duty is to present the case for the Prosecution. I do not, in any instance, serve two masters."[2] Defense counsel, much later in the proceedings, claimed unfairness,[3] but in at least one such instance it appeared that counsel had failed to protect his record.[4]

---

[1] III *Proceedings* 549. Bergold, counsel for Bormann, pointed out that paragraph 160 of the Reich Code of Penal Procedure required the prosecutor to produce evidence for the Defense as well as for the Prosecution.

[2] III *Proceedings* 551.

[3] XVII *Proceedings* 603-4. Nelte, for Keitel, claimed that the Prosecution was one-sided, submitting only incriminating evidence instead of following the Germany theory. The Tribunal took issue with the statement that "We cannot serve two masters."

[4] XVII *Proceedings* 609, 610. The Tribunal stopped Dr. Nelte from attacking the manner in which the case had been tried. Nelte claimed that the Prosecution never had shown him documents the Tribunal had ruled he was entitled to see. The Tribunal retorted that it was entirely his own fault—he should have made an application or complaint to the Tribunal. Not having done so, he cannot now complain. However, it serves to illustrate that no extra courtesies were extended by the Prosecution.

In view of the fact that the Americans had provided the physical facilities for the trial, that meant that the printing and other facilities were in its control, which placed the defense counsel frequently in the role of suppliants for copies of Prosecution documents or for the printing of their own. It will be remembered that early in the proceedings objection was made to the failure of the Prosecution to provide sufficient copies to defense counsel of the documents to be used, the Prosecution stating that it could do no more with the limited printing facilities. Thereupon the defense pointed out that the Prosecution had already delivered two hundred fifty copies of the same material to the Press.[5] Later Jackson complained that he had required 250 copies of Dr. Stahmer's document book to be printed and then found it contained much irrelevant and objectionable material, and that he was not going to extend unlimited facilities any longer. The Tribunal thereupon ruled that defense counsel must, in the future, indicate the exact passages to be translated, show them to the Prosecution, and either secure an agreement or a ruling from the Tribunal prior to printing.[6] And, still later, Jackson announced that he was forced to close the Document Room as to printing documents for the German counsel. It had just completed 107 pages for Rosenberg of, what he termed, violent anti-Jewish propaganda, and he refused to participate in spreading such dogma. Thoma, counsel for Rosenberg, protested. The Tribunal suggested there must be some error since all documents were first to be submitted to the Prosecution to be checked for relevancy. Jackson suggested that a master be appointed to rule upon documents, which suggestion the Tribunal stated it would consider, but that it would continue in the same manner for the present.[7] Apparently printing continued even after the second outburst, as no further discussion appears thereon and the speeches of defendants' counsel were printed.

It has already been observed that repeated objections were raised by the defense for failure of the Prosecution to give adequate notice of documents to be used or to furnish copies thereof.[8] At one time Dr. Stahmer requested the Tribunal to require the Prosecution to announce the following day's program together with the names of witnesses to be used. Jackson stated that the name of a particular witness had to be kept secret "for security reasons." Dr. Stahmer retorted that if this were true, it was strange that the name of the witness had already been

[5] II *Proceedings* 292.

[6] IX *Proceedings* 666-71.

[7] XI *Proceedings* 73-88.

[8] Page 95, *ante*, note 37.

given to the Press. Upon checking with his assistants, Jackson found this to be true—it having been done without his knowledge.[9]

A good illustration was presented during the trial of the advantage which could be taken of a situation where the defense was required to disclose the documents and witnesses, and matters tended to be proven by them, weeks in advance. As to one such witness the Prosecution simply took a cross interrogatory the day before the hearing and failed to notify defense counsel thereof or to show a copy to counsel.[10] And another prosecutor showed up with an affidavit from a witness the Prosecution had been unable to locate for the purpose of interrogatories submitted long before by defense counsel.[11]

In addition to the matters previously observed as to conduct of the Prosecution, it is most significant to examine the manner employed in the presentation of evidence and introduction of documents. It will be recalled that it was the function of the chief prosecutors to present the opening statements which were, and rightly so, argumentative in character. It was the function of their assistants to introduce evidence, documentary or otherwise, with the right to summarize the contents briefly, indicate the importance thereof, read important passages, and supply a connective issue of transition between varying types of evidence. This, however, if performed in a lawyer-like manner and as an officer of the court, demanded a concise, courteous, unbiased approach. Argument was not the function of these gentlemen and had no place in their presentation. However, many of these assistants, glittering in the spotlight, packed with rotund phrases, and fairly bursting with righteous indignation, took advantage of their positions to make a successive series of appeals to passion and prejudice.[12] The Americans were, perhaps,

---

[9] II *Proceedings* 435-9.

[10] XI *Proceedings* 297.

[11] XIV *Proceedings* 529-33.

[12] See, for example, certain comments in II *Proceedings* at 210 and 426. Sir David Maxwell-Fyfe was quite calm in his presentation, but his associate, Griffith-Jones, III *Proceedings* at 238 makes a mild appeal to passion. Roberts, who was rebuked by the Tribunal for such tactics in III *Proceedings* at 296, still persisted in closing at 307 with "a story of perfidy, dishonor, and shame." Dodd's presentation in III *Proceedings* 402-10, was clearly argumentative. Albrecht (U. S.) made very argumentative statements in IV *Proceedings* 529-556 and was twice requested by the Tribunal to cut his presentation short. See pp. 532, 555. Lt. Col. Baldwin (U.S.), who made a very clean presentation, was reprimanded in V *Proceedings* at 81 for misstating the purport of a document. Fauré (France) in VII at 23-25 and 49, was quite argumentative and was rebuked by the Tribunal at 25. Mounier (France) fell into the same fault in VII *Proceedings* 74-104, and was rebuked by the Tribunal at 86. Dubost was guilty of the same

the worst offenders. The Tribunal established itself as a judicial tribunal in dealing with later speakers by chiding them for such remarks, although this did not wholly cure the situation. It likewise required both Prosecution and defense to curtail remarks which were cumulative in character, in order to expedite the proceedings.[13] And the Tribunal raised a question as to the correctness of conclusions cccasionally reached by counsel.[14] However, the censure did not fall solely upon the Prosecution.[15]

These things led to that which is unfortunate in any lawsuit and that is bickering between counsel. The attitude of the Prosecution being from the beginning that the defense counsel were probably imbued with Nazi propaganda, and anxious to disseminate such propaganda and anti-Semitic arguments, some resentment occurred. At the time of Jackson's announcement of the closure of the Document Room to defendants' counsel following his experience with the Rosenberg documents, he stated bluntly, "I may be a biased judge of what ought to be done; I

---

fault in VI *Proceedings* at 418-27 but was not rebuked. Pokrovsky (Russia) was very argumentative in VII *Proceedings* at 437-87, although he had just been rebuked at 429 for the declaration that we are "not faced with the simple murder of three unarmed soldiers of the Polish Army." Smirnov (Russia) was told bluntly in VII *Proceedings* at 448 to cut out his comments after discussing the documents. And statements of Rudenko XVII *Proceedings* at 196, 197, 231 in cross-examining Fritsche were certainly reprehensible as couched in an argumentative and insulting manner. The Tribunal had previously censured a Russian interrogator for constantly asking argumentative questions and for interrupting the answers in XV *Proceedings* at 137, 143, 145 and 151.

13 Col. Storey's presentations in IV *Proceedings* at 17-160 was very clean but cumulative, and he was interrupted for that at 105, 110, 114, 145. Similarly Major Farr in IV *Proceedings* 161-230 was required to summarize much of his material instead of reading it (see 170, 173, 181, 190, 193); likewise with Albrecht in IV *Proceedings* 532, 555, Brudno V *Proceedings* 50, 53-4, 55, 61, Sprecher in V *Proceedings* at 288, 291, 292, Dubost in VI *Proceedings* at 144 for giving the details of atrocities rather than facts, and again at 338-9 upon concentration camps, the Tribunal ruling that he had now made a *prima facie* case. And Zorya in VII *Proceedings* at 331, 333 was required to shorten his presentation. M. Delpeck, on the other hand, was thanked for shortening his address in VI *Proceedings* at 20.

14 The Tribunal was unable to agree, IV *Proceedings* at 180, as to evidence upon the indicted organizations as constituting a weapon of Nazism that the persons who "formed that weapon were criminals and knew of the criminal objectives of the SS."

15 Goering in IX *Proceedings* 653-7 was stopped repeatedly by the Tribunal when he started in upon long speeches, instead of giving direct answers. Nelte, for Keitel, in IX *Proceedings* at 379-80 was censored for offering a document which had been excluded by a prior written ruling. Several defense counsel were told to eliminate certain material from their closing arguments as improper or unnecessary, and Dr. Laternser in XXI *Proceedings* at 373-408 was criticized several times for his verbosity.

never pretended to complete impartiality."[16] A remark of Rudenko in closing argument was construed to refer to one of defense counsel, Dr. Boehm, as a Nazi. Dr. Loeffler rose to the rescue of his fellow attorney and the Tribunal asked Rudenko to withdraw his statement, which was thereafter quite modified.[17]

It will be remembered that Jackson and Dodd had both suggested counsel for defendants merely offer their translated documents without reading them. Stahmer and Dix pointed out that the Prosecution had brought all of its material out before the public and the defense should have the same right. Also, since the Prosecution had consumed all of the time taken to that point, there was no particular reason to shorten the presentation of the defense. It was, as a matter of fact, this exchange which preceded Jackson's original restriction upon the printing of documents, which the Tribunal smoothed over.[18] At another time, when the same defense counsel, Dix, for Schacht, propounded a question to Jackson and Maxwell-Fyfe, the Tribunal refused to require them to answer.[19]

Dr. Babel protested a remark made by the Prosecution as intended to show that he had tried to confuse a witness. The Tribunal promptly criticized him for making a speech. Babel retorted that it was necessary since the Tribunal had not protected him from the Prosecution's reproach. The Tribunal ordered him back to the rostrum and sharply demanded an explanation. Babel stated that under German procedure defense counsel were protected from attacks by the Prosecution. The Tribunal asked what remark was made, and, following an explanation by Babel, stated that it was certain no reflection was intended.[20]

Again, Goering protested when Jackson sought to use interrogatories to impeach him that he had been informed at the time of their taking that they would not be used at the trial and that his counsel need not be present. Stahmer, his attorney, joined in the objection. Jackson desisted from their use but declared he did not believe there was any such stipulation.[21] In effect, this was calling both the defendant and his attorney liars—and if this had occurred before that prosecutor in his judicial capacity would perhaps have been punished as a contempt.

---

16 XI *Proceedings* 78.
17 XXII *Proceedings* 333.
18 IX *Proceedings* 657-74.
19 VIII *Proceedings* 473-6.
20 VI *Proceedings* 319.
21 IX *Proceedings* 551-2.

But not all the controversy arose from acts of the Prosecution. Dr. Thoma was clearly caught off base reading passages which were supposed to have been deleted and his explanation was accepted graciously.[22] The most interesting occurrence arose, however, in connection with that very entertaining and perplexing witness, Gisevius. No sooner had he been placed upon the stand than he wanted to relate what Stahmer, for Goering, had stated to Dix, for Schacht, in the Defendant's Counsel Room. Jackson insisted that the witness be heard—stating that the witness was a loyal and courageous German and that if he had been threatened the Tribunal should be informed. The effect of this testimony was that if Schacht or Gisevius, the witness is vague as to which, attacked Blomberg or told the scandal of his marriage, Goering would tell about Schacht. The witness was dying to tell the scandal concerning Blomberg's marriage and subsequently did so. Stahmer exploded against Dix for a breach of confidence as to the occurrence in the counsel room, and the relations between those particular defense counsel were strained thereafter.[23]

In addition to the quibblings described, there were frequent interruptions both by defense counsel and counsel for the Prosecution of the proceedings of the other, which were adroitly handled by the Tribunal.[24]

It must be remembered that the Press was represented during these hearings and received information from both sides.[25] As a matter of fact, the Tribunal was finally forced to stop interviews of the defendants with the Press through their counsel.[26]

[22] XI *Proceedings* 149, 152.

[23] XI *Proceedings* 176-9.

[24] VI *Proceedings* 576. Babel started to explain the purpose of cross-examination. He was reprimanded for the interruption. In VII *Proceedings* at 97 Stahmer interrupted Mounier to deny Goering's responsibility, which was censured as being out of order. In XV *Proceedings* 137, 143, 145, 151 the Russian interrogator was rebuked for repeatedly asking argumentative questions and for interrupting the answers of defendant Sauckel. In XVIII *Proceedings* Rudenko interrupted Thoma for Rosenberg, at 92, for attempting to spread fascist propaganda and was overruled. In XXII *Proceedings* the Russian counsel was again overruled upon an interruptive motion while Boehm was speaking for the SA. But in XVII *Proceedings* at 150 Rudenko's objection to Seidl's discussion of the Potsdam agreement was sustained.

[25] E. g., see II *Proceedings* 292, II *Proceedings* 437-8, IX *Proceedings* 657-74. In X *Proceedings* at 175-8 Pokrovsky objected to certain documents submitted by Horn, for Von Ribbentrop, as forged, and as slanderous against Roosevelt and other public leaders. While the Tribunal held the objections to be premature, it ruled that they could not be released to the Press until received in evidence.

[26] IV *Proceedings* 1.

But when the attention of the Tribunal was brought to threatening article in a German newspaper criticizing Dr. Marx for a certain cross-examination, it announced that Dr. Marx, as a defense counsel, was an officer of the court, that it would not tolerate criticism of the court's officers and would extend to him its full protection. The Control Council was asked to investigate the matter fully and to report to the Tribunal.[27] And by so doing, the Tribunal recognized the services performed by the defense, as well as by the Prosecution, in the interest of international law and of justice.

[27] VIII *Proceedings* 532-3.

PART III

SUBSEQUENT NUREMBERG PROCEEDINGS

The 23 defendants in the Medical Case, all SS doctors left to right: Handloser, Rostock, Schroeder, Karl Brandt (Hitler's physician); Genzken, Gebhardt, Blome, Rudolf Brandt, Mrugowsky, Poppendick; (second row) Rose, Ruff, Brack, Romberg, Becker-Freyseng, Weltz, Schaefer, Hoven, Beiglboeck, Pokorny, Oberheuser, and Fischer.

XX

CASE NO. 1 (Medical Case)

Judges (Presiding Judge marked by*)

*Walter B. Beals, Chief Justice of the Supreme Court of Washington

Harold L. Sebring, Justice of the Supreme Court of Florida

Johnson Tal Crawford, formerly Judge of the District Court of Oklahoma

Victor C. Swearingen, alternate, former Special Assistant Attorney General of the United States

Prosecution

Chief of Counsel—Brigadier General Telford Taylor, 61 Broadway, New York City

Chief Prosecutor—James M. McHaney, Little Rock, Arkansas

Associate Counsel—Alexander G. Hardy, Cochituate, Massachusetts; Arnost Horlik-Hochwald, Leigh-On-Sea, England

Assistant Counsel—Glen J. Brown, Salt Lake City, Utah
Esther Jane Johnson, Vancouver, Wash.
Jack W. Robbins, Denton, Texas
Daniel J. Shiller, Waterbury, Connecticut

Medical Consultant—Dr. Leo Alexander, West Newton, Mass.

Indictment

Counts: (1) Conspiracy to commit war crimes and crimes against humanity;
(2) War crimes;
(3) Crimes against humanity;
(4) Membership in SS.

Defense

Defendant	Chief Defense Counsel	Counts on which sentenced	Sentence
1. Karl Brandt	Dr. Robert Servatius, Dr. Rudolph Schmidt	2, 3, 4	Death
2. Karl Gebhardt	Dr. Alfred Seidl, Dr. Georg Gierl	2, 3, 4	Death

Defendant	Chief Defense Counsel	Counts on which sentenced	Sentence
3. Rudolf Brandt	Dr. Kurt Kauffmann	2, 3, 4	Death
4. Joachim Mrugowsky	Dr. Fritz Flemming	2, 3, 4	Death
5. Wolfram Sievers	Dr. Josef Weisgerber, Dr. Erich Bergler	2, 3, 4	Death
6. Viktor Brack	Dr. Georg Froeschmann	2, 3, 4	Death
7. Waldemar Hoven	Dr. Hans Gawlik, Dr. Gerhard Klinnert	2, 3, 4	Death
8. Siegfried Handloser	Dr. Otto Nelte	2, 3	Life Imprisonment
9. Oskar Schroeder	Dr. Hanns Marx, Dr. Walter Dehner	2, 3	Life Imprisonment
10. Karl Genzken	Dr. Rudolf Merkel, Dr. Alfred Brenner	2, 3, 4	Life Imprisonment
11. Gerhard Rose	Dr. Hans Fritz	2, 3	Life Imprisonment
12. Fritz Fischer	Dr. Alfred Seidl, Dr. Georg Gierl	2, 3, 4	Life Imprisonment
13. Herman Becker-Freyseng	Dr. Hanns Marx, Dr. Walter Dehner	2, 3	20 years
14. Herta Oberheuser	Dr. Alfred Seidl, Dr. Georg Gierl	2, 3	20 years
15. Wilhelm Beiglboeck	Dr. Gustav Steinbauer	2, 3	15 years
16. Helmut Poppendick	Dr. Georg Boehm, Dr. Helmut Duerr	4	10 years
17. Paul Rostock	Dr. Hans Pribilla		Acquittal
18. Kurt Blome	Dr. Fritz Sauter		Acquittal
19. Siegfried Ruff	Dr. Fritz Sauter		Acquittal
20. Hans Wolgang Romberg	Dr. Bernd Vorwerk		Acquittal
21. Georg August Weltz	Dr. Siegfried Wille		Acquittal
22. Konrad Schaefer	Dr. Horst Pelckmann		Acquittal
23. Adolf Pokorny	Dr. Karl Hoffmann, Dr. Hans Gunther Seraphim		Acquittal

The Indictment was filed in the first proceeding upon October 26, 1946, and served upon the defendants upon the 6th day of November. They were arraigned upon November 21, and the trials actually opened upon December 9. The order of procedure in these cases was the same as that followed before the International Military Tribunal, in that the Prosecution made its opening statement explaining the charges brought in the Indictment and then presented its evidence in support of those charges. In this particular case the Prosecution consumed 25 trial days, examined 32 witnesses, and introduced 570 documents. Following the close of the Prosecution's case, the procedure was that defense counsel would then open with statements, followed by their evidence in support of the theory of the defense. In view of the fact that in most of the proceedings there were many defendants and, in turn, numerous counsel, the order in which such statements would be made and evidence introduced was generally determined by agreement between the various defense counsel and approved by the Tribunal, the Tribunal acting as arbitrator if defense counsel were unable to agree as to the order of procedure. The defense counsel first proceeding would complete his original statement and evidence prior to the next counsel commencing his defense.

The defense counsel opened their defense in this case upon January 29, 1947, and consumed almost six months, or a total of 107 actual trial days, during which time they placed 30 witnesses upon the stand and introduced 901 documents. Following the presentation of the defense and rebuttal evidence, the Prosecution summed up the case, followed by closing arguments for the defense, after which the Prosecution had an opportunity to reply. As in the proceedings before the International Military Tribunal, each defendant was given an opportunity for a short statement to explain his conduct or actions, his excuses or justifications, or anything which he had to say which might affect the judgment of the Tribunal. The closing statements for the Prosecution were completed on July 14, 1947, and the case taken under advisement until the rendition of judgments upon August 19 and 20, 1947, those judgments being confirmed subsequently upon November 22. The proceedings were lengthy, the transcript, in the English edition, running 11,538 pages, of which the judgment occupied 179 pages.

This case is generally termed colloquially the "Medical Case." Count One, which was based upon conspiracy to commit war crimes and crimes against humanity, met with little approval by the Tribunal, and no defendant was found guilty upon that count. The chief counts were Counts Two and Three, which were very similar in character. While Count Two refers to war crimes and Count Three to crimes against humanity, actually both of them involved the killing or maiming of vast numbers of persons through medical experimentation of one type or another. The defendants themselves were, for the most part, medical men. The defendant Karl Brandt had at one time been a personal physician to Adolf Hitler, and had later occupied the highest medical position in Germany, that of Reich Commissioner for Health and Sanitation. As such he had supervisory authority over all military and civilian medical services. General Handloser was chief of the medical services of the Wehrmacht; General Schroeder was chief of the medical services of the Luftwaffe; Dr. Gebhardt was president of the German Red

Cross; Dr. Rostock was dean of the medical faculty of the University of Berlin; and Gerhard Rose was an internationally known specialist in tropical medicine. The other doctors were chiefly staff doctors or consultants allegedly having direct contact with the medical experiments.

The term "medical experiments" sounds relatively harmless. Actually, to anyone reading the mass of evidence in the proceedings before the International Military Tribunal and also the proceedings in this case, a much different picture appears. There seems to be no evidence throughout the trial to the effect that these various acts were not committed—practically all of the evidence is devoted to disproving or attempting to disprove any supervision or responsibility on the part of the individual defendant, or to establish justification upon the basis of necessary research, or that it was performed upon "volunteers." Therefore, it is not improper to consider the nature of the charges as being proved and to examine into the acts committed and the philosophy underlying them.

A portion of the evidence relates to studies in anthropology being conducted by certain defendants. For some reason it was considered desirable to secure skeletons of Jews in order to compare the backward characteristics of the skulls and body types with those of the advanced Aryans. Consequently, when skeletons were desired, it did not occur to those defendants to secure skeletons from dead bodies. Instead, living persons were selected as proper body types. They were slaughtered, the flesh stripped from the bones by approved methods, and the skeletons placed in a museum for study. These were destroyed when the fall of Germany became imminent, but correspondence concerning these activities was introduced in evidence.

The freezing experiments actually involved some rather nightmarish activities. A subject would be brought to the point of unconsciousness from immersion in ice water or exposure to winter weather while naked. The subject might then be placed in a room with normal temperature and extensive notes made on the length of time it took for him to revive, assuming that he would regain consciousness. However, the experimenters even went to the fantastic lengths of surrounding the frozen victim with the naked bodies of living prostitutes, and made detailed scientific notes on the length of time required for revival. An amusing result of this test was that it showed that a single prostitute was more effective than two, because she seemed to concentrate more upon the task than when in competition with another.

Another fantastic product of the Nazi imagination was revealed in the techniques evolved for sterilization. For some reason the defendants did not seem to want to disclose to the victims what was about to happen to them, whether the particular act was to result in death, maiming, or sterilization. Consequently, it was suggested that a long counter could be placed in a room where Jews would be sent to get supplies. An X-ray machine would be placed just below the counter. The victim would then be told that he would have to fill out a questionaire, and the person in back of the desk would ask him questions for several minutes, operating the X-ray machine with his foot. It was suggested that a whole battery of such X-ray machines could be placed behind a long counter, and, by efficient operation, several thousand persons could be sterilized in a single day and would not even suspect until much later that anything had even occurred.

Of course, the evidence was not limited to merely these fantastic contrivances. There was a great deal of evidence concerning the murder rooms and murder cars where victims would be herded and gas poured into the enclosed space until all the victims were dead. They would then be taken out and stripped of any jewelry or valuables, which included knocking out the gold fillings in their teeth, after which the bodies were cremated or buried in huge ditches. Other victims were shot or even buried while alive. Still others were injected with all types of tropical and other communicable diseases, in order to test vaccines and other drugs. In some cases, bone grafts were made to test new techniques, or the skin of the victim was abraded and infected in order to test new drugs. Still others were forced to drink sea water, both treated and untreated, in order to determine the effectiveness of the chemical treatment and the length of time it would take such a victim to die or to be driven insane.

This is only a brief summary of the evidence which actually appeared in the proceedings. The opening statement for the Prosecution outlines in a concise and clear manner the acts which occurred, which formed the basis for the charges. The introductory portion of this presentation for the Prosecution gives the reason why the charges were brought in all of the subsequent Nuremberg cases, and particularly in this case. It is as follows:

> The defendants in this case are charged with murders, tortures, and other atrocities committed in the name of medical science. The victims of these crimes are numbered in the hundreds of thousands. A handful only are still alive; a few of the survivors will appear in this courtroom. But most of these miserable victims were slaughtered outright or died during the course of the tortures to which they were subjected.
>
> For the most part they are nameless dead. To their murderers, these wretched people were not individuals at all. They came in wholesale lots

and were treated worse than animals. They were 200 Jews in good physical condition, 50 Gypsies, 500 tubercular Poles, or 1,000 Russians. The victims of these crimes are numbered among the anonymous millions who met death at the hands of the Nazis and whose fate is a hideous blot on the page of modern history.

The charges against these defendants are brought in the name of the United States of America. They are being tried by a court of American judges. The responsibilities thus imposed upon the representatives of the United States, prosecutors and judges alike, are grave and unusual. They are owed not only to the victims, and to the parents and children of the victims, that just punishment be imposed on the guilty, and not only to the defendants, that they be accorded a fair hearing and decision. Such responsibilities are the ordinary burden of any tribunal. Far wider are the duties which we must here fulfill.

These larger obligations run to the peoples and races on whom the scourge of these crimes was laid. The mere punishment of the defendants, or even of thousands of others equally guilty, can never redress the terrible injuries which the Nazis visited upon these unfortunate peoples. For them it is far more important that these incredible events be established by clear and public proof, so that no one can ever doubt that they were fact and not fable, and that this Court, as the agent of the United States and as the voice of humanity, stamp these acts, and the ideas which engendered them, as barbarous and criminal.

We have still other responsibilities here. The defendants in the dock are charged with murder, but this is no mere murder trial. We cannot rest content when we have shown that crimes were committed and that certain persons committed them. To kill, to maim, and to torture is criminal under all modern systems of law. These defendants did not kill in hot blood, nor for personal enrichment. Some of them may be sadists, who killed and tortured for sport, but they are not all perverts. They are not ignorant men. Most of them are trained physicians and some of them are distinguished scientists. Yet these defendants, all of whom were fully able to comprehend the nature of their acts, and most of whom were exceptionally qualified to form a moral and professional judgment in this respect, are responsible for wholesale murder and unspeakably cruel tortures.

It is our deep obligation to all peoples of the world to show why and how these things happened. It is incumbent upon us to set forth with conspicuous clarity the ideas and motives which moved these defendants to treat their fellow men as less than beasts. The perverse thoughts and distorted concepts which brought about these savageries are not dead. They cannot be killed by force of arms. They must not become a spreading cancer in the breast of humanity. They must be cut out and exposed, for the reason so well stated by Mr. Justice Jackson in this courtroom a year ago:

> "The wrongs which we seek to condemn and punish have been so calculated, so malignant, and so devastating that civilization cannot tolerate their being ignored because it cannot survive their being repeated."

To the German people we owe a special responsibility in these proceedings. Under the leadership of the Nazis and the war lords, the German nation spread death and devastation throughout Europe. This the Germans now know. So, too, do they now know the consequences to Germany. Defeat, ruin, prostration, and utter demoralization. Most German children will never, so long as they live, see an undamaged German city.

To what cause will these children describe the defeat of the German nation and the devastation that surrenders them? Will they attribute it to the overwhelming weight of numbers and resources that was eventually leagued against them? Will they point to the ingenuity of enemy scientists? Will they perhaps blame their plight on strategic and military blunders by their generals?

If the Germans embrace these reasons as the true cause of their disaster, it will be a sad and fatal thing for Germany and for the world. Men who have never seen a German city intact will be callous about flattening English or American or Russian cities. They may not even realize that they are destroying anything worthwhile, for lack of a normal sense of values. To reestablish the greatness of Germany, they will pin their faith on improved military techniques. Such views will lead the Germans straight into the arms of the Prussian militarists to whom defeat is only a glorious opportunity to start a new war game. "Next time it will be different." We know all too well what that will mean.

This case, and others which will be tried in this building, offer a signal opportunity to lay before the German people the truc causes of their present misery. The walls and towers and churches of Nurnberg were, indeed, reduced to rubble by Allied bombs, but in a deeper sense Nurnberg had been destroyed a decade earlier, when it became the seat of the annual Nazi Party rallies, a focal point for the moral disintegration in Germany, and the private domain of Julius Streicher. The insane and malignant doctrines that Nurnberg spewed forth account alike for the crimes of these defendants and for the terrible fate of Germany under the Third Reich.

A nation which deliberately infects itself with poison will inevitably sicken and die. These defendants and others turned Germany into an infernal combination of a lunatic asylum and a charnel house. Neither science, nor industry, nor the arts could flourish in such a foul medium. The country could not live at peace and was fatally handicapped for war. I do not think the German people have as yet any conception of how deeply the criminal folly that was Nazism bit into every phase of German life, or of how utterly ravaging the consequences were. It will be our task to make these things clear.

These are the high purposes which justify the establishment of extraordinary courts to hear and determine this case and others of comparable importance. That murder should be punished goes without the saying, but the full performance of our task requires far more than the just sentencing of these defendants. Their crimes were the inevitable result of the sinister doctrines which they espoused, and these same doctrines sealed the fate of Germany, shattered Europe, and left the world in ferment. Wherever those doctrines may emerge and prevail, the same terrible consequences will follow. That is why a bold and lucid consummation of these proceedings is of vital importance to all nations. That is why the United States has constituted this Tribunal.

The defendants for the most part attempted to disassociate themselves as far as possible from responsibility for the acts committed. Some pleaded entire ignorance of these matters, while others relied upon the doctrine of *respondeat superior* and claimed that they could do nothing to change the course of action. All of them were represented by able counsel. Twelve of the chief counsel had represented defendants before the International Military Tribunal, while four had acted as assistant counsel in those proceedings. One may assume that if they had been retained to represent either the organizations indicted in the earlier proceedings or the leading military and political figures in Germany that they were among the best qualified men available at the German bar. The skill demonstrated both earlier and in this trial showed them to be outstanding men involved in a very difficult type of case to defend. By reason of their former experience, they were also eminently familiar with the form of procedure. Only three of the chief counsel had had no prior experience before the International Military Tribunal. It is interesting to observe that, of those three attorneys, two of them secured acquittal for their clients while the other client was hung.

So far as the court procedure was concerned, the same general technique was followed as in the earlier trial. Affidavits were permitted introduction, subject to the right of opposing counsel to have those witnesses produced personally for cross-examination. Twenty-four hours' notice was required to be given either for the production of documents or witnesses. Verification of affidavits by a proper person was required. Rulings upon the evidence were fairly and competently handled.

It is apparent that the Tribunal was more shocked by the charges and evidence in this case than most of the tribunals in subsequent cases. While the tendency of later tribunals was to acquit defendants or let them off with light sentences where they were in a position of prominence, the inclination was here, as well as later, to deal more severely with the persons personally concerned with the executions or atrocities. Where there was a close question of guilt or innocence, it was resolved in this case in favor of the defendants, and the acquittals of Ruff, Romberg, and Weltz were based squarely upon the premise that the Prosecution had failed to prove personal guilt "beyond all reasonable doubt." The Tribunal in its decision laid down certain rules for medical experimentation and its legality which should be of great benefit in the future. They are as follows:

> "The great weight of the evidence before us to the effect that certain types of medical experiments on human beings, when kept within reasonably well-defined bounds, conform to the ethics of the medical profession generally. The protagonists of the practice of human experimentation justify their views on the basis that such experiments yield results for the good of society that are unprocurable by other methods or means of study. All agree, however, that certain basic principles must be observed in order to satisfy moral, ethical and legal concepts:

"1. The voluntary consent of the human subject is absolutely essential.

"This means that the person involved should have legal capacity to give consent; should be so situated as to be able to exercise free power of choice, without the intervention of any element of force, fraud, deceit, duress, overreaching, or other ulterior form of constraint or coercion; and should have sufficient knowledge and comprehension of the elements of the subject matter involved as to enable him to make an understanding and enlightened decision. This latter element requires that before the acceptance of an affirmative decision by the experimental subject there should be made known to him the nature, duration, and purpose of the experiment; the method and means by which it is to be conducted; all inconveniences and hazards reasonably to be expected; and the effects upon his health or person which may possibly come from his participation in the experiment.

"The duty and responsibility for ascertaining the quality of the consent rests upon each individual who initiates, directs or engages in the experiment. It is a personal duty and responsibility which may not be delegated to another with impunity.

"2. The experiment should be such as to yield fruitful results for the good of society, unprocurable by other methods or means of study, and not random and unnecessary in nature.

"3. The experiment should be so designed and based on the results of animal experimentation and a knowledge of the natural history of the disease or other problem under study that the anticipated results will justify the performance of the experiment.

"4. The experiment should be so conducted as to avoid all unnecessary physical and mental suffering and injury.

"5. No experiment should be conducted where there is an *a priori* reason to believe that death or disabling injury will occur; except, perhaps, in those experiments where the experimental physicians also serve as subjects.

"6. The degree of risk to be taken should never exceed that determined by the humanitarian importance of the problem to be solved by the experiment.

"7. Proper preparations should be made and adequate facilities provided to protect the experimental subject against even remote possibilities of injury, disability, or death.

"8. The experiment should be conducted only by scientifically qualified persons. The highest degree of skill and care should be required through all stages of the experiment of those who conduct or engage in the experiment.

"9. During the course of the experiment the human subject should be at liberty to bring the experiment to an end if he has reached the physical or mental state where continuation of the experiment seems to him to be impossible.

"10. During the course of the experiment the scientist in charge must be prepared to terminate the experiment at any stage, if he has probable cause to believe, in the exercise of the good faith, superior skill and careful judgment required of him that a continuation of the experiment is likely to result in injury, disability, or death to the experimental subject."[1]

The sentences were confirmed by the Military Governor upon November 22, 1947, and an attempt was made to carry the case to the United States Supreme Court. By a five to three vote, Justice Jackson not participating, that court declined to review the proceedings, and the executions were duly carried out at Landsberg prison where the prison terms of the remaining defendants are now being served.

---

[1] Transcript 8063, 8065-6.

Defendant Milch is seated at table in right foreground betwen U. S. Army guard and his defense counsel.

XXI

CASE NO. 2 (Milch Case)

Judges (Presiding Judge marked by*)

Robert M. Toms, Judge of Circuit Court of Michigan
F. Donald Phillips, Judge of Superior Court of North Carolina
*Michael A. Musmanno, Judge of Court of Common Pleas of Pennsylvania
John L. Speight, Alabama, alternate

Prosecution

Clark Denney, 1 West 54th Street, New York City
James Conway, Yonkers, New York
Henry T. King, Jr., Meriden, Connecticut
Raymond J. McMahon, Jr., Pawtucket, Rhode Island
Maurice C. Myers, Los Angeles, California
Paul Niederman, Chicago, Illinois
William F. Raugust, Alexandria, Virginia
Adolph G. Dahl
Dorothy Hunt
Robert Rosenthal

Indictment

Counts: (1) Slave labor;
(2) War crimes;
(3) Crimes against humanity.

Defense

Defendant	Chief Defense Counsel	Counts on which sentenced	Sentence
Erhard Milch	Dr. Friedrich Bergold, Dr. Werner Milch	1, 3	Life Imprisonment

* Judge Musmanno is a colorful trial judge in Pittsburgh, well known to trial lawyers. He also possesses a sense of humor. Recently a man was brought in before him charged with striking his wife on the head with a rolling pin. Judge Musmanno, in addressing the defendant, declared: "From time immemorial cartoonists have portrayed the henpecked husband fleeing from the irate housewife, rolling pin armed. You are trying to break down humorous tradition and a legend of comedy. It is incredible that a husband should hit his wife with a rolling pin. This is revolutionary and cannot be tolerated." (Indianapolis Star, March 25, 1950, p. 1.)

Upon November 13, 1946, the Prosecution filed the Indictment against Erhard Milch, the only case conducted in Nuremberg in which a single defendant was tried. The Indictment was served on November 14, the defendant arraigned December 20, and the Prosecution opened its case upon January 2. The Prosecution consumed only eight actual trial days, in which time it placed three witnesses on the stand, and introduced 570 documents. The defense opened its case on January 27, consuming 28 trial days, placing 27 witnesses upon the stand, and introducing 901 documents. Final argument for the Prosecution was made upon March 26. The transcript ran 2528 pages, of which 36 comprised the judgment of the Tribunal.

The counsel for the defendant Milch was Dr. Friedrich Bergold, who had had the easy task of representing Bormann, the absent or deceased defendant in the proceedings before the International Military Tribunal. He was assisted by Dr. Werner Milch, who was the brother of the defendant.

Milch held the rank of Field Marshal in the Luftwaffe and was Goering's principal deputy in the Air Ministry. He was also a member of the central planning board which Hitler had established on November 29, 1942, to have complete control of German production and the allocation and development of raw materials. He was charged both with participation in the forced labor program and with participation in the medical experiments conducted at Dachau for the benefit of the German Air Force.

In view of the fact that this was the only such case in which a single defendant was tried and was the first case actually to proceed to judgment, it affords an excellent opportunity to study the procedure followed by these subsequent tribunals in examining the fairness and thoroughness of those trials. Consequently, more attention will be paid to those phases of this trial than most of the subsequent proceedings.

The Prosecution brought out repeatedly threats by Milch with reference to killing prisoners, persons in concentration camps, and persons in his command. It showed him to be a man of ungovernable temper. The defense concentrated upon this particular phase of the testimony and had testimony by witness after witness to the effect that Milch was actually a likeable old codger, whose bark was worse than his bite. Milch himself testified that he never meant what he said when he would declare that he would have such and such a person killed. He stated that all of his underlings knew the situation and understood it and never took him seriously; and that, as a matter of fact, no person had ever been executed by his orders. It was pointed out that he had intervened time and again to save persons from execution or from concentration camps.

The explanation was given by the defense that this apparent uncontrolled temper resulted from a series of brain concussions which Milch had suffered earlier in life. This is of particular interest in view of the fact that Milch had testified somewhat differently before the International Military Tribunal. There, he claimed that his apparent loss of memory and confusion as to events was caused through heavy blows on his head received at the time of capture.[1] It now appeared that he claimed his brain injuries were of much earlier origin. At any rate the Tribunal seemed to believe the testimony of the defense in this regard, and Milch was excused as to Count Two. The judgment, which was rendered upon April 16 and 17, 1947, and which was confirmed upon November 22, found the defendant guilty only as to participating in the forced labor program. He was sentenced to life imprisonment.

The conduct of the trial was on a high plane in practically every regard. With only a few exceptions, the utmost courtesy prevailed between counsel, and the procedure previously used in the proceedings before the International Military Tribunal prevailed here. The Tribunal was quick to grant witnesses to the defense and to require witnesses who had given affidavits for the Prosecution to appear for the purpose of cross-examination by the defense.[2] Upon occasions when defendant's counsel desired recesses for the purpose of preparing particular portions of his case, they were readily granted, one such vacation extending for twelve days.[3] And even though the Tribunal insisted that it would not permit leading questions by defendant's counsel,[4] it obviously permitted defendant's counsel to persist in his usual practice of asking leading questions.[5] At one particular point Mr. Denney objected that he had "been listening to Dr. Bergold testify for about forty-five minutes," which was approximately correct, but his objection was overruled.[6]

At one point the Tribunal ruled that hearsay evidence was admissible, which is directly contrary to the American concep-

---

1 IX *Proceedings* 108.

2 Transcript 361, 409-410, 625-8, 887.

3 Transcript 485, 1472.

4 Transcript 723, 866.

5 Transcript 885. It will be remembered that in the proceedings before the International Military Tribunal the defense counsel would ask questions running a paragraph or even a page in length and merely requiring a "yes" or "no" answer, the most flagrant type of leading question. While censured by the Tribunal, the practice was not entirely stopped. This obviously arose from the unfamiliarity of German counsel with the practice of interrogation and cross-interrogation of witnesses.

6 Transcript 885.

tion of evidence.[7] The Tribunal ruled properly that impeachment of a witness would be permitted only upon a material point,[8] but later held that it was proper to impeach one witness by another witness under circumstances somewhat inconsistent with the prior ruling.[9]

It would not be proper to give the impression that there were no controversies arising between counsel at all. Complaint was made upon several occasions by defense counsel to the effect that documents were not served upon him by the Prosecution in compliance with the rules, or that they were not properly translated, necessitating considerable labor upon his part.[10] He also complained that at one time the Prosecution had tied up one of his witnesses for eight days, so that he was not allowed to talk to the witness. The Prosecutor stated that the Prosecution also had wanted to talk to the witness, and an agreement was worked out satisfactorily between the counsel and the Tribunal.[11] Upon other occasions errors in translation of documents were pointed out, but the correct translations were agreed upon with the utmost cordiality between counsel.[12]

In every trial there are certain points of humor or of interest which occur. At one point the Prosecutor Mr. Denney became quite indignant because of the evasiveness of the witness and demanded that the Tribunal require the witness to answer the question directly. The Tribunal replied as follows:

> "The Tribunal will admonish the witness to answer the questions as simply as possible, and the Tribunal also admonishes Mr. Denney to watch his rising blood pressure."[13]

The Prosecutor apologized to the Tribunal, and the proceedings continued harmoniously. At another point Dr. Leo Alexander, medical consultant for the Prosecution, was on the witness stand under cross-examination by Dr. Bergold. He was asked the following question and made the following answer, to some interest of omnivorous readers of American literature:

> Q: "You know of a book of Paul De Kruif, don't you?"
> A: "I know not only Paul De Kruif but also his reputation for veracity, and I would not believe a word Paul De Kruif says."[14]

---

[7] Transcript 1502.

[8] Transcript 1534.

[9] Transcript 1598.

[10] Transcript 59, 71, 535.

[11] Transcript 711-716.

[12] Transcript 65, 605. And a correction of the record was made by agreement of the counsel at 1187.

[13] Transcript 858-9.

[14] Transcript 1086.

Dr. Bergold at one point brought out rather dramatically the position of the German people as a nation. He declared: "May I ask the court to believe me that we in Germany were not all of us hangmen and people who delighted in other people's misery. I may say here that I think the majority of the German people are goodhearted and that they treat other people well."[15] And when the defendant, Milch, was asked about his obedience to the orders which were obviously not in accord with commonly understood principles of international law, he declared: "It was my duty toward my people to maintain my allegiance. I had sworn an oath to keep allegiance to Hitler, too."[16]

In his closing argument Dr. Bergold relied mainly upon the fact that any protest by Milch would have been unavailing. He contended that the defendant was not liable if he honestly believed that his acts were permissible. He also contended that Milch was protected by orders from superior authority, but this statement the Tribunal challenged.[17] Prosecutor Clark Denney followed this with a cogent discussion of the controlling international law, which sets out excellently the premises governing in such a case and the opinions of leading international jurists thereon.[18]

On the whole the case was well tried upon both sides and with a minimum of friction.

---

15 Transcript 1945. See also the statements of counsel in the subsequent pages and in final argument.

16 Transcript 2258.

17 Transcript 2403-6.

18 Transcript 2436-2488.

Defendants in the Justice Case. First row, left to right: Schlegelberger, Klemm, Rothenburger, Lautz, Mettgenberg, Von Ammon, Joel, Rothaug, Barnickel, Petersen, Nebelung; second row, left to right: Cuhorst, Oeschey, and Altstoetter.

XXII

CASE No. 3 (Justice Case)

Judges (Presiding Judge marked by*)

Carrington T. Marshall, former Chief Justice of Supreme Court of Ohio

*James T. Brand, Justice of Supreme Court of Oregon

Mallory B. Blair, Justice of the Court of Civil Appeals of Texas

Justin B. Harding, former Judge in Alaska and Assistant Attorney General of Ohio, alternate

Judge Marshall retired because of health, and Brand presided.

Prosecution

Hon. Charles M. LaFollette, Deputy Chief Counsel, former Congressman from Indiana, Evansville, Indiana

Alfred M. Wolleyhan, Cecilton, Maryland

Robert Douglas King, New York City

Sadie B. Arbuthnot, Orlando, Florida

Arnold Buchtal

Of Counsel: Robert M. W. Kempner, Lansdowne, Pennsylvania; Jack W. Robbins, Denton, Texas; William A. Dickinson

Research Associates: Lorenz Eitner, Henry Einstein, Karl Jacoby

Indictment

Counts: (1) Conspiracy to commit war crimes and crimes against humanity;
(2) War crimes;
(3) Crimes against humanity;
(4) Membership in SS.

Defense

Defendant	Chief Defense Counsel	Counts on which sentenced	Sentence
1. Franz Schlegelberger	Dr. Egon Kubuschok	2, 3	Life imprisonment
2. Herbert Klemm	Dr. Alfred Schilf	2, 3	Life imprisonment
3. Oswald Rothaug	Dr. Josef Koessl	3	Life imprisonment

Defendant	Chief Defense Counsel	Counts on which sentenced	Sentence
4. Rudolf Oeschey	Dr. Werner Schubert	3, 4	Life imprisonment
5. Wilhelm von Ammon	Dr. Egon Kubuschok	2, 3	10 years
6. Guenther Joel	Dr. Karl Haensel	2, 3, 4	10 years
7. Wolfgang Mettgenberg	Dr. Alfred Schilf	2, 3	10 years
8. Ernst Lautz	Dr. Heinrich Grube	2, 3	10 years
9. Curt Rothenburger	Dr. Erich Wandschneider	2, 3	7 years
10. Josef Altstoetter	Dr. Hermann Orth	4	5 years
11. Paul Barnickel	Dr. Edmund Tipp		Acquittal
12. Hermann Cuhorst	Dr. Richard Brieger		Acquittal
13. Guenther Nebelung	Dr. Karl Doetzer		Acquittal
14. Hans Petersen	Dr. Rudolf Aschenauer		Acquittal

The third trial is one of particular interest to attorneys. It was the so-called "Justice Case." As has been pointed out in the proceedings before the International Military Tribunal,[1] the courts in Germany had degenerated under Hitler to a point where they were mere enforcement agencies for his decrees. The Weimar Constitution had been suspended in its operation, and its guarantees were wholly ineffective to provide due process for any citizen in Germany. The Gestapo was a body practically independent of the courts. The courts were subject to the domination of prosecutors and a sentence of "not guilty" could be set aside or a sentence increased at the whim of those in power. Special courts were created which were not subject to the usual rules. And, under the doctrines of "analogy" and the "sound feelings of the people," it was not necessary for a conviction that a person even have violated an existing law.

Those persons charged in the justice case were persons holding high positions under the Nazi regime, charged with the administration of the courts. Franz Schlegelberger was for a time acting secretary of the Justice Ministry. Rothenburger, Klemm, Altstoetter, von Ammon, Joel, and Mettgenberg were all at one time officials in the Ministry of Justice. Ernst Lautz was the chief public prosecutor; Barnickel was his assistant; and the defendants Cuhorst, Rothaug, and Oeschey were all chief justices of special courts.

The proceedings themselves are packed with interest. Not only do they reveal the operation of the processes of justice during the entire Nazi regime and up until the termination of hostilities, but they show the method in which actual trials were conducted. A person charged with crime appearing before one of those courts was not granted justice in the American manner.

---

[1] *Ante* pages 31, 79, 81-83.

He was convicted practically before the proceedings began. At times these proceedings were so flagrant that protest was made by outstanding persons but seldom with effect. The defendant Rothaug, for example, condemned one sixty-eight year old Jew to death because he was found guilty of permitting a German girl to sit upon his lap. It was obvious that the decrees of the Nazi government could not be carried into effect without the active cooperation of those charged with the prosecution of persons indicted for crime and those in a position to pass sentence upon the persons so convicted. The Tribunal pointed out that it was reluctant to find that any members of the legal profession or judiciary could lend themselves to any program of mass extermination, but that the evidence showed beyond any question that the defendants convicted were persons who knew the intent and purpose of the pogroms and lent themselves and their offices to the carrying out of these measures.

It was because of such matters that the Indictments were filed. They were filed on January 4, 1947, and served upon the defendants the same day. The defendants were arraigned upon February 17, with the case actually opening for trial upon May 5, thereby allowing four months for preparation of the defenses. The Prosecution consumed 35 trial days, placed 47 witnesses upon the stand, and introduced 641 documents. The defendants consumed 59 trial days, interrogated 91 witnesses in chief, and introduced 1,589 documents. There were 10,936 pages in the transcript of this trial, including a judgment of 275 pages. Two of the chief counsel for the defendants had represented defendants before the International Military Tribunal, and one had acted as an assistant in those proceedings. The Prosecution completed its closing statement on October 13, judgment was entered upon December 3 and 4, 1947, and it was confirmed upon January 18, 1949.

The defendant Westphal, originally indicted, died before the commencement of trial. Because of the continued illness of the defendant Karl Engert, a mistrial was declared as to him on August 22, 1947. The proceedings opened with the Honorable Carrington T. Marshall presiding, who later withdrew because of illness, with Justice Brand taking his place and Justin B. Harding, the alternate, sitting then as a full member of the Tribunal. A motion was filed early by the defense to strike Count One of the Indictment, which was based upon conspiracy to commit war crimes and crimes against humanity. It will be recalled that in the proceedings before the International Military Tribunal, the Germany attorneys had concentrated their most vigorous efforts against a similar count in that Indictment. In those efforts they were unsuccessful, but they claimed there was nothing in the German law which was analogous to this charge as known to the Anglo-Saxons.[2] This particular charge has also met more criticism from writers in the field of international law than any of the other charges. At any rate, upon July 11, 1947, the Tribunal held that neither the Charter of the International Military Tribunal nor Council Control Law No. 10 had defined conspiracy to commit war crimes or crimes against humanity as a separate substantial crime, and that the Tribunal had no jurisdiction to try any of the defendants upon such charges. Thereafter, all evidence relating to the first count was excluded, and no defendant was found guilty on that count.

So far as the proceedings were concerned, substantially the same pattern was followed as in the other cases. The rulings upon the evidence were quite similar and skill was shown in the conduct of both the Prosecution and the defense. A great many applications for production of witnesses who had furnished affidavits to the Prosecution were filed by defense counsel, and a great majority of these were allowed. The evidence was ample to sustain convictions, actually, of all of the defendants, if the theory of the Prosecution and the Tribunal is accepted at all. However, the Tribunal held the evidence insufficient as to four of the defendants, and they were acquitted.

The position taken by the Prosecution and by the Tribunal upon the controlling law is of considerable interest and subject to some criticism. At one point it was declared that the controlling military powers had legal authority to pass laws and to create judicial tribunals because of the complete breakdown of the German government, and to this effect eminent writers in the field of international law were quoted at length.[3]

The Hague Rules were declared not to be applicable where there had been a complete surrender. A great deal of time was spent trying to justify Council Control Law No. 10. It was pointed out that the governing power had the task of reorganizing the German government and of punishing persons guilty of crimes against humanity committed against the nationals of that nation. Then, however, it was declared that the Tribunal was not sitting as a German court or dependent on German law, but drew its full power and jurisdiction from the will and command of the four occupying powers.[4] It might be seriously questioned as to what law such a court was supposed to administer, if not the law of that country or the principles accepted under prevailing rules of international law.

---

[2] See the discussion of this particular charge, *ante* pages 40-45.

[3] Transcript 10,614-5.

[4] Transcript 10,620-1.

Again, shortly later, it was stated that Council Control Law No. 10 "did not purport to establish by a legislative act any new crimes of international applicability." There seems to be a grave inconsistency in this position. If the court was sitting as a military court, then it could punish for war crimes recognized under the Hague Rules or other recognized international principles. At best, there was a very attenuated chain of circumstances creating any link between the acts committed against German nationals, either in time of peace or war, and the conduct of the war itself, or the commission of other crimes. War crimes have particular reference to offenses against the subjects of an opposing belligerent power, and particularly the members of its armed forces, whether prisoners or otherwise. The crimes charged in this case related almost exclusively to the judicial murder of subjects of Germany, which would fall almost wholly within the class of crimes against humanity. If it is admitted that Council Control Law No. 10 did not purport to establish any new crimes of international applicability, then it is necessary to draw from international law as it then existed, or to go back to the law of Germany itself. The Tribunal was not in any position to deny the applicability of German law or prior international law without then recognizing that the occupying powers and the Tribunal were creating and applying new law.

An even more sweeping statement was subsequently made when it was declared: "Surely Council Control Law No. 10, which was enacted by the authorized representatives of the four greatest powers on earth, is entitled to judicial respect when it states, 'Each of the following acts is recognized as a crime.' "[5] It is strange to find such an element of flag waving in a serious judicial proceeding, and particularly one concerning itself with the improper administration of justice by others. Furthermore, the very declaration that "Each of the following acts is recognized as a crime" implies that such law pre-existed. New law cannot be created in that manner and made retroactive. Either such law existed prior to that time, or it did not, and the methods of determining that question are simple. The mere fact that such a statement was reduced to writing by the representatives of those nations serves no legal or judicial purpose, and would not be entitled to judicial respect.

At other places, however, a better discussion is contained of the right of a nation to intervene to prevent crimes against humanity and examples of repeated interventions by the United

---

[5] Transcript 10, 626.

States are given.[6] Whether or not these would be sufficient to justify individual punishment for such crimes, rather than the prevention thereof, might be open to some legal doubt. An excellent discussion is also given of the German law as applied by the defendants and the position of Hitler in the judicial picture.

[6] Transcript 10,643-5.

Defendants in the Pohl Case. Left to right, first row; Oswald Pohl, Frank, Loerner, Fanslau, H. Loerner, Vogt, Tschentscher, Scheide, Kiefer, Eirenschmaltz; left to right, second row: Sommer, Pock, Baier, Hohberg, L. Volk, Mummenthey, Bobermin, and Klein.

XXIII

CASE NO. 4 (SS, Pohl, Case)

Judges (Presiding Judge marked by*)

*Robert M. Toms, Judge of Circuit Court of Michigan
F. Donald Phillips, Judge of Superior Court of North Carolina
Michael A. Musmanno, Judge of Court of Common Pleas of Pennsylvania
John L. Speight, of Alabama, alternate

Prosecution

James McHaney, Little Rock, Arkansas
William I. Hart, New York City
Jack W. Robbins, New York City
Baucum Fulkerson, Little Rock, Arkansas
James R. Higgins, Pottsville, Pennsylvania
Peter W. Walton, Monticello, Georgia
Daniel J. Shiller, Waterbury, Connecticut
Julius I. Rudolph, Jr., Chicago, Illinois
Hans Froechlich

Research Assistants: Erik T. Ortmann, Kurt L. Ponger, Paul S. Siebenschein, Howell Webb, Manfred Wolfson, Larry L. Young

Indictment

Counts: (1) Conspiracy to commit war crimes and crimes against humanity;
(2) War crimes;
(3) Crimes against humanity;
(4) Membership in SS.

Defense

Defendant	Chief Defense Counsel	Counts on which sentenced	Sentence
1. Oswald Pohl	Dr. Alfred Seidl	2, 3, 4	Death
2. Franz Eirenschmalz	Dr. Bolko von Stein	2, 3, 4	Death
3. Karl Sommer	Dr. Eduard Belzer	2, 3, 4	Death
4. Georg Loerner	Dr. Carl Haensel	2, 3, 4	Death (commuted to life imprisonment on review)

Defendant	Chief Defense Counsel	Counts on which sentenced	Sentence
5. August Frank	Dr. Gerhard Rauschenbach	2, 3, 4	Life imprisonment
6. Karl Mummenthey	Dr. Georg Froeschmann	2, 3, 4	Life imprisonment
7. Max Kiefer	Dr. Erich K. Mayer	2, 3, 4	Life imprisonment (commuted to 15 years on review)
8. Heinz Fanslau	Dr. Curt F. von Stackelberg	2, 3, 4	25 years (commuted to 15 years on review)
9. Hans Bobermin	Dr. Hans Gawlik	2, 3, 4	20 years (commuted to 15 years on review)
10. Erwin Tschentscher	Dr. Hans Pribilla	2, 3, 4	10 years
11. Leo Volk	Dr. Hans Gawlik	2, 3	10 years
12. Hans Loerner	Dr. Gerhard Rauschenbach	2, 3, 4	10 years
13. Hermann Pock	Dr. Paul Ratz	2, 3, 4	10 years
14. Hans Baier	Dr. Stefan Fritsch	2, 3, 4	10 years
15. Hans Hohberg	Dr. Ernst Schulte	2, 3	10 years
16. Joseph Vogt	Dr. Wilhelm Schmidt		Acquittal
17. Rudolf Scheide	Dr. Karl Hoffmann		Acquittal
18. Horst Klein	Dr. Friedrich Bergold		Acquittal

Note: The original sentences were pronounced November 3, 1947, and the Tribunal reconvened July 12, 1948, to consider additional evidence which formed the basis for the reduction of the four sentences above noted.

The Indictment in Case Four was filed January 13, 1947, and served upon the various defendants the same day. The defendants entered their pleas upon March 10, and the trials opened upon April 8. The Prosecution consumed 16 actual trial days, introducing 21 witnesses and 472 documents. The defense opened its case upon May 14, consuming 65 actual trial days and introducing 45 witnesses and 614 documents. The case closed upon September 17, and judgments were rendered on November 3, 1947. The transcript consisted of 8,201 pages, of which the judgment occupied 152 pages.

With reference to the sentences in this case, the matter was handled somewhat differently than in the other cases. The defense counsel filed customary petitions for reduction of sentence with the military governor under the provisions of Ordinance No. 7. When these petitions were brought to the attention of the Tribunal, it elected to deal with them as petitions for rehearing. The defense counsel were permitted to furnish supplemental briefs, and the Tribunal reconvened July 12, 1948 to consider additional evidence. As a result thereof, four sentences were reduced, one of which had previously been a death penalty, as shown in the preceding table.

Case Four is commonly called the "SS" or "Pohl Case." Oswald Pohl was the chief of the economic and administrative department of the SS, commonly called the WVHA, as an abbreviation of *Wirtschaft und Verwaltungshauptamt*. The other defendants were officials of this same division. As such, they were responsible for the operation of concentration camps, mines, and factories maintained by the WVHA. With the exception of the conspiracy count, which received the same treatment as in Case Three, the charges consisted principally of criminal responsibility for the murders, mayhems, and ill treatment of the inmates of such concentration camps and other establishments administered by the SS. The opening statement for the Prosecution discussed the organization and growth of the SS, the various acts committed, including the various medical experiments conducted by the defendants in Case One, the sterilization, euthanasia programs, poisonous foods, and the like. In the opening statement, the administration of these camps was portrayed in detail, including the fact that the WVHA operated houses of prostitution in the concentration camps where the usual charge was two Reichsmarks, of which 75% went to the organization and a small portion to the madame and to the performer.

Much of the evidence heard by the Tribunal was repetitious of that used before the International Military Tribunal and also that relating to the defendants in Case One. The defendants in this case relied strongly upon the doctrine of *respondeat superior* and attempted to divorce themselves from much of the responsibility for the acts committed. With reference to charges that concentration camp inmates had been ill fed, they introduced considerable evidence to show that these persons worked the same hours and received the same foods as the Germans who were suffering from the blockades so effectively enforced by the Allied powers. The Tribunal in its judgment strongly condemned the principle of forced labor, irrespective of the treatment given to the persons thus subjected, and went on in sweeping terms to condemn the acts performed under the direction of the defendants.

Because of the fact that these defendants were closer in point of direct contact with the acts performed, the reaction of the Tribunal was similar to that in the medical case. Four of the defendants were condemned to death, one of these sentences later being reduced to life imprisonment. While three defendants were acquitted, the terms of imprisonment awarded to the other defendants were substantially more severe than in the case of industrialists, bankers, and others whose efforts made it possible for the Nazis to rise to power and to wage aggressive war. While one might question the wisdom of making such a distinction, it is quite clear that any judge stirred by human emotions would be considerably more affected by the type of testimony introduced in the medical case and in this case than in others dealing with political or financial machinations.

Defendants in the Flick case. Left to right: Weiss, Flick, Burkart, Kaletsch, Steinbrinck, and Terberger.

XXIV

CASE NO. 5 (Flick Case—Industrialists)

Judges (Presiding Judge marked by*)

*Charles B. Sears, retired Justice of Court of Appeals of New York

Frank N. Richman, former Justice of the Supreme Court of Indiana

William C. Christianson, former Justice of the Supreme Court of Minnesota

Richard D. Dixon, Judge of the Superior Court of North North Carolina, alternate

Prosecution

Thomas E. Ervin, New York City
Charles S. Lyon, New York City
Paul H. Gantt, Williamsburg, Virginia
Sadi J. Mase
Joseph H. Stone, New York City
Blake B. Woodson
Edwin M. Sears, Denver, Colorado
Ralph S. Goodman
Richard H. Lansdale, Washington, D. C.

Of Counsel: Drexel A. Sprecher, Cecilia Goetz

Research Assistants: Josif Marcu, Nobert Barr, Eric Kaufmann, Louise Stubin, Walter Schonfeld, Frank Esterkin

Indictment

Counts: (1) Slave labor;
(2) Spoliation;
(3) Crimes against humanity prior to the war;
(4) Cooperation with SS;
(5) Membership in SS.

Defense

Defendant	Chief Defense Counsel	Counts on which sentenced	Sentence
1. Friedrich Flick	Dr. Rudolf Dix	1, 2, 4	7 years
2. Otto Steinbrinck	Dr. Hans Flaechsner	4, 5	5 years

Defendant	Chief Defense Counsel	Counts on which sentenced	Sentence
3. Bernhard Weiss	Dr. Walter Siemers	1	2½ years
4. Hermann Terberger	Horst Pelckmann		Acquittal
5. Odilo Burkart	Dr. Otto Kranzbuehler		Acquittal
6. Konrad Kaletsch	Dr. Herbert Nath		Acquittal

The so-called "Flick Case" was the first of the cases brought against industrialists of Germany. Friedrich Flick was a powerful steel magnate, who had built up his enterprise to a leading point in German steel production. The other defendants were five of his principal associates.

The very excellently organized and indexed opening statement traces the development of the Flick combine and its role in heavy German industry. After tracing this historical development, the opening statement goes on to point out the close cooperation between the persons here charged and the Nazi regime. In addition to membership in the SS, the defendants contributed large sums of money to the party, aided in the conscription of labor, issued requests for the assignments of prisoners of war for use in factories, and subsequently considerable evidence was introduced to show an abnormally high death rate among the prisoners, which was attributed to inadequate housing, poor food, and ill treatment. The opening statement also pointed out that in one case Flick, through his intimate contact with the high officials in the Nazi regime, had himself placed in the position where he was the only one permitted to negotiate for a large plant in an occupied nation. The owners thereof were unwilling to sell and were compelled to sell at a drastic sacrifice, and Flick thereby became the owner of such added industry without competition from other industrialists. His efforts to procure other industrial plants in different territories were also traced in detail.

The Indictment was filed on February 8, 1947, and served upon the defendants the same day. It was subsequently amended upon March 18 and the amended Indictment served upon the day it was filed. The defendants pleaded "not guilty" upon April 19, and the case opened upon April 21. The Prosecution occupied 38 trial days, placing 31 witnesses on the stand, and introducing 742 documents. The defense opened its case upon July 2. The defendants were represented by able counsel, four of them having been chief counsel for defendants before the International Military Tribunal. They consumed 85 actual trial days, placed 20 witnesses on the stand, and introduced 614 documents. The Prosecution closed November 24, and judgment was rendered December 22, 1947. The transcript consisted of 11,026 pages, of which 52 pages comprised the judgment. The judgment was confirmed June 30, 1948, and an unsuccessful action for writ of habeas corpus was filed in the District Court for the District of Columbia and then appealed to that Court of Appeals, certiorari being denied by the Supreme Court after affirmance by the Circuit Court of Appeals.

The evidence itself was amply sufficient to sustain the charges brought if said charges amounted to violations of international law. The Tribunal ruled that it had no jurisdiction over the matters charged in Count Three relating to crimes against humanity committed prior to the war.[1] Therefore, acts under Count Three were not considered. The Tribunal also felt that crimes against humanity should be limited to matters affecting the lives or safety of persons and could not extend to the seizure of property.[2]

As to the procedure during the trial, the Tribunal profited by the experience of former tribunals, and the trial moved expeditiously. Counsel were stopped from reading exhibits in full and were required to summarize their contents briefly.[3] Documents were permitted introduction without the necessity of extensive preliminary proof, with little dissension by counsel.[4] The Tribunal was impatient with delays and verbosity, the following exchange occurring at one point where the transmission apparatus temporarily went out of commission:

> "Interpreter: The switch, Your Honor! I can't hear a thing.
>
> "The President: Well, you haven't missed much anyway."[5]

In its Judgment the Tribunal expressed itself definitely upon several points of law. As to the question which had been considerably argued by defense counsel in all cases, concerning the lack of international sanction for individual responsibility, the court summarily declared:

> "It can no longer be successfully maintained that international law is concerned only with the actions of sovereign states and provides no punishment for individuals."[6]

Again, the Tribunal declared:

> "Acts adjudged criminal when done by an officer of the government are criminal also when done by a private indi-

1 Transcript 11,010.
2 Transcript 11,013.
3 Transcript 9464.
4 Transcript 9470-1.
5 Transcript 9483.
6 Transcript 10,980.

vidual. The guilt differs only in magnitude, not in quality. The offender in either case is charged with personal wrong and punishment falls on the offender in *propia persona.*"[7]

However, the Tribunal gave some heed to the German doctrine of "necessity." It is believed that the Tribunal misunderstood the sense in which this term was intended by German counsel. It will be recalled from the earlier discussion[8] that the German political philosophers believe that the violation of a treaty, breach of faith, or violation of law is justified when the desired result can be accomplished in no other way. That is what is meant by Germans in speaking of the doctrine of necessity. The Tribunal, however, construed the doctrine of necessity as one of duress, which is quite a different thing. Bearing this misunderstanding in mind, we are not then surprised to find the Tribunal stating:

> "This Tribunal might be reproached for seeking vengeance rather than administering justice if it were to declare as unavailable to defendants the defense of necessity here urged in their behalf. This principle has had wide acceptance in American and English courts and is recognized elsewhere."[9]

The Tribunal then went on to speak of "a clear and present danger" which existed if the defendants had not cooperated with the government, making it clear that the Tribunal had in mind the elements of force and fear rather than what might be called the "doctrine of justification."[10]

The German counsel dealt at length with charges which they made against the allies, much as they had done in their arguments before the International Military Tribunal. They sought to show that the acts with which the defendants were charged were no more reprehensible than the bombing of industrial cities by the Americans, which resulted in the killing of many women and children. This contention having been overruled by the International Military Tribunal, little attention was paid to it by this court. However, the court was apparently unable to feel that offenses by industrialists fell into as severe a category as when committed by a common man, particularly when the latter individual actually took the final steps toward the mistreatment or killing of another human being. Three of the defendants were

---

[7] Transcript 10,981.

[8] *Ante*, pages 83, 84.

[9] Transcript 10,992.

[10] Transcript 10,993-4.

acquitted entirely, and the others drew only light sentences, receiving full credit for time served prior to the rendition of the judgment.

Defendants in the Farben case are seated in the dock. First row, left to right: Krauch, Schmitz, Von Schnitzler, Gajewski, Hoerlein, Von Knierem, Ter Meer, Schneider, Ambros, Buergin, Buetefisch; second row, left to right: Haefliger, Ilgner, Jaehne, Kuehne, Lautenschlaeger, Mann, Oster, Wurster, Duerrfeld, Gattineau, von der Heyde, and Kugler. Defendants' counsel are seated immediately in front of them, which was the arrangement in all of the trials. The ear phones worn by attorneys and defendants are clearly visible.

XXV

Case No. 6 (Farben Case)

Judges (Presiding Judge marked by*)

*Curtis G. Shake, former Justice of the Supreme Court of Indiana
James Morris, Justice of the Supreme Court of North Dakota
Paul M. Hebert, Dean of Louisiana State University Law School

Prosecution

Josiah E. Dubois, Jr., Camden, New Jersey
Drexel A. Sprecher, Washington, D. C.
Morris Amchan, Arlington, Virginia
Jan Charmatz, Havana, Cuba
Belle Mayer, Washington, D. C.
Emanuel E. Minskoff, Silver Springs, Maryland
Randolph Newman, Baldwin Harbor, Long Island, New York
Virgil Van Street, Catonsville, Maryland
Paul H. Gantt, Williamsburg, Virginia
James E. Heath, Norfolk, Virginia
(Mrs.) Mary M. Kaufman, Los Angeles, California
Moses Kove
William Zeck

Indictment

Counts: (1) Planning and waging aggressive war;
(2) Spoliation;
(3) Slave labor;
(4) Membership in SS;
(5) Conspiracy to commit aggressive war.

Defendant	Chief Defense Counsel	Counts on which sentenced	Sentence
1. Otto Ambros	Dr. Karl Hoffmann	3	8 years
2. Walter Duerrfeld	Dr. Alfred Seidl	3	8 years
3. Fritz Ter Meer	Karl Bornemann Dr. Erich Berndt	2, 3	7 years
4. Carl Krauch	Dr. Conrad Boettcher	3	6 years
5. Heinrich Buetefisch	Dr. Hans Flaechsner Dr. Hartmann	3	6 years
6. Georg von Schnitzler	Dr. Walter Siemers	2	5 years

Defendant	Chief Defense Counsel	Counts on which sentenced	Sentence
7. Hermann Schmitz	Dr. Rudolf Dix Dr. Gierlichs	2	4 years
8. Heinrich Oster	Dr. Helmut Henze	2	2 years
9. Ernst Buergin	Dr. Werner Schubert	2	2 years
10. Paul Haefliger	Dr. Wolfram von Metzler	2	2 years
11. Friedrich Jaehne	Dr. Hans Pribilla Dr. Eisenblaetter	2	1½ years
12. Max Ilgner	Dr. Herbert Nath	2	Credit for time in prison and released
13. Hans Kugler	Dr. Helmut Henze	2	Credit for time in prison and released
14. August von Knierem	Horst Pelckmann Dr. Silcher		Acquittal
15. Hans Kuehne	Dr. Herbert Nath Dr. Lummert		Acquittal
16. Carl Lautenschlaeger	Dr. Hans Pribilla Dr. Eisenblaetter		Acquittal
17. Wilhelm Mann	Dr. Erich Berndt		Acquittal
18. Karl Wurster	Friedrich Wagner Dr. Heintzeler		Acquittal
19. Heinrich Gattineau	Dr. Rudolf Aschenauer		Acquittal
20. Erich von der Heyde	Dr. Karl Hoffmann		Acquittal
21. Fritz Gajewski	Dr. Wolfram von Metzler Dr. Wegher		Acquittal
22. Heinrich Hoerlein	Dr. Otto Nelte		Acquittal
23. Christian Schneider	Dr. Hellmuth Dix		Acquittal

General Defense Staff (No particular client)

Fritz Naumann
Josef Niemann
Dr. Hugo Schramm
Dr. Hermann Walter

Special Counsel (For all defendants)

Prof. Dr. Eduard Wahl

Case Six, commonly called the "Farben Case," was concerned with the trial of twenty-four directors and officers of the I. G. Farben-industrie A. G., the enormous chemicals and synthetic combine controlling many patents throughout the world. One defendant, Brueggeman, was severed from the case for ill health, so that only twenty-three of the defendants stood trial.

The Indictment was filed on May 3, 1947, and served upon the defendants the same day. They pleaded "not guilty" upon August 14 and the case opened upon August 27, which allowed almost four months for the preparation of defenses. The Prosecution consumed 53 trial days, examining 87 witnesses and introducing 2282 documents.[1a]

Four of the defense counsel had acted as chief counsel before the International Military Tribunal, and two others had acted as assistant counsel in that case. The defense opened upon December 15, occupying 90 trial days, examining 102 witnesses, and introducing 4195 documents. Final arguments for the defendants took six and one-half days. The closing statement for the Prosecution, which took only one day, was made upon June 10, 1948, judgments were rendered upon July 29 and 30, and these were confirmed upon March 4, 1949. The transcript was 15,834 pages in length, of which the judgment occupied 205.

The judgment analyzes in a concise manner the charges brought against the defendants and the evidence in support of those charges. From the point of view of a student of the proceedings, it appears that the Prosecution's case was stronger in most respects than against the remaining industrialists. It was shown quite clearly that Farben favored a dictatorship long before Hitler came into power and wished for domination over the chemical industry of all of Europe and even beyond Europe,

---

[1a] This was the only case in which a charge was made by the Prosecution of improper conduct by defense counsel. The Prosecutors accused certain members of the German defense staff of misappropriation and destruction of tons of documentary evidence obtained from archives to which both sides had equal access. A motion seeking an accounting of all missing records, principally concerned with various phases of the administration of the Oswicim concentration camp, was filed with the Tribunal. Discovery of the missing documents was made immediately prior to the appearance on the witness stand of defendant Ambros, who was largely responsible for the operation of the Oswicim establishment. In preparation for his cross-examination, the Prosecution team went to Griesheim to examine a large number of pertinent documents. On arrival they found receipts for a large quantity of such papers ostensibly signed for by French occupation authorities then operating one of the Farben plants. The Prosecution team then made a further investigation and found that the French occupation officials denied any knowledge of such records. It finally appeared that the Germans were acting on specific instructions from Dr. Wolfgang Alt, assistant counsel for Ambros. The arrival of the Prosecution team topped off further activity. All Farben case records then on the premises were hidden in cupboards and closets, and one crate was smuggled outside an entrance and deposited in Dr. Alt's apartment. These were found after an untiring search by French security police.

The investigation team obtained affidavits showing the method employed in securing the documents and their disposition. The majority of the documents destroyed had been fed into paper shredding or pulping machines in the offices of the Farben plant at Ludwigshafen, while other records were burned.

This incident illustrates the necessity for the care taken by the Prosecution in other cases in keeping the records in the central office, with defense counsel being limited to examination of such records under supervision.

if possible. Before Hitler had seized power, Farben had arranged for support by him of their policies, and, following his rise to power, cooperated closely with him and with military leaders in their principles and preparations of a military character. The Farben leaders assisted greatly in rearmament and in making Germany self-sufficient for war purposes, correspondence between the defendants and the government officials indicating that war was definitely in the minds of certain of the defendants.

The Tribunal, however, in its majority opinion, laid down certain principles which served to exonerate the defendants upon the chief charges. It held flatly that there was no conspiracy to commit aggressive war shown in this case, despite the evidence referred to. It referred to the judgment of the International Military Tribunal and pointed out that that court had approached the concept of conspiracy with great caution. This Tribunal felt that the only persons who could be so charged were political leaders with power to control governmental policies, and that there was not shown to be any common knowledge of Hitler's plan. Consequently, all defendants were declared innocent of charges of conspiracy and of aggressive war.[1b]

[1b] Transcript 15-685-9. There has been a charge made that the members of the Tribunal, other than Justice Hebert, were sympathetic to the defense. The following is illustrative of the charges made in this regard:

"What would the reactions of the average citizen be if they saw the wife of a prominent judge sipping malted milk at the Army PX with the wife of a defendant who is standing trial before her husband? Naturally, this would cause some eyebrow-raising. . . .

"Yet this is what happened recently in Nuremberg, Germany, during the War Crimes trials against I. G. Farben.

"The wife of Judge James Morris invited Baroness von Schnitzler, whose husband was one of the chief defendants, to the PX and entertained her there frequently. It was indeed a strange sight to see both women behaving like bosom friends—eating, drinking and chatting together amiably. What an honor to be befriended by a Baroness—even if her husband is in jail charged with having committed ghastly war crimes!

"Still another amazing incident occurred in Nuremberg, one concerning Judge Curtis G. Shake, who presided at the Farben trials. This judge had the brilliant idea of inviting German defense attorneys to dinner at the Grand Hotel, where Germans were generally denied the right of admittance.

"Apparently Judge Shake was greatly impressed by his talks with the German lawyers as he let no occasion slip without pointing out what nice and brilliant people the Germans were.

"It is said that he went to Germany armed with the conviction that the trial of German industrialists was never contemplated by the Charter (Law No. 10) under which he was operating, and this despite the fact that under this particular law it was mandatory to consider guilty all persons who have committed those acts and crimes defined in the Charter.

"Incidentally, Judge Shake's picture has been prominently displayed in German newspapers after the Farben verdict. Significantly enough, the

The Tribunal further declared that the American concepts of criminal justice must be applied in that (a) there shall be no conviction without proof of personal guilt; (b) guilt must be proved beyond all reasonable doubt; (c) each defendant must be presumed innocent until so proven guilty; (d) the burden of such proof remains upon the Prosecution throughout the trial; (e) if two inferences of equal probability can be drawn, one of which is of guilt and the other of innocence, the latter must prevail.

Applying these tests, the Tribunal also held that spoliation or plunder was not a crime against humanity, nor could it be considered a war crime where committed in territory not under belligerent occupation.

There was a strong concurring opinion by Judge Hebert which dissented from the reasoning of the majority upon the issues of planning and preparing for aggressive war. He seemed to feel that the issue of fact was so close that he had serious doubt of the correctness of the majority opinion.[2] Judge Hebert also filed a dissenting opinion from that of the majority which acquitted all but five defendants on the slave labor charge. It had been shown in evidence that Farben had constructed a synthetic rubber plant adjacent to the Auschwitz concentration camp with a definite view toward using such labor. The majority found only the five defendants guilty who had shared direct responsibility for this project. Judge Hebert felt that knowledge was definitely shown on the part of all of the defendants of such activity, and that they had all willingly cooperated in the plan. He declared:

> "Under the evidence it is clear that the defendants in utilizing slave labor which is conceded to be a war crime (in the case of non-German nationals) and a crime against humanity, did not, as they assert, in fact, act exclusively because of the compulsion and coercion of the existing Governmental

---

weekly 'Christ und Welt' of Stuttgart, featured the picture with the following caption:

> 'The president of the U. S. Military Tribunal in the Nuremberg I. G. Farben trial, who excelled by his just conduct of the proceedings, by his absolute objectivity and disregard for all vindictive sentiments, as well as by his endeavor to understand the nature of German conditions between 1933 and 1945.'

"Maybe these occurrences have no significance. Perhaps nothing sinister should be derived from them. But they may shed some light on the reasons for the shocking leniency shown the Farben criminals.

"Maybe our readers know why the I. G. Farben criminals deserved so much understanding and leniency? We don't." No. 27 *Prevent World War III*, November-December 1948, Society for the Prevention of World War III, Inc., page 36.

[2] See Concurring Opinion, pages 2-3.

regulations and policies. The record does not establish by any substantial credible proof that any of the defendants were actually opposed to the Governmental solution of the manpower problems reflected in these regulations. On the contrary, the record shows that Farben willingly cooperated and gladly utilized each new source of manpower as it developed. . . .

"Willing cooperation with the slave labor utilization of the Third Reich was a matter of corporate policy that permeated the whole Farben organization. The Vorstand was responsible for the policy. For this reason, criminal responsibility goes beyond the actual immediate participants at Auschwitz. It includes other Farben Vorstand plant-managers and embraces all who knowingly participated in the shaping of the corporate policy. I find on the evidence that all Vorstand members must share the responsibility for the approval of the policy despite the fact that there were varying degrees of immediate connection among various defendants."[3]

As to the actual conduct of the trial, some of the more significant rulings are that the Tribunal struck any Prosecution affidavits from evidence where the witnesses could not be located for cross-examination, counter-affidavits or interrogatories. It also refused affidavits of deceased persons.[4] The Tribunal permitted the introduction of voluntary statements or admissions by the defendants, but ruled that if such defendant did not take the witness stand, such statement would not be admissible against the remaining defendants. In one case such admission was rejected as being procured by duress.

An extensive discussion took place at one part of the record concerning the right of one side to interrogate witnesses reserved to another. This was the question raised throughout almost all of the trials, even including the proceedings before the International Military Tribunal. The Prosecution claimed here that it had not interfered with the defense in any way, but the mere fact that a witness had been requested by one side or the other should not prevent the other from talking to him. It pointed out that otherwise the defense counsel could request that all of the leading witnesses for the Prosecution be reserved, and the Prosecution would thus be precluded from making a case. The defense counsel claimed that the International Military Tribunal had followed a different rule, and that the Prosecution should not be permitted to talk to their witnesses. The Tribunal originally reserved its ruling, but finally agreed with the Prosecution.[5]

---

[3] Dissenting Opinion of Judge Hebert, pages 4, 9-10.

[4] E.g., Transcript 4445.

[5] E.g., Transcript 1071.

At another point the defense counsel pointed out that it was necessary to send representatives to France to locate witnesses, and they could neither get clearance for such a trip nor currency to pay the necessary expenses. At that point the Tribunal took the matter under advisement and arrangements were later made to alleviate these difficulties.[6] The question was also raised as to the right of the Prosecution, on closing, to introduce a further affidavit by a witness who had already been examined.[7] This was permitted, subject to recall of the witness for further cross-examination. The Prosecution, on its part, asked the Tribunal to reconsider its ruling excluding affidavits from deceased witnesses, but the Tribunal refused to do so.[8]

An excellent task of cross-examination was performed by Dr. Frischel for the defendant Ambros of a German witness who had stressed the great importance of Farben for war purposes. The cross-examinationer adroitly brought out that war could not be waged without the cooperation of agriculture and of other fields, and that the situation with reference to Farben was the same as that of chemical plants in all other countries.[9]

As the proceedings moved along, the Tribunal took occasion to censure the Prosecution for wasting time on cross-examination as to trivialities.[10] Subsequently, the Tribunal chided the Prosecution for going too far, and at one place asked how much longer the examination would take. The following conversation followed:

"Mr. Van Street: May it please Your Honor, I am finished now.

"The President: Sorry I didn't speak sooner."[11]

The Tribunal, in this industrial case like the others, seemed less concerned with the leading business figures and industrial leaders than with the persons actually carrying out orders. Ten of the defendants were acquitted entirely, and the heaviest sentence consisted of eight years, in marked contrast to the sentences of death and life imprisonment imposed in the medical and SS cases. One may conclude that the differences in results occasionally arose from a difference in philosophy, or in the degree of shocked conscience, rather than from the quantum of evidence.

---

6 Transcript 4443.
7 Transcript 4453-9.
8 Transcript 4445.
9 Transcript 1024.
10 Transcript 8461.
11 Transcript 10,275.

The Hostages Case. The defendants are, left to right: List, Kuntze, Foertsch, Von Geitner, Von Weichs, Rendulic, Dehner, Von Leyser, Lanz, Felmy, and Speidel.

XXVI

CASE NO. 7 (Hostages)

Judges (Presiding Judge marked by*)

*Charles F. Wennerstrum, Justice of the Supreme Court of Iowa
Edward F. Carter, Justice of the Supreme Court of Nebraska
George J. Burke, of Michigan, former General Counsel of O.P.A.

Prosecution

Clark Denney, 1 West 54th Street, New York City
Theodore F. Fenstermacher, New York City
Walter H. Rapp, San Francisco, California, of counsel
Baucom Fulkerson, Little Rock, Arkansas
James R. Higgins, Pottsville, Pennsylvania
Paul Niederman, Chicago, Illinois
James M. McHaney, Little Rock, Arkansas

Interrogators:
Otto Krelisheim
Fred Kaufman

Research Associates: Marina V. Farmakis, Vincent Czeisler, Frank Freudenthal, Robert C. Blakeslee, Everett V. Cunningham, Mary E. Carter, Elizabeth M. Stewart, Thomas Rosenthal-Desmines, Mary Walker Taylor, Mark Natlacen-Malec

Indictment

Counts: (1) Mass murder;
(2) Spoliation;
(3) Illegal executions;
(4) Slave labor.

Defense

Defendant	Chief Defense Counsel	Counts on which sentenced	Sentence
1. Franz Boehme	(Committed suicide before arraignment)		
2. Wilhelm List	Dr. Hans Laternser	1, 3	Life imprisonment
3. Walter Kuntze	Dr. Georg Menzel Dr. Beier	1, 3, 4	Life imprisonment
4. Lothar Rendulic	Dr. Stefan Fritsch	1, 3, 4	20 years

Defendant	Chief Defense Counsel	Counts on which sentenced	Sentence
5. Wilhelm Speidel	Dr. Joseph Weisgerber	1	20 years
6. Hellmuth Felmy	Dr. Heinz Mueller-Torgow	1, 2	15 years
7. Hubert Lanz	Dr. Fritz Sauter	1, 3	12 years
8. Ernst von Leyser	Dr. Edmund Tipp	3, 4	10 years
9. Ernst Dehner	Dr. Hans Gawlik	1	7 years
10. Maxmilian von Weichs	Dr. Hans Laternser	Separated from case because of ill health	
11. Hermann Foertsch	Dr. Gerhard Rauschenbach		Acquittal
12. Curt von Geitner	Dr. Fritz Sauter		Acquittal

The Indictment in Case Seven, or the so-called "Hostages Case," was filed May 10, 1947, and served upon the defendants the same day. They were arraigned upon July 8, except for Franz Boehme, who had committed suicide prior to that time. The trial opened upon July 15, the Prosecution occupying 33 trial days, examining seven witnesses in chief, and introducing 721 documents. The defense attorneys, two of whom had appeared as chief counsel and two as assistant counsel before the International Military Tribunal, opened their defense upon September 15, placing 43 witnesses upon the stand and introducing 1029 documents. The closing argument for the Prosecution was made on February 3, 1948, judgment pronounced upon February 19, and the sentences were confirmed by the Military Governor upon January 18, 1949. The transcript consisted of 10,544 pages, of which the judgment occupied 125.

The persons indicted were leaders in the army who were charged with various war crimes. These are set out in detail in the very excellent opening statement for the Prosecution, tracing the position and responsibility of each defendant in connection with the entire military structure and the acts committed in each of the various counts. Field Marshal Wilhelm List had commanded the Twelfth Army, which carried out the invasion and occupation of Greece and Yugloslavia from April 1941 until October of that year when, because of illness, he was succeeded by the defendant Lieutenant General Walter Kuntze. General Lothar Rendulic commanded the Second Panzer Army in Yugoslavia in 1943 and 1944. Lieutenant General Hermann Foertsch was chief of staff to List, Kuntze, and von Weichs. The other defendants included five lieutenant generals who were army commanders in a slightly lesser degree of importance and one brigadier general in a subordinate staff position.

The opening statement pointed out the military policy established in the occupied countries, with particular reference to the ratio of persons to be shot for particular acts. It discussed the treatment of commandos and commissars, the destruction of homes and shooting of prisoners where not enough hostages were available, and the killing of Italians, who were former allies of the Germans. The Prosecution pointed out the destruction of the entire northern portion of Norway, all devastated by the Germans, and the destruction of entire villages, thirteen being destroyed at one time in retaliation for the kidnapping of a general. The Prosecution contended that the net result of these harsh acts actually was the opposite of that intended, in that the people were driven to resistance from fear, never knowing when they otherwise might be shot for some act of resistance in which they had no part. The position of the Prosecution upon the law pertaining to the execution of guerillas, commandos, and commissars is discussed, the Prosecution further contending that there was no legal right whatever to execute hostages. This position is definitely questionable both under the Hague Rules of Land Warfare and under the accepted practice of nations, although the abnormal ratio used by the Germans during the war could not be countenanced under any reasonable construction of international law.

The evidence introduced for the Prosecution followed closely the order outlined in the opening statement and strongly supported the charges brought. For the defendants, a definite effort was made to show that the practice of other nations countenanced the shooting of hostages. Other attempts were made to show that the orders originated upon a higher level and that the defendants had no power to change or to disregard the orders, although in many instances they failed to enforce them for humanitarian reasons. Both the doctrines of *respondeat superior* and of "necessity" were invoked by the defense.

With reference to the treatment of matters of evidence, there were a few points of particular interest. Objections were made by the Prosecution to portions of an affidavit offered by Dr. Sauter because the affidavit included excerpts of a letter which were not capable of verification. Dr. Sauter withdrew the objectionable portions without the necessity of a ruling of the Tribunal.[1] Dr. Laternser offered part of the argument of the Deputy Judge Advocate of Great Britain, C. L. Stirling, who acted as the law officer on the trial of Kesselring, to the effect that hostages may be shot as reprisal measures. Objection to this offer was sustained, the Tribunal ruling that such a statement was not a proper exhibit, but could be referred to in final argument.[2] And an affidavit of General Eisenhower was intro-

1 Transcript 5027.
2 Transcript 8730-1.

duced by the defense, which referred to a French decree directing the shooting of five German hostages for every French soldier shot by snipers and directing that every sniper or person aiding a sniper was to be shot without trial.[3]

While the Prosecution was proceeding with its rebuttal, vigorous objection was made by Dr. Laternser that twenty-four hours' notice was not given as to additional documents sought to be introduced. The Prosecution contended that the twenty-four hour rule did not apply to rebuttal any more than it did to cross-examination. After some interchange of personalities between counsel, the Tribunal overruled the objections and stated that the twenty-four hour rule did not apply.[4] Subsequently, both Dr. Laternser and Dr. Sauter objected to Prosecution affidavits as not being proper rebuttal but evidence in chief and upon the further grounds that the affidavits were ten months old, that the witness was still in Nuremberg, and that they invaded the province of the court.[5] The Tribunal sustained only the last objection holding that the subject matter of the affidavit dealt with a matter of law of which it was the sole judge.[6] However, the Tribunal shortly later warned the Prosecution that it would not be permitted to re-try the case on rebuttal, and that it would not receive documents which should have been offered in chief.[7] And the Tribunal also ruled that an affidavit would not be admitted until the Prosecution could show the date when the witness had left Nuremberg, counsel for the defendant pointing out that a witness had frequently disappeared after his affidavit had been taken.[8] Defense counsel also requested that when the Prosecution submitted documents it wait until all defense counsel had had an opportunity to read them, as they had to pass the documents along from one to the other.[9]

At one stage of the interrogation, one Prosecutor ceased asking questions and another took over. Dr. Laternser objected to this division of the examination. The Tribunal tentatively agreed with Dr. Laternser, whereupon the Prosecution stated that the defense had constantly divided its interrogation and requested special permission for this occasion, which was granted.[10] At another point the Prosecution attempted to get a German witness to testify about the type of warfare waged against partisans.

---

[3] Transcript 8731-2.
[4] Transcript 8887-91.
[5] Transcript 8893.
[6] Transcript 8896.
[7] Transcript 8899.
[8] Transcript 8902-3.
[9] Transcript 8911.
[10] Transcript 8946.

This was objected to as opinion evidence, and the Tribunal required the witness to restrict himself to purely factual testimony.[11] But the Tribunal also stopped defense counsel repeatedly from making personal attacks upon a witness through objections or statements.[12]

As the proceedings neared the close, Dr. Laternser pointed out to the Tribunal that assistant defense counsel were not being allowed in the court room and were not being given tickets for admittance. Mr. Rapp replied that one assistant defense counsel was now in the balcony, and that the others could go in the balcony as well. The Tribunal severely criticized this practice and stated that all practicing counsel would be permitted to be together in the court room.[13]

Among the minor incidents which occurred in the trial was a little confusion concerning the name of a witness. The Prosecution had objected to an affidavit which did not show clearly whether a witness was from Norn or Zorn.

> "Dr. Gawlik: The affiant's name is Zorn and he is also born in Zorn.
>
> "Justice Burke: Zorn, Born, Norn, but it is Zorn?
>
> "Dr. Gawlik: In Zorn he was born. His name is Zorn and he was born in Zorn."[14]

Subsequently, Dr. Gawlik wanted to know if witness Korn was to be called. Whereupon Justice Burke asked, "From Dorn?" "Dr. Gawlik: No." "Justice Burke: Fine."[15]

At another point the Tribunal felt that all counsel were paying too little attention to the proceedings in court, and the following reprimand was made:

> "At this morning's session of the court, we have been favored with the presence of one representative of the prosecution. The head of the prosecution staff, whichever individual he may be, is not present, nor has he asked to be excused.
>
> "We have had three representatives of the defense counsel present, including Dr. Tipp, who is representing the defendant now on the stand. The other defense counsel, with the exception of two, have not asked to be excused.
>
> "The Tribunal does not know whether the lack of attendance on the part of counsel is indicative of their interest in this case or their attitude toward the Tribunal. Suffice it to say, at least as far as I am concerned, it is not looked upon

[11] Transcript 8920-5.
[12] Transcript 8925, 8933-5.
[13] Transcript 8911.
[14] Transcript 8713.
[15] Transcript 8912.

with favor. The Tribunal asks to be remembered to the absent individuals."[16]

---

[16] Transcript 5709. This was the only case in which a direct and bitter conflict developed subsequently between the Prosecution and the Tribunal. The presiding judge, Charles F. Wennerstrum, took occasion to denounce bitterly the conduct of the Prosecution during the course of the trial, claiming that the case was not fairly tried, that documents were not placed at the disposal of the defense, and that in other ways the defendants were not permitted a full and fair hearing. In reply to these charges, the chief Prosecutor, Brigadier General Telford Taylor, wrote the following letter:

"Nurnberg, 21 February, 1948

"Judge Charles F. Wennerstrum
Chariton, Iowa

"My dear Judge Wennerstrum:

"It has just come to my attention that yesterday, a few hours before your departure from Nurnberg, you gave an interview to a representative of the Chicago Tribune, in the course of which you made a deliberate, malicious, and totally unfounded attack on the integrity of the very trials in which you yourself have been a presiding judge. It is clear from the nature of your remarks that you were not speaking on behalf of your Tribunal or in your official capacity, but were volunteering purely personal views. Since your remarks are subversive of the interests and policies of the United States, they must not go unanswered.

"Your personal attacks against the attorneys who conducted the prosecution before your Tribunal as 'vindictive' and pursuing 'personal ambitions' are an insult to able, conscientious, loyal Americans who are rendering devoted service to their government. But these charges against the prosecution are not nearly so important as those you have brought against the conduct of the trial before your own Tribunal over which you yourself presided. If you in fact held the opinions you are quoted as expressing, you were guilty of grave misconduct in continuing to act in the case at all. In giving vent to these baseless slanders you have now fouled your own nest and sought to discredit the very judgment which you and your two distinguished colleagues have just rendered.

"You are quoted as saying that the defense had access only to such documents as the prosecution thought were relevant to the case, and that the prosecution protested against making complete documents available to the defense. You well know that these are wantonly false accusations. Your tribunal ruled that a great mass of captured documents from the Pentagon Building, Washington, D. C., required by the defense, should be sent to Nurnberg. On the basis of the Tribunal's ruling, these documents were sent to Nurnberg in trunks and put at the disposal of defense counsel. You are quoted as saying that I tried out of court to persuade the other tribunals to rescind your ruling. This is an utter fabrication. On the contrary, I repeatedly advised the War Department that the ruling should, of course, be complied with, and the War Department went to great trouble and expense to comply.

"Your statement that these trials are teaching the Germans only that they lost the war to tough conquerers would be laughable if its consequences were not so likely to be deplorable. Your own tribunal, thanks to the wisdom, patience and judicial detachment of your colleagues, accorded the defendants a trial which can be an outstanding and sadly needed lesson to the Germans in respect to the rights of an accused person, and an

The Tribunal then adjourned until 1:30 in the afternoon. No apology from the absent counsel was found by this writer in the transcript.

The Tribunal in its judgment passed squarely upon the questions of law presented. In referring to the plea of *respondeat superior,* the court held that it could be considered only in mitigation of the offense and went on to state:

> ". . . mitigation of punishment does not in any sense of the word reduce the degree of the crime. It is more a matter of grace than of defense. In other words, the punishment assessed is not a proper criterion to be considered in evaluating the findings of the court with reference to the degree of magnitude of the crime."[17]

Upon the question of the right of a belligerent nation to execute hostages, the court held squarely that this was permissible within reasonable limits under existing international law. It declared:

> "The idea that an innocent person may be killed for the criminal act of another is abhorrent to every natural law. We condemn the injustice of any such rule as a barbarous relic of ancient times. But it is not our province to write international law as we would have it—we must apply it as we find it.

---

unshakenable demonstration that the Nurnberg trials are for justice, not for vengeance. The one great obstacle to your trial having this beneficent effect is the wanton, reckless nonsense which you yourself are quoted as uttering.

"No large enterprise is ever perfect, and I would be the last man to reject any constructive criticism of the Office of Chief of Counsel for War Crimes or the conduct of the .prosecution. Instead of making any constructive moves while you were here, you have chosen to give out a baseless, malicious attack during the last hours of your eight-months stay and then leave town rather than confront those whom you have so outrageously slandered. I would use stronger language if it did not appear that your behaviour arises out of a warped, psychopathic mental attitude. It is indeed fortunate that your unreasoning bias is so clearly on behalf of the defendants since, in that sense, it tends to reinforce the verdict of your tribunal rather than undermine it. Unfortunately, those who stand eager to use your words to discredit the trials will not stress that factor.

"The statements attributed to you will, I fear, do grave harm to our country and your own court. They will be used by all the worse elements in Germany against the best. And your own words, I am sure, will injure you yourself far more seriously than anything I could say in this letter.

Very truly yours,
Telford Taylor
Brigadier General, U.S.A.
Chief of Counsel for War Crimes."

---

[17] Transcript 10,542.

> "An examination of the available evidence on the subject convinces us that hostages may be taken in order to guarantee the peaceful conduct of the populations of occupied territories and, when certain conditions exist and the necessary preliminaries have been taken, they may, as a last resort, be shot. The taking of hostages is based fundamentally on a theory of collective responsibility. . . . The occupant may properly insist upon compliance with regulations necessary to the security of the occupying forces and for the maintenance of law and order. In the accomplishment of this objective, the occupant may, only as a last resort, take and execute hostages."[18]

The Tribunal also held, and it would seem properly, that guerrillas are not entitled to the same privileges as legitimate members of an armed force.

> "Just as the spy may act lawfully for his country and at the same time be a war criminal to the enemy, so guerrillas may render great service to their country and, in the event of success, become heroes even, still they remain war criminals in the eyes of the enemy and may be treated as such. In no other way can an army guard and protect itself from the gadfly tactics of such armed resistance. And, on the other hand, members of such resistance forces must accept the increased risks involved in this mode of fighting. Such forces are technically not lawful belligerents and are not entitled to protection as prisoners of war when captured.
>
> "We think the rule is established that a civilian who aids, abets or participates in the fighting is liable to punishment as a war criminal under the laws of war. Fighting is legitimate only for the combatant personnel of a country. It is only this group that is entitled to treatment as prisoners of war and incurs no liability beyond detention after capture or surrender."[19]

The Tribunal, however, held squarely that prior to the execution of hostages, it was first necessary that a proclamation be made, giving the names and addresses of the hostages and notifying the population that upon the recurrence of the stated acts the hostages will be shot. The number so shot may not exceed in number that necessary to deter the recurrence of the particular act. In the absence of these steps, the execution of hostages would be considered a war crime.[20]

The Tribunal acquitted two of the defendants upon the basis that their lack of authority gave them immunity as to the

---

18 Transcript 10,446.

19 Transcript 10,441-2.

20 Transcript 10,447-8.

charges made. The destruction of northern Norway was considered justifiable upon the theory of apparent necessity. As to the other charges, the remaining defendants were convicted upon various counts, except for General von Weichs, who was separated from the case prior to its conclusion because of ill health. None of the defendants was sentenced to death.

The defendants in the RuSHA case. First row, left to right: Greifelt, Creutz, Meyer-Hetling, Schwarzenberger, Huebner, Lorenz, Brueckner, Hofmann, Schwalm, Sollmann; second row, left to right: Ebner, Tesch, and Inge Viermetz.

XXVII

CASE NO. 8 (RuSHA Case)

Judges (Presiding Judge marked by*)

*Lee B. Wyatt, Justice of the Supreme Court of Georgia
Daniel T. O'Connell, Judge of the Superior Court of Massachusetts
Johnson Tal Crawford, formerly Judge of the District Court of Oklahoma

Prosecution

James M. McHaney, Little Rock, Arkansas
Knox Lamb, Greenwood, Mississippi
Harold E. Neely, Hinton, West Virginia
Daniel J. Shiller, Waterbury, Connecticut
Edmund Schwenk, Washington, D. C.
E. Jane Johnson, Vancouver, Washington

Indictment

Counts: (1) Crimes against humanity;
(2) War crimes;
(3) Membership in SS.

Defense

Defendant	Chief Defense Counsel	Counts on which sentenced	Sentence
1. Ulrich Greifelt	Dr. Carl Haensel	1, 2, 3	Life imprisonment
2. Otto Hofmann	Dr. Alfried Schwarz	1, 2, 3	25 years
3. Richard Hildebrandt	Dr. Georg Froeschmann	1, 2, 3	25 years
4. Werner Lorenz	Ernst Hesse	1, 2, 3	20 years
5. Rudolf Creutz	Dr. Rudolf Merkel	1, 2, 3	15 years
6. Heinz Brueckner	Dr. Karl Doetzer	1, 2, 3	15 years
7. Herbert Huebner	Ernst Durchholz	1, 2, 3	15 years
8. Fritz Schwalm	Dr. Willi Heim	1, 2, 3	10 years
9. Konrad Meyer-Hetling	Dr. Kurt Behling	3	Credit for time in prison and released
10. Gregor Ebner	Dr. Herbert Thiele-Fredersdorf	3	Credit for time in prison and released

Defendant	Chief Defense Counsel	Counts on which sentenced	Sentence
11. Otto Schwarzenberger	Dr. Hans Gawlik	3	Credit for time in prison and released
12. Max Sollmann	Dr. Paul Ratz	3	Credit for time in prison and released
13. Guenther Tesch	Dr. Wilhelm Schmidt	3	Credit for time in prison and released
14. Inge Viermetz	Dr. Hermann Orth		Acquittal

The Indictment in Case Eight, commonly called the "RuSHA Case," was filed July 1, 1947, and served upon the defendants upon the same day. They all pleaded not guilty upon October 10, and the Prosecution opened its case upon October 20. The Prosecution employed 14 actual trial days, placed 27 witnesses on the stand, and introduced 904 documents. The defense counsel, of whom one had been a chief attorney before the International Military Tribunal, and five others had been assistants or associates, consumed 43 trial days, interrogating 70 witnesses, and introducing 1148 documents. The transcript was somewhat shorter than the average, totalling 5408 pages, of which the judgment comprised 130.

The nickname of the case is taken from the term *Rasse und Siedlungshauptamt,* which was the "Main Race and Resettlement Office," headed at various times by the defendant Hofmann and Hildebrandt. The remaining defendants were officials of this organization, or of two other similar organizations, the Well of Life Society and the Main Office for Repatriation of Racial Germans. The defendant Greifelt occupied the office of Reich Commissioner for the strengthening of German folkdom.

These various titles sound rather innocuous. Actually they were the backbone of the Nazi racial program. The defendants were charged with the function of kidnapping suitable children from occupied countries for Germanization, the forced Germanization of other nationals who were considered "Ethnic Germans," the evacuation of foreign nationals from their homes in favor of Germans or ethnic Germans, the extermination of inferior races, such as Slavs or Jews, and the commitment to concentration camps of persons not fitting into the Germanization program.

The transcript of evidence is of considerable interest from the point of view of development of the Nazi philosophy along racial lines. The defendants attempted to disclaim knowledge of extermination measures which were taken in occupied countries, and also to disclaim the powers which the Prosecution claimed they possessed.[1] The defendant Greifelt, for example, contended that he had objected to Himmler concerning some of his orders and had even suffered a heart attack as a result of that controversy.[2]

So far as rulings upon the evidence are concerned, there were very few points of novelty. The Tribunal was extremely vigorous in excluding opinion evidence and evidence not relevant to the issues.[3] It also refused to permit each of the fourteen defense counsel to interrogate each witness at length, but required each counsel to limit his examinations to matters particularly pertaining to his client.[4] Defense counsel apparently resented the ruling of the Tribunal, Dr. Froeschmann declaring, for example, "I then see no possibility to defend my client."[5] The Tribunal also refused to permit defense counsel to go into the period prior to 1939, stating that no charges of activities prior to that date would be considered by the Tribunal. Defense counsel persisted in desiring interrogation concerning this period, on the basis that any crime must have a preparation, but objection by the Prosecution was sustained.[6]

So far as leading questions were concerned, the Tribunal was quite lenient, possibly in an effort to conserve time. As a matter of fact, when the Prosecution objected at one point to the use of leading questions by defense counsel, the Tribunal declared: "I wish you would lead a little more and get right down to facts."[7]

The only woman defendant was acquitted. Five other defendants were given credit for time already served, while awaiting trial and during trial and were released. The remaining defendants were found guilty upon all three counts of the Indictment.

---

1 Transcript 1639 *et seq.*
2 Transcript 1639 *et seq.*
3 E.g., Transcript 1771-1823.
4 Transcript 1794.
5 Transcript 1795.
6 Transcript 1792-4.
7 Transcript 1712.

Einsatzgruppen Case. The defendants are, left to right, first row: Otto Ohlendorf, Jost, Naumann, Schulz, Six, Blobel, Blume, Sandberger, Seibert, Steimle, and Biberstein; left to right, second row: Braune, Haensch, Nosske, Ott, Klingelhoefer, Fendler, von Radetsky, Ruehl, Schubert, and Graf. (Absent, Rasch and Strauch, ill.)

XXVIII

CASE NO. 9 (Einsatzgruppen Case)

Judges (Presiding Judge marked by*)

*Michael A. Musmanno, Judge of Court of Common Pleas, Pennsylvania
John L. Speight, Alabama
Richard D. Dixon, Superior Court of North Carolina

Prosecution

Benjamin B. Ferencz, Nurnberg, Germany
Arnost Horlik-Hochwald, Leigh-On-Sea, England
Peter W. Walton, Monticello, Georgia
John E. Glancey, Washington, D. C.
James E. Heath, Norfolk, Virginia

Interrogators:
Rolf Wartenberg
Alfred Schwartz

Research Analysts: Nancy Fenstermacher, Henry Sachs, Barbara Bitter, Frederick S. Burin II, Charles Ippen

Indictment

Counts: (1) Crimes against humanity;
(2) War crimes;
(3) Membership in SS.

Defense

Defendant	Chief Defense Counsel	Counts on which sentenced	Sentence
1. Emil Hausmann	Committed suicide before trial		
2. Otto Ohlendorf	Dr. Rudolf Aschenauer	1, 2, 3	Death
3. Erich Naumann	Dr. Hans Gawlik	1, 2, 3	Death
4. Paul Blobel	Dr. Willi Heim	1, 2, 3	Death
5. Heinz Schubert	Dr. Josef Koessl	1, 2, 3	Death
6. Waldemar Klingelhoefer	Dr. Erich K. Mayer, Dr. Leiz	1, 2, 3	Death
7. Martin Sandberger	Dr. Bolko von Stein	1, 2, 3	Death
8. Eugen Steimle	Dr. Erich K. Mayer	1, 2, 3	Death
9. Walter Haensch	Dr. Fritz Riediger	1, 2, 3	Death
10. Eduard Strauch	Dr. Karl Gick	1, 2, 3	Death

Defendant	Chief Defense Counsel	Counts on which sentenced	Sentence
11. Willy Seibert	Dr. Gerhard Klinnert, Dr. Hans Gawlik	1, 2, 3	Death
12. Adolf Ott	Dr. Josef Koessl	1, 2, 3	Death
13. Werner Braune	Dr. Erich K. Mayer Dr. Stueburger	1, 2, 3	Death
14. Ernst Biberstein	Dr. Friedrich Bergold	1, 2, 3	Death
15. Walter Blume	Dr. Guenther Lummert	1, 2, 3	Death
16. Gustav Nosske	Dr. Karl Hoffmann Dr. Koessl	1, 2, 3	Life imprisonment
17. Heinz Jost	Dr. Alfred Schwarz	1, 2, 3	Life imprisonment
18. Franz Six	Hermann Ulmer	1, 2, 3	20 years
19. Waldemar von Radetsky	Dr. Paul Ratz	1, 2, 3	20 years
20. Erwin Schulz	Dr. Ernst Durcholz	1, 2, 3	20 years
21. Lothar Fendler	Dr. Hans Fritz	1, 2, 3	10 years
22. Felix Ruehl	Dr. Heinrich Link	3	10 years
23. Mathias Graf	Dr. Eduard Belzer	3	Credit for time in prison and released
24. Otto Rasch	Dr. Hans Surholt	Separated because of illness	

Case Nine, or the so-called "Einsatzgruppen Case," arose out of the activities of certain special units of the SS which accompanied the German army during the invasion and occupation of Soviet Russia. It was one of the bloody trials delving into mass murders committed under the direction of the defendants.

The Indictment was filed July 30, 1947, and served upon the defendants the same day. They were arraigned upon September 15, and the case opened upon October 20. The opening statement for the Prosecution is an eloquent plea for justice on behalf of the minority peoples destroyed by these persons. It points out by the statements of the German leaders their desire to destroy all minority groups and inferior races.

This was the only trial in which the Prosecution did not put a single witness upon the stand. The Prosecution took only two days for the presentation of its evidence, which consisted wholly of 258 captured documents. The defense, on the other hand, took 61 days to present its evidence, during which time it placed 51 witnesses on the stand and introduced 748 documents. Two of the attorneys had been chief counsel before the International Military Tribunal, and six more had been assistants or associates in the earlier proceedings. The transcript totaled only 6895 pages, of which 249 pages constituted the judgment. The closing statement for the Prosecution was made February 13, 1948, and judgment was pronounced on April 8, 9, and 10. The sentences were confirmed upon March 7, 1949, without reduction.

The evidence in the case, which consisted wholly of captured documents so far as the Prosecution was concerned, showed a clear plan of procedure approved by higher authority and carried into effect by the defendants. The defendants, however, were not executioners by training. Eight of them were lawyers, one a university professor, another a dentist, and another an expert on art. One was a former minister, and another, as an opera singer, had given concerts throughout Germany before he began his tour of Russia with the Einsatzgruppen.[1]

The group proceeded with only general orders, in the majority of instances, to exterminate Jews, gypsies, and Russian commissars. Sex of the victims apparently made no difference. Age was disregarded. Yet, in the course of the trial, some of the defendants attempted to justify their acts upon other than legal grounds. Klingelhoefer, for example, claimed that his predecessor had largely cleaned out the town of Tatarsk of Jews, but admitted that he had shot all remaining male Jews. It was pointed out that women were also included in this group. Thereupon, Klingelhoefer claimed that these people were shot because of their assistance to partisans. At this point the Tribunal stepped in and personally interrogated the witness. He stumbled badly under the penetrating cross-examination of the Tribunal, and it came out that these persons had never communicated with a partisan nor taken any overt step to indicate hostility toward the occupying force. The witness had concluded through some process of mental telepathy that they would be sympathetic to the partisans if given the opportunity, and had them executed before any occasion of that type could arise.[2] Klingelhoefer's attorney, Dr. Mayer, attempted by objection and comment to coach his witness, but without great success. At one point the president commented affably to the German attorney: "I'll have to give you credit for trying hard there, but let the witness testify."[3]

The only legal justification that Klingelhoefer could have advanced, which would have been more effective than his stumbling evasiveness, would have been that under the German decree of December 4, 1941, I (4), his actions were specifically authorized.

---

[1] Transcript 6648.

[2] Transcript 3840-3853, particularly 3849-50; also 3863-70, 3872-5.

[3] Transcript 3870.

It is doubtful that the Tribunal would have accepted this as a complete legal defense, however.

Similarly, the defendant Radetsky made an incredibly bad witness. When he was cross-examined about the order for the killing of Jews, he stated that he had not realized that women and children were to be included until forty or fifty thousand Jews had been killed.[4] The defendant Ohlendorf freely admitted that this group had killed some ninety thousand Jews in the Ukraine and Crimea, defending the killings on the grounds of "necessity." When interrogated about the killing of Jewish children, he stated that this was necessary as a "permanent security because. . . . the children were people who would grow up and surely, being the children of parents who had been killed, they would constitute a danger no smaller than the parents."[5]

The enforcement of their orders, at one point, reached the heights of absurdity. In the Crimea they encountered a group called Krimtschaks. They did not know whether these people were Jews or not, learning only that these people had originally migrated into the Crimea from some Mediterranean country and spoke the Turkish language. There was a rumor that sometime in the past some Jewish blood had entered the strain of these people. An inquiry was sent back to Berlin, and the reply came back that these people were to be regarded as Jews. They were duly executed.[6]

Gypsies were slaughtered in like manner, falling under the condemnation of the Nazi decree as inferior peoples.[7] Other liquidations were pointed out in detail in the analysis of the charges by the Tribunal.[8]

The closing argument by Brigadier General Telford Taylor was very effective and made a complete analysis of the defenses advanced and the answers thereto. These may be summarized briefly as follows:

1. **Reprisals.** General Taylor pointed out that the use of reprisals are strictly limited by the laws of war. In this case these steps were planned long in advance, and therefore could not be considered reprisals. Furthermore, wherever reprisal measures are to be employed, a trial of the persons charged is required under the Hague Rules of Land Warfare. No trial was ever given to the persons so slaughtered. Furthermore, since all of the persons executed, male and female, young and old, could

---

[4] Transcript 4257, 4312.
[5] Transcript 662.
[6] Transcript 6653-4.
[7] Transcript 6653-4.
[8] Transcript 6659-72.

not possibly have been partisans, the steps taken could not be considered as reprisal measures.

2. **Superior orders.** This could not be considered a defense where the order itself was palpably criminal. General Taylor referred to the Leipzig decision of the German Supreme Court in 1921 in the Llandovery Castle case, and referred also to Council Control Law No. 10. Nor, he argued, could this be considered in mitigation of these offenses, since these were educated men acting in cold blood and not in the heat of battle.

3. **No personal participation.** General Taylor pointed out that military and political leaders seldom themselves shoot a gun or even take part in a battle or an execution. In any event, they must be considered as controlling personnel or, at least, accessories.

4. **Necessity.** General Taylor pointed out that under no circumstances could these acts be considered as a vital part of warfare or justifiable under any existing rules of international law. There was no threat to the success of the war by the mere existence of these persons who were not engaged in partisan warfare or inimical activities.

5. **That the laws of war were obsolete.** The defense counsel had argued at length, as had the defendants in their statements to the International Military Tribunal, to the effect that bombing raids and other acts by the allies showed that the Hague Rules of Land Warfare were no longer controlling. General Taylor claimed that the bombing of urban or industrial centers was a part of accepted modern warfare, and that, as a matter of fact, the Germans had taken the initiative in such bombing raids. He pointed out also that the extermination of Jews and other racial groups was not in retaliation of such bombing raids, but had been planned long in advance. The defendants also had no military objective in mind in the commission of these crimes.

In addition to the foregoing matters, General Taylor pointed out that the acts charged against the defendants had long been a violation of local penal law, and amounted to the crime of murder. Therefore, irrespective of the rules of international law, the defendants could be punished by the occupying powers for these crimes against innocent nationals of other lands.

The Tribunal felt that the offenses had been proved beyond all reasonable doubt and declared:

> "Although the principal accusation is murder and, unhappily, man has been killing man ever since the days of Cain, the charge of purposeful homicide in this case reaches such fantastic proportions and surpasses such credible limits

that believability must be bolstered with assurance a hundred times repeated."[9]

With the exception of the defendant Emil Haussman, who committed suicide after indictment but prior to trial, and the defendant Otto Rasch, who had been severed from the trial because of illness, no defendant was acquitted. The defendant Mathias Graf was found guilty only as to Count Three, given credit for time previously spent in prison, and released. Fourteen of the defendants were condemned to death, two to life imprisonment, and the remainder to long prison terms.

---

[9] Transcript 6648.

Krupp case. The defendants are, left to right: Alfried Krupp, Houdremont, Mueller, Janssen, Pfiirsch, Ihn, Eberhardt, Korschan, Buelow, Lehmann, and Kupke, (Ewald Loeser absent, ill.)

XXIX

CASE NO. 10 (Krupp Case)

Judges (Presiding Judge marked by*)

*Hu C. Anderson, Justice of the Court of Appeals of Tennessee
Edward J. Daly, Judge of the Superior Court of Connecticut
William J. Wilkins, Judge of the Superior Court of Washington

Prosecution

Joseph W. Kaufman, 36 W. 44th Street, New York City
Rawlings Ragland, Lexington, Kentucky
W. Russell Thayer, New York City
Max Mandellaub, Washington, D. C.
Cecelia H. Goetz, New York City
Maurice C. Myers, Los Angeles, California
Maxmilian Koessler, Forest Hills, Long Island, New York
Irving G. Brilliant, Brooklyn, New York
John A. Bowler, Bradford, Pennsylvania
Maurice O. Huebsch, Chicago, Illinois
Richard Lansdale, Washington, D. C.

Of Counsel:

Herbert Goldenberg, Brooklyn, New York
Josif Marcu, Jr., Special Consultant

Interrogators:

Eric Kaufman
Manfred A. Isserman
Arthur T. Cooper
Paul H. Katscher
Joseph Schneider

Research Associates: Henry A. Buxbaum, Cornelius M. Cosman, Emile Skraly, Kaete H. Baumann, Leo Brondes, Vincent Czeisler, Fred Frantschi, Ernest Hegmann, Otto Lowengart, Joseph C. Pallenberg, Walter Pollitzer, Frederick A. Rager, Hanns Schade, Walter J. Steen, Max M. Austein, Bernard B. Fall, Lucette L. Von Halle, Ursula Hirsch, Marcel Lobel, Rudolph Popper, Ernest A. Reich, Vassily K. Targoni, Ernst L. K. Tislowitz, Vladimir Mandl.

Indictment

Counts: (1) Crimes against peace by planning and waging aggressive war;
(2) Spoliation;
(3) Slave labor;
(4) Conspiracy to commit crimes against peace.

Defense

Defendant	Chief Defense Counsel	Counts on which sentenced	Sentence
1. Alfried Krupp von Bohlen und Halbach	Dr. Otto Kranzbuehler		
	Dr. Geisseler	2, 3	12 years and forfeiture of property
2. Erich Mueller	Dr. Heinrich Link		
	Dr. Reintzenstein	2, 3	12 years
3. Friedrich von Buelow	Dr. Wolfgang Pohle		
	Dr. Maschke		
	Joseph T. Robinson of New York City	3	12 years
4. Friedrich Janssen	Dr. Alfred Schilf	2, 3	10 years
5. Prof. Eduard Houdremont	Dr. Kurt Peschke	2, 3	10 years
6. Max Ihn	Dr. Otto Kranzbuehler		
	Dr. Hennig	3	9 years
7. Karl Eberhardt	Dr. Walter Siemers		
	Dr. Weiz		
	Dr. Gollnik		
	Dr. Arndt	2, 3	9 years
8. Ewald Loeser	Dr. Kurt Behling		
	Dr. Wendland	2, 3	7 years
9. Heinrich Lehmann	Dr. Heinz Wolf	3	6 years
10. Heinrich Korschan	Dr. Erich Wandschneider		
	Dr. Heinzke	3	6 years
11. Hans Kupke	Dr. Alfred Behringer	3	Credit for time in prison and released
12. Karl Pfirsch	Dr. Bernd Vorwerk		Acquittal

Special Counsel (For all defendants)

Dr. Walter Ballas

Case number Ten was the last of the industrialist cases. It will be recalled that Gustav Krupp von Bohlen und Halbach had been indicted in the proceedings before the International Military Tribunal as representing the position of German industry.

The Prosecution in that case was bitterly disappointed when medical examination showed his physical condition to be such that he could not possibly stand trial, and his mental state to be almost that of a gibbering idiot. A motion had been made by the Prosecution to substitute Alfried Krupp von Bohlen und Halbach as a party defendant, which was refused by the Tribunal.[1] Consequently, Alfried Krupp von Bohlen und Halbach, the son, and his associates conducting the Krupp industries were made defendants in the subsequent proceedings.

The Indictment against the defendants was filed August 17, 1947, and served upon the defendants the following day. They were arraigned upon November 17 and the case opened December 8. The Prosecution occupied 46 trial days, placing 80 witnesses on the stand, introducing 1471 documents in evidence, and having an additional 145 documents marked "for identification," which was the procedure the Tribunal used in this case to distinguish those documents of which it would take judicial notice. The defense opened its case upon March 22, 1948, consuming 44 trial days, placing 97 witnesses on the stand, and introducing 2829 documents in addition to 318 marked "for identification." The final argument for the defense took five days and the briefs of defense counsel, two of whom had been attorneys before the International Military Tribunal, were more than 1500 pages in length. The closing statement for the Prosecution was made June 24, 1948. The transcript consisted of 13,454 pages, of which the judgment occupied 223, the judgment being rendered upon July 31, 1948.

There is a slight discrepancy in the number of witnesses as listed above, which was the summary by the Judge Advocate General's office and that stated in the judgment of the Tribunal. In its judgment the Tribunal referred to the number of witnesses stating that 117 had testified in open court for both sides, and 134 additional witnesses before commissioners, or a total of 251 instead of 177. It is very interesting to note that the total number of witnesses does not include any of the defendants, as not a single defendant in this case took the witness stand. This may have been due partially to the recalcitrant attitude both of the defendants and their counsel, or it may have been due to the Tribunal's early ruling that the affidavit of any defendant would not be considered as evidence against any other defendant unless the affiant was placed upon the witness stand.[2] The defendants, however, did not even avail themselves fully of the right to make a final statement to the Tribunal. Only one of

---

1 See p. 92, *ante*.

2 Transcript 1029.

the defendants made a final statement for himself alone; one other defendant made a final statement on behalf of himself and the other ten defendants.

The opening statement for the Prosecution is a well organized document from an historical point of view, tracing the developments in Germany from the period of the Versailles Treaty through the war period. It traces extensively the part of the Krupp industries in the rearmament of Germany, and in the preparation and plans for aggressive war. These form the basis of Counts One and Four of the Indictment. However, on March 12, 1948, the defendants filed a joint motion for a verdict of not guilty as to Counts One and Four, and on April 5, 1948, this motion was sustained, and these counts were dismissed. The reason for the dismissal of those counts was not the same in the minds of all of the judges. Apparently reliance was placed upon the acquittals of Schacht and Speer by the International Military Tribunal upon the ground that those defendants were not shown to have had sufficient knowledge of Hitler's plans for war. Presiding Justice Hu C. Anderson expressed himself more definitely to the effect that he felt that criminal liability for conspiracy, planning or waging of aggressive war had to be restricted to persons in a policy-making capacity, without extension to industrialists and private citizens, who may participate in the war effort but have no voice or control in the initiation or conduct of a war. Judge Wilkins, on the other hand, felt that while these counts were an excellent historical indictment against the Krupp industries they were not pertinent in the charges brought against the particular defendants on trial. He pointed out that these persons had risen to power in the industries only a short time before the outbreak of the war, had no control over the firm's policies prior to that time, and, therefore, all of the data introduced by the Prosecution relating to acts immediately after Versailles or in the growth of the Nazi party was wholly irrelevant. If Gustav Krupp had been the defendant upon trial, Judge Wilkins inferred that he would have voted differently as to the dismissal of these counts.[3]

Accordingly, the only evidence considered by the Tribunal related to Counts Two and Three of the Indictment. The evidence under these counts is well summarized in the judgment of the Tribunal. The Tribunal definitely agreed with the Prosecution that a warring nation cannot expropriate property of an occupied country indiscriminately. All of the charges of spoliation had to do with factories and machines. The Rothschild plant was one of those involved. The Berndorfer industries in Austria

---

[3] Transcript 13,435-7.

were another example upon which the majority opinion does not apparently rest a responsibility, but upon which Judge Wilkins, dissenting, felt that liability should have been imposed.

The story of that deal is that immediately after the Anschluss, negotiations were opened by Krupp to purchase this plant. A substantial interest was owned by a leading bank by way of trust. The bank had no desire to sell, and, if a sale had been contemplated, it would have been far in excess of the amount which Krupp desired to pay. Personal contacts were made by Krupp with Goering, there being some evidence to indicate that contact had been made with reference to the Berndorfer plant prior to the Anschluss. Goering issued orders that the interest in the Berndorfer plant must be sold, and that bids would be received. It was then arranged that no one except Krupp would be able to bid upon the plant, and he secured these vast Austrian industries at his bid price. Within a short time after the absorption of these plants, they were carried on the corporate balance sheets at a figure several times larger than that of the purchase price. Judge Wilkins definitely felt that these incidents should have been considered.[4] The majority opinion also ignored like offenses in Yugoslavia, Greece, and the Soviet Union apparently upon the basis of lack of jurisdiction.[5]

The Tribunal dealt more satisfactorily in its judgment with Count Three, dealing primarily with the use of forced labor, violations of the Hague Rules of Land Warfare with reference to the misuse of prisoners and the failure to properly protect, lodge, feed, and clothe the persons who were the subject of forced labor. The defendants contended that no person, including the German workers, was safe from the allied bombing raids. However, it appeared that a definite discrimination was made in this regard, and that, while German workers usually had bombproof shelters to which they could go, the forced labor had to rely upon slit trenches or no protection whatever. The Tribunal at one point declared that it was no answer to say that because of the bombing attacks and the military situation in general, life for everyone in Essen, including Germans, had become dangerous and difficult. The prisoners of war, concentration camp inmates, and, in large part, the foreign civilian workers were not in Essen by choice. They had been brought there to an enemy country against their will and kept there in a state of involuntary servitude. They were utterly unable to help themselves and were absolutely dependent upon the officials of the Krupp firm for protection and for their every need.[6]

---

[4] Transcript 13,408.

[5] Transcript 13,293.

[6] Transcript 13,315.

The Tribunal went on to point out that, by reason of this situation, the defendants were absolutely responsible for the conditions under which these workers served and under a duty to provide ample food, lodging, and safe conditions. Persons attempting to escape were recaptured and arrested, and these persons received cruel treatment and brutalities with knowledge of the plant leaders. The inadequate housing conditions were treated at length. The Tribunal even pointed out that Ihn and Lehmann arranged for the destruction of a group of Hungarian Jewesses rather than to permit their repatriation by the allies. In view of this conclusion by the Tribunal, it is amazing that these defendants received sentences of only nine years and six years, respectively, when other tribunals had condemned defendants to death for like offenses. The Tribunal went on to say in this regard, "In this connection it is argued that the defendants had scant knowledge of the persecutions of the Jews by Nazi leaders. . . . . . The fact was common knowledge not only in Germany but throughout the civilized world."[7] The Tribunal pointed out evidence introduced by the defendants themselves which showed such knowledge. For example, an affidavit of Mickenschrieber had been offered. The Tribunal stated: "It was offered along with other documents to show that the officials of the firm were not in accord with the attitude of the Nazi regime toward Jews. But it shows also without doubt they knew of that abominable policy as early as 1936."[8] The Tribunal stated also that the letters introduced in evidence showed a great desire upon the part of the Krupp officials to employ Russian prisoners of war and to conscript Belgian and Dutch workers when their voluntary contracts expired, thus making them parties to the entire forced labor program. Krupp maintained labor offices in France and other nations, and drafted workers for employment in their plants, even going so far as to enter into direct negotiations with concentration camps for the services of the inmates.

The defendants again relied upon the doctrine of "necessity." The Tribunal pointed out that all that probably would have happened in the event of disagreement with the Nazi regime was nationalization of the plant by the government. None of the defendants, except Krupp, could be considered as an owner of the plant, and therefore had nothing to lose but a job. This was hardly sufficient, it felt, to justify a claim of necessity. In reply to the argument, the Tribunal declared:

---

[7] Transcript 12,380-1.

[8] Transcript 13,381-2.

". . . . . the question from the standpoint of the individual defendants resolves itself into this proposition: To avoid losing my job or the control of my property, I am warranted in employing thousands of civilian deportees, prisoners of war, and concentration camp inmates, keeping them in a state of involuntary servitude; exposing them daily to death or great bodily harm, under conditions which did in fact result in the deaths of many of them; and working them in an undernourished condition in the production of armament intended for use against the people who would liberate them and indeed even against the people of their homelands.

"If we may assume that as a result of opposition to Reich policies, Krupp would have lost control of his plant and the officials their positions, it is difficult to conclude that the law of necessity justified a choice favorable to themselves and against the unfortunate victims who had no choice at all in the matter. Or, in the language of the rule, that the remedy was not disproportioned to the evil. In this connection it should be pointed out that there is a very respectable authority for the view that the fear of the loss of property will not make the defense of duress available.

"But the extreme possibility hinted at was that Gustav Krupp and his officials would not only have lost control of the plant but would have been put in a concentration camp had they refused to adopt the illegal measures necessary to meet the production quotas.

". . . . . . in all fairness it must be said that in any view of the evidence the defendants, in a concentration camp, would not have been in a worse plight than the thousands of helpless victims whom they daily exposed to danger of death and great bodily harm from starvation and the relentless air raids upon the armament plants to say nothing of involuntary servitude and the other indignities which they suffered. The disparity in the number of the actual and potential victims is also thought provoking."[9]

With reference to the conduct of the trial, there were several points of confusion. The first major difficulty arose with reference to the doctrine of judicial notice, and this was never entirely clarified. In the early stages of the trial, an objection was made by defense counsel to certain documents that were offered under the theory of judicial notice, at which time the Tribunal pointed out that when it took judicial notice of an instrument, it did not consider it as evidence.[10] Immediately thereafter the Prosecution referred to a part of the record of the International Military Tribunal and the provisions of the Council Control Law

[9] Transcript 13,396-7.
[10] Transcript 959-962.

that "The Tribunal shall take judicial notice of the records and findings of military and other tribunals of the United Nations."[11] Defense Attorney Geisseler then pointed out that the Tribunal in the Jurists' case, case number three, had held that evidence submitted in the International Military Tribunal proceedings would have to be submitted again as evidence if considered to have any probative value.[12] The Prosecution took the position that Tribunal III was the only one giving a narrow construction to the doctrine of judicial notice.[13] Judge Daly declared that such documents would be assigned numbers only "for identification" and would not be received, in this particular instance the material referring to a speech of Hitler which he felt could not be admissible against the present defendants.[14] Judge Wilkins then stated that he had misled the Prosecution by announcing that all exhibits, even those for judicial notice, would be admitted, but added that he had announced later that same day, after consultation with the other members of the Tribunal, that he had been reversed on this point.[15] Judge Daly then stated that records of tribunals, other than the International Military Tribunal, would be treated in the same manner.[16] Justice Anderson next raised the question as to whether the Tribunal must take judicial notice of all evidence, as well as findings in those cases. The Prosecution replied in the affirmative.[17] Judge Wilkins then stated that this would have to be limited to evidence considered pertinent in that case.[18] The Prosecution agreed that it would not ask the court to take judicial notice of anything of which it did not furnish photostatic copies.[19]

Defense counsel at that point informed the Tribunal that it was thoroughly confused. In the first place, what right did defense counsel have to object to such exhibits? Second, what right did the Prosecution have to read such documents if they were not offered as exhibits? Third, what weight would be given to such documents?[20] The Tribunal then stated that it would confer upon this matter and determine later as to the effect to be given documents recognized under the doctrine of judicial notice.[21] After this question was clarified, both parties availed

---

[11] Transcript 964.
[12] Transcript 965, 978 *et seq.*
[13] Transcript 990-1.
[14] Transcript 980.
[15] Transcript 981.
[16] Transcript 982.
[17] Transcript 982.
[18] Transcript 983-4.
[19] Transcript 984.
[20] Transcript 987.
[21] Transcript 991-3.

themselves of that form of procedure, and the court apparently gave some weight to such documents, but not the same effect as given to those pertaining directly to the defendants themselves.

It has already been observed that affidavits of defendants not taking the witness stand were not considered in evidence against the remaining defendants. At one point, Defense Attorney Geisseler objected to an affidavit of Alfried Krupp upon the basis that it had been procured by deceit. The objection was overruled, the Tribunal holding that such matters were proper to show only when introducing the defense.[22] At another point Geisseler objected to such an affidavit upon the ground that it did not show that it was made in the presence of an official authorized to accept affidavits. The Tribunal inquired if the document bore Krupp's signature. When this was admitted, the court held the grounds of the objection to be immaterial.[23] However, at another place when Dr. Link denied that an offered document was connected with his defendant, and pointed out that there was no affidavit to establish validity, the Tribunal required the Prosecution to produce the person capturing such document to prove its validity.[24] Again, defense counsel objected that by the time a document was submitted by the Prosecution, and the time it became available to defense counsel to examine, a lapse of fourteen days to three weeks occurred. The prosecutor stated that the delay was due to the intervention of a holiday period. Defense counsel stated that it never took less than eight to ten days under ordinary circumstances. The Tribunal instructed the secretary general to check into the matter and to expedite the receipt of such materials by defense counsel.[25]

One of the most interesting occurrences in all of these proceedings arose from a contempt charge filed against the defense counsel individually. There had been discussions between the Prosecution, Defense, and Tribunal as to possibly shortening the proceedings by having certain of the evidence taken before a commissioner, as had been done in some of the other trials, including the proceedings before the International Military Tribunal at Nuremberg. Upon this particular day the Tribunal had apparently arranged to have a commissioner available for hearing certain evidence that afternoon. Justice Wilkins asked Mr. Thayer of the Prosecution staff if he could arrange for evidence to be taken before the commissioner at such time. Thayer replied that he could if defense counsel were agreeable.[26] Defense

---

[22] Transcript 1106-7.

[23] Transcript 1012-3.

[24] Transcript 1025-8.

[25] Transcript 1180.

[26] Transcript 1788.

counsel Wecker stated that all defense counsel and all defendants wanted to be present at that time and claimed that they had such a right under Ordinance 7. Wilkins stated that he was incorrect.[27] A short time later defense counsel Pohle again raised the question about the commissioner, stating that all defendants insisted upon their right to be present.[28] Defense attorney Schilf then arose and wanted to make a statement. The exact statements which occurred then were as follows:

"P. J. Daly: There will be no further discussion on that. We will proceed with the document book. Proceed with the document book, please.

"Dr. Schilf: Your Honor—

"P. J. Daly: Proceed with the document book—

"Dr. Schilf: Your Honor, I protest that I am not permitted to go on—

"P. J. Daly: Did you hear me say, counsellor, that there will be no further discussion on the question of the commissioner's hearing?

"Dr. Schilf: Yes, and I protest against this ruling and request that a decision of another court—

"P. J. Daly: You will please take your seat or I will order you removed from the courtroom.

"Dr. Schilf: I request that that be done.

"P. J. Daly: All right, you can remove yourself, then. Proceed."[29]

What happened immediately thereafter must be reconstructed solely from the statements of persons afterward. In this particular case the defendants themselves frequently were absent from many of the hearings, and anywhere from three to eight defense counsel would be present at some time or another. As Schilf turned away from the rostrum, he apparently had an afterthought and turned back toward the Tribunal. He was checked by the marshal, who beckoned for him to leave. He then picked up his documents and left and was followed from the court room by other German counsel. The morning was almost gone, and the Tribunal noticed nothing strange about the occurrence. That afternoon the Tribunal reconvened, and the Prosecution started in with other documents. Not a single defendant or defense counsel was present. After this had continued for about an hour, the Tribunal instructed the marshal to see where the defendants and defense counsel were and to tell them to come down to the court room.[30] The Tribunal then proceeded to

[27] Transcript 1788-9.
[28] Transcript 1817-8.
[29] Transcript 1818.
[30] Transcript 1855.

interrogate the defense counsel and to lecture them upon their conduct, pointing out that the Prosecution had been introducing evidence while the defendants were wholly unrepresented by any attorney.[31] Becoming increasingly irate about the matter, the Tribunal then ordered the marshal to take into custody defense attorneys Wecker, Reitzenstein, Schilf, Gollnik, Geisseler, and Pohle.[32] Attorney Geisseler, a young Nazi with no prior trial experience, tried twice to make a statement and was stopped by the Tribunal.

These counsel were detained over the weekend in custody and were brought before the Tribunal on Monday for determination of steps to be taken. Prior to that time none of the tribunals had had disciplinary questions arise to any substantial degree. In the first case, the Medical Case, one witness had been sentenced to ninety days' imprisonment for attacking a defendant. In the Justice Case, grave irregularities by an attorney and his assistant were discovered by the Tribunal, and the lawyer was sentenced to thirty days' imprisonment and disqualified from acting as defense counsel. This was the first time, however, in which an entire group of defense counsel had taken concerted action.

Upon reconvening the Tribunal had the record read, together with its admonishments, to defense counsel.[33] Dr. Kranzbuehler, admittedly one of the most brilliant of all German defense counsel to appear in the various proceedings, who had been absent at the time of the prior occurrence, acted as defense counsel for the accused attorneys. He promptly filed a challenge to the jurisdiction of the court to pass upon this matter, which was overruled.[34] Dr. Schilf was then placed upon the stand and examined at length.[35] The marshal was then examined by Dr. Kranzbuehler and the Tribunal.[36] Dr. Wecker testified,[37] followed by defense attorney Geisseler.[38] While the other defense counsel had taken a rather restrained position, Dr. Geisseler refused to adopt that view. The other attorneys stated that they had been disturbed and apprehensive as to the treatment accorded Dr. Schilf and had followed him from the court room in order to draft a petition to the Tribunal to reconsider the question of appearances before the commissioner and to explain their

[31] Transcript 1857-1870.
[32] Transcript 1870.
[33] Transcript 1872-80.
[34] Transcript 1881-4.
[35] Transcript 1884-1938.
[36] Transcript 1939-43.
[37] Transcript 1944-85.
[38] Transcript 1989-2011.

desire for further argument on this matter. They realized that the defendants were left without representation, but felt this other matter to be of paramount importance, and had no intention of showing any contempt for the Tribunal. Geisseler, on the other hand, stated that he felt that the defense counsel were being abused and mistreated, and that he would act the same way if the occasion arose again. With the exception of Geisseler, the other defense counsel apologized for their conduct.[39] Dr. Kranzbuehler then went into extended argument with the Tribunal concerning the position of his clients, upholding Geisseler's position vigorously.[40] When the Tribunal stated that the incident probably would not have occurred if Kranzbuehler had been present, he disagreed, stating that he had felt that Geisseler's position was not abnormal and reiterating his dissatisfaction with an earlier ruling of the Tribunal where it had refused to permit the American law firm of Foley & Carroll to join as defense counsel. The Tribunal clarified its position as to this law firm, and then entered judgment discharging all of the attorneys from custody,[41] but with reprimands,[42] and barring Geisseler from all further participation in the proceedings.[43] Attorney Wendland, who was not present at the time of that hearing, subsequently stated his position and was also purged of contempt.[44]

As in the case of the other industrialists, no defendant received a sentence more severe than a mere prison term, with the exception of Alfried Krupp, whose property was confiscated, the only defendant to receive such a penalty in any of the

---

39 Transcript 2012-2019.

40 Transcript 2019-2040.

41 Transcript 2042-5.

42 Transcript 2053.

43 Transcript 2050-2.

44 Transcript 2056-7. This was an unfortunate instance which probably would not have occurred had the Tribunal members been familiar with the differences existing in courtroom decorum in the United States and other nations. One of the other judges wrote to me as follows: "It is the rule, however, as I understand it, both in England and in some continental countries, that counsel has the right whenever he feels that he has been insulted or that his client is being unjustly dealt with, to throw up his brief and retire. I remember that Marshall Hall did that on at least one occasion before the Court of Appeals and that Judah P. Benjamin did the same thing when arguing a case before the House of Lords. I'm quite sure that if the tribunal had been advised that this was a customary right exercised by counsel that they probably would not have issued the citation or proceeded with it. On the other hand, if the tribunal had made clear to defense counsel that it did not recognize that right, then I'm quite sure that the German lawyers would not have withdrawn or attempted to do so.

"There was a very real feeling of regret in the Palace of Justice that this unfortunate affair occurred * * * * *."

Nuremberg proceedings. Judges Wilkins and Daly agreed upon the sentences fixed. Judge Anderson concurred only in the prison sentences for Krupp and Kupke. The others he thought were too severe, because of mitigating circumstances not mentioned in the judgment. He felt that Loeser should have been released because of his efforts in cooperation with the underground to overthrow Hitler and the Nazi regime, which he felt had been convincingly established.[45] He also dissented from the order forfeiting Alfried Krupp's property.

In connection with the confiscation decree, there has been an interesting subsequent development which has not yet been fully crystallized. Gustav Krupp actually was not a member of the Krupp line. He married into the Krupp family and had been permitted by special dispensation of Kaiser Wilhelm to take the name Krupp. He was a very active and successful executive who built the business to even greater heights than it had previously enjoyed. His wife, Bertha, after whom the first great cannon was named, was an original member of the line. When Gustav's health began to fail, he and his wife, Bertha, were permitted to make a tax-free transfer of the interests represented by this great enterprise to Alfried Krupp, who actually did not come into power in the business until around 1943. Alfried actually appears to be somewhat of a weak sister. At any rate, following the order of confiscation, Bertha has brought an action to rescind the original transfer claiming that the enterprises really belonged to her, and were, therefore, not subject to forfeiture as Alfried's property. Whether or not she will be successful in this regard, only time can tell. But if it was the intention of the Tribunal to break up the great industry of Krupp from a point of view of preventing Germany from rebuilding for future wars as quickly, some question might be legitimately raised as to why such steps were not taken in the case of other industrialists. Of course, another question might be raised that if the members of the Krupp firm were guilty of spoliation, as was also established in the Flick case, by taking over plants and machinery in occupied countries, why does not this same charge apply to Soviet Russia, which has stripped countries occupied by it, including Germany, of like plants and material?

---

[45] Transcript 13,451-2.

Ministries Case. The defendants are shown, first row, left to right: Weizsaecker, Steengracht, Keppler, Bohle, Woermann, Ritter, Erdmannsdorff, Veesenmayer, Lammers, Stuckart, Darre; second row, left to right: Dietrich, Berger, Schellenberg, Schwerin-Krozigk, Puhl, Rasche, Koerner, Pleiger, and Kehrl. (Otto Meissner absent, ill.)

XXX

CASE NO. 11 (Ministries Case)

Judges (Presiding Judge marked by*)

*William C. Christianson, former Justice of the Supreme Court of Minnesota
Leon W. Powers, former Justice of the Supreme Court of Iowa
Robert F. Maguire, Portland, Oregon

Prosecution

Robert M. W. Kempner, Lansdowne, Pennsylvania
Morris Amchan, Arlington, Virginia
Frederick H. Bird, Boston, Massachusetts
Arnold Buchtal
William H. W. Caming, New York City
Meyer L. Casman, Philadelphia, Pennsylvania
Frank A. Esterkin, London, England
Arthur Fanta, Carlisle, Cumberland, England
James M. Fitzpatrick, Washington, D. C.
Paul H. Gantt, Williamsburg, Virginia
Ralph J. Goodman, New York City
R. Quentin Haden, Ava, Missouri
Alexander G. Hardy, Washington, D. C., Cochituate, Massachusetts
Paul L. Horecky, London, England
Irvin M. Kent, Poughkeepsie, New York
Walter Klein
Maximilian Koessler, Forest Hills, Long Island, New York
Alvin Landis, Beverly Hills, California
John Lewis, Suffern, New York
Charles S. Lyon, New York City
Max Mandellaub, Washington, D. C.
Mrs. Dorothea G. Minskoff, Silver Springs, Maryland
Virginia Miller
Donald C. Noggle, Pontiac, Michigan
Herbert W. Nurnberg, Chicago, Illinois
Walter W. O'Haire, Pittston, Pennsylvania
Arthur L. Petersen, New York City
John J. Posner, Brooklyn, New York
Walter J. Rockler, Chicago, Illinois
Rawlings Ragland (Deputy Chief of Counsel), Lexington, Kentucky

Herbert Schonfield, New York City
Walter Speyer, London, England
Drexel A. Sprecher
Joseph H. Stone
H. Russell Thayer, New York City
Foster Adams, Economic Consultant

Indictment

Counts:
(1) The planning, initiating, and waging of aggressive war;
(2) Conspiracy to commit crimes against peace;
(3) Murder and mistreatment of prisoners of war;
(4) Atrocities against German nationals from 1933-1939;
(5) Atrocities against civilian population;
(6) Plunder and spoliation;
(7) Slave labor;
(8) Membership in SS.

Defense

Defendant	Chief Defense Counsel	Counts on which sentenced	Sentence
1. Gottlob Berger	Dr. Georg Froeschmann	3, 5, 7, 8	25 years
2. Hans Heinrich Lammers	Dr. Alfred Seidl	1, 3, 5, 7, 8,	20 years
3. Edmund Veesenmayer	Dr. Karl Doetzer	5, 7, 8	20 years
4. Paul Koerner	Dr. Justus Koch, Dr. Gerhard Rauschenbach	1, 6, 7, 8	15 years
5. Paul Pleiger	Dr. Robert Servatius	6, 7	15 years
6. Hans Kehrl	Dr. Heinrich Grube	5, 6, 7, 8	15 years
7. Wilhelm Keppler	Dr. Werner Schubert	1, 5, 6, 8	10 years
8. Lutz Schwerin von Krozigk	Dr. Stefan Fritsch	5, 6	10 years
9. Ernest Weizsaecker	Hellmut Becker Warren E. Magee of Washington, D. C.	1, 5	7 years
10. Richard Walther Darre	Dr. Hans Merkel	5, 6, 8	7 years
11. Otto Dietrich	Dr. Friedrich Bergold	5, 8	7 years
12. Ernst Woermann	Dr. Alfred Schilf	1, 5	7 years
13. Karl Rasche	Dr. Egon Kubuschok	6, 8	7 years
14. Gustav Adolf Steengracht von Moyland	Dr. Carl Haensel	3, 5	7 years

	Defendant	Chief Defense Counsel	Counts on which sentenced	Sentence
15.	Walter Schellenberg	Dr. Fritz Riediger	5, 8	6 years
16.	Emil Puhl	Dr. Hans Gawlik	5	5 years
*17.	Ernst Wilhelm Bohle	Dr. Elisabeth Gombel	8	5 years
18.	Karl Ritter	Dr. Egon Kubuschok	3	4 years
19.	Wilhelm Stuckart	Dr. Hans Von Zwehl	5, 6, 8	Credit for time in prison and released
20.	Otto Meissner	Dr. Fritz Sauter		Acquittal
21.	Otto von Erdmannsdorff	Dr. Bernd Vorwerk		Acquittal

Special Consultant, Dr. Werner von Schmieden

The Indictment in Case Eleven, commonly called the "Ministries Case," was filed November 1, 1947, and served upon the defendants November 4. The defendants were arraigned upon December 20, and much to the amazement of the Tribunal, Prosecution, and all persons concerned, one defendant pleaded guilty. The defendant Ernst Wilhelm Bohle pleaded guilty to membership of the SS with knowledge of its criminal activities, and incidentally, was found guilty only upon this one count and sentenced to five years' imprisonment. One wonders whether the fact that he had a woman counsel had anything to do with his decision to enter the plea of guilty.

The remaining defendants pleaded not guilty, and the case opened for trial on January 6, 1948. The Prosecution occupied 51 trial days, put 109 witnesses on the stand, and introduced 4372 documents. The defense counsel, which included five of the chief attorneys and three associate or assistant counsel appearing before the International Military Tribunal, opened the defense on May 3 and occupied 110 trial days, introducing 246 witnesses and 4695 documents. Closing arguments for the Prosecution were made November 9, 1948, the total transcript of the proceedings, exclusive of judgment, totaling 28,085 pages. The judgment itself occupied 833 pages and was not given until April 14, 1949, or more than five months later.

To understand this case, it is necessary to understand the position which the defendants occupied and their relationship to the entire plan of the war. In the opening statement[1] an excellent analysis was made of the charges brought and the place of each defendant in relationship to the acts charged.

---

* Bohle later married his counsel, who is now in the United States.

1 Transcript 1-110.

Upon the charges relating to war economy, the Prosecution placed the defendants Koerner, Pleiger, Kehrl, and Keppler in that category. Koerner was deputy to Goering in the office of the Four Year Plan; Pleiger, the dominant figure in the huge Hermann Goering Works, a great industrial plant participating in this program. Kehrl held various high governmental economic positions, and Keppler was affiliated with the Foreign Office. Upon the banking aspects, the defendants Rasche, who was chairman of the Vorstand of the Dresdner Bank, and Emil Puhl, vice president of the Reichsbank, were those charged. As to government ministries, the defendants were Hans Lammers, Reich Minister and Chief of the Reich Chancellery; Darre, minister for food and agriculture; von Krozigk, minister of finance; Dietrich, assistant to Goebbels in the propaganda ministry; Meissner, chief of the Presidential Chancery, and Wilhelm Stuckart.

And, as influential in the foreign office in shaping the policies thereof, were such persons as von Weizsaecker, who had been minister to Switzerland and Norway, and who later became undersecretary of the German foreign office; Ernst Bohle, chief of the foreign department of the Nazi party; and Steengracht, Keppler, Woermann, Ritter, von Erdmannsdorff, and Veesenmayer, all of whom were influential in their positions. In addition, Lieutenant General Berger, who had headed the SS main office with administrative authority over the Waffen SS, and Brigadier General Schellenberg, who headed the foreign intelligence branch of the SS, were indicted.

The Prosecution in its opening statement compared the broad scope of the charges to those of the International Military Tribunal. There is much justification for the comparison. The persons charged ranged from leaders in the SS to bankers and to politicians. The charges were sweeping and extensive in character. All of the defendants were influential persons. The effect of the foreign office and of the particular defendants were traced through the Czechoslovakian, Austrian, Polish, and other incidents, so as to tie them in with a common knowledge of the entire plan. The Tribunal, however, felt that there was no justification for the inclusion of the charges under Count Four, and this count was dismissed upon the motion of the defendants. This is consistent with the rulings of the other tribunals that it was not within their province to examine into crimes committed prior to the outbreak of the war. This, it will be seen, is contrary to the principle advanced throughout by the Prosecution that these courts were sitting in the place and stead of German courts with full rights to examine into crimes committed against German nationals. In view of the fact that there was actually no system of justice in Germany, either prior to or during the time of the war, which could effectively punish such persons, there would seem to be some moral justification for the position of the Prosecution, even though the legal theory is somewhat attenuated.

Despite the length of the transcript and the corresponding length of the judgment, there are no procedural points of particular interest in the case. The hearing was conducted dispassionately, and the rulings upon evidentiary matters were consistent with accepted rules of evidence, giving rise to no freak or unusual declarations requiring comment. There are some excellent statements in the judgment itself concerning certain of the charges brought. The decision was not a unanimous one, Judge Powers filing a lengthy dissenting opinion, although he did concur in the judgment of the Tribunal under Counts Seven and Eight of the Indictment.

With reference to the determination of the Tribunal upon the charges concerning crimes against peace, the following interesting declaration was made:

> "Obviously, no man may be condemned for fighting in what he believes is the defense of his native land, even though his belief be mistaken. Nor can he be expected to undertake an independent investigation to determine whether or not the cause for which he fights is the result of an aggressive act of his own government. One can be guilty only where knowledge of aggression in fact exists, and it is not sufficient that he have suspicions that the war is aggressive.
>
> "Any other test of guilt would involve a standard of conduct both impracticable and unjust."[2]

The Tribunal also declared:

> "We may not, in justice, apply to these defendants because they are Germans, standards of duty and responsibility which are not equally applicable to the officials of the Allied Powers and to those of all nations. Nor should Germans be convicted for acts or conduct which, if committed by Americans, British, French, or Russians would not subject them to legal trial and conviction."[3]

The Tribunal also pointed out, however, that it was wholly unfair that the private citizens should always suffer, because of the loss of a war by a nation, and the leaders escape unscathed.[4] The Tribunal went on to state:

> "No one would question the right of any country to use its armed forces to halt the violator in his tracks and to

[2] Transcript, page 41 of judgment.

[3] Transcript, page 7 of judgment.

[4] This supports the contention of the author made *ante*, pp. 10, 57.

rescue the country attacked. Nor would there be any question but that, when this was successfully accomplished, sanctions could be applied to the individuals by whose decisions, cooperation and implementation the unlawful war on invasion was initiated and waged. Must the punishment always fall on those who were not personally responsible? May the humble citizen, who knew nothing of the reasons for his country's action, who may have been utterly deceived by its propaganda, be subject to death or wounds in battle, held as a prisoner of war, see his home destroyed by artillery or from the air, be compelled to see his wife and family suffer privations and hardships; may the owners and workers in industry see it destroyed, their merchant fleets sunk, the mariners drowned or interned; may indemnities result which must be derived from the taxes paid by the ignorant and the innocent; may all this occur and those who were actually responsible escape?

"The only rationale which would sustain the concept that the responsible shall escape while the innocent public suffers, is a result of the old theory that 'the King can do no wrong' and that 'war is the sport of Kings.' "[5]

However, one finds it difficult to agree with the Tribunal's blanket statements with reference to the role of bankers as innocent bystanders in such a situation, when their functions are of equal importance with those of members of the government. The Tribunal declared:

> "The real question is, is it a crime to make a loan, knowing or having good reason to believe that the borrower will use the funds in financing enterprises which are employed in using labor in violation of either national or international law? . . . A bank sells money or credit in the same manner as the merchandiser of any other commodity. It does not become a partner in enterprise. . . . Loans or sale of commodities to be used in an unlawful enterprise may well be condemned from a moral standpoint and reflect no credit on the part of the lender or seller in either case, but the transaction can hardly be said to be a crime. Our duty is to try and punish those guilty of violating international law, and we are not prepared to state that such loans constitute a violation of that law. . . ."[6]

With the exception of Count Four, which was dismissed on motion of the defendants, and Count Two on conspiracy, as to which this Tribunal and the previous tribunals had looked with skepticism, at least one or more defendants was found guilty

[5] Transcript, page 14-15 of judgment.

[6] Transcript, page 485-6 of judgment.

upon each of the remaining counts. Only the defendants Meissner and Von Erdmannsdorff were found not guilty. Wilhelm Stuckart, whose health would not have permitted him to serve a prison term, was given a sentence which permitted his release upon receiving credit for time already served. The remaining sentences varied from four years to twenty-five years.

High Command Case. Court scene showing defense counsel in foreground and defendants at right rear. First row, left to right: Von Leeb, Von Kuechler, Hoth, Reinhardt, Von Salmuth, Hollidt, Schniewind; second row, left to right: Warlimont, Woehler, and Lehmann.

XXXI

CASE NO. 12 (High Command Case)

Judges (Presiding Judge marked by*)

*John C. Young, former Chief Justice of the Supreme Court of Colorado
Winfield B. Hale, Justice of the Tennessee Court of Appeals
Justin W. Hardin, former Judge in Alaska and Assistant Attorney General of Ohio

Prosecution

James McHaney, Little Rock, Arkansas
Paul Niederman, Chicago, Illinois
Eugene H. Dobbs, New York City
Paul L. Horecky, London, England
Morton M. Barbour, New York City
James R. Higgins, Pottsville, Pennsylvania
Baucom Fulkerson, Little Rock, Arkansas
Arnost Horlik-Hochwald, Leigh-On-Sea, England
Walter H. Rapp, San Francisco, California (of counsel)

Interrogators:
Benno H. Selcke
Fred Kaufman
Curt Ponger
Ivan Devries

Research Associates: Louis A. Bornemisza, Frank Freudenthal, Elisabeth M. Hardy, Leo Loeb, Mary W. Taylor, Marshall F. Webster, Frank W. Young

Indictment

Counts: (1) Planning and waging of aggressive war;
(2) War crimes and crimes against humanity; against enemy belligerents and prisoners of war;
(3) War crimes and crimes against humanity; against civilians;
(4) Conspiracy.

Defense

	Defendant	Chief Defense Counsel	Counts on which sentenced	Sentence
1.	Walter Warlimont	Dr. Paul Leverkuehn	2, 3	Life imprisonment
2.	Hermann Reinecke	Dr. Hans Surholt	2, 3	Life imprisonment
3.	Georg Karl von Kuechler	Dr. Kurt Behling, Dr. Mueller	2, 3	20 years
4.	Hans von Salmuth	Dr. Kurt Gollnick	2, 3	20 years
5.	Karl von Roques	Dr. Edmund Tipp	2, 3	20 years
6.	Hermann Hoth	Heinz Mueller-Torgow	2, 3	15 years
7.	Hans Reinhardt	Dr. Friedrick Frowein	2, 3	15 years
8.	Otto Woehler	Dr. Gerhard Rauschenbach	2, 3	8 years
9.	Rudolf Lehmann	Dr. Rupprecht von Keller	2, 3	7 years
10.	Karl Hollidt	Dr. Stefan Fritsch	2, 3	5 years
11.	Wilhelm von Leeb	Dr. Hans Laternser, Dr. Leer	3	Credit for time in prison and released
12.	Johannes Blaskowitz	Heinz Mueller-Torgow	(committed suicide)	
13.	Hugo Sperrle	Dr. Kurt Gollnick		Acquittal
14.	Otto Schniewind	Dr. Hans Merkel		Acquittal

The Indictment in case twelve, the so-called "High Command Case," was filed on November 28, 1947, and served upon the defendants the next day. All of them pleaded not guilty upon December 30. The trial opened on February 5, 1948, and upon that day General Johannes Blaskowitz committed suicide. The trial proceeded against the remaining thirteen defendants, the Prosecution using 26 actual trial days, placing 23 witnesses on the stand, and introducing 1778 documents. The defense opened its case upon April 12, taking up 85 trial days and introducing 66 witnesses and 2122 documents. One of the defense counsel had acted as chief counsel and another as assistant counsel in the proceedings before the International Military Tribunal. The closing statement of the Prosecution was made August 10, and the judgment of the Tribunal was rendered October 27, 1948. The transcript consisted of 10,316 pages, of which the judgment comprised 332.

The opening statement covered the entire period of German history from 1919 down through the entire course of World War II. It first traced the rearmament of Germany and the gradual disregard of the provisions of the Treaty of Versailles, the establishment of the Third Reich, the overrunning of the Rhineland, Czechoslovakia and Austria, and the conquest of Europe. It went into extensive detail as to the war crimes, particularly the orders for the shooting of civilians without trial (the night and fog decree); and the decrees for the killing of commissars who were special officers representing the Communist party, accompanying the Soviet armies, responsible for the political indoctrination and morale of the troops, these men wearing uniforms, carrying arms, and fighting as any other soldier (the commissar decree); the orders for the killing of low flying aviators (the terror flier decree). In addition to these decrees, reference was made to the orders for extermination of Jews, the shooting of hostages and other reprisal measures, and the mistreatment of belligerents and prisoners of war.

It is important to examine the positions held by the defendants, in order to determine their relationship to the various offenses charged. Wilhelm von Leeb was the senior of the German field marshals charged as defendants in this case. He had held the western front while von Bock and von Rundstedt overran Poland, and later led the northern groups of German armies across the Baltic countries to Leningrad while von Bock and von Rundstedt overran the central and southern portions of Russia, respectively. Field Marshal von Kuechler had commanded an army in Russia under Leeb, and in 1942 succeeded him as army group commander. With the exception of Hugo Sperrle, who was field marshal of the Luftwaffe, heading the German air forces in Western Europe, and Admiral Otto Schniewind, chief of the Naval War Staff under Raeder, the remaining defendants were all high military leaders, none of a lesser rank than that of Lieutenant General.

The Prosecution took the position that many of the defendants had personally attended major conferences in which Hitler had disclosed his plans to invade Poland, Luxembourg, Holland, Belgium, and other nations and that this conduct made them participants in the crimes against peace. The particular defendants who had not attended such conferences all had knowledge of mobilization and other plans in the event of the existence of a state of war with neighboring nations, and some of the defendants had helped to prepare such plans.

The Tribunal again felt that responsibility in a charge of conspiracy, or in a charge of planning, initiating, or waging aggressive war should rest solely upon the political leaders. It felt that mere knowledge by military leaders of such plans did not make them personal participants therein, but that it was also necessary that the person possessing such knowledge should be in a position to shape or influence the policy that brings about the initiation of war or its continuation, once started.[1] As a

[1] Transcript 10,034.

result, none of the defendants were found guilty on either Counts One or Four.[2]

With reference to the war crimes alleged, it will be recalled that the evidence before the International Military Tribunal tended to show that neither the German air force nor the navy acted with any particular ungallantry. Admiral Nimitz had testified in those proceedings by deposition that the United States had acted exactly as Admiral Doenitz had acted, and Admiral Doenitz was found not guilty on those charges. Here, also, the air force and navy representatives were found not guilty upon those charges and were, therefore, acquitted. The other defendants were in a different position. They were actually in charge of armies which had carried out the commando and commissar decrees. The army had aided in deporting hundreds of thousands of persons from occupied nations to forced labor in Germany; it had transported and billeted the Einsatzgruppen while it carried on its program of extermination of Jews and other noncombatants. There was no question that the military leaders had knowledge of these things going on while they were in command of the particular forces, or while acting upon an administrative level. Whether or not they could have done anything to prevent the enforcement of these decrees might be a different question.

To some extent these questions pose a philosophical problem which is difficult to resolve. The mere fact of the establishment of rules of warfare seems to put a state of war in the same category as a medieval tournament. Actually war is not a sporting thing. Its object is to kill. To kill quickly and with sufficient effectiveness that another nation will be forced into submission, irrespective of the relative right or wrong of the conquering nation's position. Military success does not necessarily mean that God was on the side of the victors. If war can be condoned at all, perhaps rules of chivalry should be abandoned and war carried on with a maximum efficiency, in order that the invading nation may exterminate everyone who may stand in the way of success. Talk about the rules of war, as correct as it may be legalistically, seems to be an absurd anachronism. If humanity is to survive extermination, and if principles of justice are to be recognized in international relations, as well as in the relations between individuals, the only solution to the problem is the absolute prevention of war.

Irrespective of the philosophical aspects of this question, the Tribunal found the defendant von Leeb guilty only as to the third count and released him by applying credit for time already

---

[2] Transcript 10,038.

served in prison. All remaining defendants, other than those previously named, were found guilty upon both Counts Two and Three and given prison terms ranging from five years to life imprisonment.

The only rule of particular interest upon procedural questions arose early in these proceedings as to the admissibility of statements or affidavits taken from the defendants. It has long been considered desirable in the English speaking countries that a defendant be warned of the effect of a statement to be given by him, and that it might be used in evidence against him. True, voluntary admissions or confessions are admissible where no duress is applied, but where the prosecution seeks to secure a confession or plea, it is usually considered necessary that the person be fully advised of his rights. In this case, objection was made to the introduction of statements upon the ground that the defendants had not been told that they were under no compulsion to make incriminating statements, it appearing that it had been represented to them that they would be used only as witnesses and not as parties defendant. The Tribunal held such statements admissible but ruled that the defendants might show any duress or any promise of immunity, that the statements were rashly or inconsiderately made, or that they did not conform to the facts.[3] The Tribunal pointed out also that, in ruling upon objections made, it was not required to follow rules of evidence ordinarily applied in courts of the United States, and also not bound by technical rules so far as either side of the case was concerned.

---

[3] Transcript 1348-9.

PART IV

INTERNATIONAL MILITARY TRIBUNAL FOR THE FAR EAST

View of the court room, IMTFE. Left foreground are the eleven presiding Judges, with defense counsel in the right foreground and defendants on the extreme right hand side.

—*Courtesy of U. S. Army Signal Corps.*

XXXII

INTERNATIONAL MILITARY TRIBUNAL FOR THE FAR EAST

Members of the Tribunal

Sir William F. Webb, Australia, presiding judge
E. Stuart McDougall, Canada
Ju-Ao Mei, China
Henri Bernard, France
Delfin Jaranilla, The Philippines
Bernard Victor A. Roling, Netherlands
Erima Harvey Northcroft, New Zealand
I. M. Zaryanov, Russia
Lord Patrick, Great Britain and North Ireland
John P. Higgins, United States; replaced by Major General Myron C. Cramer
R. M. Pal, India

Prosecution Staff

This was headed by Joseph B. Keenan of the United States, with one chief prosecutor representing each nation. Each of the chief prosecutors was assisted by his own staff, a total of seventy-two serving the prosecution.

Defense Staff

The defense staff was headed by Captain Beverly M. Coleman, U.S.N., with four American associates representing all defendants, with one chief Japanese counsel for each accused. A total of twenty-five American and seventy-nine Japanese counsel acted for the defense.

Indictment

There were 55 counts, dealing with crimes against peace and war crimes.

There were no charges of membership in criminal organizations and no crimes against humanity except where they bore directly upon war crimes.

Defendants	Sentence
Kenji Dohihara	Death
Koki Hirota	Death
Seishiro Itagaki	Death
Heitaro Kimura	Death

Defendants	Sentence
Iwane Matsui	Death
Akira Muto	Death
Hideki Tojo	Death
Sadao Araki	Life
Kingoro Hashimoto	Life
Shunoku Hata	Life
Kiichiro Hiranuma	Life
Naoki Hoshino	Life
Okinori Kaya	Life
Koichi Kido	Life
Kuniaki Koiso	Life
Jiro Minami	Life
Takasumi Oka	Life
Hiroshi Oshima	Life
Kenryo Sato	Life
Shigetaro Shimada	Life
Toshio Shiratori	Life
Teiichi Suzuki	Life
Yoshijiro Umezu	Life
Shigenori Togo	20 years
Mamoru Shigemitsu	7 years
*Yosuke Matsuoka	
*Osami Nagano	
**Shumei Okawa	

The International Military Tribunal for the Far East was first contemplated by the Cairo Declaration of December 1, 1943. Further references were made in the Declaration of Potsdam of July 26, 1945, the Instrument of Surrender of September 2, 1945, and the Moscow Conference of December 26, 1945. On January 19, 1946, General Douglas MacArthur, as Supreme Commander, established the International Military Tribunal for the Far East for the trial of offenses similar to those charged at Nuremberg, including crimes against peace. Its constitution, jurisdiction, and functions were approved by him the same day. It provided for not less than six nor more than eleven judges, who were to be appointed by the Supreme Commander from names submitted by the signatory powers, namely, the United States, China, United Kingdom, Soviet Union, Australia, Canada, France, the Netherlands, and New Zealand, and, in addition, India and the Philippines. The instruments also provided for the appointment by the Supreme Commander of the

* Died prior to close of proceedings.
** Found to be insane and separated.

president of the Tribunal, a secretary general, and the chief of counsel, each nation with whom Japan had waged war being authorized to appoint associate counsel. The Charter provided that decisions should be made by majority vote of the Tribunal, and the Tribunal was entrusted with drafting and amending rules of procedure. The Supreme Commander was authorized to reduce, but not to increase, sentences.

The Tribunal actually was officially organized on April 29, 1946, and convened for the purpose of arranging for the issuance of an Indictment. The defendants were arraigned upon May 3, upon which date the Prosecution made its opening statement, commencing its evidence on June 3, 1946, and closing January 24, 1947. The defense opened February 24, 1947, and closed on January 12, 1948, an adjournment having been granted from June 19 to August 4 to permit counsel to coordinate their work. The rebuttal and reply evidence took until February 10, 1948. The arguments opened February 11, 1948, and closed April 16. The court adjourned to November 4, 1948, and then reconvened to read its judgment, taking seven days for that purpose. During the course of the evidence, 419 witnesses testified in court, 779 additional witnesses by deposition and affidavits. Four thousand three hundred thirty-six exhibits were admitted. There were 3915 exhibits not copied into the record, containing some 30,000 additional pages. The transcript of evidence, inclusive of the judgment, covers 49,858 pages. The Prosecution took 192 days, of which 160 were spent on direct evidence, 3 to reply to the defendants' motion to dismiss, 14 on rebuttal, and 15 on summation. The defense took 225 days, of which 187 were on direct evidence, 3 in argument on the motions to dismiss, 4 on surrebuttal, and 31 on summation.

After examining the proceedings of the International Military Tribunal at Nuremberg and the subsequent hearings, the proceedings before the International Military Tribunal for the Far East seem strangely disorganized. There was also definitely observed a tendency of the presiding justice to be autocratic and overbearing in his manner. There seemed to be somewhat of a feeling upon his part that history would fail to recognize the importance of his position and might belittle the importance of that Tribunal because of the great attention which had been devoted to the hearings at Nuremberg. This self-conscious attitude betrayed itself in many ways.

Early in the proceedings, when one of defense counsel presented a motion, the following dialogue occurred:

> "Mr. Logan: If the Tribunal please, I wish to present a matter at this time on behalf of all of the accused, which we

believe to be of vital importance in this case. This Tribunal has upon several occasions based its rulings on precedents which had been established at the Nuernberg Trials, and I wish to call your attention to a ruling which was made at the Nuernberg trial with respect to admission of interrogatories of the accused.

"The President: You are wrong in assuming we have been following Nuernberg slavishly. I have not read the decisions until the last day or two. We are always pleased to have their guidance, and I think in some matters we have followed them. I do not remember any matter in which we have given a different ruling. * * *I will tell you one matter Lord Patrick has reminded me several times that we are far more liberal to the defense than they are at Nuernberg. * * * We are not slavishly following Nuernberg."[1]

The statement of the president that the rulings were far more liberal to the defense is wholly inaccurate.

Very shortly after this dissertation, the president voluntarily made another comment upon that situation:

"Talking about Nuernberg decisions, I want to remind you, for what it is worth, that there are four nations represented at Nuernberg; those four are represented here and seven others besides, and you are wrong if you think we are going to slavishly follow Nuremberg."[2]

At other places the president comments upon differences in the two Charters.[3] Shortly after, the Tribunal stated:

"In receiving affidavits we have exercised more liberality than has been displayed at Nuernberg. The court will continue to exercise its judgment in each case."

And in his separate concurring opinion, the president belittled the proceeding at Nuremberg on the ground that, after calling aggressive war the supreme crime, that tribunal permitted certain of the defendants found guilty on that charge to escape with mere sentences, whereas some of those found guilty of crimes against humanity were executed.[4] However, Mr. Webb forgot that there were varying degrees of participation in each offense, and that even mere crimes against humanity may constitute murder.

The president of the Tribunal seemed much more concerned about his personal comfort than the conduct of the case. He

---

1 *Proceedings*, IMTFE, pp. 2225-6.
2 *Proceedings*, IMTFE, p. 2228.
3 *Proceedings*, IMTFE, pp. 2353, 7201.
4 Judgment of the IMTFE, Vol. IV, p. 6.

complained bitterly of the heat, even adjourning court on that account.[5] At the next session the president commented upon the extreme temperature, stating that it was due to the fact that the court was held in the well of the building with no ventilation, and that the court room was crowded, with the heat increased by constantly blazing lights.[6] The court shortly thereafter commented that the morning relief had been merely temporary, as the temporary air conditioning equipment had been stopped because of the lack of water, and that court would adjourn until the Supreme Commander had made arrangements for permanent air conditioning.[7] The court remained in recess for one week, until air conditioning was installed, which seems a little strange in view of the difficulty which defense counsel encountered in securing a recess for the initial preparation of the defense case.

At the opening of the defense case, challenges were made by Kiyose, representing Tojo, to each member of the Tribunal.[8] The president, Mr. Webb, was challenged on the ground that he had investigated Japanese atrocities in New Guinea, and therefore was familiar with such matters and would have preconceived notions with reference thereto. The Tribunal ruled that no objection to the person of any member could be sustained, as Article 2 of the Charter provided that the members were to be appointed by the Supreme Commander, and the Tribunal had no authority to unseat anyone so appointed.[9] Later certain of the defense counsel challenged Major General Myron C. Cramer, who was named to succeed Chief Justice Higgins of the Massachusetts Supreme Court, who had withdrawn. The grounds for the challenge were that (1) there was no provision in the Charter for additional appointments and that General Cramer would constitute the twelfth appointee; (2) it would cloud the trial since the new appointee had not been present at prior hearings; (3) having served as a high ranking general, the new justice's concept of impartiality might be incompatible with his former duties; (4) there was no evidence that he had been nominated by a signatory of the surrender instrument. The motion asked for a mistrial and for a new tribunal to be appointed.[10] Several of the defense counsel refused to join in the motion and welcomed General Cramer to the bench. The Tribunal pointed out that the French appointee was the second

[5] *Proceedings*, IMTFE, pp. 2267, 2284.

[6] *Proceedings*, IMTFE, pp. 2286-7.

[7] *Proceedings*, IMTFE, p. 2294.

[8] *Proceedings*, IMTFE, pp. 93-8.

[9] *Proceedings*, IMTFE, p. 98.

[10] *Proceedings*, IMTFE, pp. 2342-63.

representative of that nation,[11] which was answered by defense counsel to the effect that the second appointee had been named before the Tribunal had been duly constituted and begun hearing evidence and that was the reason no objection had been made. The Tribunal then ruled that while the Nuremberg charter expressly precluded changes after a certain time, there was no limitation in this Charter, and that the Supreme Commander could amend the Charter at any time in any respect. Objections of defense counsel were overruled.[12]

When defense counsel stated that they wanted to preserve certain points to argue before the Supreme Court of the United States, the president pointed out that it was a matter of indifference what proceedings they filed in any court of any nation, that the courts of any one of the signatory powers would have as much right to review the case as any other.[13] On the surface, this would seem sound, although defense counsel later argued that the courts of the United States would have more reason to assume jurisdiction since the Tribunal was constituted by its agent, General Douglas MacArthur, acting as Supreme Commander.

A peculiar situation arose in the very opening of the case. Although the chief defense counsel had been appointed by the Supreme Commander, whose word seemed to be law to the dominant members of the Tribunal, those judges refused to recognize his appointee. When the Tribunal was convened upon April 29, 1946, the Prosecution announced that the indictment was then being translated and would be lodged within a few hours. Captain Beverly M. Coleman of the Navy, chief of the defense division, requested that arraignments be not held earlier than two weeks after indictments were served.[14] The Tribunal told Captain Coleman that it would not hear his request unless he spoke for a Japanese accused. Captain Coleman pointed out that as yet there were no accused, since the indictments had not been lodged, but the Tribunal refused to hear him further. It set May 3 for the date of arraignment. Again, after Japanese counsel had been introduced, the Tribunal held that the American defense attorneys had no standing unless or until they were specifically nominated by an accused.[15] Following this time, the accused filed affidavits with the Tribunal indicating their willing-

---

11 *Proceedings*, IMTFE, pp. 2348, 2351.

12 *Proceedings*, IMTFE, p. 2353.

13 *Proceedings*, IMTFE, p. 16,267.

14 *Proceedings*, IMTFE, p. 5.

15 *Proceedings*, IMTFE, p. 80.

ness and desire to have the American counsel assist, and this basis of objection by the Tribunal was terminated.[16]

It was early pointed out by Major Warren of the defense staff, when the Tribunal wanted evidence to start within one month of arraignment, that the Prosecution had had many months for preparation of its case, whereas the defense staff then did not even have desks at which the attorneys could work.[17] This, and other requests for additional time, were overruled.[18]

The only certain way to secure a continuance or severance was by reason of death or mental incapacity. When Matsuoka was removed for serious illness, defense counsel asked for a severance of the case against him,[19] which was objected to by the Prosecution,[20] and refused by the Tribunal.[21] However, Matsuoka overruled the Tribunal by dying. Nagano was also subsequently discharged because of death.[22] Okawa, upon the day of the arraignment, closed his eyes and started to pray, then rocked back and forth in his seat, and suddenly leaned forward and slapped Tojo vigorously upon the head.[23] Rather than a sign of sanity, this was taken to be a lack of mental incompetence and a psychiatric examination was conducted.[24] It was later discovered that Okawa was insane, as well as suffering from extreme physical disability, and proceedings were suspended as to him.[25]

The attitude of the president of the Tribunal throughout toward defense counsel was one not consistent with the standards commonly observed in courts of the United States. While American attorneys are expected to observe high principles of ethical conduct and courtesy toward the court, the court is considered to have an equal duty toward counsel practicing before it. Arrogance on the part of the court by reason of its exalted

---

[16] *Proceedings*, IMTFE, p. 307.

[17] *Proceedings*, IMTFE, p. 115.

[18] At *Proceedings*, IMTFE, pp. 1847-53, Major Warren and other counsel pointed out that the defense staff did not have sufficient time and opportunity properly to prepare its defense. The Prosecution had many months and great assistance of personnel in digging up material, while defense counsel had to be in the court room to attend the hearings. Subsequently, however, a recess was given to permit counsel to coordinate their material (June 19 to August 4, 1947).

[19] *Proceedings*, IMTFE, p. 327.

[20] *Proceedings*, IMTFE, p. 330.

[21] *Proceedings*, IMTFE, p. 377.

[22] *Proceedings*, IMTFE, p. 14,307.

[23] London Times, May 4, 1946, p. 3.

[24] *Proceedings*, IMTFE, pp. 62-4.

[25] Judgment of Tribunal, Vol. I, pp. 2-6.

position is considered in this country to be a violation of judicial ethics, and an indication of the weakness of the man presiding. If this is used as a test of the competence of the Tribunal in question, it leaves one with marked distaste for the judicial tactics employed. The insults to defense counsel were frequent.[26]

Lest we be thought too harsh in our criticism in this regard, a few examples may help to illustrate this point. After counsel for Tojo had made a masterly attack upon the Indictment, another defense counsel, in raising other points, referred to attorney Kiyose's presentation as "brilliant." The Tribunal abruptly told him to omit the compliments. At another place the Tribunal read a formal statement criticizing defense counsel,[27] just as in the judgment the Tribunal added the following comment: "To these delays was added a tendency for counsel and witnesses to be prolix and irrelevant."[28] At another place, when the Tribunal had ruled that the restoration of tranquillity in occupied territory constituted no defense, defense counsel asked if the Tribunal considered it immaterial if Japanese action had followed as a result of agreements between nations. The president stated that counsel had missed the point. Defense counsel asked if the rulings of the Tribunal on this question constituted its judgment upon the question of certain steps as constituting aggressive war. The president declared:

> "You are very impertinent. You know that I did not pronounce any judgment. What I said can be read and reread, and there is nothing in the nature of a judgment in it. It is a mere warning to counsel as to what is their duty. Your observations are gratuitous, and we will deal with you if necessary."[29]

The observations of counsel seemed very pertinent, and the statements of the court a clear abuse of its powers. As a matter of fact, the author has been informed that several counsel refused to take this continued abuse, withdrew from the case, and returned to the United States.

---

[26] A few of the examples will be found at the following pages of *Proceedings*, IMTFE: 196, 2155, 2264-7, 2290, 2511, 2512, 2517, 2535, 2545, 2740, 2746, 3700, 6091, 16,271, 18,408-9, 21,720-3, 38,489; Judgment, Vol. I, p. 17. There are many others. In view of the vast number of such instances, it is surprising that upon two occasions the president was guilty of courtesy toward counsel. See p. 16,284. And at another place when counsel pointed out an objection to a certain type of procedure, the president actually said, "There is a lot to be said for that view." (p. 30,406)

[27] *Proceedings*, IMTFE, pp. 21,720-3.

[28] Judgment of IMTFE, Vol. I, p. 17.

[29] *Proceedings*, IMTFE, p. 2155.

In a similar vein, when defense counsel had made an objection to certain evidence, the president declared:

> "This looks like organized interruption to me, and I shall know how to deal with it. This Bench will know how to deal with it. I tell you your objection comes too late and we will not hear you further."[30]

At another place, when the president of the Tribunal objected to argument of the defense counsel in support of what was termed the "Supreme Commander's motion," the Tribunal stated that there was no need publicly to challenge the position of General MacArthur. It finally added that defense counsel would be allowed argument, "but you will do it as a respectful legal argument and not as a political harangue. This is not the floor of Congress or the floor of the Senate of the United States or the floor of any other parliament."[31] Defense counsel Smith objected to the remark of the Tribunal, which objection seemed to be in order. Defense attorney Smith was later barred from further appearing in these cases by reason of his vigorous defense and refusal to apologize to the Tribunal for a remark which it considered objectionable. Defense attorney Cunningham was also barred for discussing the conduct of the Tribunal at the American Bar Association meeting in Seattle in 1948, prior to the rendition of the decision by the Tribunal.

At another place, defense attorney Logan stated that he viewed certain rulings of the Tribunal with alarm. The Tribunal stated that counsel was out of order, adding "You would not dare take that stand in the United States Supreme Court." The president went on to state that the rulings of the Tribunal were honest ones, and that the president himself had voted against counsel. "I make no apologies," he declared, "and it is a matter of sheer indifference to me what attitude you take or anybody takes. We will not be intimidated."[32]

This does not mean that defense counsel were always gracious in their attitude. At one point counsel objected to the introduction of portions of a speech by one of the defendants, which had been reprinted in a newspaper, claiming that it was incomplete and amounted to a suppression of evidence by the Prosecution.[33] The Prosecution challenged the statement, claiming that it was an attack upon the integrity of the Prosecution and demanded that counsel apologize.[34] Defense counsel pointed

[30] *Proceedings*, IMTFE, p. 6091.
[31] *Proceedings*, IMTFE, p. 16,271.
[32] *Proceedings*, IMTFE, pp. 18,407-8.
[33] *Proceedings*, IMTFE, p. 2200.
[34] *Proceedings*, IMTFE, p. 2201.

out that fuller statements from the speech had been contained in other publications and were easily available; that defense counsel had merely sent out and gotten other copies of the same speech. After discussion, defense counsel finally withdrew the accusations that the Prosecution had a full copy of the speech which was being deliberately withheld. The Tribunal accepted the apology and declared: "You didn't do it very gracefully."[35]

In arguments upon the motion to quash the Indictment, defense attorney Kiyose advanced some ingenious arguments. He pointed out that both the allies and Japan were bound by the Potsdam Declaration which referred to "all war crimes," and stated nothing about crimes against peace or crimes against humanity. He referred to current definitions of "war crimes" and stated that the Supreme Commander had no power to increase the offenses charged. Since Japan had accepted the terms of the Instrument of Surrender, authorizing trial of these offenses, he felt that a binding contract had been established which could not be enlarged by one party against the will of the other contracting party. This, he stated, was particularly true since Article V of the Potsdam Declaration declared: "Following are our terms. We shall not deviate from them."[36]

Mr. Keenan made an excellent reply, pointing out that the Potsdam Declaration expressly referred to the elimination of the authority and influence of those who had misled Japan into war.[37] Other arguments by defense counsel which followed helped to develop the defenses which were later argued more fully on the motions to dismiss.[38]

The following defenses were those which were principally raised and argued by defense counsel throughout the hearing:

1. Existing international law did not recognize the offenses charged, particularly those pertaining to aggressive war, crimes against peace, crimes against humanity, and conspiracy.[39] Reference was made to Hall and Oppenheim as to the status of existing international law up to that time and to the British Manual of the Laws of War, Article 441.

2. International law makes no provision for the liability of individuals but only for the responsibility of nations.[40] This was particularly pointed out with reference to the concept of aggressive war.

---

[35] *Proceedings*, IMTFE, p. 2208.

[36] *Proceedings*, IMTFE, pp. 120-137.

[37] *Proceedings*, IMTFE, pp. 139, 140.

[38] *Proceedings*, IMTFE, pp. 196-234. See also motion for mistrial and other motions, p. 16,262 *et seq.*

[39] *Proceedings*, IMTFE, p. 120 *et seq.*

[40] *Proceedings*, IMTFE, p. 187.

3. Aggressive war had never been established or recognized as a violation of international law.[41] Defense counsel strongly urged the point that the failure of nations to enter into specific treaties upon this point and the steps which had been taken in an effort to outlaw aggressive war, which had been pointed out by the Tribunal at Nuremberg, actually showed a disapproval, rather than approval, of any binding principle by nations in today's civilization.

4. Conspiracy was not a recognized concept of international law imposing liability upon individuals.[42] It was vigorously argued that persons operating in widely scattered theaters and with widely divergent responsibilities could not be considered to have conspired together, particularly when a number of the defendants had been violently opposed to entry into war. This defense was particularly argued as to violations charged against camp commanders and others similarly situated, as to whose actions and conduct many of the defendants would have no knowledge, and over whom they would have no power of control. The Prosecution's attitude as to this charge was that the acts in various theaters were so similar in character as to show an over-all understanding and method of procedure in such instances.

5. The doctrine of *ex post facto* was repeatedly raised and argued.[43] The arguments which had been raised in detail by defense counsel at Nuremberg were reiterated along the same line by both the American and Japanese defense attorneys.

6. There was no provision in international law for the establishment of an international tribunal.[44] It was the position of defense counsel that the only provision in international law was for the establishment of a military court by the occupying power for the purpose of trying offenses in violation of recognized rules of land warfare. This argument was rejected for the same reasons as the similar argument at Nuremberg.

7. Prisoners of war were entitled to trial by court martial under the rules of the Geneva Protocol.[45] This would require notice to the protecting power and also an adherence to rules of procedure established for the conduct of courts martial. It was rejected for the reasons advanced in the *Yamashita* case.[46]

8. There had been no acceptance of the terms and conditions under which the charges were brought, or the trial conducted,

---

41 *Proceedings*, IMTFE, p. 196 *et seq.*, p. 16, 284 *et seq.*

42 *Proceedings*, IMTFE, pp. 231; 16,304 *et seq.*

43 E.g., *Proceedings*, IMTFE, p. 188.

44 *Proceedings*, IMTFE, p. 196 *et seq.*

45 See particularly the discussion of this in the Judgment, Vol. I, p. 24.

46 See Keenan's argument, *Proceedings*, IMTFE, pp. 299-301.

by the vanquished power.[47] Attorney Kiyose argued that the treaty of surrender differed from the Versailles treaty which provided for the trial of the Kaiser, which Germany had accepted and signed, but that there was no similar provision in the Potsdam Declaration.

9. A binding contract had been established under the Potsdam Declaration which neither the Tribunal nor the Prosecution were at liberty to ignore.[48] It was argued by defense counsel that Nuremberg was no precedent, as different declarations had preceded the establishment of that charter. Here an offer had been made to Japan, which was accepted as a basis of surrender, and the terms and conditions of that contract were believed to be binding.

10. The Potsdam Declaration referred to "war crimes" and not to crimes against peace or crimes against humanity.[49] It was argued that the Supreme Commander had no power to go beyond the scope of this declaration, or to add new crimes for the purpose of trial.

11. Victor nations cannot give a fair trial.[50] It was argued that the members of the Tribunal were there, not as impartial judges, but as representatives of victor nations to see that punishment was duly meted out to their enemies. In reply, Mr. Keenan pointed out that there are no true neutrals where an entire world is embroiled in a state of war.[51]

12. War crimes cannot be committed prior to the existence of a state of war.[52] This resulted from the Prosecution going back to the beginning of the century to trace the imperialistic aims of Japan, and in the course of that journey bringing in charges of war crimes committed against China and Russian nationals prior to the outbreak of World War II.

13. Incidents which have been settled by treaty cannot be reopened or investigated.[53] Again this referred to the extensive exploration conducted by the Prosecution of historical incidents. Russia was particularly anxious to have Japan found to be in the wrong as to certain border clashes. The Japanese attorneys pointed out that the Lake Khasan incident had been settled by an agreement of August 1938, and the Kholkin Gol River incident was settled in September 1939. The Prosecution's attitude as to this was that the society of nations had a broad general

---

[47] *Proceedings*, IMTFE, p. 186.

[48] *Proceedings*, IMTFE, p. 125 *et seq.*

[49] *Procedings*, IMTFE, pp. 120-5.

[50] *Proceedings*, IMTFE, p. 193 *et seq.*

[51] *Proceedings*, IMTFE, p. 235.

[52] *Proceedings*, IMTFE, pp. 221-2.

[53] *Proceedings*, IMTFE, p. 130 *et seq.*

interest in this matter, which could not be foreclosed by a treaty entered into by the two nations involved.

14. Killings are normal incidents of war and not murder.[54] While it is true that killings do normally occur in time of war, the attitude of the Tribunal was that investigation must be made as to the legality of the war in making this determination.

15. The United States and not Japan was the aggressor. The defense introduced a top secret United States dispatch alerting the Navy on November 28, 1941, but specifically instructing its high personnel to "undertake no offensive action until Japan has committed an overt act."[55] Justice Pal, in his dissenting opinion, spoke very bitterly of the United States, accusing Roosevelt and Hull of fostering the war.[56] Instead of limiting their actions to the protection of the Philippines, these persons purported, he stated, to declare what should be done in the entire Pacific. He believed the United States was the aggressor against Japan by aiding the Chinese throughout in their struggles. He went on to say: "The evidence does not entitle us to characterize the Japanese attack as a sudden unexpected, treacherous act committed while relations between the two countries were peaceful. We have seen to what extent the United States was at peace with Japan, and how she was actually engaged in a peace conference with Japan's envoys. There was no treachery on the part of Japan in this respect. It does not matter whether there was any maneuvering anywhere to make Japan commit the first overt act."[57]

16. There is a duty of obedience which excuses those following lawful orders.[58] This is similar to the defense of *respondeat superior* advanced in the German proceedings. Captain Robinson made an excellent reply to this argument.[59] Justice Pal, on the other hand, felt that even an officer of the government had no duty to resign or to refuse to follow orders given, stating "According to the prosecution every member of a government owes a duty to bring such matters before the cabinet and to resign if he fails thereby to get satisfaction."[60]

17. *Mens rea.*[61] It was argued that there must be a criminal intent prior to a finding of guilt, and that there had been no

---

54 See the discussion of this in the Judgment of IMTFE, Vol. I, p. 24.
55 *Proceedings*, IMTFE, pp. 25,630-1.
56 Judgment, Vol. VIII, p. 875.
57 Judgment, Vol. VIII, p. 978.
58 *Proceedings*, IMTFE, pp. 15,030, 16,317 *et seq.;* also pp. 41; 701-2.
59 *Proceedings*, IMTFE, pp. 41; 701-2.
60 Judgment, Vol. VIII, p. 1160.
61 *Proceedings*, IMTFE, p. 16,275 *et seq.*

showing of any feeling of guilt on the part of any of the defendants.

18. Civilian officers are not responsible for war crimes. This point was particularly emphasized by Justice Pal in his dissenting opinion.[62]

In addition to the defenses particularly raised, as listed above, specific attack was also made upon certain counts of the Indictment, as not stating proper offenses, or as being too vague and general properly to apprise the defendants of the charges against them. The Indictment did not follow the form used at Nuremberg, but was quite inexpertly drawn, consisting of fifty-five counts, many of which were duplicitous and vague in their terminology. While the Tribunal refused to strike these counts at the time of argument, a number of them were dismissed from the consideration of the Tribunal at the time of judgment.[63]

The Tribunal held, however, that the defendants would not be relieved of liability by showing that they had restored peace and order in China, but that such evidence would be considered only in mitigation of the offenses. It was up to the defendants to establish their authority to so act or to justify their conduct.[64] And the fact that Generalissimo Chiang Kai-Shek had approved the Japanese treatment of the wounded and prisoners of war was held inadmissible.[65]

As to questions of procedure, the court held that it would not take judicial notice either of national constitutions,[66] or of events.[67] As to evidence offered by the Prosecution, relevancy was to be presumed.[68] Where an answer seemed to be improper, the president ruled that such answers would not be stricken, stating: "No answer will be stricken out unless it is scandalous. I do not know any practice of striking out answers."[69] The statement of the Tribunal is clearly inconsistent with recognized trial practice followed in the United States. It appears also that the Tribunal let in practically all evidence "on the usual terms," but there was considerable confusion as to what were "the usual terms." For example, defense attorney Brooks moved to strike

---

[62] Judgment, Vol. VIII, p. 1160. See above note 60.

[63] The Tribunal dismissed 37, 38, 44, and 53 as conspiracy counts not related to the charge of conspiracy to wage aggressive war, on the ground that the Tribunal had no jurisdiction over other types of conspiracy. Counts 39 to 43 and 44 to 52 were held to be obscure and duplicitous and not to be considered for that reason. Judgment, Vol. I, pp. 24-38.

[64] *Proceedings*, IMTFE, p. 2154.

[65] *Proceedings*, IMTFE, p. 21,806.

[66] *Proceedings*, IMTFE, p. 16,264.

[67] *Proceedings*, IMTFE, p. 379.

[68] *Proceedings*, IMTFE, p. 2032-3.

[69] *Proceedings*, IMTFE, p. 865.

Exhibit 2206A, which was a file of United States newspaper clippings. The prosecutor stated that the exhibit had been admitted without objection. Brooks stated that he had a right to raise this question by a motion to strike, declaring: "That is the meaning of 'admitted on the usual terms'." He was overruled by the Tribunal. Mr. Brooks then asked to have an understanding from the Tribunal as to what was meant by this language, but was unable to secure any definite information.[70] Both defense counsel and this author are confused by the use of this term.

Even though all evidence was presumed to be relevant, the Tribunal still gave lip service to the best evidence rule.[71] These rulings were criticized by Justice Pal, who thought that it was absurd to speak of a best evidence rule when, under the Charter, anything was admitted having probative value.[72]

As to documents, the twenty-four hour notice rule, which had been established at Nuremberg, was adopted also by this Tribunal, for the purpose of requiring notification of opposing counsel and service of a copy of the document proposed to be introduced.[73] However, when defense counsel called this ruling to the Tribunal's attention, upon at least one occasion where it had not been observed, the Tribunal hedged and stated that it might have to modify its ruling.[74]

With reference to the introduction of documents, the Tribunal several times held that introduction of a part only of the document was proper practice.[75] Thus, the Tribunal stated that where the Prosecution read only two sentences from a total of six pages that the whole document was in evidence, but that only two sentences were presently in the record.[76] When defense counsel objected at one point to the failure of the Prosecution to read the portions of a document favorable to the accused, the Tribunal stated that the whole document should be filed, and the defense given facilities to copy the portions desired, with complete copies of all affidavits to be furnished to the interested defendant within one month.[77]

The failure of the Tribunal to make clean-cut rulings on this matter led to one misunderstanding with defense counsel. Mr.

---

[70] *Proceedings*, IMTFE, p. 13,914.

[71] *Proceedings*, IMTFE, p. 18,975. See ruling of Tribunal at pp. 21, 720-3.

[72] Judgment, Vol. VI, p. 308 *et seq.*

[73] *Proceedings*, IMTFE, p. 1013.

[74] *Proceedings*, IMTFE, p. 2293.

[75] *Proceedings*, IMTFE, pp. 1854, 1860, 1922-3, 5932.

[76] *Proceedings*, IMTFE, p. 5932.

[77] *Proceedings*, IMTFE, p. 1860.

Logan of the defense insisted that the Prosecution was duty bound to introduce the entire affidavit, in order that defense counsel could examine it, and then the Prosecution should indicate the portions to be offered. He referred to decisions 80, 81, 82 at Nuremberg. The president was apparently unable to grasp his reasoning and thought counsel was charging fraud or suppression of evidence by the Prosecution. Mr. Logan was very patient and tried to explain his position to the Tribunal. The Tribunal finally disagreed with him and stated that it would not require the production of additional matters in relevant documents, unless the defense charged suppression of evidence, and that counsel would be required to prove such charges very strictly.[78] Upon another occasion, defense counsel pointed out that they were not being furnished with translations of entire documents, where a part only of such documents had been read. The Tribunal cut off the statement of defense counsel abruptly and refused to hear him further upon the matter.[79]

As to copies of documents, it was pointed out by defense counsel that the paper shortage was holding up the reproduction of necessary instruments.[80] Where an affidavit was introduced referring to documents which had been burned, the president was quite arbitrary in his reception of such affidavit, indicating that the documents would not have been burned if they had been favorable to the defense, and indicating that it would be very difficult for the defense to supply an affidavit which would satisfy him.[81]

It was early held that affidavit evidence could be used in the same manner as it had been used a+ Nuremberg.[82] Justice Pal was quite bitter about the use of affidavit evidence, his reaction being the same in that regard as to the use of hearsay evidence and leading questions.[83] The Tribunal did hold that affidavit evidence could not be used where the witness was available, spoke English, and possessed an excellent education.[84]

The Prosecution was permitted to introduce captured documents without the necessity of certificates of authenticity.[85] Even letters by private individuals to the war ministry were allowed introduction, characterized as "crank letters" by the defense.[86] But the Tribunal refused admission to press releases

[78] *Proceedings*, IMTFE, pp. 2229-31.
[79] *Proceedings*, IMTFE, pp. 2737-40.
[80] *Proceedings*, IMTFE, p. 21,825.
[81] *Proceedings*, IMTFE, pp. 21,648-58; also pp. 21,756-7.
[82] *Proceedings*, IMTFE, pp. 915-939.
[83] Judgment, Vol. VI, pp. 299-302.
[84] *Proceedings*, IMTFE, pp. 2528-30; 2549-50.
[85] *Proceedings*, IMTFE, p. 379.
[86] *Proceedings*, IMTFE, p. 2198.

which the defense sought to introduce in countering like evidence which the Prosecution had offered and which had been received.[87]

The statements of one defendant in the form of an affidavit were held not to be considered as evidence against another defendant, although statements made upon the witness stand were to be considered as against any defendant.[88] Thus, testimony in its general phases by one defendant was considered to be evidence by all defendants as to that phase, unless such other accused expressly dissented.[89] Any objections by defense counsel that abuse or misleading statements had been used to obtain affidavits or admissions from the defendants, and objections based upon the incorrectness of such statements, were, however, overruled, the Tribunal holding that such testimony could be heard only as a part of the defense case.[90] It was, of course, apparent that numerous errors arose in translation which occasionally resulted in a change in meaning of the words used.[91]

The Nimitz affidavit, which had been offered and received in evidence before the International Military Tribunal at Nuremberg, was offered in evidence in these proceedings. It was withdrawn by agreement of counsel, after the Prosecution had withdrawn the charges of offenses toward civilian populations.[92] One of the more interesting occurrences arose with reference to John B. Powell's book, "My 25 Years in China." Powell had been called as a witness for the Prosecution. The defense then sought to introduce excerpts from his book. The Tribunal originally inferred that this would be admissible,[93] but then changed the rule and excluded such evidence.[94] Defense counsel Logan remonstrated with the Tribunal and was roughly reprimanded by the president.[95] Almost immediately thereafter a different book was offered with a similar attitude shown by the president. One of the members of the Tribunal then requested a conference and court recessed.[96] Upon reconvening, this offer was also rejected.[97] Mr. Logan then reoffered other excerpts from such books and a discussion ensued. They were rejected on the presi-

---

87 *Proceedings*, IMTFE, pp. 21,546-8; also pp. 21,720-3.
88 *Proceedings*, IMTFE, pp. 25,662-9.
89 *Proceedings*, IMTFE, pp. 25,875-94.
90 *Proceedings*, IMTFE, p. 5153.
91 E.g., see *Proceedings*, IMTFE, p. 30; also p. 10,055.
92 *Proceedings*, IMTFE, p. 34,772; also p. 34,819.
93 *Proceedings*, IMTFE, p. 18,403.
94 *Proceedings*, IMTFE, p. 18,407.
95 *Proceedings*, IMTFE, pp. 18,407-10.
96 *Proceedings*, IMTFE, p. 18,410.
97 *Proceedings*, IMTFE, p. 18,414.

dent casting his own ballot to break a tie.[98] Then Logan offered Powell's book, and it was admitted.[99] Other documents were rejected subsequently,[100] but, after the president had announced rejection of one document on his casting a vote, he received another vote from a member of the Tribunal and was forced to change his ruling.[101]

On rebuttal, objection was made by defense to an attempt of the Prosecution to introduce documents which should have been introduced in chief. The Tribunal commented that if other counsel did not object that the documents could be admitted as to them. Defense attorney Brooks pointed out that the Tribunal would then have a parade of counsel, all making separate objections. The Tribunal admitted that the point had merit and the Prosecution withdrew the document.[102]

Leading questions were held to be proper and are found throughout the proceedings.[103] Hearsay evidence was approved.[104] Even a conversation with a deceased person was held admissible.[105] And opinions and conclusions of a witness were originally held to be perfectly proper,[106] although the Tribunal later ruled that such evidence would not be received unless it was expert in character.[107] However, by this time, the ruling seemed to have application only to the defense. And character questions were held to be proper.[108]

Where objections were made to portions of Cordell Hull's affidavit as being too remote and not relevant to the proceedings, the Tribunal stated that it would regard only such matters as were relevant.[109] Elsewhere the Tribunal was quite caustic when defense counsel objected to evidence on the basis of irrelevancy.[110] Where proof was offered of the commission of atrocities, in an attempt to prove conspiracy, the defense objected to such evidence on the basis of lack of foundation, no link having been shown in evidence to establish any common agreement or purpose. The Tribunal ruled that such link could be shown either

---

98 *Proceedings*, IMTFE, p. 18,419.
99 *Proceedings*, IMTFE, p. 18,419.
100 *Proceedings*, IMTFE, p. 18,425.
101 *Proceedings*, IMTFE, p. 18,426.
102 *Proceedings*, IMTFE, p. 30,406.
103 E.g., *Proceedings*, IMTFE, pp. 3752-3.
104 *Proceedings*, IMTFE, pp. 2032-3; also p. 2535.
105 *Proceedings*, IMTFE, pp. 2011-8.
106 *Proceedings*, IMTFE, pp. 955-2324.
107 *Proceedings*, IMTFE, pp. 21,720-3.
108 *Proceedings*, IMTFE, p. 14,391.
109 *Proceedings*, IMTFE, p. 10,110.
110 *Proceedings*, IMTFE, pp. 2264-7.

at that time or later,[111] and where defense counsel objected to the use of epithets by the Prosecution of prejudicial-type words, such as "massacres," the Tribunal commented, "You are unduly sensitive."[112]

The Tribunal held that it was proper for a witness to use notes while testifying, even though it appeared that he was actually merely reading therefrom.[113] It also imposed very severe limitations upon cross-examination.[114] Its general rulings were that cross-examination must be limited to matters covered in chief,[115] and that it must be non-repetitious.[116] The president referred, in addition, to a doctrine, which is certainly not the American rule, which, in itself, imposed severe limitations upon cross-examination. He stated: "Well, we cannot stop your cross-examination on those lines. You mean to tell us you will observe what is certainly the British rule, that your questions will be such that you will be able to prove that subject matter, if necessary, or you hope to be able to, and they are not mere speculative questions."[117] This would seem to be an absurd rule and would place a most severe obstacle in the path of counsel trying to determine the truth. It is often obvious that a witness is concealing evidence or is distorting facts, but counsel, in starting his interrogation, has no idea at what point he will be able to break the witness down or crash through the fabrication. The cross-examination starts as a purely speculative matter, but often results in a determination of the truth. To be able to guarantee that counsel will be able to prove a certain subject is to guarantee that he will win a lawsuit. In every case one counsel must lose, and the ruling would be highly inconsistent if applied to both sides of a case.

At another point the Tribunal in effect told defense counsel that they could not call a witness, testifying by affidavit, for cross-examination unless they could prove he was a liar.[118] How any attorney could make such a guarantee prior to cross-examining the witness and learning the sources of his information and the conclusion he drew therefrom, is difficult to see. Of course, this does not mean that the Tribunal refused to produce all witnesses for cross-examination.[119] But a witness was also per-

111 *Proceedings*, IMTFE, pp. 2628-9.
112 *Proceedings*, IMTFE, p. 2290.
113 *Proceedings*, IMTFE, pp. 3752-3.
114 E.g., *Proceedings*, IMTFE, pp. 866; 38,470; 38,480; 38,487.
115 *Proceedings*, IMTFE, p. 2515.
116 *Proceedings*, IMTFE, p. 866.
117 *Proceedings*, IMTFE, p. 38,306.
118 *Proceedings*, IMTFE, p. 11,733.
119 *Proceedings*, IMTFE, pp. 14,228; 14,282-4.

mitted to refuse to answer certain questions on the basis that such information was confidential and constituted a military secret.[120] As might be suspected, this was a Russian.[121] At another point the Russian prosecutor, Vasiliev, objected to cross-examination of a Russian witness.[122] The Tribunal finally stopped defense counsel, after telling Vasiliev that he could not prevent bad things being said about his country. However, the fact remains that it did stop the cross-examination.[123]

Objections were made to the Stimson affidavit and to the Grew affidavit, which were offered by the Prosecution. The defense demanded that former Ambassador Grew be produced for cross-examination, claiming that his affidavit was misleading and contradicted by his own books "Ten Years in Japan" and "Report from Tokyo."[124] The defense pointed out that they had no funds with which to take any deposition, but would try to arrange payment of necessary expenses. Defense counsel Levin stated that if Mr. Grew would be produced for examination by deposition, that Major Furness would be going to the United States and could cross-examine him.[125] The Tribunal ruled that there was no necessity to have Mr. Grew present at the trial, but that counsel could present an application for interrogatories and also for the items of required expense.[126]

The Russian opening statement was quite verbose and was objected to by defense counsel. It was pointed out that the first twenty pages dealt with a period from 1900 to 1922, which was beyond the scope of the Indictment, that the next twenty pages were pure argument instead of detailing the nature of the expected evidence, the next twenty pages were spent in justifying Russian activities in Manchuria and adjoining areas, and only about five pages were devoted to the expected proof by witnesses and documents.[127] The president pointed out that Rudenko's opening statement at Nuremburg had many of the same faults,[128] but that there was a material difference in the Charters. The Tribunal went on to rule that the defendants could not object to the whole statement but merely to the objectionable parts, stating reasons.[129] It then ruled that it would permit the entire statement to be read with the right to object to those portions.

120 *Proceedings*, IMTFE, pp. 38,309-11.
121 *Proceedings*, IMTFE, pp. 38,309-11.
122 *Proceedings*, IMTFE, pp. 38,481-4.
123 E.g., *Proceedings*, IMTFE, pp. 38,485-6.
124 *Proceedings*, IMTFE, p. 10,083.
125 *Proceedings*, IMTFE, pp. 10,086-7.
126 *Proceedings*, IMTFE, p. 10,088.
127 *Proceedings*, IMTFE, pp. 7196-7211.
128 *Proceedings*, IMTFE, p. 7201.
129 *Proceedings*, IMTFE, p. 7204-11.

The speech was given, objections made, and the Tribunal then held that there was no necessity to make a ruling at all, as it would only consider those parts which were justified by the evidence to follow.[130] The defense counsel were forced to request copies of the opening addresses, which the Prosecution objected to supplying, but which were finally turned over to defense counsel.[131]

In addition to severely limiting the opportunity of defense counsel to cross-examine, and displaying open hostility toward them, the Tribunal made several peculiar rulings of interest to trial lawyers. At one place, Mr. Warren, for the defense, objected to a certain question. The objection was sufficiently clear that the Tribunal stated that it would hear from the Prosecution upon the objection. After the Prosecution had stated its position, Warren stated that he would reply to it, and the following conversation occurred:

> "Mr. Warren: Your honor, may I be heard on that before I am overruled.
>
> "The President: Oh, no, it is obviously a matter upon which evidence can be received. We have heard enough, Mr. Warren."[132]

At another place, where defense counsel wanted to make an offer of proof, the Tribunal refused even to permit such offer to be made.[133] At another point, where counsel made a motion for mistrial, the Tribunal refused to permit such motion to be filed, the president stating that he had never heard of such a practice.[134]

The Tribunal was also very displeased about the attitude of the American Army newspaper, The Stars and Stripes. At one point it asked General MacArthur to give protection against the "lying misrepresentations" of that paper. One of the occurrences in which the newspaper was involved was in printing a speech of defense counsel prior to its delivery in court. The defense attorney stated that copies had been given to the newspapers, but that they were not to be printed until delivered. The Tribunal promptly held a contempt hearing upon the matter,[135] and severely reprimanded the editor.[136]

---

[130] *Proceedings*, IMTFE, p. 7294.

[131] *Proceedings*, IMTFE, p. 8180.

[132] *Proceedings*, IMTFE, p. 2545.

[133] *Proceedings*, IMTFE, p. 38,487.

[134] *Proceedings*, IMTFE, p. 16,262.

[135] *Proceedings*, IMTFE, pp. 17,000-3.

[136] *Proceedings*, IMTFE, pp. 17,029-32. And see *New York Times*, May 14, 1947, p. 20.

The Prosecution protested bitterly at one point when one of the Japanese defense counsel wanted to quote President Truman, although the Prosecution had previously quoted Stalin and others.[137] Defense counsel, upon another occasion, pointed out the Russian technique of acquiring territory by merely changing the boundaries upon a map.[138] Of course, all defense counsel did not agree upon all points throughout the trial.[139]

Judgment of the Tribunal

The judgment of the Tribunal is very lengthy and of considerable interest. The majority opinion gives a history of the establishment of the Tribunal and discusses the nature of the counts in the Indictment. It pointed out that the proceedings had been unduly protracted, ascribing part of the blame to the attorneys[1] and commenting also upon the lack of candor of the witnesses.[2]

As to the law of the case, the majority declared, "In our opinion the law of the Charter is decisive and binding on the Tribunal."[3] It stated that the members of the Tribunal had no jurisdiction except that expressly found within the Charter, but added, "In the exercise of their right to create tribunals for such a purpose and in conferring powers upon such tribunals, belligerent powers may act only within the limits of international law."[4]

The Tribunal also related the various grounds of attack which had been made upon jurisdictional grounds, including such matters as lack of individual criminal responsibility, *ex post facto,* the lack of any pre-existing concept of aggressive war, and similar grounds. It held that the law of the Charter was conclusive, and that such contentions must be dismissed.[5] However, after making this sweeping statement, the court went on to quote from the reasoning of the Tribunal at Nuremberg and to adopt that reasoning. As to the defenses based upon the Geneva Convention, it referred to the Yamashita decision at some length.

---

137 *Proceedings,* IMTFE, pp. 188-95.

138 And this seems to have been admitted by Russia. *Proceedings,* IMTFE, pp. 38,342-3.

139 E.g., see *Proceedings,* IMTFE, p. 2350 as to challenges of Major General Myron C. Cramer.

1 Judgment, Vol. I, p. 17.

2 Judgment, Vol. I, p. 20.

3 Judgment, Vol. I, p. 23.

4 Judgment, Vol. I, p. 23.

5 Judgment, Vol. I, p. 24.

Upon the question of mistreatment of prisoners, the Tribunal held that the defendants would be responsible if they had knowledge that such crimes were being committed, or if the defendants were at fault in failing to acquire such knowledge. It dismissed counts 37, 38, 44, and 53 as based upon conspiracy other than conspiracy to wage aggressive war, upon the basis that the Tribunal had no jurisdiction over those charges. Counts 39 to 43 and 45 to 52, inclusive, were held obscure and duplicitous and not to be considered.

The judgment then went on to discuss in detail early Japanese history and treaties, prior to the commission of offenses charged in the Indictment, the development of political and military personalities, and their powers. It stated that it was unnecessary to determine if Japan had attacked without warning or whether killings committed constituted murder, since its findings were that Japan did commit aggressive war.[6] It did add that Japan's warning note was not delivered until after the attack on Pearl Harbor.[7] It specifically found Japan to be the aggressor and not to be acting under economic compulsion.[8] It found this true also as to the hostilities with the Netherlands, which had declared war first upon Japan, since the evidence showed that Japan had planned to attack the Netherlands.

It declared that the atrocities followed such a pattern in all theaters that they were obviously either ordered or wilfully committed. It detailed the killings, rapes, abuses, murders and mistreatment of prisoners which occurred in all theaters, stating that massacres were "ordered."[9] The judgment pointed out that certain defendants admitted knowing of these acts, and that they received protests, but did nothing about them. The court was particularly shocked by evidence of various tortures, such as those by water, electric shock, burning, suspension, knee spread, vivisection, and by such acts as cannibalism and the maintenance of unwholesome conditions upon prison ships. It found that there was a conspiracy to commit wars of aggression and sentenced seven defendants to death, two to prison for varying terms of years, and the remainder of the defendants to life imprisonment.

There was a separate concurring opinion of the president filed, which adds little to the field of international law. A dissenting opinion by M. Bernard, the French jurist, is of consid-

---

[6] Judgment, Vol. III, pp. 985-6.
[7] Judgment, Vol. III, p. 988.
[8] Judgment, Vol. III, pp. 991-1000.
[9] Judgment, Vol. III, p. 1041.

erable interest, and presents what might be called the Catholic point of view. He points out that the majority opinion rejects the defendants' pleas to the jurisdiction because the Tribunal felt it was bound by the Charter, although the Tribunal immediately thereafter stated that the Charter represented the law in its existing state. He contended that the Tribunal was competent to examine the legality of the Charter provisions and to reject them if they did not conform to existing international law.[10] He agreed with the legal conclusions because of the natural law which was binding upon nations, and not because the law had been reduced to writing in the Charter.

As to the Lake Khasan and like incidents, he agreed with the majority for a different reason, which is of considerable interest. He stated that two individuals cannot dispose of the right of society to prosecute crimes; and that two nations similarly cannot dispose of the right of the community of nations to settle controversies arising in international law.[11]

He disagreed sharply with the sweeping majority conclusion as to persons responsible for the mistreatment of prisoners. He felt that one can be held liable only for his own acts and that a guilt arising from omission can exist only where the commission of crime is said to follow from the omission charged. He felt that a causal connection should have been established, and that the circumstances existing at that time must be shown.[12]

M. Bernard was the only one of the judges to criticize the procedure followed by the Tribunal as between the judge themselves. He pointed out that the defendants had not been given an opportunity to obtain and to assemble the necessary elements for defense by hearing before an independent magistrate, which is the French procedure; that the Prosecution was not carried out in an equal and fair manner as to all defendants; that the eleven judges were never called together to discuss the judgment orally, but that the proceedings were dominated by a small faction, and the others were not even called into consultation.[13]

M. Bernard also expressed grave doubt as to the sufficiency of proof of conspiracy and certain other charges, but declared that he was unable to formulate an opinion thereon when he felt the defendants had not had a fair trial.[14] In discussing the law applicable, he gave an extremely interesting discussion of the application of international morality. He declared:

---

10 Dissenting Opinion of Bernard, Judgment, Vol. IV, p. 9.

11 Dissenting Opinion of Bernard, Judgment, Vol. IV, p. 11.

12 Dissenting Opinion of Bernard, Judgment, Vol. IV, pp. 13-15.

13 Dissenting Opinion of Bernard, Judgment, Vol. IV, pp. 15-17.

14 Dissenting Opinion of Bernard, Judgment, Vol. IV, p. 17.

"Several times in expressing my opinion I preferred the expression of natural or universal law to that of international law. The latter has been used too often to define the whole of the rights and obligations of nations as a result either of custom, social convention, treaties, or agreements. This whole can or cannot conform to the law shared by all individuals and all nations but does not identify itself with it. It is to this law that I have reserved the qualification of 'natural' and 'universal.' It exists outside and above nations. If opinions differ as to its nature, its existence is not seriously contested or contestable and the declaration of this existence is sufficient for our purpose."[15]

A separate concurring opinion was filed by the Philippino, Jaranilla. He discussed at length the concept of conspiracy or common plan to commit crimes against humanity, and in this regard it is considerably stronger than the majority opinion.[16] He resented the dropping of counts 6 to 17, and 18 to 26, as well as 39 to 52, inclusive.

Jaranilla's principal thesis was that the victorious nation has the power to punish, and it is upon this ground that he justified the legal composition of the Tribunal. He quoted extensively from Oppenheim, Garner, Hall, and Kelsen upon the application of international law. He referred also to Jessup's concept of individual responsibility and to the case of *Ex Parte Quirin*.[17] However, he went off upon one rather bad tangent, in referring to the dissenting opinion of Justice Pal of India. He criticized Pal for attacking jurisdiction of the Tribunal, upon the following reasoning: If the Charter was invalid, then the appointment of Pal as a member was invalid, and he had no right to question the Charter.[18] This is, of course, absurd. One may be validly appointed as a judge and yet be in a position to declare invalid certain legislation embodied in the instrument which creates the court. As a judge, whether *de jure* or *de facto*, it is his duty to apply the law as it exists and not as it is desired. The appointment may still be valid upon the basis of the underlying agreements, even if portions of the final instrument are invalid.

The strongest opinion, in many ways, was the dissenting opinion of Roling of the Netherlands. With reference to the law of the Charter, he declared:

"In the Nuremberg judgment it is stated. . . . and in our case the prosecution and the majority of the Tribunal have held the same view—that the Tribunal is bound by its

[15] Dissenting Opinion of Bernard, Judgment, Vol. IV, p. 18.
[16] Concurring Opinion of Jaranilla, Judgment, Vol. IV, pp. 1-7.
[17] Concurring Opinion of Jaranilla, Judgment, Vol. IV, pp. 13-23.
[18] Concurring Opinion of Jaranilla, Judgment, Vol. IV, p. 29.

Charter. This is true in the sense that never could the Tribunal have power 'to try and punish' beyond the Charter. But it does not, and cannot, imply that the Tribunal would be bound to follow the Charter in case it should contain provisions in violation of international law."[19]

Referring to Jaranilla's statement, he pointed out that the majority also took the view that the members could only refuse office if they felt the Charter transgressed those limits and leave their places to judges prepared to agree with the Charter. This view, he felt, was not only dangerous for the future, but incorrect. It would be extremely dangerous if an international tribunal, called upon to mete out justice, were required to follow the views of the Supreme Commander of the victors, without the power or duty to inquire if it were applying rules of justice at all.[20] The Tribunal could only decide if certain crimes, acknowledged as such in international law, came within the jurisdiction of the Tribunal. It had no power to make certain activities criminal by the Charter.[21] The Tribunal also had power only to try war crimes arising from this war, not every war waged in the Far East.[22]

This author differs with Justice Roling upon his next conclusion, however, as to the legality or illegality of aggressive war. He discussed extensively the steps taken seeking to outlaw war and came to the conclusion that aggressive war actually is not recognized as a crime, that no tribunal was ever contemplated for punishment, and that each nation was left to determine for itself the doctrine of self-defense.[23] As to acts of omission, he felt that these were not sufficiently definite to be punishable. After referring to the *Yamashita* case he laid down the following tests which he believed must all be shown to establish guilt: (1) the defendant must have known or should have known of the commission of acts charged; (2) he must have had the power to prevent them; (3) he must have had the duty to prevent them.[24]

Justice Roling felt that none should be sentenced to death for a crime against peace at this stage of the law. He felt that others who were guilty of conventional war crimes who had received only life imprisonment should have been executed, but felt that five of the defendants whom he named should be ac-

---

19 Dissenting Opinion of Roling, Judgment, Vol. V, p. 3.
20 Dissenting Opinion of Roling, Judgment, Vol. V, pp. 4, 5.
21 Dissenting Opinion of Roling, Judgment, Vol. V, p. 7.
22 Dissenting Opinion of Roling, Judgment, Vol. V, p. 8.
23 Dissenting Opinion of Roling, Judgment, Vol. V, pp. 10-44.
24 Dissenting Opinion of Roling, Judgment, Vol. V, p. 54 *et seq.*

quitted. Hata, he felt, was purely a military man following his duties, and was not required to question orders.[25] Hirota was an elder statesman, who tried to prevent the occurrences.[26] Kido, he felt, was in no position to prevent the occurrence of these acts.[27] Shigemitsu[28] and Togo[29] had not been proven guilty of crime.

Justice Pal's dissenting opinion is lengthy and seems to be a translation of Ghandi's theory of passive resistance or of no resistance into judicial terminology. He was obviously unhappy about the entire trial and its outcome. He opened his discussion by stating the chief questions to be (1) whether aggressive wars were or became criminal during the period in question; (2) whether any *ex post facto* law could be or was enacted, making these acts criminal; (3) whether individuals were criminally liable for such acts.[30] He quoted from Kelsen at length, feeling that the trial was based upon a thirst for vengeance. He definitely felt that the Tribunal was not limited to the law set forth in the Charter, and that the Charter might be *"ultra vires."*[31] He felt that the Tribunal had a right to see if the law was correctly stated in the Charter, and that a belligerent has no right, as Glueck contends, to create new international law.[32] He severely criticized Justice Lawrence's language as to the Charter "making" something the law.[33] He also criticized the doctrine of natural or universal law.[34]

All efforts to outlaw war, he felt, were merely using public opinion as a sanction.[35] He referred to the difficulty of defining aggression,[36] and severely criticized the rules of procedure and evidence followed by the Tribunal.[37] He stated that the Tribunal had abandoned all rules developed by civilized tribunals, including hearsay evidence,[38] the introduction of private papers,[39] leading questions and affidavit evidence,[40] opinions, beliefs and

---

[25] Dissenting Opinion of Roling, Judgment, Vol. V, pp. 178-190.
[26] Dissenting Opinion of Roling, Judgment, Vol. V, pp. 190-211.
[27] Dissenting Opinion of Roling, Judgment, Vol. V, pp. 211-227.
[28] Dissenting Opinion of Roling, Judgment, Vol. V, pp. 228-243.
[29] Dissenting Opinion of Roling, Judgment, Vol. V, pp. 248-249.
[30] Dissenting Opinion of Pal, Judgment, Vol. VI, pp. 1-15.
[31] Dissenting Opinion of Pal, Judgment, Vol. VI, pp. 26-38.
[32] Dissenting Opinion of Pal, Judgment, Vol. VI, p. 44.
[33] Dissenting Opinion of Pal, Judgment, Vol. VI, pp. 50-51.
[34] Dissenting Opinion of Pal, Judgment, Vol. VI, pp. 147-151.
[35] Dissenting Opinion of Pal, Judgment, Vol. VI, p. 90.
[36] Dissenting Opinion of Pal, Judgment, Vol. VI, pp. 227-279.
[37] Dissenting Opinion of Pal, Judgment, Vol. VI, pp. 280-348.
[38] Dissenting Opinion of Pal, Judgment, Vol. VI, pp. 282-283.
[39] Dissenting Opinion of Pal, Judgment, Vol. VI, pp. 283-295.
[40] Dissenting Opinion of Pal, Judgment, Vol. VI, p. 299.

conclusions,[41] and that it had placed undue limitations upon cross-examination.[42] He also criticized the Tribunal for refusing to admit evidence, and applying certain rules with great strictness, when all evidence having probative value was supposed to have been admitted.[43]

He felt that the Tribunal's ruling upon the matter of conspiracy was unreasonable that, if a person were once in a government, thereafter he was responsible for everything ever done even long after he was separated from it, or conversely, that he would be liable for anything occurring prior to such connection.

Justice Pal then referred at great length to the situation existing between the United States and Japan, and directly accused Roosevelt and Hull of fostering the war.[44] Instead of limiting their activities to the protection of the Philippines, he declared they purported to advocate what should be done in the entire Pacific. He believed that the United States was the aggressor against Japan throughout in its struggles. As pointed out in the earlier discussion,[45] Justice Pal's judgment may have been influenced by the fact that he felt that the western nations had stepped out of their sphere in interfering in the affairs of the Pacific.

The judgment may be summarized in its contribution to international law by stating that it definitely raises the question of the law to be applied by such tribunals. The better opinion would be that such a tribunal cannot go beyond its charter, but can apply only existing rules of international law which are within the scope of the charter. The judgment does not aid greatly in straightening out the questions of what constitutes present international penal jurisprudence. Probably the majority opinion, following closely upon the heels of the Nuremberg and other trials, would be considered as advancing the concepts of aggressive war as criminal and of individual responsibility. With reference to the procedure to be followed, the trial leaves much to be desired, and it would seem essential that future bodies crystallize in advance the nature of evidence to be introduced, rules of procedure to be followed, and the respective duties owing by counsel to the tribunal and by the tribunal to the counsel.

---

41 Dissenting Opinion of Pal, Judgment, Vol. VI, pp. 302-5.

42 Dissenting Opinion of Pal, Judgment, Vol. VI, pp. 305-8.

43 Dissenting Opinion of Pal, Judgment, Vol. VI, pp. 302-5, 308.

44 Dissenting Opinion of Pal, Judgment, Vol. VIII, p. 875.

45 Infra, p. 249.

PART V

MILITARY COMMISSIONS AND OTHER TRIBUNALS

XXXIII

INTRODUCTION

There has been some tendency for persons not familiar with the recent post-war trials to belittle the conduct and importance of the hearings before military commissions. Frequently such persons are wholly unaware of the number of such trials actually conducted, the number of persons tried therein, and the nature of the evidence introduced. There has been so much publicity given to the major international trials, and to a few of the military commission hearings, that the labors expended in the many hundreds of other cases tend to be forgotten.

Not all of such hearings have been reported, and no information has been received by this author of hearings conducted by the Soviet Union or its satellites. Apart from the International Military Tribunal at Nuremberg, the International Military Tribunal for the Far East, and the subsequent Nuremberg trials, there were 2,116 known hearings before military commissions or corresponding tribunals, divided as follows: United States, 950; Great Britain, 541; Australia, 275; France, 271; the Netherlands, 35; Poland, 25; Norway, 11; Canada, 5; China, 2; Greece, 1. Undoubtedly there have been many more such hearings of which no record is presently available. The number of cases handled by military commissions of the United States may be tabulated as follows:

	Europe	Japan	China	Manila	Italy	Pacific Islands	Total
No. of Cases	491	317	11	97	9	25	950
Defendants tried	1,682	993	75	215	14	116	3,095
Convictions	1,416	850	67	195	11	108	2,647
Acquittals	266	143	8	20	3	8	448
Death Sentences	428	124	10	92	7	28	689

It can readily be seen that complete trials of 3095 persons by commissions of one nation alone involve a tremendous task. This required the preparation of prosecution and defense data in 950 separate hearings. Reference will be made to many of these hearings in the following discussion, as well as to those of other nations. Since a number of the trials conducted by various allied nations have been meticulously studied by the United Nations War Crimes Commission, reference to the fifteen-volume set published by that organization will be cited as "U. N. 30," or whatever the case number may be, and the volume and page number will be found under the appropriate reference. Other leading cases not specifically reported in those volumes will be cited as "Supp. Cases 14, 18," or according to the number in the tabulation hereinafter contained, with appropriate page references.

From sheer mass of material alone, these trials cannot be minimized. International law exists, fundamentally, in the conscience of civilized nations as so called "customary" law. The holdings of such tribunals, where uniform, demonstrate the concept of such nations of customary law and are, accordingly, of great significance. International law, like continental law, does not adhere rigidly to the doctrine of stare decisis. That legal doctrine, furthermore, is not conclusive even in this country, and our national courts do not hesitate to overthrow precedent where necessary to accomplish substantial justice. However, while these decisions will not be wholly conclusive upon future tribunals, they do serve a valuable function in determining the construction of doctrines of international law and their application to specific factual situations. Determinations so made are very persuasive. While the general controlling principles of law and procedure were established at Nuremberg, only a few major offenders were tried by that international court, and not all potential questions were settled. The vast number of other trials required the decision of procedural questions of almost every conceivable type, as well as the adjudication of similar and wholly different criminal acts. Whatever opinion one may have concerning the conduct of post-war trials, they are *faites accompli,* and thus constitute constructions of international law which will be observed in the future.

Some criticism has been made of the composition of the tribunals, upon the ground that they were not composed of trained jurists. It was obviously impossible to secure skilled criminal court judges to preside in more than two thousand hearings, some of which consumed many months of time. However, even if such personnel had been available, the criticism assumes that such judges would have more knowledge of international law than would trained military officers. It must not be forgotten that military officers are trained in the rules of land warfare and in controlling treaties and conventions, which are not ordinarily a part of a jurist's background.

Such officers are also familiar with court martial procedure, which is similar to, although not identical with, that followed by military commissions. A trained legal officer was assigned in almost every instance to the court for its guidance. We Americans make juries, composed of laymen, the sole judges of guilt or innocence of a person indicted under our criminal laws, even for offenses as serious as murder. Under our system of justice, we accept the fact that laymen are competent to judge the truth or falsity of testimony, to weigh the evidence, and arrive at a just result. It seems rather inconsistent, therefore, to criticize military tribunals upon the ground that not all of their personnel were attorneys.

As a matter of fact, an examination of the trial records themselves discloses, with a few exceptions, remarkable consistency in procedure and fairness in the rulings of such tribunals. This will be discussed at greater length subsequently, after an analysis of certain of the controlling cases. While it is obviously impossible to discuss all of the reported cases, in view of space limitations and because of the unavailability of much of such material, the following tabulation lists the cases which will be referred to in the ensuing chapters as representative of such hearings.

LAW REPORTS OF TRIALS OF WAR CRIMINALS

United Nations War Crimes Commission
His Majesty's Stationery Office
London, England

No. of Case	Name of Case	Presenting Nation	Place of Presentation	Date of Trial	Vol.	Pages
1	Kapitanleutnant Heinz Eck and 4 others (Peleus Trial)	Great Britain	Hamburg	Oct. 17-20, 1945	I	1- 21
2	General Anton Dostler	United States	Rome	Oct. 8-12, 1945	I	22- 34
3	Otto Sandrock and 3 others (Almelo Trial)	Great Britain	Almelo, Holland	Nov. 24-26, 1945	I	35- 45
4	Alfons Klein and 6 others (Hadamar Trial)	United States	Wiesbaden	Oct. 8-15, 1945	I	46- 54

No. of Case	Name of Case	Presenting Nation	Place of Presentation	Date of Trial	Vol.	Pages
5	Oberleutnant Gerhard Grumpelt (Scuttled U-Boats Case)	Great Britain	Hamburg	Feb. 12, 13, 1946	I	55– 70
6	Rear Admiral Nisuke Masuda and 4 others of Imperial Japanese Navy (Jaluit Atoll Case)	United States	Kwajalein Island	Dec. 7-13, 1945	I	71– 80
7	Karl Amberger (Dreierwalde Case)	Great Britain	Wuppertal	Mar. 11-14, 1946	I	81– 87
8	Erich Heyer and 6 others (Essen Lynching Case)	Great Britain	Essen	Dec. 18-19, 21-22, 1945	I	88– 92
9	Bruno Tesch and 2 others (Zyklon B Case)	Great Britain	Hamburg	Mar. 1-8, 1946	I	93–103
10	Josef Kramer and 44 others (Belsen Trial)	Great Britain	Luneburg	Sept. 17-Nov. 17, 1945	II	1–156
11	Karl-Hans Hermann Klinge	Norway		Dec. 8, 1945-Feb. 27, 1946	III	1– 14
12	Richard Wilhelm Hermann Bruns and 2 others	Norway		Mar. 20 & July 3, 1946	III	15– 22

No. of Case	Name of Case	Presenting Nation	Place of Presentation	Date of Trial	Vol.	Pages
13	Robert Wagner and 6 others	France	Strasbourg	Apr. 23-May 3, 1946; July 24, 1946	III	23– 55
14	Gunther Thiele and Georg Steinert	United States	Aubsberg	June 13, 1945	III	56– 59
15	Peter Back	United States	Ahrweiler	June 16, 1945	III	60– 61
16	Albert Bury and Wilhelm Hafner	United States	Freising	July 15, 1945	III	62– 64
17 & 18	Anton Schosser and of Josef Goldbrunner and Alfons Jacob Wilm	United States	Dachau	Sept. 14-15, 17, 1945	III	65– 66
19	Erich Killinger and 4 others	Great Britain	Wuppertal	Nov. 26-Dec. 3, 1945	III	67– 75
20	Yamamoto Chusaburo	Great Britain	Kuala Lumpur	Jan. 30-Feb. 1, 1946	III	76– 80
21	General Tomoyuki Yamashita	United States	Manila	Oct. 8-Dec. 7, 1945; Feb. 4, 1946	IV	1– 96

No. of Case	Name of Case	Presenting Nation	Place of Presentation	Date of Trial	Vol.	Pages
22	S. S. Brigadefuhrer Kurt Meyer (Abbaye Ardenne Case)	Canada	Aurich	Dec. 10-28, 1945	IV	97–112
23	Major Karl Rauer and 6 others	Great Britain	Wuppertal	Feb. 18, 1946	IV	113–117
24	Kurt Student	Great Britain	Luneberg	May 6-10, 1946	IV	118–124
25	Lieutenant-General Shigeru Sawada and 3 others	United States	Shanghai	Feb. 27, 1946-Apr. 15, 1946	V	1– 24
26	Sergeant-Major Shigeru Ohashi and 6 others	Australia	Rabaul	Mar. 20-23, 1946	V	25– 31
27	Captain Eitaro Shinohara and 2 others	Australia	Rabaul	Mar. 30-Apr. 1, 1946	V	32– 36
28	Captain Eikichi Kato	Australia	Rabaul	May 7, 1946	V	37– 38
29	Karl Buck and 10 others	Great Britain	Wuppertal	May 6-10, 1946	V	39– 44
30	Karl Adam Golkel and 13 others	Great Britain	Wuppertal	May 15-21, 1946	V	45– 53
31	Werner Rohde and 8 others	Great Britain	Wuppertal	May 29-June 1, 1946	V	54– 59

No. of Case	Name of Case	Presenting Nation	Place of Presentation	Date of Trial	Vol.	Pages
32	Lieutenant General Harukei Isayama and 7 others	United States	Shanghai	July 1-25, 1946	V	60– 65
33	General Tanaka Hisakasu and 5 others	United States	Shanghai	Aug. 13-Sept. 3, 1946	V	66– 81
34	Haupsturmfuhrer Oscar Hans	Norway		Jan. 1947; Aug. 1947	V	82– 93
35	Josef Alstotter and others (Justice Trial)	United States	Nuremberg	Feb. 17-Dec. 4, 1947	VI	1–110
36	Gerhard Friedrich Ernst Flesch	Norway		Nov.-Dec., 1946 and Feb. 1948	VI	111–120
37	Hauptsturmfuhrer Amon Leopold Goeth	Poland	Cracow	Aug. 27-31; Sept. 2-5, 1946	VII	1– 10
38	Obersturmbannfuhrer Rudolf Franz Ferdinand Hoess	Poland	Warsaw	Mar. 11-29, 1947	VII	11– 26
39	Erhard Milch	United States	Nuremberg	Dec. 20, 1946-Apr. 17, 1947	VII	27– 66

No. of Case	Name of Case	Presenting Nation	Place of Presentation	Date of Trial	Vol.	Pages
40	Gustav Becker, Wilhelm Weber and 18 others	France	Lyon	Concluded July 17, 1947	VII	67–73
41	Jean-Pierre Lex	France	Nancy	Concluded May 13, 1946	VII	74–75
42	Heinrich Gerike and 7 others (the Velpke Children's Home Case)	Great Britain	Brunswick	Mar. 20-Apr. 3, 1946	VII	76–81
43	General von Mackensen and General Maelzer	Great Britain	Rome	Nov. 18-30, 1945	VIII	1–8
44	Albert Kesselring	Great Britain	Venice	Feb. 17-May 6, 1947	VIII	9–14
45	Carl Bauer, Ernst Schrameck and Herbert Falten	France	Dijon	Completed Oct. 18, 1945	VIII	15–21
46	Franz Holstein and 23 others	France	Dijon	Completed Feb. 3, 1947	VIII	22–33
47	Wilhelm List and others (Hostages Trial)	United States	Nuremberg	July 8, 1947-Feb. 19, 1948	VIII	34–92

No. of Case	Name of Case	Presenting Nation	Place of Presentation	Date of Trial	Vol.	Pages
48	Friedrich Flick and 5 others	United States	Nuremberg	Apr. 20-Dec. 22, 1947	IX	1- 59
49	Hans Szabados	France	Clermont-Ferrand	Judgment, June 23, 1946	IX	59- 61
50	Alois and Anna Bommer and their daughters	France	Metz	Judgment, Feb. 19, 1947	IX	62- 66
51	Karl Lingenfelder	France	Metz	Judgment, Mar. 11, 1947	IX	67- 68
52	Christian Baus	France	Metz	Judgment, Aug. 21, 1947	IX	68- 71
53	Philippe Rust	France	Metz	Judgment, Mar. 5, 1948	IX	71- 74
54	Karl-Heinz Moehle	Great Britain	Hamburg	Oct. 15-16, 1946	IX	75- 82
55	Helmuth von Ruchteschell	Great Britain	Hamburg	May 5-21, 1947	IX	82- 90
56	Otto Skorzeny and others	United States	U. S. Zone of Germany	Aug. 18-Sept. 9, 1947	IX	90- 94

No. of Case	Name of Case	Presenting Nation	Place of Presentation	Date of Trial	Vol.	Pages
57	Carl Krauch and 22 others (I. G. Farben Trial)	United States	Nuremberg	Aug. 14, 1947-July 29, 1948	X	1– 68
58	Alfried Felix Alwyn Krupp von Bohlen und Halbach and 11 others (Krupp Trial)	United States	Nuremberg	Nov. 17, 1947-June 30, 1948	X	69–181
59	Tanabe Koshiro	Netherlands	Macassar	Feb. 5, 1947	XI	1– 4
60	Martin Gottfried Weiss and 39 others	United States	Dachau	Nov. 15-Dec. 13, 1945	XI	5– 17
61	Generaloberst Nickolaus von Falkenhorst	Great Britain	Brunswick	July 29-Aug. 2, 1946	XI	18– 30
62	Max Wielen and 17 others (Stalag Luft III Case)	Great Britain	Hamburg	July 1-Sept. 3, 1947	XI	31– 52
63	Lieutenant General Kurt Maelzer	United States	Florence	Sept. 9-14, 1946	XI	53– 55

No. of Case	Name of Case	Presenting Nation	Place of Presentation	Date of Trial	Vol.	Pages
64	Lieutenant-General Baba Masao	Australia	Rabaul	May 28-June 2, 1947	XI	56– 61
65	Tanaka Chuichi and 2 others	Australia	Rabaul	July 12, 1946	XI	62– 63
66	Franz Schonfeld and 9 others	Great Britain	Essen	June 11-26, 1946	XI	64– 73
67	Johannes Oenning and Emil Nix	Great Britain	Borken	Dec. 21 & 22, 1945	XI	74– 75
68	Hans Renoth and 3 others	Great Britain	Elten	Jan. 8-10, 1946	XI	76– 78
69	Arno Heering	Great Britain	Hannover	Jan. 24-26, 1946	XI	79– 80
70	Willi Mackensen	Great Britain	Hannover	Jan. 28, 1946	XI	81– 82
71	Eberhard Schoengrath and 6 others	Great Britain	Burgsteinfurt	Feb. 7-11, 1946	XI	83– 85
72	Wilhelm von Leeb and 13 others (German High Command Trial)	United States	Nuremberg	Dec. 30, 1947-Oct. 28, 1948	XII	1–127

No. of Case	Name of Case	Presenting Nation	Place of Presentation	Date of Trial	Vol.	Pages
73	Ulrich Greifelt and others	United States	Nuremberg	Oct. 10, 1947-Mar. 10, 1948	XIII	1- 69
74	Gauleiter Artur Greiser	Poland	Poznan	June 21-July 7, 1946	XIII	70–117
75	Albert Wagner	France	Rastatt	Judgment, Nov. 29, 1946	XIII	118–121
76	Washio Awochi	Netherlands	Batavia	Judgment, Oct. 25, 1946	XIII	122 125
77	Susuki Motosuke	Netherlands	Amboina	Judgment, Jan. 28, 1948	XIII	126–130
78	Wilhelm Gerbsch	Netherlands	Amsterdam	Judgment, Apr. 28, 1948	XIII	131–137
79	Shigeki Motomura and 15 others	Netherlands	Macassar	Judgment, July 18, 1947	XIII	138–145
80	Heinz Hagendorf	United States	Dachau	Aug. 8-9, 1946	XIII	146–148
81	Erich Weiss and Wilhelm Mundo	United States	Ludwigsburg	Nov. 9-10, 1945	XIII	149–150

No. of Case	Name of Case	Presenting Nation	Place of Presentation	Date of Trial	Vol.	Pages
82	Max Schmid	United States	Dachau	May 19, 1947	XIII	151–152
83	Takashi Sakai	China	Nanking	Aug. 29, 1946	XIV	1– 7
84	Lothar Eisentrager and others	United States	Shanghai	Oct. 3, 1946-Jan. 14, 1947	XIV	8– 22
85	Dr. Joseph Buhler	Poland	Cracow	June 17-July 10, 1948	XIV	23– 48
86	Hans Paul Helmuth Latza and 2 others	Norway		Feb. 18, 1947; Dec. 3, 1948	XIV	49– 85
87	Josef Hangobl	United States	Dachau	Oct. 17-18, 1945	XIV	86– 88
88	Hans Albin Rauter	Netherlands	Hague	May 4, 1948; Jan. 12, 1949	XIV	89–138
89	Willy Zuehlke	Netherlands	Amsterdam	Aug. 3, 1948; Dec. 6, 1948	XIV	139–151

SUPPLEMENTAL CASES

(References either to official transcripts, other publications, or United Nations War Crimes Commission's Law Reports where merely referred to but not reported)

1 The Peleus Trial, J. Cameron, 1 War Crimes Trials, William Hodge & Co., Ltd. (Same as U. N. Case 1)

2 The Belsen Trial, Raymond Phillips, 2 War Crimes Trials, William Hodge & Co., Ltd. (Same as U. N. Case 10)

3 Trial of Gozawa Sadaichi and 9 others, Colin Sleeman, 3 War Crimes Trials, William Hodge & Co., Ltd. (Same as Supplementary Case 46)

4 The Hadamar Trial, Earl W. Kintner, 4 War Crimes Trials, William Hodge & Co., Ltd. (Same as U. N. Case 4)

5 The Natzweiler Trial, Anthony M. Webb, 5 War Crimes Trials, William Hodge & Co., Ltd.

6 Trial of Nikolaus von Falkenhorst, E. H. Stevens, 6 War Crimes Trials, William Hodge & Co., Ltd. (Same as U. N. Case 61)

No. of Case	Name of Case	Presenting Nation	Place of Presentation	Date of Trial	Vol.	Pages
7	United States v. Kurt Goebbel and others (Borkume Island Case)	United States	(References to Official Transcript)			
8	United States v. Josias Prince Zu Waldeck et al.	United States	(References to Official Transcript)			
9	United States v. Johann Melchior and Walter Hirschelman	United States	Ludwigsburg	Jan. 24, 1946	U. N. V	17
10	United States v. Alphonse Klein and 6 others (Hadamar Case)	United States	Dachau	Oct. 8-15, 1945	(References to official transcript)	

No. of Case	Name of Case	Presenting Nation	Place of Presentation	Date of Trial	Vol.	Pages
11	United States v. Hans Altfuldisch and others (Mauthausen Concentration Case)	United States	Dachau	Mar. 29-May 13, 1946	(References to official transcript)	
12	United States v. Karl Neuber	United States	Ludwigs-burg	Apr. 26, 1946	U. N. V	17
13	United States v. Friederich Becker and others (Flossenberg Trials)	United States	Dachau	May 14, 1946-Jan. 22, 1947	U. N. XV	44
14	United States v. Franz Umstatter	United States	Dachau	Aug. 26-27, 1946	U. N. XV	47
15	United States v. Jurgen Stroop and 21 others	United States	Dachau	Jan. 10-Mar. 2, 1947	(References to official transcript)	
16	United States v. Erwin Schienkiewitz	United States	Dachau	Feb. 13, 1947	U. N. XIII	66
17	United States v. Hans Seibold and 2 others	United States	Dachau	Mar. 5-7, 1947	U. N. XIII	66

No. of Case	Name of Case	Presenting Nation	Place of Presentation	Date of Trial	Vol.	Pages
18	United States v. Eduard Erb	United States	Dachau	Mar. 25-Apr. 2, 1947	U. N. XV	15
19	United States v. Joaquin Espinosa	United States	Dachau	May 9-12, 1947	U. N. XV	46
20	United States v. Erich Wippermann	United States	Dachau	May 16-23, 1947	U. N. XV	47
21	United States v. Hans Heitkamp	United States	Dachau	Aug. 7-8, 1947	U. N. XV	47
22	United States v. Anton Stinglwagner and Max Lengfelder	United States	Dachau	Aug. 12-14, 1947	U. N. XV	43
23	United States v. Josef Remmele	United States	Dachau	Sept. 9-15, 1947	U. N. XV	44
24	United States v. Kingoro Fukuda and 7 others	(References to official transcript)				
25	United States v. Nichizawa and 6 others	United States	Yokohama	(References to official transcript)		
26	United States v. Yuichi Sakamoto	United States	Yokohama	Feb. 13, 1946	U. N. IV	86

No. of Case	Name of Case	Presenting Nation	Place of Presentation	Date of Trial	Vol.	Pages
27	United States v. Jutaro Kikuchi	United States	Yokohama	Apr. 20, 1946	U. N. XIII	152
28	United States v. Chogo Hashinoto	United States	Yokohama	Feb. 12-17, 1947	U. N. XV	44
29	United States v. Tomoyuki Yamashita	United States	Manila	Oct. 8-Dec. 7, 1945	(References to official transcript)	
30	United States v. Shiyoku Kou	United States	Manila	Apr. 18, 1946	U. N. IV	86
31	United States v. Yoshio Makizawa	United States	Shanghai	May 9-10, 1946	U. N. XV	101
32	United States v. Yoshio Tachibana and 4 others	United States	Guam	Aug. 1946	U. N. IV	86
33	United States v. Tachibana Yochio and 13 others	United States	Marianas	Aug. 2-15, 1946	U. N. XIII	66
34	Trial of Kapitanleutnant Ehrenrich Stever	Great Britain	Hamburg	July 17-18, 1946	U. N. XV	13

No. of Case	Name of Case	Presenting Nation	Place of Presentation	Date of Trial	Vol.	Pages
35	Trial of Hans Wickman	Great Britain	Hamburg	Nov. 29, 1946	U. N. XV	133
36	Trial of Johannes Schwarzhuber and 15 others (Ravensbruck Trial)	Great Britain	Hamburg	Dec. 5, 1946-Feb. 3, 1947	U. N. XV	46
37	Trial of Willi Tessmann and others	Great Britain	Hamburg	Sept. 1-24, 1947	U. N. V XV	73, 76 94, 177
38	Trial of Karl Rath and Otto Schutz	Great Britain	Hamburg	Jan. 14-22, 1948	U. N. XV	122
39	Trial of Carl Rath and Richard Thiel	Great Britain	Hamburg	Jan. 23-29, 1948	U. N. XV	184
40	Trial of Valentin Fuerstein and others	Great Britain	Hamburg	Aug. 4-24, 1948	U. N. XV	173
41	Trial of Oscar Hans	Great Britain	Hamburg	Aug. 18-25, 1948	U. N. XV	198, n. 3
42	Trial of Erwin Wieczorek	Great Britain	Hamburg	Aug. 25-Nov. 6, 1948	U. N. XV	186

No. of Case	Name of Case	Presenting Nation	Place of Presentation	Date of Trial	Vol.	Pages
43	Trial of Georg Tyrolt and others	Great Britain	Helmstedt	May 20-June 24, 1946	U. N. XV	61, 86, 92
44	Trial of General Victor Seeger	Great Britain	Wuppertal	July 10-11, 1946	U. N. IV XV	88, 89 68-69
45	Trial of Gustav Alfred Jepson	Great Britain	Luneberg	Aug. 13-23, 1946	U. N. XV	46
46	Trial of Gozawa Sadaichi and others	Great Britain	Singapore	Jan. 21-Feb. 4, 1946	U. N. XV	175
47	Trial of Tomomo Shimio	Great Britain	Singapore		U. N. I II	106 128
48	Trial of Mitsugu Toda	Great Britain	Hong Kong	May 7-28, 1947	U. N. X	167-168
49	Trial of Yoshimasa Nishisama and Sadeharo Haratake	Great Britain	Maymyo	July 18-Aug. 1, 1947	U. N. XV	43
50	Trial of August Bauer	France	Metz	June 10, 1947	U. N. IX	65
51	Trial of Heinrich Weber	France	Metz	Aug. 21, 1947	U. N. IX	70-71

No. of Case	Name of Case	Presenting Nation	Place of Presentation	Date of Trial	Vol.	Pages
52	Trial of Pitz	France	Metz	Oct. 8, 1947	U. N. VII	69, 71
53	Trial of Ferrarese	France	Metz	Oct. 8, 1947	U. N. VII	69, 71
54	Trial of Karl Benz and wife	France	Metz	Nov. 4, 1947	U. N. IX	65
55	Trial of Jean Georges Stucker	France	Metz	Nov. 25, 1947	U. N. VI VII XV	109 73 89
56	Trial of Willi Buch	France	Metz	Dec. 2, 1947	U. N. IX	65
57	Trial of Elisabeth Neber	France	Metz	Apr. 6, 1948	U. N. IX	65
58	Trial of Elisa Kespar	France	Metz	Apr. 6, 1948	U. N. IX	71
59	Trial of Lucien Fromes	France	Lyon	Nov. 23, 1945	U. N. XV	45
60	Trial of Albert Raskin	France	Lyon	Jan. 16, 1947	U. N. XV	46
61	Trial of Horst Hebestreit	France	Lyon	Jan. 16, 1947	U. N. XV	91
62	Trials of Piffer and Tschander	France	Lyon	Oct. 30, 1947	U. N. VII	69
63	Trial of Gallina	France	Lyon	Apr. 8, 1948	U. N. VII	69
64	Trial of Paul Korber	France	Restatt	Nov. 27, 1946	U. N. XIII	120
65	Trial of Lendines Monte	France	Paris	Apr. 25, 1947	U. N. XV	45

No. of Case	Name of Case	Presenting Nation	Place of Presentation	Date of Trial	Vol.	Pages
66	Trial of Henri Georges Stadelhofer	France	Marseilles	Apr. 15, 1948	U. N. VI XV	106 90-91
67	Trial of Hermann Roechling	France	German Zone	June 30, 1948	U. N. X	56, 57, 171
68	Trial of Abraham Robert Esau	Netherlands	s'-Hertogenbosch		U. N. XV	128
69	Trial of Ahlbrecht	Netherlands	Arnhem	June 19, 1946; Feb. 17, 1947	U. N. XI	89, 90
70	Trial of Friedrich C. Christianson	Netherlands	Arnhem	Aug. 12, 1948	U. N. XIV	128
71	Trial of Minoru Hatada and 2 others	Netherlands E. I.	Macassar		U. N. XV	132
72	Trial of Mizuo Katsuno	Netherlands E. I.	Medan	May 7, 1947	U. N. XV	132
73	Trial of Albert Forster	Poland			U. N. XIV	46
74	Trial of Ludwik Fischer and Ludwik Leist	Poland		Mar. 3, 1947	U. N. XIV	42-45
75	Trial of Wilhelm Artur Konstantin Wagner	Norway			U. N. V	17
76	Trial of Ernest Weiman and others	Norway		Sept. 1946; Aug. 1947	U. N. IV	95-96

No. of Case	Name of Case	Presenting Nation	Place of Presentation	Date of Trial	Vol.	Pages
77	Trial of Robert Holzer and 2 others	Canada	Aurich	Mar. 25-Apr. 6, 1946	U. N. V	15, 16, 21
78	Trial of Generals Mueller and Braeuer	Greece	Athens		U. N. XV	62
79	Trial of Yoshio Taki and others	Australia	Rabaul	Dec. 13, 1945	U. N. XV	200
80	Trial of Col. Satoru Kikuchi	Australia	Rabaul	Mar. 28-29, 1946	U. N. V	76
81	Trial of Masao Kudo and others	Australia	Rabaul	Mar. 30-Apr. 1, 1946	U. N. XV	8
82	Trial of Tomiyasu Tisato	Australia	Rabaul	Apr. 2, 1946	U. N. XIII	152
83	Trial of Tsuziji Matsumoto and others	Australia	Rabaul	Apr. 6, 1946	U. N. XV	200
84	Trial of Hiroe Sakoda	Australia	Rabaul	Apr. 26-29, 1946	U. N. XV	200
85	Trial of Jiro Sakata	Australia	Rabaul	Apr. 29-30, 1946	U. N. XV	200
86	Trial of Toma Ikeba and others	Australia	Rabaul	May 15-16, 1946	U. N. VII	61
87	Trial of Shoichi Yamamoto and others	Australia	Rabaul	May 20-27, 1946	U. N. XI XV	80 83

No. of Case	Name of Case	Presenting Nation	Place of Presentation	Date of Trial	Vol.	Pages
88	Trial of Daijiro Yamasaki	Australia	Rabaul	June 3-4, 1946	U. N. XV	8
89	Trial of Kazuyoshi Shimida	Australia	Rabaul	June 26, 1946	U. N. XV	200
90	Trial of Lt. Gen'l. Artachi Hatazo	Australia	Rabaul	Apr. 1947	U. N. XI	60
91	Trial of Hitoshi Imamura	Australia	Rabaul	May 1-16, 1947	U. N. IV	87
92	Trial of Teruma Hiranaka and 1 other	Australia	Rabaul	May 13, 1947	U. N. VII	61
93	Trial of Kunito Hatakeyama and 1 other	Australia	Rabaul	July 14-17, 1947	U. N. VII	61
94	Trial of Lt. Kazuhiko Imamura	Australia	Rabaul	July 25, 1947	U. N. XII	101
95	Trial of Tazaki Takehiko	Australia	Wewak	Nov. 30, 1945	U. N. XIII	152
96	Trial of Maj. Gen'l. Endo Shimichi	Australia	Mortai	Jan. 1946	U. N. XI	59, 60
97	Trial of Kishio Uchiyama and Mitsugu Fukuda	Australia	Singapore	Apr. 18-29, 1947	U. N. XI XV	80 n. 1 83-84
98	Trial of Takashi Sakai	China	Nanking	Aug. 27, 1946	U. N. IV XIV	88 7

The crematorium at the Dachau concentration camp. The crematory is filled with bodies awaiting to be burned.
—*Courtesy of U. S. Army Signal Corps.*

XXXIV

NATURE OF CRIMES CHARGED

The nature of war crimes in general and other offenses forming the basis of the post-war trials following World War II has already been examined in detail in the discussion of the International Military Tribunal at Nuremberg. Those same charges were, in addition to others, examined at additional length in the subsequent proceedings at Nuremberg and in the many trials before military commissions. There were also proceedings of particular interest which were heard by special tribunals in certain of the allied countries, in which the charges were not of a character to receive any consideration where the trials of only major war criminals were involved. In view of the fact that these various hearings constitute adjudications which may be of future benefit in like hearings, an effort will be made to cover the general scope of any charges raised in the reported hearings.

The concept of aggressive war as a crime against peace, including the planning, preparation, initiation, and waging of hostilities, and acts in concert toward these ends, was established fundamentally by the International Military Tribunal at Nuremberg. This concept was explained in detail by the International Military Tribunal for the Far East and in the various subsequent hearings at Nuremberg, including particularly the Ministries Case.[1] This concept was also necessarily involved in certain of the hearings before military commissions, and it was uniformly held that crimes against peace constituted violations of international law.[2] In one of these cases the effect of the doctrine was limited, in that that court held that, even though the war was illegal, not all acts committed by members of the enemy army would constitute war crimes.[3] Doubtless this is true, properly construed, in that the acts in themselves may be legal and therefore not subject to question. Inasmuch as the charges involved acts which were highly extraordinary and ordinarily in violation of the penal law, however, the result may be questioned. A person is usually subject to punishment under the ordinary penal laws for acts permitted in war time, such as the shooting of an enemy. If the war is itself illegal, so as not to constitute

---

1 See infra, pp. 22-28.

2 U. N. 57, 58, 72, 74, 83, 84.

3 U. N. 89.

an excuse for such shooting, it would seem that the ordinary penal rules would apply.[4]

The question of crimes against humanity has evoked considerable discussion among jurists and lawyers. As evidenced by the prior discussion, crimes against humanity have long been recognized by international law, and intervention has occasionally been required in order to terminate such offenses.[5] In so far as the punishment of individuals for such offenses are concerned, international authority has generally been lacking prior to this time. It must be recognized that the expression is more sweeping than that of war crimes, but that the two may overlap, as a single offense may be both a war crime and a crime against humanity.[6]

The language of many of the cases is rather loose. In order to constitute a crime against humanity, the offenses must be general in character, widespread, systematic, and based upon political, racial, or religious grounds. Isolated acts may constitute crimes under a penal code of the nation where the act is committed, or they may constitute war crimes, but they cannot constitute crimes against humanity unless they meet the tests stated above. Conversely, the fact that such acts meeting these tests constitute crimes against humanity does not prevent each separable act from being criminal, either as a war crime or as a violation of municipal law. The greatest significance of the development of the separate concept of crimes against humanity is that it permits the punishment of genocide or other acts against citizens or subjects of the enemy nation.[7] While one of those cases[8] states that those acts committed before the outbreak of war are not relevant to the court's jurisdiction, this holding was not by way of limitation upon criminal responsibility, but was evolved because of the limitations imposed upon the jurisdiction of the tribunal by Council Control Law No. 10. If the controlling law establishing the tribunal is sufficiently broad, then offenses committed prior to the outbreak of hostilities could be adjudged equally with those committed thereafter.[9] The outbreak of war was not a necessary corollary to the commission of such crimes and violators could be brought to justice whether or not hostilities ever developed.

In view of the fact that crimes against humanity frequently involved control of courts and of the judicial process, it is ap-

[4] See discussion infra, pp. 35, 39, 53.
[5] See prior discussion, infra, pp. 25, 36.
[6] See general discussion, U. N. XV, pp. 134-138.
[7] U. N. 35, 41, 78, 85; also discussion in U. N. XV, pp. 87-88.
[8] U. N. 41, p. 26.
[9] U. N. 41, pp. 47-48.

parent that such acts could not be committed under any system where persons are protected in their life, liberty, and property by due process of law. The question, then, of the denial of a fair trial may be presented either in the instance of crimes against humanity or in the case of war crimes committed either against members of an enemy force or against civilians. In view of the overlapping character of such offenses, no effort will be made to break down the citations as to the situation of the victim.

Frequently, such offenses were shown to have been committed where prisoners of war or civilians were executed without a prior trial at all, or under such circumstances as to make the trial a mockery. If these were widespread in character and such as to show a general course of conduct as to a particular people or group of people, whether allied or enemy nationals, they may constitute crimes against humanity. In the last great war, this arose where Jews were condemned en masse, irrespective of their place of residence. When such acts are committed against allied nationals, whether civilian or members of an army, they constitute war crimes. If the war is illegal so as to constitute no defense for the commission of the act, the unlawful restraint or killing may also constitute penal offenses against the law of the place of commission.

As a general rule, the requirements of a fair trial are these:[10]

(1) The accused must be told that he is being tried, and must be apprised of the exact nature of the charge preferred against him.

(2) The facts upon which an accused is tried must be adequately investigated and an honest effort made to determine all of the facts, both favorable and unfavorable.

(3) The accused must be given an opportunity to defend himself, and given adequate opportunity to investigate the facts and present a proper defense.

(4) The accused must be allowed to select or be assigned competent defense counsel whose sole interest is the protection of the accused's rights.

(5) The proceedings must be conducted in a language familiar to the accused or translated for his benefit.

(6) The accused must be shown any and all documents introduced in evidence against him.

(7) The accused must be given an opportunity for confrontation of hostile witnesses where reasonably possible, and where such testimony is of major importance.

---

[10] See general discussion U. N. V, pp. 70-81.

(8) The charges and evidence must involve real offenses properly based upon the law and not supported by false, fictitious, or misleading evidence.

(9) The Tribunal must take adequate time for deliberation of the facts before passing sentence, and such finding must be based upon an honest interpretation of the facts in evidence.

(10) If the charge is a capital one, there should be an opportunity, where possible, given for review of the findings.

In many of these cases it will be found that certain of the defendants claimed to have given a fair trial to prisoners where no evidence whatsoever was taken or any discussion had with any of the accused. Two of the defendants would, perhaps, meet together and merely decide what punishment to give the accused. Often there were no defense counsel; in several instances the trials were conducted in Japanese, and the accused did not even know that they were upon trial. In practically all instances where such charges were brought, the evidence indicated clearly that the accused persons had never had a legitimate opportunity to be heard in accordance with common principles of justice, whether those applied by this nation or by any of the other allied nations whose hearings are reported in the discussion of these particular tribunals.[11] Even suspected spies[12] or saboteurs[13] must be given a fair trial, even though the sentence may be one of death if such accused are found guilty.

Proceeding over to war crimes, in their more ordinary aspects, many of the charges were based upon the unlawful killing of prisoners of war.[14] In many cases, this involved the killing of prisoners who had just been captured; frequently these were aviators who had landed by parachute upon enemy terrain. In other cases the executions were performed in prisoner of war camps or concentration camps. In certain of the hearings, the evidence showed that the action of the particular defendant was close to the borderline of propriety. For example, in one instance[15] the prisoners were escaping over the border into Switzerland. However, the defendant there admitted that he gave no adequate warning before firing or that he fired simultaneously with the giving of a warning. Other examples will be discussed in greater detail in dealing with the defenses asserted by the defendants.

---

[11] U. N. 21, 25-36, 61, 66, 77, 86; Supp. Case 80.

[12] U. N. 3, 30, 31, 66.

[13] U. N. 26, 27, 45.

[14] U. N. 2, 3, 6-8, 10, 13-18, 22-25, 29, 30, 32, 33, 45, 60, 61, 64, 67, 68, 70-72, 74, 81, 82, 87; Supp. Cases 9, 16, 17, 33, 47, 64, 77, 80, 82.

[15] Supp. Case 64.

In connection with killings, some confusion has arisen where the charge contained the term "murder." It is clear from prior discussion that the crime of murder may be committed, although a state of war exists.[16] The continuation of hostilities does not suspend all penal codes. It merely creates a justification or defense for an act which would amount to murder unless rightfully committed in a legal war. If the war is illegal, then this justification or excuse may disappear and the penal laws be rendered active. If the act constitutes a war crime, then, being unjustified by the laws of war, the penal code may again apply. Thus, in two cases handled by military tribunals, the indictment or charge sheet was based upon "murder," but the judgment of conviction found the defendants guilty of "manslaughter."[17] In those two cases it appeared that the prosecuting nation, Australia, used these terms loosely, as no violation of any penal law of the place where the acts were committed was charged. Only a war crime was charged, but the municipal law concept was carried over. As opposed to this, a British Judge Advocate[18] pointed out that the term "murder" could be used only if all members of the tribunal and counsel understood its particular employment. He declared that technically the term "murder" requires the killing of a person under the King's peace. The Netherlands held that municipal law was wholly inapplicable under any circumstances,[19] which conclusion seems far too sweeping to be correct.

In view of the fact that one cannot with impunity execute a prisoner of war, he cannot produce such death through medical experimentation, irrespective of whether or not such a result was contemplated.[20] The Hague Rules and the Geneva Convention impose certain standards recognized by civilized nations which must be followed in the treatment of prisoners. Any violation of these standards constitutes a war crime.[21] Thus, a prisoner who has escaped but is recaptured is not subject to execution.[22] And it is illegal to shoot prisoners in order to prevent their escape, even though their intention to so escape may be common knowledge.[23]

In addition to the requirements of the Hague Rules and of the Geneva Convention prohibiting the execution of prisoners

---

16 Infra, pp. 35, 39, 53, 292.

17 Supp. Cases 81, 88.

18 U. N. 8.

19 Supp. Case 69.

20 U. N. 60.

21 U. N. 20, 24, 59, 61, 64, 65, 69.

22 Supp. Case 86.

23 Supp. Cases 92, 93.

without just cause, certain standards are imposed to insure the well-being of such prisoners. In view of these requirements, ill treatment of such persons by torture or beating, or by providing inadequate and unsanitary quarters, or by depriving such persons of food or medical supplies, constitute war crimes. Many of the charges brought were based upon such offenses.[24] Other charges were based upon abuses or violations resulting from the interrogation of prisoners and attempts to secure information from them by wrongful acts.[25] Other offenses resulted from mistreatment in places where the prisoners were required to work,[26] and from exposure of the prisoner to insults and humiliation.[27] Other trials dealt with the compelling of prisoners to work upon implements of war or in places aiding the war effort of the enemy,[28] although one tribunal disregarded such charges where it did not appear that the prisoners were to be exposed to danger.[29] It should be recognized that the compelling of prisoners to aid the war effort of the enemy is itself a war crime, irrespective of the hazards thereby incurred, just as the forcing of prisoners to work in a place of danger and failing to take precautions for their safety is a separate war crime.[30]

Whether or not turning over prisoners to another command or arm of the government constitutes a war crime may depend upon the knowledge possessed as to the fate awaiting such prisoner.[31] The transportation of a prisoner for execution is an initial step in the wrongful act and may form the basis for a charge.[32] In addition to these acts, violation of one's duty towards sick and wounded is a war crime,[33] as is the infringement of religious beliefs of prisoners.[34] The only reported case in the European theater of the mutilation of dead bodies was when a surgeon detached a skull for research purposes.[35] In the Pacific theater such charges were common,[36] and convictions were even had upon the express charge of cannibalism.[37]

---

[24] U. N. 11, 19, 24, 39, 57, 58, 60, 61, 63, 64, 65, 69, 70, 72, 74, 75; Supp. Cases 31, 48.

[25] U. N. 19 (as to civilian prisoners see U. N. 11).

[26] Supp. Case 48.

[27] U. N. 63.

[28] U. N. 24, 39, 48, 57, 59, 72; Supp. Case 94.

[29] U. N. 72.

[30] U. N. 24, 72; Supp. Case 94.

[31] U. N. 72 (in Germany the army often turned prisoners over to the SD, knowing they would be executed).

[32] U. N. 60.

[33] U. N. 22, 60; Supp. Cases 24, 25.

[34] U. N. 65.

[35] U. N. 82.

[36] Supp. Cases 27, 32, 95.

[37] Supp. Cases 32, 33, 82, 95.

Other charges of war crimes in the European theater arose from such matters as the denial of quarters to troops desiring to surrender,[38] improper firing upon ships,[39] and the killing of shipwrecked survivors.[40] The improper use of captured uniforms,[41] the abuse of Red Cross protection,[42] and bombing of Red Cross ships[43] formed the bases of other charges.

In addition to the duties imposed upon a belligerent nation as to the soldiers of an enemy force, the Hague Rules of Land Warfare impose stringent requirements for the protection of civilian inhabitants.[44] The killing of such civilians without just cause, therefore, constitutes a war crime.[45] Nor may such persons be killed indiscriminately as hostages under the guise of reprisals.[46] And while genocide is itself illegal as a crime against humanity, it further constitutes a war crime when committed against the citizens of an occupied country.[47]

Certainly the use of such persons for medical experimentation is one of the horrible examples of a breach of the Hague Rules.[48] The shooting of civilian prisoners who have escaped and been recaptured has constituted a ground for indictment.[49] But where the guarantees of fair trial are observed, execution of a person for war treason will carry no penalty.[50]

The employment of systematic terrorism by the occupying nation violates not only the dictates of international morality but the Hague Rules of Land Warfare, and renders those responsible liable to punishment.[51] Thus, it is found that the ill-treatment of the civilian population in an occupied nation, or of civilian prisoners, including such acts as torture and brutalities, was one of the common charges upon which guilt was found.[52] This would include brutalities inflicted in an effort to secure informa-

---

38 U. N. 22.

39 U. N. 55.

40 U. N. 1, 54, 55. See the excellent discussion of duties at sea, U. N. IX, pp. 86-90, and upon submarine warfare IX, pp. 78-82.

41 U. N. 56.

42 U. N. 80.

43 U. N. 24.

44 See discussion, infra, pp. 29-39.

45 U. N. 3, 4, 11, 12, 21, 26-28, 37, 38, 40, 45, 60, 74, 75, 77-79, 85, 86; Supp. Cases 38, 85, 89.

46 U. N. 34, 36, 43, 44, 46, 47, 49, 88.

47 U. N. 9, 10, 35, 37, 38, 60, 73, 74, 85, 88; Supp. Case 75.

48 U. N. 9, 35, 38, 60.

49 U. N. 75.

50 U. N. 47.

51 U. N. 40, 79, 85.

52 U. N. 10, 11, 31, 35, 36, 38-40, 46, 60, 74, 78, 79, 89; Supp. Cases 53, 63, 79, 83, 84.

tion,[53] as well as acts committed in concentration camps,[54] although one prosecutor admitted the necessity of showing a connection with the prosecution of the war.[55] While this connection would seem to be necessary so far as violation of the Hague Rules are concerned, the same result would not necessarily follow in so far as crimes against humanity or violations of municipal law are charged.

Acts of reprisal[56] or failure to provide medical treatment and care[57] may raise a question of guilt. Deportation of civilian populations except in cases of extreme military necessity constitutes a war crime.[58] Employment of civilians as slave labor is also criminal.[59] In this respect, lines of distinction must be carefully drawn. It is not illegal for an occupying power to require civilians to work in order to maintain their own existence or their internal economy. It is, however, improper to transport them from their own land, to place them in hazardous employment, to require them to work to aid the efforts of the aggressor in its belligerencies, or to require them to do any act demanding disloyalty toward their own nation. If such persons are employed, they must receive adequate remuneration, and adequate housing, food, and clothing must be provided. It was not until clear violation of all of these requirements was shown that the term "slave labor" came into general use by these tribunals, and it is in that sense that the term is employed in this discussion.

A combination crime consisting of deportation for purposes of slave labor, thus embodying two offenses, formed a common basis for indictment.[60] Use upon illegal work was punishable.[61] And transportation for execution, as in the case of prisoners of war previously examined, constituted one step in a crime series which itself rendered the actor responsible.[62]

The imposition of collective penalties is forbidden by international law, except under very narrow and strictly construed circumstances.[63] The misuse of authority,[64] unlawful arrest and

---

[53] U. N. 11; Supp. Case 76.

[54] U. N. 4, 9, 10.

[55] U. N. 10 at page 106.

[56] E.g., U. N. 36.

[57] U. N. 36, 60.

[58] Supp. Case 52 (as to the crime of causing deportation by denunciation, U. N. 41).

[59] Supp. Case 67.

[60] U. N. 13, 39, 40, 41, 43, 48, 57, 58, 72, 74, 85, 88.

[61] U. N. 53.

[62] U. N. 60; Supp. Case 75.

[63] U. N. 88.

[64] U. N. 77, in this case amounting to incitement to murder.

detention,[65] attempting to secure arrests,[66] illegal recruiting,[67] or attempts to recruit illegally[68] all are acts recognized for decades as violations of international law. Enforced prostitution constitutes an offense,[69] as does the forcible separation of children from their parents,[70] or failure to safeguard such children thereafter.[71] And the unnecessary putting aside of the usual courts of the occupied nation and disregard of legal process,[72] or the invasion of religious rights[73] constitute violations of the Hague Rules.

In addition to penal responsibility for the infliction of personal indignities, such responsibility may be incurred for wrongful acts regarding property. These may include, for example, the economic exploitation of occupied territory and its resources, contrary to the Hague Rules.[74] The indiscriminate destruction of property,[75] or monuments[76] is unlawful. Looting, pillage, seizure, or confiscation of public or private property renders the wrongdoer liable,[77] even though a legal formality may be followed or some inadequate consideration paid for the transfer.[78] Acts of theft,[79] receipt of stolen goods,[80] and, as termed by the French, "abuse of confidence," similar to the American "confidence game" charge[81] resulted in sentences to various offenders. Clearly the first two of such charges could be in the nature either of war crimes or violations of municipal law. The last could fall only in the municipal law category.

Other crimes charged were of a more unusual nature. Denunciation of a citizen to the occupying authority was considered criminal.[82] The incitement of citizens to take up arms against their own nation was punished.[83] Upon a broader scale, de-

---

65 U. N. 10, 35, 40, 46, 79, 88, 89; Supp. Cases 52, 53, 62, 63.
66 Supp. Case 55.
67 U. N. 13.
68 Supp. Case 52.
69 U. N. 76.
70 U. N. 42.
71 U. N. 42; Supp. Case 43.
72 U. N. 35, 72; see also note 10, supra.
73 U. N. 88, 89.
74 U. N. 74, 85.
75 U. N. 46, 49.
76 U. N. 48, 51.
77 U. N. 21, 37, 38, 46, 47, 48, 53, 57, 58, 85, 88; Supp. Case 68.
78 U. N. 48, 57, 58.
79 U. N. 50, 52; Supp. Cases 50, 54, 56, 57.
80 U. N. 50, 52; Supp. Cases 50, 54.
81 U. N. 52; Supp. Cases 51, 58.
82 U. N. 41.
83 U. N. 13.

nationalization,[84] Germanization of a conquered people,[85] annexation of occupied territory,[86] destruction of the culture and education of the occupied nation,[87] insulting and deriding of that nation and its citizens,[88] creation of a puppet state from its territory,[89] and the wrongful demand for the withdrawal of troops[90] were held to be indictable offenses. And, of course, a violation of the rights of neutrals is punishable.[91]

The giving of illegal orders may constitute a war crime, even though such orders are never enforced.[92] Thus, an order to troops to take no prisoners and to execute all prisoners taken is *ipso facto* illegal, though occasion never arises to act accordingly.[93] The breach of terms of a surrender agreement or armistice is a war crime.[94] One of the most interesting of such trials arose in China where a group of ex-Nazis ignored the German surrender and actively aided the Japanese. These persons were captured after the Japanese surrender, adroitly rounded up, and tried. Guilt was established.[95] And the waging of hostilities by a civilian is punishable.[96]

---

[84] U. N. 37, 73.
[85] U. N. 74.
[86] U. N. 74.
[87] U. N. 74, 85.
[88] U. N. 74.
[89] U. N. 83.
[90] U. N. 83.
[91] U. N. XV, p. 84, note 1.
[92] U. N. 22, 61, 67, 72 at pp. 118-123; Supp. Case 35.
[93] Supp. Case 35.
[94] U. N. 5, 84; Supp. Cases 34, 71, 72.
[95] U. N. 84.
[96] U. N. 87.

XXXV

PARTIES DEFENDANT

It is not the purpose of this chapter to deal exhaustively with all persons who have been charged with war crimes, but merely to illustrate the general types of situations, with appropriate examples, as a corollary to the preceding chapter. As will appear, any person may be a war criminal, whether or not in the actual military service. The same, of course, holds true as to the concepts of aggressive war, crimes against humanity, and other criminal acts previously discussed.

Military officers, whether Army or Navy, have thus been arraigned upon such charges.[1] Staff officers may be adjudged guilty,[2] and have been so found as a result of drafting illegal orders normally issued of their own volition.[3] A staff officer would not necessarily be held punishable, however, by his possession of knowledge of illegal acts which he did not order and could neither prevent nor punish.[4]

Civilians may be liable equally with personnel of the armed forces.[5] Such persons may occupy particular posts, such as party officials and administrators,[6] or members of the Gestapo.[7] Businessmen, industrialists, and bankers have all been found in the dock.[8] Judges[9] and prosecutors,[10] doctors and nurses[11] have been parties defendant. And the same is true of concentration camp employees,[12] and executioners.[13]

Nor is the power of the nation sitting in judgment limited to the trial of enemy nationals. Neutrals, as well, may be subject to punishment. Thus, the United States had occasion to try

---

1 U. N. 1, 2, 5, 6, 21-23, 33, 39, 47, 48, 54, 55, 66, 72; Supp. Cases 6, 44, 78.

2 U. N. 32, 33; IMTFE Judgment, p. 1186.

3 U. N. 47 at pp. 113-118.

4 U. N. 47 at pp. 75-76.

5 U. N. 8-10, 14, 16, 62, 68, 87.

6 U. N. 13, 35; Supp. Cases 73, 74. Compare U. N. 78 at pp. 136-137.

7 Supp. Case 75.

8 U. N. 9, 48, 57, 58. See also infra pp. 6, 7, 171, 177, 207.

9 U. N. 13 at p. 27; 31, 32, 35, 42, 86.

10 U. N. 13, 25, 27, 28, 33, 35.

11 U. N. 4, 10, 42; Supp. Case 43 and see infra pp. 141-151.

12 U. N. 10; Supp. Cases 11, 13.

13 U. N. 10, 31; Supp. Cases 11, 13, 41.

allied nationals,[14] citizens of Yugloslavia,[15] the Netherlands,[16] and Spain.[17] Great Britain tried nationals of Poland,[18] Denmark,[19] and Switzerland.[20] France tried citizens of Luxembourg,[21] Spain,[22] and Belgium.[23]

The question logically arises as to the liability of defendants who have acted in conjunction with others toward a common end, or who have engaged in crimes requiring action by more than one person. As has been seen, the International Military Tribunal at Nuremberg established membership in a criminal organization as punishable per se. This concept was followed by the military commissions.[24] Poland even held the occupation government of that nation to be a criminal group.[25]

The United States likewise had introduced the concept of conspiracy into the first international hearing.[26] This view was followed only to a limited degree in that precise form.[27] One case even held that no proof of advance preparation need be shown, that a conspiracy might be deduced from the acts of the parties.[28] There is, in addition, discussion of situations involving so called "group crimes."[29] France, in a similar vein, posed penalties for association with wrongdoers.[30]

For the most part, use of the term "conspiracy" was not in the best odor. The indictments normally referred to some aspect of a "common design" or "concerted action."[31] The British were prone to use the term "concerned in" to include accessories and persons not physically present at the time of commission.[32] The

---

14 Supp. Case 11.

15 Supp. Case 13.

16 Supp. Case 13.

17 Supp. Case 19.

18 U. N. 10.

19 Supp. Case 45.

20 Supp. Case 36.

21 Supp. Case 59.

22 Supp. Case 65.

23 Supp. Case 60.

24 U. N. 35, 37, 48, 57, 74, 89.

25 Supp. Cases 73, 74.

26 Infra pp. 40-45.

27 See comments in U. N. 62, 74; Supp. Cases 61, 66. But compare stringent restrictions imposed by U. N. 35 at p. 5, also pp. 105-109.

28 U. N. 10.

29 U. N. 79; Supp. Case 7 at pp. 494-509 and Supp. Case 11, pp. 51-63.

30 Supp. Case 66.

31 U. N. 3, 8, 10, 35, 60, 66; Supp. Cases 10, 11, 13, 37. Compare U. N. 68 at pp. 76-77.

32 U. N. 30, 31, 66; compare U. N. 62 at pp. 43, 44, 46.

French referred also to "complicity,"[33] and the United States carried over the concept of principals and accessories.[34]

The instigation or incitement of offenses, or encouragement thereof, renders the individual liable.[35] Aiding and abetting may bring similar results.[36] Arranging for poison gas, although not acting as a supplier thereof, for an improper use was held to be criminal.[37] And one may be an accessory after the fact.[38]

It will thus be seen that one need not personally participate in a killing in order to be responsible therefor.[39] He may have a liability if he fails to stop a beating or murder which he has the power to prevent.[40] The difficulty arises and much heated argument has ensued over drafting the boundary lines of guilt resulting from inaction or from an act of omission. One defeated defense counsel wrote a book largely upon this subject which, while subject to much pertinent criticism upon certain conclusions and upon general bias, ably presents the view usually taken by defendants upon this subject.[41]

In order to understand this problem properly, it is necessary to consider to some degree the functions of a field commander in time of war. If a civilian, such as Scarface Al Capone, for example, had turned loose three hundred machine gunners in Cicero, with no instructions whatever, he should not have been too amazed if a few violations of law occurred. Soldiers are armed also and possess this advantage, plus an important psychological factor of being in control of a certain area, over prisoners of war and civilians. It may be expected that disorders and even killings will result in the absence of capable and strict supervision. The Army expects to provide that supervision through its chain of command, and by the instillation of discipline into its soldiers. In the chain of command, each officer, whether commissioned or non-commissioned, is directly responsible for the acts of any soldier under his command, and may be removed from his command or punished by court martial for any improper act. The captain is not relieved of responsibil-

[33] U. N. 13, 40. The Norwegian and Dutch law also expressly recognized this term.

[34] U. N. 35, 57, 66, 68, 79. See also U. N. XV, pp. 52-53.

[35] U. N. 8, 77, 83.

[36] Supp. Case 12. In that case leading prisoners to the place of execution.

[37] U. N. 9.

[38] U. N. XV, p. 53.

[39] U. N. 8, 9, 30.

[40] U. N. 68.

[41] A. Frank Reel, The Case of General Yamashita, 1949, University of Chicago Press.

ity by the neglect of a sergeant or lieutenant—each officer is responsible along the scale, and none may excuse himself by an effort to shift the blame.

In order to protect himself from the consequences of irresponsible acts, the field commander takes several steps. (1) He selects or secures responsible junior officers and non-commissioned officers. (2) He issues strict orders as to the conduct to be observed by the men in the field. (3) He instills discipline into the men by training, drills, censure, punishment, reward, and promotion. (4) He keeps close contact with daily occurrences in order to determine offenders and, by creating examples, to deter others from offending. If a commander does all of these things, he has little cause for concern upon the question of criminal guilt. But the cases treated in the following discussion, and over which much fury has arisen, are those where the commander did nothing whatever, even in the nature of issuance of orders; or he merely issued orders and took no steps to secure their enforcement. The question is then squarely presented as to whether a person having such responsibility can fold his hands, close his eyes, and merely say "I did not know."[42]

As a spy knows that he may be executed if captured, a field commander knows that the patriotic duty he performs exposes him to certain penalties if he fails to control his troops. Neither the spy nor the officer may desire the task or ask for the responsibility; many a soldier is sent upon a suicide mission against his will, and many a civilian loses his life in a bombing raid; but these are the responsibilities of war. So long as nations adhere to this form of barbarism, these responsibilities must be accepted. Those responsibilities of the commanding officers are imposed in order to hold at a minimum the barbarities and oppressions which otherwise must occur, to fix the responsibility for violations of the rules of warfare upon those who, by their own integrity and use of their extensive powers, can prevent such violations or hold them to a minimum.

The military tribunals were quite uniform in imposing penalties upon field commanders whose neglect to control their troops permitted the occurrence of atrocities,[43] or deaths of prisoners.[44] This is, of course, true where such acts are permitted and

---

[42] See Moore's International Law Digest, Vol. VI, p. 919; American Rules of Land Warfare, Article 347; Wharton's Criminal Evidence, Vol. I, Section 88.

[43] U. N. 21, 64; Supp. Cases 26, 32, 91.

[44] U. N. 8, 10, 21, 25, 48, 64, 72; Supp. Cases 90, 96.

[45] U. N. 21, 22; Supp. Case 30.

sanctioned,[45] instigated,[46] or condoned.[47] If the commander has knowledge, there can be no reasonable argument in his defense.[48]

Some cases have inferred that knowledge on the part of such a defendant must be shown before guilt can be adjudged.[49] Without proof of knowledge of the wrongful act contemplated or committed, acquittal upon that count may be directed under this view.[50] Negligence, it has even been held, is insufficient no matter how gross it may be.[51]

This seems to be a singularly unrealistic view, completely disregarding the duties of field commanders, and placing an almost insurmountable burden upon the prosecution. It is almost impossible to show one's state of mind; it is, at best, difficult to show direct knowledge. This would seem more aptly to be a defensive matter to show lack of knowledge, when the circumstances show the chain of command and the commission of acts which are criminal in character by persons under that commander.

Other cases have held that one may be charged with knowledge of such acts under a proper showing.[52] Nor is lack of knowledge any defense where one has a duty to know what is going on and the legality of the act.[53] Certainly if the defendant had reasonable grounds for supposing that wrongful acts might occur and failed to take all reasonable steps to prevent them, he will be held responsible.[54] And while one will not be liable where he has no authority or physical power to prevent an occurrence,[55] this has been held no defense to the commanding general of occupied territory.[56] A chief of staff, however, would not have the same responsibility as a commanding general.[57]

---

46 U. N. 23.

47 U. N. 23.

48 U. N. 64; Supp. Cases 44, 90, 96. This responsibility is also fixed where knowledge is shown by the laws of China, U. N. XIV, p. 158; France, U. N. III, p. 94; Luxembourg, Article 3 of Law of August 2, 1947; and the Netherlands, U. N. XI, pp. 100-101, XV, p. 68.

49 U. N. 72 at pp. 110-111; Supp. Case 44.

50 U. N. 33, 39 at pp. 88-91. See also U. N. VII, pp. 63, 64.

51 U. N. 19.

52 U. N. 9, 35, 39; Supp. Case 98.

53 U. N. 21 at p. 35; 40, 47, 72; Supp. Case 98. Also see discussions of Medical Case in U. N. IV, pp. 91-93 and the Pohl Case, U. N. XV, p. 72; IMTFE, Judgment, p. 72.

54 U. N. 66.

55 U. N. 21 at pp. 42-44. See also U. N. 47, 72.

56 U. N. 72 at pp. 107-110.

57 U. N. 72.

XXXVI

DEFENSES ASSERTED

1. **To Jurisdiction.** In general, the right to try enemy combatants has been well established, as pointed out in the prior proceedings at the International Military Tribunal at Nuremberg, which discusses the controlling law. Punishment of individuals for piracy, brigandage, espionage, sabotage, treason, and other offenses has long been accepted. The Hague Rules provide expressly for trials by the military authority of the belligerent nations of war crimes. Since it is obvious that a commanding general can not sit in judgment upon an enemy state, the liabilities of which are ordinarily determined by treaty, the trials of individuals for war crimes were clearly contemplated since 1907, if not before. The Treaties of Versailles of June 28, 1919,[1] St. Germain of September 10, 1919,[2] and Trianon of June 4, 1920,[3] all expressly provided for individual responsibility. The Report of the Commission appointed after the First World War made such recommendations.[4] A like reference is found at the close of the Boer War, which preceded the Hague Convention.[5] Many individual instances could be cited.[6]

As will be indicated later, some defense counsel raised the defense of lack of individual liability. Others were, however, concerned with the manner of trial. One defendant asserted that he was entitled to trial by an international court rather than a commission.[7] As a matter of fact, there were some holdings to the effect that a commission appointed as a result of four-nation agreement in dividing the responsibilities of government and trials is itself an international tribunal,[8] although a Far Eastern commission regarded itself as an administrative and not a judicial body.[9]

---

1 Article 228.

2 Article 173.

3 Article 157.

4 March 9, 1919. See 14 *American Journal of International Law* 95, 121, also memorandum at page 141.

5 95 British and Foreign State Papers (1901-1902), p. 160.

6 See references in Colby, *War Crimes*, 23 Mich. Law Review 482, 496, 497.

7 U. N. 88.

8 U. N. 39, 48.

9 Supp. Case 29 at p. 101, where the tribunal stated, perhaps erroneously, that it was "not a judicial body . . . it is an executive tribunal set up

Some authorities have felt that such trials might be held before regular municipal courts.[10] Since the Hague Rules provide only for trials by courts-martial or military commissions, it is the author's conviction that trials by municipal courts would be proper only (1) if the offense were a violation of the law of such state, committed within the jurisdiction of that state;[11] or (2) if the international law has been embodied in the organic or statutory law of the prosecuting state, or made a part thereof by treaty. As a matter of fact, both Norway and Denmark expressly require that there be a violation of their municipal law before they will assume jurisdiction over one accused of war crime in their tribunals. The mere fact that such act is a violation of international law has been held by them to be insufficient.[12] France will not assume jurisdiction in courts created within its boundaries unless the offense was committed in France or to the prejudice of persons specifically enumerated in its ordinance,[13] although a broader rule was followed in tribunals supervised by France as an occupying power under the Four Power agreement. As to whether or not municipal law or municipal law concepts will carry over, there is a difference of opinion.[14]

The defense was raised in hearings conducted by the United States that Congress had not delegated authority to military commissions to try enemy nationals for war crimes.[15] Other defendants claimed the right to trial by court-martial, in which hearings a stricter procedure is followed, more beneficial to the defense.[16] One such defendant based his claim upon the theory that he, as a prisoner of war, had greater rights than a mere civilian.[17] Another insisted upon a right to trial by persons of equal or superior rank.[18] One might assume, if this reasoning is correct, that a trial of Hitler could have been conducted by no lesser personages than Truman, Churchill, DeGaulle, and Joseph Stalin, as their nations' commanders-in-chief. It must be re-

---

by the Commander-in-Chief . . . it is an executive body, and not a judicial body."

[10] See discussion in U. N. XV, pp. 28-48.

[11] Jurisdiction not necessarily being co-extensive with or limited by geographical boundaries.

[12] See discussion in U. N. XV, p. 32.

[13] U. N. 13.

[14] Netherlands, for example, holds that municipal law has no application whatever: Supp. Case 69. Australia holds differently: Supp. Cases 81, 88. See the discussion *ante*, pp. 79-81, 295, 299.

[15] U. N. 6, 25; Supp. Case 29.

[16] U. N. 2; Supp. Case 7.

[17] Supp. Case 7.

[18] U. N. 63.

emphasized that these are not courts-martial but military commissions, with rigid formalities removed, but with one prime requisite—that of the administration of justice.

A defendant in a case in Poland insisted that there was no valid law or decree permitting his trial, contending that the decree in question referred only to Poles and not Germans.[19] Another claimed that his acts, which consisted merely of the murder of some thousands of varied nationals in a hospital, were not war crimes, and that a military tribunal could not try him for such acts.[20] Such acts are, of course, in addition to being crimes against humanity, also war crimes and violations of municipal law which could be tried by a military commission per se, or as a general court if sitting as a body created by the occupying power in the absence of appropriate national tribunals for that purpose. Another defendant argued that the particular commission was not legally established;[21] a different defendant objected to the venue.[22] The objection was also made that another nation, in these instances China, had prior jurisdiction to try the offenders,[23] and that there had been no sufficient consent by that nation to waive such prior jurisdiction.[24] It would seem that if such nations had concurrent jurisdiction, it is for the nation first obtaining custody of such persons to proceed in the absence of objection by the other nation or of an agreement to the contrary.

An objection in an American trial that the acts in question occurred prior to America's entry into the war was overruled upon the ground that they were committed while war was being waged.[25] This seems correct upon the premise that the tribunal of the United States was one constituted by international agreement to represent all four powers, three of which were at war at the time of the crimes. An objection that the acts occurred outside of the American Occupation Zone, and that this nation had thereby lost jurisdiction, was overruled for like reasons.[26] And this was true even of a charge that the offense was committed against an allied national in the Russian Zone.[27]

It was likewise argued that an American tribunal had no jurisdiction to evaluate offenses against Chinese nationals.[28] A

19 U. N. 37.
20 U. N. 4.
21 U. N. 2.
22 U. N. 6.
23 U. N. 25, 84.
24 U. N. 2, 25, 84.
25 Supp. Cases 8, 23.
26 Supp. Case 8, pp. 4-9, 14, 15.
27 Supp. Case 18.
28 Supp. Case 24 at pp. 15, 18, 548.

similar confusion appeared in many of such hearings. These tribunals, however, uniformly enforced the rule that so far as war crimes alone were concerned, the nationality of the victim was immaterial, provided he was an allied national.[29] Thus, the United States tried cases where the victims were Canadian,[30] Polish and Czechoslovakian,[31] and the British tried cases where the victims were Chinese and Indian.[32] Nor did it matter to a British tribunal that the victim was an American who had been killed in French Indo-China.[33]

The killing or ill-treatment of allied nationals in enemy territory may thus be adjudicated.[34] Crimes against former enemy nationals have been tried,[35] although in three of these cases it will be found that the offenses actually constituted crimes against humanity, as to which there would be little question arising upon this jurisdictional ground.[36] One tribunal refused jurisdiction, however, even though the offense was one which might constitute a violation of the municipal law.[37] Offenses against neutrals have been held within the tribunals' jurisdiction.[38]

It has similarly been held immaterial that the place of the offense was not one then, or even previously, held by the particular power conducting the tribunal. The United States has adjudicated cases where the offenses occurred in the Russian Zone,[39] the French Zone,[40] the British Zone,[41] China,[42] and Hong Kong, a British Crown Colony.[43] Great Britain has taken a like view,[44] as has Canada.[45] Certainly someone must take jurisdiction over offenses committed upon the high seas.[46] And it is not even of particular moment that the place of the offense be specified for judicial purposes,[47] although it may be required

---

[29] U. N. 3, 4, 9, 10, 22, 42, 60, 70, 71, 77; Supp. Cases 4, 8, 18, 22, 23, 24, 28, 49.

[30] Supp. Case 28.

[31] Supp. Case 22.

[32] Supp. Case 49.

[33] Supp. Case 47.

[34] U. N. 4, 10, 42, 78; Supp. Cases 2, 4, 43.

[35] U. N. 10, 35, 39, 48.

[36] U. N. 10, 35, 48.

[37] U. N. 77.

[38] Supp. Case 38.

[39] Supp. Case 18.

[40] Supp. Case 21.

[41] Supp. Case 20.

[42] U. N. 25.

[43] U. N. 33.

[44] U. N. 3.

[45] U. N. 22.

[46] Supp. Case 1.

[47] Supp. Case 14.

for reasons of information to the defense. In addition to the reasons previously advanced for these conclusions, there is the quite well recognized doctrine of the universality of jurisdiction over war crimes.[48] In other words, where nations are joined in combat with and later in judgment upon a wrongdoer, the offenses are regarded as offenses against all of the allied nations, and may be punished by any of them, irrespective of geographical boundary lines.

Other jurisdictional defenses were (1) that Russia was not a signatory to the Geneva Convention, and violations of that treaty as to Russian prisoners were not war crimes;[49] (2) that China was not a party to the Hague Convention and was not within its protection;[50] (3) that Poland as a conquered nation was not within the protection of the Geneva Convention, but subject exclusively to the rules of the occupying force, thereby making German law apply;[51] (4) that Japan had not signed by the Geneva Convention and was not bound by its provisions as to the treatment of prisoners.[52] In reply to these defenses, it should be observed that the Geneva Convention did no more than to recast already well accepted customary law of nations in this regard, as demonstrated by the Hague Rules and other conventions. In addition to this, Japan, in February 1942, agreed to observe the Geneva Convention as to certain nations "mutatis mutandis."[53]

The Geneva Convention was given another twist defensively, defense counsel objecting that jurisdiction of several tribunals was non-existent because of failure to give notice to the protecting powers of Germany or Japan, depending upon the nationality of the defendant. It was succinctly pointed out that notice was required only as to offenses committed by prisoners of war and not as to crimes committed by belligerents prior to capture.[54]

---

48 Cowle's, "Universality of Jurisdiction over War Crimes," 33 *California Law Review*, 177 (1945); I Wheaton's *International Law*, 6th Ed., p. 269; U. N. 47, 84.

49 Supp. Case 4.

50 Supp. Case 24.

51 Supp. Case 4.

52 Supp. Case 3.

53 U. N. 59, 64.

54 U. N. 2, 6, 13, 47, 60, 72, 88; Supp. Case 11 at pp. 8-11; Supp. Case 15 at pp. 29-36; Supp. Case 24 at p. 935; Supp. Case 29 at pp. 95-97. See particularly the discussion in U. N. 88, pp. 114-118 and the language of the United States Supreme Court in *In Re Yamashita*, quoted in U. N. IV at pp. 46-49. Also see p. 78 of that volume. But compare the inconsistent argument of the prosecutor in U. N. 30, where he charged as a failure to give a fair trial the defendant's failure to notify the protecting power of British airmen tried and convicted by the persons accused.

Nor is a tribunal deprived of jurisdiction by the fact that the alleged crime was committed after the cessation of hostilities.[55]

2. **Customary Defenses.** One of the delightful matters in connection with all of the post-war trials is the intensity of the defenses made by appointed counsel. Attorneys take their duties seriously, and fight bitterly for the rights of an accused whom they may represent, however much they may detest his personal views and conduct. Only through a complete presentation of all proper defenses can complete justice be administered.

Of course, such appointed counsel were not experts in the field of international law, and many of the defenses had no sound basis in such jurisprudence. Unless otherwise indicated in the following discussion, the defenses raised were not usually upheld. They are, however, of considerable legal interest, and an examination of these questions may save considerable time in any future hearings.

It was contended, for example, that charges of crimes against humanity represented good morals but were not the law.[56] British counsel contended that concentration camp offenses were not violations of international law and could not be made such by Royal Warrant.[57] And, of course, the cry of *ex post facto, nullem crimen sine lege,* and like expressions referring to the same doctrine were heard repeatedly.[58]

It was contended that international law provided for no individual responsibility.[59] Likewise, an individual was claimed to have no responsibility for war crimes.[60] Again, it was argued that one could not be held responsible for that which it was beyond his power to prevent,[61] such as where he had no control over state police, the real offenders.[62] The doctrine of Act of State, invoked at Nuremberg, appeared again.[63] Many defendants relied upon superior orders,[64] one defendant being acquitted upon this ground alone,[65] and it being held a valid defense as to

---

55 U. N. 20.

56 Supp. Case 10 at pp. 4-6.

57 U. N. 10.

58 U. N. 1, 6, 10, 11, 35, 46-48, 57, 58, 72, 74, 88. And see ruling at U. N. 47, p. 52.

59 U. N. 10; Supp. Case 10 at pp. 4-6.

60 U. N. 62; Supp. Case 24 at pp. 18, 19.

61 U. N. 21, 23. (And this would probably be valid, if shown.)

62 U. N. 74.

63 U. N. 35, 74, 85.

64 U. N. 2-6, 10, 12, 13, 14, 16, 20, 25, 30, 31, 34-39, 44, 45, 47, 49, 57, 58, 61, 62, 68, 69, 72-74, 79, 85, 88, 89; Supp. Case 7 at pp. 1178-1185; Supp. Case 9; Supp. Case 10 at pp. 385-394; Supp. Case 15 at pp. 787-789; Supp. Case 75.

65 U. N. 13 (defendant Luger).

one particular order in the High Command Case.[66] In general, however, the rule adopted at Nuremberg applied, and this defense was considered only in mitigation and not in exoneration of guilt.[67]

Obviously, no question of guilt can arise if the order which the defendant claimed to have obeyed was a legal one. The validity of such a defense arises only where the order was illegal. It is interesting to observe, therefore, that Goebbels stated May 28, 1944, in a German newspaper: "No international law of warfare is in existence which provides that a soldier who has committed a mean crime can escape punishment by pleading as his defense that he followed the commands of his superiors. This holds particularly true if those commands are contrary to all human ethics and opposed to the well established international usage of warfare."[68]

This statement can hardly be improved. If the actor knows that his act violates positive law, or is inherently immoral, the plea is no valid defense. One defendant pleaded the inherent duty of obedience,[69] referring to the American work Winthrop, *Military Law*, in addition to the fact that he did believe the orders to have been proper and justified.[70] Other defendants used the defenses of fear, duress, and coercion as interchangeable concepts,[71] some cases referring to that doctrine as that of "superior force."[72] In fact, the theory of mass hypnosis was even admitted in one case.[73]

In connection with the theory of duress, however expressed, some interesting language appears in the Stroop case. One defendant pointed out that he had received orders from Kaltenbrunner and declared: "I fully realized at that time and lately in this court it is my deepest conviction that I would have suffered the most severe penalty, that is, the death penalty if I refused to carry out this order."[74] Subsequently, he added "I would have been shot."[75]

Such expressions convey the belief of certain of the defendants as it existed at that time. Most refreshing is the frank

---

[66] U. N. 72 at p. 98.

[67] U. N. 25, 36, 37, 39, 45, 47, 72; Supp. Cases 9, 75.

[68] U. N. 3 at p. 40.

[69] Supp. Case 15 at pp. 1222-12227.

[70] Supp. Case 15 at pp. 1254, 1255, 2179.

[71] U. N. 10, 12, 47, 48, 57, 58, 61, 62, 72, 74; Supp. Case 1 at p. 92; Supp. Case 10 at pp. 243-244; Supp. Case 15 at pp. 2162-2179; Supp. Cases 40, 45, 46, 77. And see the dissenting opinion in U. N. 57 at p. 62.

[72] U. N. 3, 4.

[73] Supp. Case 15 at pp. 1966-1972.

[74] Supp. Case 15, pp. 2161-2162.

[75] Supp. Case 15, p. 2179.

cowardice of Dr. Wahlman in the Hadamar trial. After frankly admitting his part in the death of thousands of victims sent to the hospital, the following interrogation occurred:

> "Q. Now, one further question. You mentioned to the Commission that you were afraid of death.
> "A. Yes, I was afraid of death.
> "Q. Did it ever occur to you that some of those Russians and Poles that were killed in your institution may have been afraid of death.
> "A. Yes, but my death comes closer to me."[76]

It had previously been established, however, through pointed interrogation, that Dr. Klein and his associates could have resigned, without loss of their lives.

The question has been argued bluntly in legal circles ever since the advent of these trials concerning the merit of that defense. In many of these cases the defendants testified that they feared disfavor if they failed to carry out an order. Others feared death or harm for themselves or their families. To some extent, it is a question of legal philosophy. Suppose a man holds a gun to your head and threatens to pull the trigger unless you burglarize a filling station. Would you feel like a criminal if you complied? Probably not. But suppose the same individual ordered you to strangle your wife—no, that might not be a valid example, in all cases. Some might comply readily. Let us take your child. What then? You would disobey the order, although it meant your death. And, in even that close proximity of fear, it was held such coercion was no defense where the act was clearly illegal.[77]

The confusion surrounding the use of the term "necessity" has already been indicated.[78] While "military necessity" will excuse certain types of conduct,[79] it does not justify the abandonment of the rules of international law.[80] Where the act is not justifiable either by private morality or by international law, military necessity is no defense,[81] despite the reasoning of one German philosopher.[82]

The plea of self-defense has been raised in some of these cases,[83] and, while unsuccessful in two instances,[84] resulted in

[76] Supp. Case 10, pp. 311-312.
[77] Supp. Case 77.
[78] Infra, pp. 174, 187, 193, 202, 203, 213; see also U. N. 4.
[79] See discussion in U. N. VIII, 174-175.
[80] U. N. 47, 58.
[81] U. N. 1, 14, 37, 72, 88.
[82] Clausewitz, *infra*, p. 84.
[83] U. N. 81; Supp. Case 37. Compare U. N. 88 at p. 129.
[84] U. N. 20, 87.

the acquittal of one defendant.[85] Somewhat similarly, a prisoner attempting to escape could be fired upon, after due cry to halt, and killed with impunity.[86] Such prisoner may not, however, be killed in order to prevent his attempting to escape,[87] nor where he is forced to attempt an escape to save his life,[88] nor may he be executed upon recapture.[89]

Somewhat similar defenses have been raised by a plea that a death was caused accidentally,[90] or by an independent intervening cause following the initial wrongful act.[91] It has been argued that the result produced must be reasonably foreseeable,[92] and that, if the result would have happened anyway, the defendant should not be found guilty.[93] It has also been argued that acts of omission do not constitute crimes.[94] And in two cases counsel moved for dismissal of the charges upon the ground that the prosecution could not produce the *corpus delictus*.[95] Needless to say, this motion was not allowed.

3. **Legal and Personal Defenses.** More intriguing, in a way, were some of the provocative attacks upon the controlling law. In several cases it was argued without success that the acts alleged were legal acts under the municipal law of Germany,[96] but in one case the defense was upheld in part upon the ground that euthanasia was legalized in Germany.[97] In fact, it was hotly argued in the Belsen Case that if there was a conflict between international law and municipal law, it was the duty of the defendant to obey the latter.[98]

Vagueness or uncertainty of the law of nations has been rejected,[99] as has been the contention, made also at Nuremberg, that the doctrines of international law are obsolete.[100] Ignorance

---

85 U. N. 82.

86 U. N. 7, 12, 39; Supp. Case 42. Compare U. N. 67.

87 U. N. 39.

88 U. N. 39.

89 U. N. 35, 39, 72.

90 U. N. 55.

91 U. N. 15.

92 Supp. Cases 7, p. 495.

93 Supp. Case 7, pp. 1194-1207.

94 See discussion, *infra*, pp. 259-262, 303-305, 351.

95 Supp. Case 24 at pp. 548-571; Supp. Case 25 at pp. 162-177, overruled 190A.

96 U. N. 4, 10, 35, 61.

97 U. N. 73; compare the interesting but unsuccessful argument in Supp. Case 10, pp. 394-404.

98 Supp. Case 2, p. 498, referring to *Mortensen v. Peters*, 43 *Scottish Law Reports* 872; *Fong Yue Ting v. United States*, 149 U. S. 698, 37 L. ed. 905.

99 U. N. 47.

100 U. N. 139, 48, 49.

of the law of nations was held to constitute no defense, although where the belief was not an unreasonable one, it was actually considered in mitigation.[101] Lest this be thought the imposition of a massive burden upon an ignorant soldier, it should be recalled that his opportunities for selection of choice are generally between that which is moral and that which is immoral, since the same selection has generally resulted in that decision being codified by rules of international law or accepted as customary international law. If the accused was ignorant of the circumstances imposing a duty, such as the terms of an armistice, more kindly consideration has been given.[102] The validity of this defense would depend largely upon the particular circumstances.[103]

The doctrine of legitimate reprisal received only lukewarm reception from the tribunals.[104] This was in large part due to the factual circumstances giving rise to the asserted reprisals, as well as to the grotesque disproportion between the wrong claimed and the vengeance taken. Such defense was asserted in one case upon the theory of a violation of Germanic decree by the Dutch,[105] and in another case because of the illegal resistance by the occupants of the conquered nation.[106]

In one case it was asserted that the victim, by his acts, had lost his civil status;[107] in another, that the victim had lost his nationality by joining the Japanese Army, and this was upheld.[108] Again, it was claimed that Indian victims were voluntary collaborators who possessed no rights as prisoners and were guided by Japanese regulations.[109] With less merit, the Germans claimed that the nationals of occupied countries became German subjects.[110] This was rejected upon the ground that any annexation was not valid while armies were still in the field in resistance to the occupying power. The defense counsel in the Belsen Case[111] pointed to the Potsdam Declaration recognizing an annexation by Russia while Japanese troops were still fighting. His argument, while not valid to legalize the annexations claimed by Germany, certainly pointed out the illegality of the annexation to which he made reference.

---

101 U. N. 1, 29, 39, 48, 72, 86.

102 U. N. 5, pp. 69, 70.

103 U. N. 3, 29, 47, 58, 62; Supp. Case 39.

104 U. N. 2, 12, 28, 36, 43, 44, 46, 47, 64, 72, 88; Supp. Case 15 at pp. 1160-1170.

105 U. N. 88.

106 Supp. Case 70.

107 U. N. 30.

108 U. N. 77.

109 Supp. Case. 3.

110 U. N. 10, 35, 74.

111 U. N. 10.

It was claimed also that the execution of commandos was not illegal.[112] This is probably true, as the minute such persons donned civilian garb for the commission of a hostile act, as distinguished from an attempt to escape, they were subject to execution, conditioned, however, upon a fair trial first to prove the charges brought. A similar defense as to the execution of guerillas was held invalid, but if a proper trial had first been given, that decision would not be in accord with international law.[113] This requirement of fair trial was imposed even where espionage was the claimed offense.[114]

Other defenses asserted were upon matters of mens rea,[15] provocation,[116] drunkenness,[117] lack of premeditation,[118] mental incapacity,[119] mental instability from head injuries and overwork,[120] and extreme youth.[121]

112 U. N. 61.
113 U. N. 45.
114 U. N. 3, 31.
115 U. N. 3, 5, 23, 62, 64, 85, 88.
116 U. N. 20.
117 U. N. 20.
118 U. N. 15.
119 U. N. 15, 78; Supp. Case 15.
120 U. N. 39.
121 U. N. 50, 67 (15 years of age in each case—in the first case acquitted as "acting without judgment;" in the second, receiving a sentence of only 8 years for murder).

XXXVII

THE TRIBUNALS; INDICTMENTS

It will be recalled that the International Military Tribunal for the Far East expressed great indignation at the thought that counsel might be presumptous enough to challenge the fairness of its composition. Even though the president, and perhaps others, were shown to be definitely biased in that case, the tribunal refused to entertain any question as to its sanctity.[1] This was not true in the military tribunals to the same degree, at least in the hearings conducted by the United States. It was a customary question to inquire whether any member of the tribunal had visited the scene of an alleged atrocity,[2] or had any preconceived notion of the guilt of any defendant,[3] perhaps by reason of heated radio or press reports.[4] However, challenges to the jurisdiction upon the ground of prejudice of a member or members seemed largely to have been overruled.[5] Actually, in the only instance where a member of a tribunal indicated a closed mind during the conduct of the case, he was withdrawn from the court and transferred.[6] In contrast to the lack of judicial proceedings permitted prisoners of the Nazis or Japanese, which constituted one of the charges in certain trials,[7] it is interesting to observe the safeguards afforded the accused in these hearings. In each of them the president of the tribunal announced to the accused their complete right to a full hearing. A typical example of this is as follows:[8]

---

1 *Infra*, pp. 241, 258, 261.

2 Supp. Case 11, p. 4.

3 Supp. Case 8; Supp. Case 11, p. 5.

4 Supp. Case 8, pp. 16, 17.

5 Supp. Case 7, p. 4; Supp. Case 24, pp. 2-8. In the first of these cases, the defense motion for leave to interrogate the court as a basis for challenge was overruled. In the second case, the defense did interrogate Colonel Wang, a Chinese member. The defense brought out a 3½ hour discussion held with this person about the cases, indicating that Colonel Wang had gotten the Chinese minister to change his mind twice to rescind a permission previously granted. After asking Colonel Wang to withdraw voluntarily in order to avoid a challenge for cause, the defense was overruled by the tribunal, which stated that the motion had been discussed in chambers and was denied.

6 Hearing before Senate Subcommittee, Malmedy Massacres investigation, p. 1414.

7 *Infra*, pp. 293, 297.

8 Supp. Case 15, pp. 26, 27.

"President: You are advised that under the law of Military Government you are entitled in this court to the following:

"1. To have, in advance of trial, a copy of the charges upon which you will be tried.

"2. To be present at your trial, to give evidence, and to examine or cross-examine any witnesses.

"3. To consult counsel before trial and to conduct your own defense or to be represented at the trial by counsel of your own choice, subject to the right of this court to debar any person from appearing before it.

"4. In any case in which a sentence of death may be imposed to be represented by a member or civilian attorney of the United States Forces and such other counsel as the accused may designate.

"5. To bring with you to this trial such material witnesses in your own defense as you may wish, or to have them summoned by the court at your request, if practicable.

"6. To apply to the court for an adjournment where necessary to enable you to prepare your defense.

"7. To have the proceedings translated when you are otherwise unable to understand the language in which they are conducted.

"8. In the event of conviction, to file a petition for review to the appointing authority setting forth grounds why the findings and sentence should be set aside or modified."

In addition to American counsel assigned to the defendants, they were permitted to secure counsel of their own choice. In the case of German defendants, such national attorneys were housed and fed by the prosecuting government, paid a regular monthly stipend, and received extra privileges of value, such as cigarettes and additional food. Since many of these attorneys were Nazis, this meant the securing of an excellent livelihood where otherwise they were disqualified from practice. Yet their actions in these hearings showed that their entire allegiance was to their clients, which is wholly proper, as was the case with American counsel, who fought even more bitterly against the prosecution. Permission would be granted in each case for the appearance of German counsel properly appointed.[9]

The greatest legitimate criticism which can be made of hearings before military commissions arises from the fact that several, and sometimes many, defendants were tried at a single time. This was perhaps necessary in the interests of expediency, but it did not always lead to justice. As a result, defense counsel would frequently be assigned to represent a group of defendants,

[9] E.g., Supp. Case 15, p. 4.

perhaps with varied interests. Let us say, for example, that Schwartz, a captain, gave orders to Sgt. Krauss to execute an American prisoner. Krauss takes the prisoner to the woods and requires Faust, a private, to do the shooting. Schwartz says "I have no responsibility for this act. I was not present when the man was shot. I did not pull the trigger. I merely passed along Hitler's orders." Krauss says "I did not shoot him. I merely passed along my superior's orders to Faust." Faust says "What else could I do? I did not want to shoot him, but I would have been executed had I refused."

It can readily be seen that it was to the interest of each defendant to throw complete blame upon another, and in many cases such defendants were at each other's throats. One defendant represented by the same counsel who represented other defendants would take the stand and attempt to throw the responsibility upon another client of such attorney. Each time he made such a statement, that defense counsel was acting as an assistant prosecutor against his other client. Yet, if he refused to interrogate fully, then he was not rendering the highest service to the client upon the witness stand. It is true that many defendants were tried together at Nuremberg, but each was represented by individual counsel. Even in that hearing, if the same attorney had represented both Schacht and Goering at the time of their fracas, to which would he have owed his duty? Must he act as a judge between them?

This is no purely academic question. For example, in the Malmedy Massacres case,[10] one group of counsel represented all officers, another group represented all non-commissioned officers, and a third group represented all enlisted personnel. The situation became so ludicrous and and terrifying to defense counsel that they finally had to refuse to permit any of the defendants to take the stand in his own behalf. Prior to such refusal, each witness who took the stand created additional evidence for the prosecution and aided in the conviction of all groups.

There is a rule in legal ethics, as there is in common morals, that no man can serve two masters. An attorney owes undivided allegiance to his client, and cannot perform his full duty when forced to divide his powers and sympathies. In view of the unsatisfactory character of this representation in certain cases, it is hoped that this mistake will never be repeated in any such hearings in the future.

Conflicts arose also between American and German counsel, which controversies were determined in each instance favorably

---

[10] See report of the Subcommittee on the Malmedy Massacres investigation, pp. 25, 26.

to the contention of the German counsel, who represented one client alone.[11]

Motions for severance of hearings, although it would seem they should have been allowed where conflicts of interest appeared, were almost uniformly overruled.[12] Such a motion was granted where an irreconcilable conflict appeared,[13] and where illness of a defendant necessitated such severance.[14] Continuances or recesses were frequently granted,[15] although refused where the tribunal felt that defense counsel had had adequate time to meet the charges.[16] A claim that evidence was not within the Bill of Particulars and thereby took the defense by surprise was held insufficient grounds for a continuance,[17] although the tribunal prohibited the prosecution in one case from putting in evidence to support additional charges, in order to give the defense an opportunity to prepare its case thereon.[18]

It will be recalled that the Nuremberg trial permitted the prosecution to proceed against Bormann *in absentia*. This also occurred elsewhere.[19] Conversely, the prosecution was not permitted to *nolle prosse* a charge over objection by the defense.[20]

As to the indictments upon which convictions were sought, it will be recalled that technicalities were not looked upon with favor, since there were no juries to be confused by shadings in verbiage. Therefore, attacks made upon indictments as vague and insufficient were generally overruled where giving substantial information, upon the ground that customary formalities and precision were not required.[21] Such rulings were not, however, automatic. In the *Fukuda* case, for example, while certain objections were overruled,[22] the tribunal required a more specific statement of certain charges, stating that they would otherwise be stricken, whereupon the prosecution consented to such striking.[23] Later the tribunal required the prosecution to furnish the names of persons alleged to have been beaten.[24]

---

11 Supp. Case 10, pp. 313-317; Supp. Case 15, pp. 1697-1699.

12 U. N. 13, 60; Supp. Case 7, pp. 4, 5; Supp. Case 11, pp. 67-75; Supp. Case 24, pp. 14, 15; Supp. Case 25, pp. 6-9.

13 U. N. 17, 18.

14 U. N. 10, 58.

15 E.g., Supp. Case 15, pp. 394-397.

16 Supp. Case 29, p. 85.

17 Supp. Case 11 at pp. 1729, 1738.

18 Supp. Case 29 at pp. 188, 198, 1175, 1176, 1456.

19 U. N. 13 as to Huber.

20 Supp. Case 24 at pp. 546-548.

21 U. N. 10, 35, 60, 61; Supp. Cases 10, 11, 25.

22 Supp. Case 24 at p. 27.

23 Supp. Case 24 at p. 29.

24 Supp. Case 24, pp. 45, 46.

After the prosecution stated its inability to do so, it was given leave to withdraw the Bill of Particulars and substitute other paragraphs. Later, most of those additional allegations were stricken.[25] Upon objection in another case, the words "divers other persons" were stricken, referring to victims of concentration camps.[26] In the much mooted *Yamashita* hearing, the prosecution contended that the tribunal had no jurisdiction to hear a motion to quash. This was promptly overruled, and arguments were heard upon the matter.[27] Defense counsel thereafter moved for a Bill of Particulars, which motion the tribunal allowed.[28] After the original motion had in effect been waived by defense counsel,[29] it was overruled after the hearing of further arguments.[30]

Attacks upon the indictments as not stating any offense were generally overruled,[31] although sustained in some of the subsequent Nuremberg proceedings.[32] Where references were made to persons not accused,[33] these were withdrawn by the prosecution. In one hearing, defense counsel were granted permission to object to the validity of the charges at a later date, since counsel were unfamiliar with international law and wanted to associate an expert in the defense.[34] An objection that testimony was not connected adequately with the defendants was overruled.[35] But a contention made by one prosecutor that a military tribunal had no power to dismiss a charge, since it constituted a military order, is obviously erroneous, and would seem even to constitute a contempt of court.[36]

---

[25] Supp. Case 24 at pp. 144, 145.

[26] Supp. Case 8, pp. 36, 37.

[27] Supp. Case 29, p. 34.

[28] Supp. Case 29 at p. 36.

[29] Supp. Case 29, p. 58.

[30] Supp. Case 29, pp. 78-82.

[31] U. N. 10 at p. 70; U. N. 21 at pp. 7, 8, 11-14; Supp. Case 25 at pp. 156-158.

[32] *Infra*, pp. 143, 173 and elsewhere; Supp. Case 15, pp. 481-483.

[33] Supp. Case 15 at pp. 489, 493.

[34] Supp. Case 2, pp. 6, 7.

[35] Supp. Case 15, pp. 189, 190.

[36] See argument and ruling, Supp. Case 29, p. 92.

XXXVIII

PROCEDURE AND GENERAL FAIRNESS OF HEARINGS

As a general rule the procedure employed in hearings before military tribunals was fair and resulted in adequate presentation of both sides of the case, although such hearings were usually conducted expeditiously and without regard to technicalities. Because of the natural argumentativeness of American counsel and their desire to leave no stone unturned in the defense, as was proper, the American hearings usually were somewhat more protracted than the others. Occasionally, however, there were slight slips from the high standards of justice sought, and these should be examined in discussing trial technique and procedure.

It was obviously necessary for the defense, for example, to be familiar with the prosecution's case, in order to prepare any type of defense. However, in one case where tons of documents were involved and the Bill of Particulars was very sketchy and inadequate, the prosecution refused to make any disclosure of its evidence, and the defense motion to require additional information was overruled.[1] In a Pacific case the prosecution stated "There is no provision in the SCAP rules that the prosecution has to turn over every document that they have pertaining to the case to the defense."[2]

Evidence before commissioners was not employed by military tribunals other than in the subsequent hearings at Nuremberg.[3] The doctrine of judicial notice was also particularly employed in the Nuremberg hearings,[4] although judicial notice was taken elsewhere of the rulings made by the International Military Tribunal at Nuremberg.[5] But technical rules of evidence developed at common law and followed particularly by the United States, much to the abhorrence of lawyers steeped in those traditions, were wholly disregarded, one counsel even challenging the entire application of the SCAP rules because of this.[6]

In this regard, it should be remembered that these hearings were not conducted by the United States alone. A uniform pro-

1 Supp. Case 8, p. 38.
2 Supp. Case 24, p. 198.
3 U. N. 58, p. 76, n. 1.
4 U. N. 53, pp. 67, 68. See discussion *infra*, pp. 213-215.
5 Supp. Case 15, p. 237.
6 U. N. 6.

cedure was attempted to be evolved for the first major hearings, and such rules were adopted through the joint collaboration of the four major powers participating in those hearings. International law does not prescribe that rules of Anglo-Saxon nations control, and there is a vast difference in the procedure followed in continental European and Asiatic countries from that employed in the United States. Attorneys from those nations would, perhaps, be as shocked as many American attorneys are now if the United States had insisted solely upon the procedure peculiar to its system of justice, instead of the compromise method which attempted to include most of the provisions common to the jurisprudence of the various nations involved.

For example, hearsay evidence was frequently admitted,[7] even though such evidence was originally from a dying man and, therefore, twice removed.[8] However, where such testimony was very inconclusive,[9] or amounted to mere rumor,[10] it was stricken, in one case by agreement between the prosecution and defense.[11] The admission of such evidence did not mean, of course, that the tribunals gave the same weight to such evidence as to that of eye witnesses, and it is apparent that they did not.[12] Circumstantial evidence was held admissible,[13] and it was held that a conspiracy might be deduced from the acts and conduct of the parties, instead of being established by direct evidence.[14]

Another distinct variation from conventional American methods of evidence arose in the use of affidavits in lieu of the direct testimony of witnesses. This precedent was established at Nuremberg with the right in defense counsel to procure cross-interrogatories or production of the witness for personal cross-examination where feasible. In most cases, this resulted in saving weeks of time, with no substantial loss of rights to the defendants. An objection was early raised that Article 25 of the Articles of War of the United States prohibited the use of depositions in a capital case.[15] This objection was overruled by the commission, and its ruling would seem to be proper in view of the subsequent holding of the Supreme Court to the same

---

[7] U. N. 6; 7 at p. 85; 10 at pp. 86 and 138; 21 at p. 23; 48 at p. 6; Supp. Case 10 at p. 35; 11 at pp. 190, 1972; 29 at pp. 175, 915-946, 2303.

[8] Supp. Case 1, pp. 15, 16.

[9] Supp. Case 29, pp. 1585, 2305, 2857.

[10] Supp. Case 11, p. 188.

[11] Supp. Case 15, pp. 489-492.

[12] U. N. XV, pp. 197-199.

[13] U. N. 7 at p. 84; 35 at pp. 88, 89; 59 at p. 4.

[14] U. N. 10 at pp. 108, 109.

[15] Supp. Case 29, p. 123.

effect, but the commission refused to give its reason for such holding.[16]

Affidavits of witnesses as to facts in controversy were, accordingly, held admissible as the direct evidence of such witnesses.[17] This was true although the witnesses were not produced[18] or were dead.[19] The *Yamashita* tribunal originally imposed too great a burden upon the prosecution by refusing to receive affidavits except in support of witnesses,[20] but later reversed this ruling and adhered to the usual rule.[21] Where witnesses had erroneously been permitted to leave, the tribunal and prosecution were ordinarily most cooperative in securing their return for use by the defense.[22]

Where affidavits were introduced and the witnesses were not available for cross-examination, such evidence was regarded as of limited probative value.[23] In the *Belsen* case, for example, the judge advocate made it clear that witnesses who had been confined in a concentration camp had a definite bias, and that this must be considered in weighing their evidence.[24] Other judge advocates gave similar warnings.[25] Another tribunal

---

16 Supp. Case 29 at p. 127.

17 U. N. 1, 3, 7, 9, 10, 13, 19, 21, 30, 45, 47, 48, 64-66.

18 Supp. Case 15 at pp. 229, 230, where French authorities failed to produce witnesses held in the French Zone.

19 Supp. Case 15 at pp. 1688, 1689; objection by prosecution overruled to use of such affidavit by defense.

20 Supp. Case 29 at pp. 642, 643.

21 Supp. Case 29, pp. 1124, 1463, 1464.

22 Supp. Case 15, pp. 387-390.

23 Supp. Case 2, pp. 630-641.

24 Supp. Case 2, pp. 630-641.

25 For example, see Supp. Case 41, where the judge advocate stated:

"Another matter of general warning that I must draw your attention to relates to the documentary evidence which has been given. It is, as I think you may have heard me say earlier in these proceedings, a rule of English law that the Court must have the best evidence, and of course the best evidence of a person who is alleged to have seen something is the spoken testimony of that person given in court. You have in many cases here not got that particular person before you, but only some document, either an affidavit made by him or some other document, and we will deal with them all as we go through them, which has come into existence at some time outside the confines of this Court, and which, of course, nobody has had any opportunity in this Court of testing. Documents of that kind are subject to the criticism that the defense have been denied the opportunity of cross-examining about them, of investigating them further, of knowing anything of the circumstances in which they were taken, of being in any other way able to probe their reliability, and, therefore, I should tell you this, that in the ordinary procedure of the English Courts, many of these documents would not be admissible as evidence at all for that particular reason, and no doubt you know from your experience of administering Military Law in Courts-Martial, such documents would not be

stated bluntly that an affidavit would not carry as much weight as oral testimony,[26] but in a different case the judge advocate seemed to feel that sworn affidavits of the defendants were of more value than their testimony in court, after they had had an opportunity to compare stories with others of the accused.[27] In that case several of such persons recanted in court and withdrew many of their prior admissions.

Such pre-trial admissions would, of course, be effective either against the deponent himself,[28] or against another defendant,[29] although defense counsel invoked the rule that the testimony of an accomplice should be regarded with suspicion.[30] If a defendant told a story different from that contained in his affidavit, cross-examination was permitted as of a hostile witness.[31] But one could not contradict a witness by affidavits unless such witness was first cross-examined upon the discrepancy and given an opportunity to explain.[32]

An offer of part only of a document was held proper, whether offered by the prosecution[33] or by the defense.[34] Objections made upon the basis of the best evidence rule, because of the originals not being produced, were overruled,[35] although objections for lack of foundation were sustained.[36] And an objection to an exhibit as not corresponding with the description upon the original envelope in which it was contained was sustained.[37]

---

admissible. By special regulations made for the conduct of these Courts here for the trial of war criminals, an exception to the main rule of evidence has been made, and these documents are made admissible, but it is my duty to warn you that that is an exception, and that you must not necessarily accept them at their face value. You must have regard to each particular document and consider what weight you ought to attach to it. If you think, in spite of that warning, that the contents of the documents are true, then you are entitled to treat them as well as any other evidence. If you feel doubts about them, that may reduce the value which you give to them."

26 U. N. 19.

27 U. N. 30 at pp. 47, 48.

28 U. N. 10, 19, 62, 68, 71.

29 U. N. 10, 16.

30 U. N. 31, 62.

31 Supp. Case 3, p. 80. In this case the result seems erroneous, since the witness testified that he had protested that the statement was wrong, but was told he was lying. His statement in this regard was later confirmed by the officer taking his statement.

32 Supp. Case 2, pp. 261-267.

33 Supp. Case 15 at p. 55.

34 Supp. Case 25 at pp. 906, 907.

35 Supp. Case 29, pp. 114, 117, 121, 342.

36 Supp. Case 29, p. 2365.

37 Supp. Case 15, pp. 372, 373.

A witness was held, but not with any consistency, to have the right to refer to notes[38] or the original affidavit[39] to refresh his recollection. A statement of a witness constituting a conclusion[40] or invading the province of the court[41] was either stricken or held to have little weight. If it had no probative value, it was permitted to stand, with such weight being ascribed to it as the tribunal may see fit.[42] And at least one question which was clearly objectionable upon such grounds was permitted to be answered.[43] But the term "massacre" was stricken as being inflammatory and a conclusion.[44]

Witnesses were excluded prior to giving their testimony in court.[45] After testifying, they were permitted to remain in the courtroom.[46] However, a disturbance by spectators was summarily punished,[47] and an order of the tribunal was necessary in one case to require the military police to permit the defendants to whisper during the conduct of the case.[48]

The rule against leading questions ordinarily enforced with vigor in more usual types of trials did not meet with rigid enforcement.[49] The right to attack the credibility of a witness depended upon the particular circumstances,[50] and defense counsel were permitted, over objection of the prosecution, to impeach their own witnesses.[51]

Ordinarily, counsel were limited in their cross-examination of witnesses to the scope of direct evidence,[52] unless such person was a party defendant, in which case the usual rules of complete

---

38 U. N. 19 at p. 74; contra U. N. 10 as to witness Gertrud Neumann; U. N. 23 as to defendant Karl Rauer.

39 Supp. Case 29, p. 1156; contra Supp. Case 29, pp. 2417, 2418.

40 Supp. Case 29, p. 1147.

41 Supp. Case 24, p. 55, referring to an investigator's report.

42 Supp. Case 25 at pp. 21, 23, 25 and also pp. 837-839 where a long hypothetical question was employed.

43 Supp. Case 15, p. 225, the following question was asked, and objection made to it was overruled: "Can you agree with this statement, 'Stroop was a little Himmler and Trummler was his field commander'?"

44 Supp. Case 29 at p. 392.

45 Supp. Case 8 at p. 2.

46 U. N. 10, pp. 145, 146.

47 Supp. Case 10, p. 111.

48 Supp. Case 15 at p. 217.

49 Objection sustained, Supp. Case 10, p. 24; objection overruled s.c., p. 20.

It is perhaps fortunate for the defense that the tribunals were lenient, as German defense counsel seemed incapable of examining witnsses except by the use of leading questions.

50 Permitted, Supp. Case 24, pp. 198-222; refused, Supp. Case 11, p. 790.

51 Supp. Case 15, p. 1654.

52 Supp. Case 10, pp. 34, 59, 76, 78, 82, 94, 96, 106; Supp. Case 11, pp. 899, 1020, 1478, 1479; Supp. Case 15, p. 518; Supp. Case 25, pp. 431, 432.

examination applied.[53] But it was held that a witness does not lose his privilege by testifying,[54] and a defendant effectively stopped the prosecution from detailed interrogation by merely declining to answer.[55]

Defense counsel ordinarily were not permitted to make a witness one for the defense, so as to go into new material, while the witness was testifying for the prosecution,[56] although this result was actually required in one case.[57] As to the scope of cross-examination, while in certain instances the tribunal seemed to restrict examination unduly, such rulings applied to both sides equally.[58] Counsel were not permitted to resort to an argumentative type of cross-examination,[59] but more than one defense counsel was permitted to interrogate a single witness where necessary to aid the cause of justice.[60]

It is believed that any restriction in the cross-examination of such hearings arose because of a lack of understanding upon the part of non-legally trained judges of the importance of cross-examination as a weapon for the solicitation of truth and

[53] Supp. Case 11, p. 1742; Supp. Case 15, p. 766; Supp. Case 25, p. 219, but see pp. 431, 432.

[54] Supp. Case 25, pp. 405, 406.

[55] Supp. Case 15, pp. 766-772 and 823-826.

[56] Supp. Case 15, p. 575.

[57] Supp. Case 8, pp. 551-552. Defense counsel Lewis pointed out that he was forced into this action because of the prosecution's habit of excusing a witness after completion of his evidence and permitting him to leave the vicinity.

[58] Supp. Case 29, pp. 129, 130; also p. 599, where the point of the cross-examination by Sandberg was to prove that navy, not army, personnel was involved, and he had almost driven the witness to such an admission when the tribunal interrupted with this statement: "In the opinion of the Commission this cross-examination has been carried on to an absurdity, and the Commission will accept that in the mind of this witness he believed the personnel he has been discussing were members of the Japanese Army." At p. 879 the tribunal refused to permit cross-examination initially as to guerilla activities, but changed its ruling at p. 888 and adhered to the more liberal rule thereafter. See also pp. 1607-1614, 2193. Another instance of such changed rulings will be found at pp. 1504 and 1607. It stopped counsel for defense from continuing the cross-examination where the subject had been exhausted, or dealt with an immaterial issue: pp. 1790-1791, 2229, 2360. See also p. 3109. However, the prosecution was also restricted in the scope of its cross-examination, so that the rulings were not one-sided: pp. 1597, 1598, 1599, 1600, 1601, 2367, 3108.

As another instance of undue restriction of cross-examination, see Supp. Case 8, pp. 776, 777. In that same case, however, although defense counsel was warned "not to lecture the witness," p. 801, prosecution objections to the scope of cross-examination were overruled: pp. 1146, 1908, 4824. But see the severe limitations imposed in Supp. Case 10, pp. 77, 78, 83, 94-98.

[59] Supp. Case 11, p. 210.

[60] Supp. Case 11, p. 229.

the discovery of prejudice. A skilled cross-examiner usually has considerable success in exposing a liar, and in ascertaining the true facts. It is suggested that in future hearings such tribunals give greater leeway both to defense counsel and to the prosecution in this regard.

Counsel appointed for the defense were surprisingly able when one considers their prior backgrounds and experience, or lack of experience, as trial lawyers. For example, when neglect of prisoners or maltreatment by camp doctors was charged as a cause for deaths, American medical evidence was introduced to show that the treatment rendered was proper.[61] Upon cross-examination, other interesting matters were developed. In one case, after a witness had identified certain defendants positively, he was shown to have bad eyesight and was not wearing glasses, so that he was unable to read a chart twenty feet away.[62] Since the prisoners in the dock bore numbers upon placards on their chests, one defense counsel pointed out that the witness merely remembered the numbers of the prisoners and was unable to identify the person.[63] In that same case a witness was forced to admit upon cross-examination that he had never seen any of the accused commit a single act charged.[64] And in the *Stroop* case it was brought out that there was a complete blackout at the time the witness testified to having seen certain occurrences.[65]

A brilliant task of impeachment of a witness by documents, prior testimony, and affidavits was performed in the *Fukuda* case.[66] In a different case where a witness testified to a state of facts wholly different from those contained in his affidavit, he was pinned down to claiming that both sets of facts were true, which practically destroyed his usefulness as a witness.[67] And, again referring to the *Fukuda* case, it was brought out upon cross-examination by defense counsel that, instead of the accused having executed a camp cook, the Chinese prisoners had killed him because he had been receiving better living conditions and because he had been giving extra food to the Japanese.[68]

As a matter of fact, in that same case, when defense counsel pointed out that the unsanitary conditions under which the Chinese existed was due to their refusal to use latrines, the

---

[61] Supp. Case 25, pp. 909-918.
[62] Supp. Case 15, pp. 509-518.
[63] Supp. Case 11, p. 3033.
[64] Supp. Case 11, pp. 227, 228.
[65] Supp. Case 15, pp. 509-518.
[66] Supp. Case 24, pp. 198-222.
[67] Supp. Case 15, p. 1936.
[68] Supp. Case 24, p. 282.

tribunal interrupted to state that such was a matter of common knowledge.[69]

Upon other occasions of brilliant cross-examination, the effectiveness was destroyed by refusal of the tribunal to require the witness to answer. In the *Hadamar* case, for example, a prosecution witness made much of the fact that the acts performed were illegal and secret. Defense counsel inquired whether the witness, since he believed the acts to be illegal, had reported them to the police.[70] Also, if the acts were secret, how did the civilian population gain knowledge of them, which knowledge the witness admitted?[71] And, when the civilian population discussed these matters openly, were they arrested?[72] The Tribunal also refused to permit the defense to cross-examine to find out the rest of the names of inmates claimed to have been killed or the cause of their deaths.[73] But the defense did then establish that this same witness had previously been committed as a lunatic and practically destroyed his testimony.[74] And, in the *Fukuda* case, defense counsel brought out that an investigator, who was much imbued with the importance of his findings, had interviewed only twelve to fifteen people out of five hundred eighty-one, and that he had destroyed his original notes and could not produce them.[75]

Of course, not all of the excellent cross-examination was limited to the defense counsel. One of the most telling instances occurred in the cross-examination by the prosecution of Dr. Wahlman in the *Hadamar* case. He had admitted his acts in putting inmates to death, but stated that he had acted under duress for fear of his own life. The following cross-examination occurred:

> "Q. Now, one further question. You mentioned to the commission that you were afraid of death.
>
> "A. Yes, I was afraid of death.
>
> "Q. Did it ever occur to you that some of these Russians and Poles that were killed in your institution may have been afraid of death.
>
> "A. Yes, but my death comes closer to me."[76]

---

[69] Supp. Case 24, p. 87.

[70] Supp. Case 10, pp. 77, 78.

[71] Supp. Case 10, p. 83.

[72] Supp. Case 10, p. 83.

[73] Supp. Case 10, pp. 94-98.

[74] Supp. Case 10, p. 101.

[75] Supp. Case 24, pp. 61, 63, 75.

[76] Supp. Case 10, pp. 311-312.

Of interest also is the fact that Dr. Wahlman stated: "Today we all know that we were sold out."[77]

In the *Peleus* trial Admiral Schnee had testified for the defendant Eck, who admitted that he had machine-gunned shipwrecked survivors. He testified to generalities as to the doctrine of necessity, but when pinned down specifically as to whether he, the witness, would have committed a like act, he was compelled to answer "No."[78] When pressed as to any reason for Eck's action, he stated bluntly that the naval officer must have lost his nerve.[79] In the same case, the defendant Hoffman admitted that while he felt at the time that the acts were justifiable, he did not think so at the time of trial.[80] And one peculiar defendant (Lentz) testified that he took a machine gun away from the defendant Schwender, because he had a bad moral character, and fired the gun himself.[81] In still another case, when the prosecution was trying to establish that the defendant Eichel had snatched a scarf in anger from the neck of an allied flyer, he was interrogated and stated, "I explained this morning I wasn't mad, I was angry."[82]

Defense counsel constantly rode the prosecution with spurs. One of the most striking examples was in the *Fukuda* case,[83] where two Irishmen, O'Connell and O'Brien, made the prosecutor's lot a miserable one. Their performance was masterly upon the elements of proof, but apart from that they seemed to heckle from the pure love of combat.[84] At one point where the prosecution had interrogated in detail as to methods of torture, defense counsel suggested that a demonstration be performed upon the prosecutor.[85] In another case, a defense counsel referred to an assistant prosecutor, one Dr. Leiss, as "Dr. Louse," and upon vehement objection by the prosecution, claimed ignorance of the man's true name.[86] Again, when defense counsel had offered proof by a German lawyer as an expert upon German law as to the legality of certain acts, the following exchange occurred:

> "Captain Vance: May I ask the defense counsel, if these books are not in existence and around, where did he copy this law from.

---

[77] Supp. Case 10, p. 319.
[78] Supp. Case 1, p. 70.
[79] Supp. Case 1, p. 70.
[80] Supp. Case 1, p. 76.
[81] Supp. Case 1, pp. 85-89.
[82] Supp. Case 15, p. 1717.
[83] Supp. Case 24.
[84] E.g., see Supp. Case 24, pp. 147, 192.
[85] Supp. Case 24, p. 288.
[86] Supp. Case 11, p. 1470.

"Defense Counsel: They made it up out of their own little heads, Captain."[87]

Perhaps such interchanges are not always desirable, but they are as familiar in our adversary system of trial practice as the act of breathing. They are given here merely as representative examples to show how seriously defense counsel took their duties, and how intensely they represented the interests of their former enemies. The British trials, on the other hand, were calmly conducted with the utmost courtesy between the tribunal, prosecution, and defense. On the whole, those hearings consumed less time than those of the United States, where counsel battled vigorously each day. One cannot say that one system is better than another—both types of hearings, upon the whole, were exceedingly fair. One might conclude that the difference in national temperament was reflected in the conduct of the hearings.

With reference to testimony by a defendant, there was early some confusion in the American hearings as to the right of a defendant to testify under oath. After holding that a defendant's only right was to give unsworn testimony,[88] it was pointed out that the Manual controlling the procedure had been changed upon February 1, 1947, to permit an accused to elect to make either a sworn or an unsworn statement,[89] and such election was permitted thereafter.[90] One witness claimed immunity from testifying under oath by reason of having taken an oath of allegiance to the Reich. This was overruled upon the ground that the former Reich was no longer in existence, and the prior oath was discharged.[91] In a British proceeding it was held that a defendant had the option of taking oath and subjecting himself to cross-examination or of simply making a statement and not being subject to interrogation by the prosecution.[92] This obviously seems the correct rule. The United States, however, held that even though the testimony of the defendant was not under oath, he was subject to cross-examination,[93] which seems completely erroneous.

In one case it was held that a defendant might be cross-examined as to other crimes in order to prove a course of con-

---

[87] Supp. Case 15, pp. 2335-2338.

[88] E.g., Supp. Case 7, p. 598; Supp. Case 15 at pp. 107, 109, 374, 384-387, 469-475, 484, 585; 586.

[89] Supp. Case 15, p. 1182.

[90] E.g., Supp. Case 10 at pp. 263, 297, 336; Supp. Case 15, p. 1182; Supp. Case 25, p. 976.

[91] U. N. 60.

[92] Supp. Case 2, p. 145.

[93] U. N. 16, 60.

duct, provided it did not incriminate others.[94] It has also been stated that the prosecution was at liberty to comment adversely upon an accused's failure to testify.[95] In view of the fact that no jury trial was involved, and the purpose of the proceedings was to secure adequate justice, this would seem to be an advance over the stricter rules usually followed in this country.

In certain instances, there was no testimony on behalf of an accused but his own.[96] In one case the defendant did not testify and offered no witnesses, but merely cross-examined the prosecution witnesses.[97] A plea of guilty did not, however, necessarily mitigate a sentence.[98] One defendant admitted complete responsibility for everything occurring in a concentration camp, whether he knew of it or not,[99] while another defendant accepted partial responsibility.[100] Following his conviction by the use of two former co-defendants as prosecution witnesses, one defendant admitted that he had lied upon his trial and confessed to entire guilt, exonerating the others.[101] And character evidence, it was held, could be introduced prior to resting.[102]

It was held that a defense attorney might call himself as a witness,[103] although this practice, as in more usual proceedings, is extraordinary. One stubborn defense counsel refused to use English, but insisted upon his right to use the German language.[104] And it was held that where the defendant put in no evidence his counsel was entitled to close.[105]

Although it was customary for the tribunal to fix the sentences upon completion of the trial, often without any written opinion, in one case, at the request of the prosecution, special findings of fact were adopted.[106] No trial was considered invalid after its completion for technical faults in procedure which caused no injustice.[107] In addition to personal sentences, judg-

---

[94] U. N. 71.

[95] U. N. 16.

[96] U. N. 19, 54, 68.

[97] U. N. 38.

[98] U. N. 70.

[99] U. N. 38.

[100] U. N. 79.

[101] U. N. 18.

[102] Supp. Case 15 at pp. 715, 716. The tribunal held that reputation was admissible in this regard, but that specific acts of the individual were not. However, it then allowed considerable leeway and permitted evidence of factual matters: Supp. Case 15, pp. 1210, 1211.

[103] U. N. 9.

[104] U. N. 5.

[105] U. N. 68. See also U. N. 69.

[106] Supp. Case 15, pp. 2590-2638; see also U. N. 10 at pp. 147, 148.

[107] See comments in U. N. I, pp. 109, 110; U. N. III, p. 120; U. N. IV, p. 130; U. N. V, p. 101.

ments for confiscation of property were occasionally entered.[108] And in many cases sentences imposed were commuted upon review by higher authority, or reversed upon appeal to a higher court,[109] so that the rights of the defendants were adequately preserved.

As to the effect of judgments by similar tribunals, it was held that they were persuasive, although not binding, since each case had been determined upon its own facts.[110] Since these various adjudications arrive at markedly similar results upon the controlling law, the result is the creation of a vast body of jurisprudence available for future tribunals. This is conditioned, of course, upon the assumption that such decisions were fairly rendered upon the law and the facts. It is necessary, therefore, to examine into some complaints of unfairness to see if these corrupted the results reached.

Certain criticisms have already been made by this author of particular hearings, especially upon the failure to appoint individual counsel for each defendant, in order to avoid conflicts in interest, and, also because of somewhat undue restriction of the right of cross-examination. Other charges, however, were also levelled by defense counsel or by critics of these trials. As in trials conducted in the United States and elsewhere, defendants occasionally claimed that confessions or admissions had been obtained from them by misrepresentation or brutalities. Since these accusations have been widely publicized, it is of the greatest importance to determine the exact facts in this regard as bearing upon the fairness of the hearings. It is necessary to examine the transcripts of evidence to determine under what circumstances such affidavits or admissions were used and the evidence concerning the circumstances of their taking.

It had been held that an affidavit of an accused might be admitted, although the officer taking it did not appear and testify.[111] Normally, throughout the hearings, an affidavit or admission would be admitted as a part of the prosecution's case, with the right in the defense, in its turn, to show the circumstances under which the document was procured, in order to destroy or minimize the effect.[112] The right to attack a deposition or confession was definitely recognized.[113]

---

[108] U. N. 13, 37, 38, 41, 58, 74, 85.

[109] U. N. 5, 11, 14, 22, 23, 24, 26, 27, 32, 33, 34, 43, 44, 55, 60-63, 86, 87, 89.

[110] U. N. 48.

[111] U. N. 68. Accused later admitted that such statement was voluntary.

[112] U. N. 16; Supp. Cases 10, 11, 15.

[113] U. N. 16; Supp. Cases 10, 11, 15.

The duty to warn a defendant that he was not required to incriminate himself was not recognized at the British hearings.[114] The United States seemed to feel that such warning was not material prior to the time of indictment,[115] but was material thereafter.[116] The logic of this distinction is difficult to follow. Usually such a failure to warn, it was claimed, accompanied pressure methods used to procure statements,[117] although this was flatly contradicted by the investigating officers.[118] And it was admitted by one defendant that errors in his statement were his own fault.[119]

It was considered proper for defense counsel, even during the prosecution's case, to inquire whether or not the witness had been promised immunity.[120] In the *Yamashita* trial the tribunal sustained an objection of defense counsel to a witness's statement that influence had been brought to bear to prevent his testifying for the prosecution.[121] But where a witness testified to pressure to prevent her from testifying for the defense, another tribunal insisted upon a complete examination into the matter, and the prosecution insisted upon a report being made to the Chief of the War Crimes Division.[122]

Much more serious than these matters were the not infrequent references in hearings conducted by this nation as to trickery or force used to obtain confessions.[123] While such acts were grossly exaggerated, there was a solid germ of truth in certain instances, all apparently arising either through acts of the C.I.C. or where refugee prosecutors, not native Americans, assisted in the prosecutions. In one case, for example,[124] a defendant testified that the investigator required him to stand at attention and repeat many times "I am a liar." Other parties in the same case testified to like acts,[125] one of them testifying that the investigator made a hanging gesture to frighten him into talking.

---

[114] U. N. 10, 19, 68, 71.

[115] Supp. Case 10 at p. 132; Supp. Case 15 at pp. 374-378, 384-387.

[116] Supp. Case 15, p. 387.

[117] E.g., Supp. Case 11, pp. 1533-1544, 1673, 1675, 1839-1844, 2967, 3260, 3261.

[118] Supp. Case 11, pp. 1356, 3255, 3256, 3259.

[119] Supp. Case 11, p. 3063, where Grimm stated, "I cannot blame Lieutenant Guth because I am the one who wrote this silly nonsense."

[120] In Supp. Case 10 permission was refused initially at p. 63, but this ruling was changed at p. 64.

[121] Supp. Case 29, p. 2274.

[122] Supp. Case 8, pp. 1991-1994.

[123] Only one such charge was found in the British trials examined. See U. N. 62.

[124] Supp. Case 11, pp. 1533-1544.

[125] Supp. Case 11, pp. 1673-1675, 1839-1844, 2967.

In another case a defendant testified that the investigator forced him to do continuous knee bends, required him to hold weights outstretched in his hands, forced water down his throat, struck him in the face knocking out a tooth, presented a loaded gun and threatened to kill him, and later threatened him with hanging and struck him.[126] Another witness testified that he was beaten and his face was swollen.[127] When an American court reporter was called to testify about the circumstances surrounding the statement taken from the last witness, he testified as follows:[128]

"A. It could have happened that I told him that he doesn't have to be afraid.

"Q. Why would it be necessary for you to make such a statement?

"A. Because he said that he was beaten before and I told him . . . it is very well I could have told him that we don't use methods like this.

"Q. Did he tell you who had beaten him before?

"A. Yes. He said that some agents of the C.I.C.

* * * * *

"A. He slammed him against the wall, yes.

* * * * *

"Q. Did Zinn (the investigator), at any time, tell Lassak what the truth in the case really was?

"A. Yes, he did."

The same witness also admitted that the statement of the accused was taken in English, although he understood only German, but claimed that it was translated verbally to him.[129]

One witness who testified as to abuse in this case was, however, badly shaken. A woman, Mrs. Meter, testified that she was cursed, beaten, slapped, and had cold water poured on her to procure her statement. Upon cross-examination, she admitted that she had talked to Captain Vance of the prosecution three times and gone over her statement with him, yet had never mentioned any mistreatment. Finally she admitted that her testimony as given in court, which was in complete accord with her statement, was entirely true.[130] In a different case, it appeared definitely that no coercion was used upon any witness,[131]

---

[126] Supp. Case 15, pp. 880-887.
[127] Supp. Case 15, pp. 946-948.
[128] Supp. Case 15, pp. 570-571.
[129] Supp. Case 15, p. 977.
[130] Supp. Case 15, pp. 1326-1333.
[131] Supp. Case 7, p. 218.

but one defendant testified that he signed his statement solely because he was ordered to do so by his superior officer.[132]

The most notorious of the various cases in this regard is the Malmedy Massacres case, in which defense counsel became so incensed over charges by their clients of trickery and brutality that their continuing indignation finally evoked a Senate investigation. In this regard, it should be observed that the prosecution was hampered by assistants who were of alien birth. For example, in one instance, it was charged that one such assistant prosecutor, while the defendants were absent from their quarters, climbed over the fence, went into the bunker house, stole the defendant's private papers and documents, and took them into the prosecution offices for translation.[133] No one but a shyster would be guilty of such misconduct, and it scarcely reflects credit upon this nation. Even more serious were other charges made growing out of this trial, and such charges must be scrutinized with great care to determine where the truth lies. Some of these charges were that the accused were given inadequate accommodations, inadequate food, little water, and that they were held in solitary confinement. It was also charged that they were subjected to mock trials held in darkened rooms, with a crucifix and burning candles upon a table, and in which hearings one of the prosecutors would pretend to be a judge, another prosecutor an attorney, and a third a defense counsel to lead the prisoner into a belief that he should confide in such pseudo-defense counsel; that the prisoners were hooded and led with ropes around their necks into such hearing rooms and told that they were on trial for their lives. Other charges were that the prisoners were threatened with hanging if they failed to talk, that a sweetening-up process was used by furnishing magazines, candy, cigarettes, and polite attentions to secure confessions; that they were lied to and told that other prisoners had confessed and incriminated them, and that beatings, kickings, and stabbings were resorted to "to soften up a prisoner."

It is difficult always to sift the truth from the falsehoods. Each side has emphasized its evidence overmuch. The evidence taken before the Senate Subcommittee is not entirely complete, and it is extremely bulky. The author has also made personal interrogations among persons present at such times, in addition to reading the evidence at the time of trial and available in other forms. His conclusions as to the nature and truth of the charges are as follows:

---

132 Supp. Case 7, pp. 1192-1194.

133 See the admission of this attorney at p. 683 of Hearings before Senate Subcommittee Malmedy Massacre Investigation. See also p. 1569.

1. The cell accommodations were more than adequate. The vast majority of cells even had private toilets, which is far more than most American jails can boast. As a matter of fact, the families of many of the accused were brought to the place of trial and were billeted and fed at the expense of the American government.

2. Food was adequate.

3. Drinking water was not provided at sufficiently frequent intervals, but no physical hardship was worked thereby upon the prisoners.

4. Solitary confinement was used occasionally, but sparingly, and not to a degree which would have extorted a confession from any prisoner unwilling to confess.

5. Threats were used. Some of the testimony of the prosecution staff denying this statement is manifestly incredible under the particular circumstances involved.

6. The sweetening-up process was definitely employed with considerable consistency. Of course, there is nothing illegal about this, if false representations were not made.

7. Mock trials were used in this case with great consistency. It should be observed that the suggestion for this procedure came from one of these recently converted Americans assisting the prosecution. While such trials have occasionally been used in America, they are roundly condemned, and a confession obtained as a result thereof is usually worthless. Hoods were admittedly used to conceal the prisoner's identity. The placing of ropes around the necks of the prisoners led into hearing rooms cannot be substantiated. The candle and crucifix technique was employed, and the presence of a bull-whip was referred to by some of the affiants. However, the trials usually took place in a room sufficiently well lighted for a court reporter to take testimony, there was no physical coercion, but the prisoner was definitely misled as to the reason for his presence and the nature of the proceedings.[134]

8. Physical violence was committed in a few cases, but not in the majority. This occurred only rarely at the instance of the prosecution, but was chiefly administered by Polish guards of their own volition, probably because of the sufferings of their people at the hands of the Nazis. It is doubtful that the chief of the prosecution ever knew of such instances prior to the

---

[134] This and other trickery was admitted. See Hearings before Subcommittee, Malmedy Massacre Investigation, pp. 42, 356, 397, 565, 668, 676, 692, 723, 1271, 1290, 1426. As a matter of fact, some of the testimony was so unsatisfactory that Senator McCarthy suggested that the witnesses, including members of the prosecution, submit themselves to lie-detector tests: pp. 629-639.

question being raised at the time of trial. Testimony as to stabbing and more aggravated brutalities requiring medical attention was almost wholly false. The leading witness in this regard was established to be a pathological liar, and other witnesses had a very deep interest which seemed to color their testimony.[135] It must also be concluded that some of the early sensational "relevations" were promoted by publicity seekers building an edifice of straw upon a few grains of sand, with a somewhat careless regard for the truth—although this does not apply to defense counsel who acted without ulterior motive and with a solid foundation for their beliefs.

One must consider the questions of such techniques from the standpoints of both equity and of expediency. As one court reporter commented, "Would Colonel Everett have the prosecution sit down with these killers at tea and say 'Now, boys, how about giving me the information—please, or pretty please.' "[136] This is the same problem constantly confronting police and prosecutors in this country. Shall they beat an accused to obtain a confession, sweeten him up, shine bright lights in his eyes while pumping questions at him machine-gun fashion, plant a stool pigeon or a concealed mike in a cell, trick him into believing another has confessed, lie to him—just where is the line to be drawn? We know that a confession is not admissible where induced by force or duress; where trickery or misrepresentation is employed, the confession often will stand, but each case must be considered in the light of the particular facts. Law enforcement officers do not desire, so they say, to use such methods but are forced to do so or to turn the guilty loose. Perhaps that is true. Again, many innocent persons have confessed to crimes which they did not commit under one type of influence or another. It may be that some type of truth serum, properly administered under skillful care, would be the logical answer in criminal hearings, even those held in this country, if appropriate constitutional amendment were made. One would, of course, have to avoid the hypnotics so widely used by Russia and its satellites to secure false confessions by persons acting under post-hypnotic suggestion, and who knows whether, even in this country, such a process might not be misused by corrupt or over-eager officials, if the bars against self-incrimination were once lowered.

The point is that this is again a philosophical problem and the approach of the prosecution in the Malmedy case and others

---

[135] Report of Senate Subcommittee Malmedy Massacre Investigation, pp. 12-14.

[136] Letter of Sally Rose Hayett to Henry P. Luce, January 14, 1949, p. 3.

must be weighed in the light of one's personal convictions. There, a particularly knotty problem was presented. In the concentration camp trials, it was relatively simple to prove the crimes. The crematoriums were in physical existence, the murders were easy to establish, and the chain of responsibility was scarcely open to question. In a situation like the Malmedy Massacres case, it was the intention of the German forces to exterminate all survivors. There would, then, have been left no victims to testify as to who gave the orders and who pulled the triggers. Actually, six allied victims survived. But, these were Americans who did not speak nor understand German, who did not know the members of the army capturing them, and who were not in the hands of the Germans long enough to know the persons intimately. Certainly the testimony of these six survivors alone would have been sufficient to establish the occurrence of the crime, and, perhaps, to identify a few of the offenders. However, other evidence was clearly required, and admissions by the defendants or testimony of such persons against others of the accused were clearly indicated. Anyone condemning the members of the prosecution for over-enthusiasm must place himself in the same position prior to passing judgment. Of course, brutalities and other matters raised by defense counsel are subject to less equivocal judgment.

Another accusation of the gravest type was made by a former defense counsel appointed to aid in the defense of General Yamashita. A reading of his publication indicates the following general charges: (1) that the tribunal was incompetent; (2) that the tribunal had a completely closed mind upon the subject of guilt and innocence from the inception of the trial; (3) that the procedure was a mockery; (4) that substantially no rulings favorable to the defense were made by the tribunal; (5) that there was no evidence of guilt; (6) that improper evidence was considered, and improper rules of law were applied; (7) that these matters occurred at the direct instance of the Commander-in-Chief, General MacArthur.[137] These are more serious and far-reaching charges and should be scrutinized carefully to see if they are justified.

A check of legal rating services does not disclose that either prosecution or defense counsel have, on the whole, received the highest rating as trial lawyers, based upon their experiences in civilian practice. In view of the fact that the tribunal also was not composed of seasoned lawyers, it would not be surprising if some errors occurred in the trial. A reading of the transcript

---

137 Reel, *The Case of General Yamashita*, 1949, University of Chicago Press.

The trial of General Yamashita. The defendant is seated at the extreme left in dark uniform with his defense counsel.

—*Courtesy of U. S. Army Signal Corps.*

convinces this author that some errors were made; however, far fewer than those indicated by the defense counsel to whom reference is made.

Taking the matters in the order previously mentioned, apart from the judicial inexperience, and it must be recalled that all high-ranking officers are well versed in military law and have had considerable experience in court-martial procedures, there is nothing in the record to indicate incompetence. As to the second point, again there is nothing in the record to show that the tribunal had a closed mind upon the subject, except Mr. Reel's statement that various newspaper reporters had predicted a different result. This author has won many cases which courtroom attendants and newspaper reporters thought he would lose, and has lost some which even the trial court had believed would result differently. Mr. Reel refers to a script followed by the court as indicating what its ruling would be in advance. He failed to mention that this was merely the agenda sheet used in all such trials, indicating the order in which arguments and evidence would be heard, which was, of course, not indicative of the court's attitude.

Points (3) and (4) can be discussed together. One gathers that the rulings uniformly were unfavorable to the defense. Rulings which might be considered unfavorable to the defense occurred in a number of places.[138] It should be observed that many of these rulings were upon motions to dismiss the charges, or to strike the Bill of Particulars, which the tribunal had held sufficient. Many of the others were upon objections based upon the hearsay rule, best evidence rule, or use of affidavit testimony which rulings, as already has been observed, are consistent with the procedure followed by all other courts in such cases. Only a few of such rulings are of a type that might be considered erroneous in this type of a hearing, and upon several occasions the tribunal reversed such rulings, so as to give the defense greater leeway.[139] Mr. Reel's reference to the film "Orders from Tokyo" shows, from an examination of the record, that the objection was not to the film, but to the sound track, which could not easily be separated from the film itself, and it was admitted for any probative value as it might be found to deserve.[140] The question might be raised as to how any court hearing a matter, whether with or without a jury, could pass upon evidence until it has had an opportunity either to weigh it or hear it.

[138] Supp. Case 29, pp. 34, 78, 82, 85, 94, 97, 113, 121, 127, 129, 130, 342, 599, 879, 915-946, 1124, 1156, 1463, 1464, 1504, 1565, 1705, 1790, 1791, 2229, 2265, 2360, 2428, 2582, 2856, 2889, 2954, 2956, 3109, 3226, 3755.

[139] E.g., Supp. Case 29, pp. 879, 888.

[140] Supp. Case 29, p. 2428.

On the other hand, it has been found that rulings of a character favorable to the defense were somewhat more numerous than were unfavorable rulings.[141] This included sustaining many objections by the defense to evidence offered by the prosecution, either by witnesses or by way of documents, limitations placed upon cross-examination by the prosecution, stopping the prosecution from offering evidence upon the Supplemental Bill of Particulars until defense counsel had adequate opportunity to prepare thereon, and other matters.

Upon the fifth point of Mr. Reel that there was no evidence of guilt, we must differ with defense counsel. His conclusion is based upon the conviction that a crime of omission is not a crime, upon which the Supreme Court of the United States and various military commissions have ruled differently.[142] Mr. Reel's contention is based upon the further theory that there was no evidence in the record showing that the defendant Yamashita had any responsibility for or control over such actions of the Japanese forces, which Mr. Reel claimed were committed wholly by members of the Japanese navy.

Some of the witnesses testified as to the commission of acts by members of the Japanese army. Certain of the acts referred to occurred in Manila while General Yamashita was still in that city. Other were committed by army men at scattered points in the extermination of so-called guerillas, in which number were included many women and children. As to the commission of acts by navy personnel, General Yamashita himself testified that he had one hundred sixty army ships under his command, which would seem to include some sea-going personnel within the realm of his responsibility. As to the chain of command and the scope of his actual duties, there was a clear conflict of evidence in the record, which it was the function of the tribunal to determine under all of the circumstances.

The manner in which this case was tried by defense counsel is of considerable interest, and perhaps some of the responsibility for the result should be shared by them, if the result is criticized as being erroneous. It has already been seen that in trials conducted in the European theater, the defense documents and witnesses usually far exceeded those of the prosecution. In this case, the prosecution evidence consumed approximately 2900 pages, the defense only 724. The defense apparently took the position throughout that the prosecution had established no

---

[141] Supp. Case 29, pp. 27, 33, 34, 188, 198, 392, 642, 888, 1147, 1176, 1179, 1328, 1329, 1456, 1476, 1477, 1585, 1597, 1598, 1599, 1600, 1601, 1607, 2193, 2303, 2365, 2367, 2417-2418, 2480, 2555, 2561-2569, 2694-2698, 2773, 2805, 2816, 2857, 2977, 3108, 3150, 3155, 3694, 3727.

[142] *Infra*, pp. 259-262, 303-305, 351.

case, which is always a dangerous gamble for a trial lawyer. It was content largely to tear down the prosecution evidence instead of building up affirmative proof to establish its contentions. Reasonable men may differ in their construction of evidence. If the tribunal believed the prosecution witnesses, there was ample evidence to justify the conviction.

Nor were defense counsel taken by surprise at the charge of a crime of omission. Charge 31 of the Bill of Particulars expressly specified: "unlawfully disregarded and failed to discharge his duty as commander to control the operations of the members of his command, permitting them to commit brutal atrocities and other high crimes against the people of the United States and of its allies and dependencies, particularly the Philippines, and he, General Tomoyuki Yamashita thereby violated the laws of war."

The defense counsel not only did not move to dismiss this charge, but announced that the defendant was ready to plead thereto.[143] This would seem to indicate a recognition that the charge was valid, if established by proof. And when the evidence considered by the International Military Tribunal for the Far East of similar acts in other theaters is examined upon like charges and atrocities, it is apparent to students of legal history that the failure to maintain discipline was a widespread fault in the Japanese high command.

Point Six of Mr. Reel's objections as to the consideration of improper evidence overlooks the differences in hearings before military commissions, courts-martial, and criminal courts acting under municipal law. As has been seen, similar evidentiary objections were overruled by all other tribunals, including the International Military Tribunal at Nuremberg. As to the defenses raised of required notice to the protecting power and other matters, these also have been adjudicated many times, as pointed out in the foregoing discussion.

As to the very serious charges presented against General MacArthur, by innuendo as well as by direct statement, this author makes no comment. He has no knowledge upon that subject and seriously questions the extent of Mr. Reel's knowledge in that regard.

CONCLUSIONS

Undoubtedly mistakes were made in the conduct of some military commission hearings, which should not be repeated in

---

143 Supp. Case 29, p. 58.

future tribunals. The recommendations which this author would make as to future hearings are as follows:

1. That the procedure established in these hearings be largely followed as workable and now well defined.

2. That no refugee or former enemy alien be retained as a member of a prosecution staff.

3. That no admission or confession of a defendant be permitted introduction into evidence until a determination has been made by an impartial investigating body, upon which defense counsel are represented, that such affidavit was not procured by fraud or duress.

4. That severances of hearings be granted where necessary to promote the ends of justice.

5. That in every case where there is the slightest possibility of any conflict of interest, individual attorneys be assigned to each defendant, instead of to classes of defendants.

6. That all indictments be supported by bills of particulars, specifying as minutely as possible the dates, places, and nature of the offenses charged.

7. That all prosecution documents and a list of witnesses be made available to defense counsel upon the filing of the bill of particulars.

8. That at least thirty days be granted, subsequent to the filing of the bill of particulars, prior to the commencement of trial, for the preparation of the defense case.

9. That all facilities be offered, as in the past, to secure witnesses and documents required by the defense.

10. That a special corps of law officers of high caliber and with greater training than now exists, be trained and developed to aid military tribunals in the future.

Despite these recommendations, it is the conclusion of this author that a most remarkable work was performed by these bodies. The offenses committed were widespread. Many persons were involved in their commission. In many cases all, or nearly all, of the victims were dead. In the aftermath of war, witnesses were scattered and documents lost or destroyed. Yet, with all of these handicaps, the missing information was carefully assembled, the offenders determined and apprehended, and the facts carefully and ably presented. It is an astounding commentary that in not a single instance was there a claim of completely mistaken identity. In the overwhelming majority of the cases, the defendants admitted their commission of the acts charged, but relied upon some doctrine of law or factual situation to exonerate them or to mitigate their responsibility. It is probably the greatest display of talent in legal research and organization which has ever been demonstrated. Equally remarkable is the fact that these tribunals, composed of officers who had been at war with the nations of those accused only a short time before, or who were judges of occupied countries which had suffered at the hands of the enemy, were able to lay aside passion and prejudice and rule fairly upon the law and the evidence, and even acquit many of those whose guilt seemed clear, but which they did not deem had been established beyond all reasonable doubt. Defense attorneys, as has already been seen, performed brilliantly and with as much passion as if their dearest friends had been on trial. Friendships between prosecution and defense counsel ceased abruptly when the appointments had once been made. The defense attorneys took their duties so seriously that many of them became embittered at the loss of a case consuming their abundant energies. When nations have attorneys, military officers, and judges imbued with this passion for fairness, the doctrine of justice will prevail in post-war trials, as well as in courts of the United States.

XXXIX

THE UNITED STATES SUPREME COURT

It must be remembered in considering the cases cited in this chapter that there was a procedure for review provided from the decision of all military courts, however constituted, except that of the International Military Tribunal at Nuremberg. Thus, even the judgments of the International Military Tribunal at Tokyo were subject to review by MacArthur. As has already been seen, many judgments were altered and sentences reduced upon review.[1] The records were carefully read in every case upon which review procedure was sought and subjected to rigid tests to determine whether or not a fair trial had been had, whether the evidence completely supported the judgment, and whether the sentence was a just one. In many instances where the judgment or sentence did not seem to be completely supported by the evidence, or where the procedure seemed to have been unfair, the benefit of the doubt was definitely given to the accused.

It would seem that this safeguard provided by the military forces would be sufficient to insure against injustice. However, American defense attorneys were generally determined to exhaust the last possible remedy for their clients, and in many cases German defendants, upon their own initiative, sought to secure further action. Most of the steps were of a similar type, although there was considerable variation in the documents actually filed. In general, most of the instruments were considered to be in the nature of petitions for habeas corpus and were construed in the light of the legal principles controlling that procedure.

It should be observed that the decisions of the United States Supreme Court split along very definite lines, and one is inclined to suspect that such a divergence arose, at least so far as certain dissenting judges were concerned, along emotional lines. This is not intended in any derogatory sense. Those judges valued highly the concepts of liberty and justice as understood in the ordinary American judiciary system, and were reluctant to see any deviation from such high standards, even in trials of a wholly different character. As will be pointed out subsequently, much of the language of minority judges in speaking of due process reflects this reaction. One might say that those opinions were idealistic rather than realistic.

---

[1] *Infra*, p. 333.

It was almost a uniform procedure to find the Supreme Court rulings upon petitions for habeas corpus splitting on a four to four basis, with two exceptions. In the Medical Case,[2] Justice Douglas did not dissent, which might indicate that he was sufficiently shocked by the known evidence in that case as not to feel inclined to stay the hand of justice. In the *Stroop* case, there was no dissenter, but this may have been because of the form of the petition.[3] After a long series of such deadlocks resulting from such petitions in German cases, Justice Jackson, who had theretofore taken no part in such decisions, finally broke the tie upon presentation of a Japanese case, in order that the court might conclude once and for all what its position would be upon the merits of such controversies.[4]

The most essential point of law to be remembered in this connection is that military commissions are not courts of the United States.[5] In other words, while the writ of habeas corpus may frequently be allowed in cases where imprisonment has resulted through the action of a regular judicial tribunal, the same rules do not follow as to imprisonment resulting from the action of a military commission. The power to review the proceedings of military commissions is not by certiorari but by the methods of review fixed by the law controlling those proceedings, and which is generally to a superior reviewing officer.[6] It is clear that a military commission created by international authority is not a court of the United States,[7] and that the

---

[2] *Brandt v. United States* and 13 companion cases, 333 U. S. 836, 68 S. Ct. 603, 92 L. Ed. 1119.

[3] *In re Eichel,* 333 U. S. 865, 68 S. Ct. 787, 92 L. Ed. 1144.

[4] *Koki Hirota v. General of the Army MacArthur et al., Kenji Dohihara v. General of the Army MacArthur, Koichi Kido et al. v. General of the Army MacArthur et al.,* 335 U. S. 876, 69 S. Ct. 157, 93 L. Ed. 418. Justice Jackson pointed out that the stalemate existing in the court was extremely embarrassing from a point of view of international diplomacy, and while there were evils to be considered both in denying such a petition and in granting it, that he felt the lesser of the two evils would be to air the case upon the merits and thus establish a precedent in other situations.

[5] *Ex parte Vallandigham,* 68 U. S. 243, 1 Wall. 243, 17 L. Ed. 589; *In re Vidal,* 179 U. S. 126, 21 S. Ct. 48, 45 L. Ed. 118; *Ex parte Quirin,* 317 U. S. 1, 63 S. Ct. 2, 87 L. Ed. 3, affirming 47 F. Supp. 431; *Application of Yamashita; Yamashita v. Styer,* 327 U. S. 1, 66 S. Ct. 340 at p. 344, 90 L. Ed. 499; *Application of Homma; Homma v. Styer,* 327 U. S. 759, 66 S. Ct. 515, 90 L. Ed. 992.

[6] *Ex parte Vallandigham,* 68 U. S. 243, 1 Wall. 243, 17 L. Ed. 589; *Application of Homma; Homma v. Styer,* 327 U. S. 759, 66 S. Ct. 515, 90 L. Ed. 992.

[7] *Koki Hirota v. General of the Army MacArthur et al.,* 338 U. S. 197, 69 S. Ct. 197, 93 L. Ed. 1902.

United States would have no power to review the proceedings of any international court.[8]

As a practical matter, it may be queried as to how our Supreme Court could handle the volume of litigation which would arise if it accepted, or had the power to accept, original jurisdiction in such habeas corpus cases. There were several hundred of such petitions filed as the result of the judgments of military commissions. To examine the records in each of such cases would be a phenomenal task and would double the work of any tribunal accepting original jurisdiction. From the standpoint of expediting work in the court, it is perhaps fortunate that the United States Supreme Court has no original habeas corpus jurisdiction. Any cases coming to the attention of that court must arise by way of review of the action of a lower court. Since the overwhelming majority of such petitions filed in the Supreme Court were erroneously filed as original proceedings, and did not arise upon review, the dismissal of such proceedings followed as a matter of course, although not without dissent.[9]

---

[8] *Koki Hirota v. General of the Army MacArthur et al.*, 338 U. S. 197, 69 S. Ct. 197, 93 L. Ed. 1902; *Flick v. Johnson*, 174 F. (2d) 983, certiorari denied 338 U. S. 879, 70 S. Ct. 158, 94 L. Ed. 114, rehearing denied 94 L. Ed. 259.

[9] *Milch v. United States*, 332 U. S. 789, 68 S. Ct. 92, 92 L. Ed. 371; *Brandt v. United States and 13 companion cases* (Medical Case), 333 U. S. 836, 68 S. Ct. 603, 92 L. Ed. 1119; *In the matter of Eichel, Fuehr and Goss* (Stroop Case), 333 U. S. 865, 68 S. Ct. 787, 92 L. Ed. 1144; *Everett on behalf of Bersin and 73 others v. Truman* (Malmedy Massacre Case), 334 U. S. 824, 68 S. Ct. 1081, 92 L. Ed. 1753; *In the matter of Krautwurst and 11 companion cases*, 334 U. S. 826, 68 S. Ct. 1328, 92 L. Ed. 1754; *In the matter of Girke*, 334 U. S. 836, 68 S. Ct. 1491, 92 L. Ed. 1762; *In the matter of Ehlen "et al.,"* 334 U. S. 836, 68 S. Ct. 1491, 92 L. Ed. 1762; *In the matter of Gronwald "et al.,"* 334 U. S. 857, 68 S. Ct. 1522, 92 L. Ed. 1777; *In the matter of Hohler*, 335 U. S. 805, 69 S. Ct. 19, 93 L. Ed. 362; *In the matter of Stattmann and 3 companion cases*, 335 U. S. 805, 69 S. Ct. 18, 93 L. Ed. 362; *In the matter of Weiss*, 335 U. S. 805, 69 S. Ct. 26, 93 L. Ed. 362; *Eckstein v. United States; In re Eckstein*, 335 U. S. 841, 69 S. Ct. 60, 93 L. Ed. 392; s. c. 335 U. S. 851, 69 S. Ct. 79, 93 L. Ed. 399; *In the matter of Fulsche*, 335 U. S. 841, 69 S. Ct. 61, 93 L. Ed. 392; *In the matter of Grill*, 335 U. S. 841, 69 S. Ct. 62, 93 L. Ed. 392; *In the matter of Hans*, 335 U. S. 841, 69 S. Ct. 64, 93 L. Ed. 392; *In the matter of Pfeiffer and Landwehr*, 335 U. S. 841, 69 S. Ct. 61, 93 L. Ed. 392; *In the matter of Unrecht*, 335 U. S. 841, 69 S. Ct. 60, 93 L. Ed. 392; *In the matter of Vetter and 6 companion cases*, 335 U. S. 841, 69 S. Ct. 59, 93 L. Ed. 392; *In the matter of Heim*, 335 U. S. 856, 69 S. Ct. 126, 93 L. Ed. 404; *In the matter of Schallermair*, 336 U. S. 922, 69 S. Ct. 644, 93 L. Ed. 1084; *In the matter of Dammann and 4 companion cases*, 336 U. S. 922-3, 69 S. Ct. 644, 93 L. Ed. 1084; *In the matter of Puhl*, 336 U. S. 923, 69 S. Ct. 646, 93 L. Ed. 1084; *In the matter of Schmidt*, 336 U. S. 923, 69 S. Ct. 646, 93 L. Ed. 1084; *In the matter of Seidel*, 336 U. S. 923, 69 S. Ct. 645, 93 L. Ed. 1084; *In*

The next ground upon which cases were held inapplicable presents a closer question upon the law. In view of the fact that this question may arise in the future, it is important to realize the extent of its application. It was held by the majority in the *Eisentrager* case[10] that the writ of habeas corpus is not applicable to an alien enemy who was never within the territorial jurisdiction of the court. Justice Jackson pointed out that alien enemies within the United States in time of war are subject to definite curtailments of their rights and privileges; that even American citizens in our armed forces lose the benefit of the Fifth Amendment; and that it would be anomalous to grant greater rights to an enemy alien abroad than to an American citizen. In this particular case, the accused had never been in territory occupied by the United States, they were not imprisoned in United States territory, nor were they within the territorial jurisdiction of the Federal Court of the District of Columbia, in which court the proceedings had been filed. Justice Black, dissenting, felt that the majority opinion was wholly inconsistent with the *Quirin* and *Yamashita* results (where, however, the enemy aliens were upon territory of the United States or under its jurisdiction), and felt that a more liberal construction of the term "jurisdiction" should be applied.[11] While the majority opinion is probably justified in the light of earlier decisions defining the jurisdiction of a court, the author believes that the dissent has considerable merit in pointing out the extension of those earlier decisions by the *Quirin* and *Yamashita* cases. It seems a somewhat attenuated distinction to speak of jurisdiction when a man is imprisoned in the Philippines and to speak of no jurisdiction when he is imprisoned within the American occupation zone of Germany. There were stronger reasons available for the majority opinion, and it is felt that not too much reliance should be placed upon this single ground.

It is clear, of course, both under the Hague Rules and under the Congressional laws applying to such situations that a military commission may be appointed by any field commander.[12]

---

the matter of Muhlbauer and 57 companion cases, 336 U. S. 964, 69 S. Ct. 930, 93 L. Ed. 1115; *In the matter of Felsch*, 337 U. S. 953, 69 S. Ct. 1523, 93 L. Ed. 1754; *In the matter of Buerger*, 338 U. S. 884, 70 S. Ct. 183, 94 L. Ed. 118; *In the matter of Lammars*, 339 U. S. 976, 70 S. Ct. 1008, 94 L. Ed. 919.

10 *Johnson v. Eisentrager*, 339 U. S. 763, 70 S. Ct. 936 at pp. 938-945, 94 L. Ed. 1255.

11 *Johnson v. Eisentrager*, 339 U. S. 763, 70 S. Ct. 936 at pp. 950-952, 94 L. Ed. 1255.

12 *Application of Yamashita; Yamashita v. Styer*, 327 U. S. 1, 66 S. Ct. 340 at p. 345, 90 L. Ed. 499.

So far as the military commissions trying war criminals were concerned, it is clear that such tribunals were lawfully created.[13] This was even acknowledged by Justice Murphy, who dissented in the *Yamashita* case.[14] Only Justice Rutledge dissented as to this conclusion, and that was upon the basis that fundamental deviations from due process in setting up the rules and procedures to guide the commission vitiated its original creation.[15]

Assuming that the majority is correct in determining that such commissions were properly established, the writ of habeas corpus merely brings up the question of the power of such a commission to try the petitioner and not the validity or propriety of its judgment.[16] The writ fundamentally tests only the question as to whether or not there was jurisdiction in that particular body to detain and to try the person in custody.[17] It seems to be clear that military tribunals ordinarily have jurisdiction to try a person in military custody. It is clear also that military tribunals have jurisdiction to try and punish offenders against the laws of war.[18] And the power to conduct such trials exists from the time that war is declared until the proclamation of peace, irrespective of whether hostilities are still in progress or whether they have terminated.[19]

In considering the question of what constitutes a war crime, because of the lack of decisions by our Supreme Court upon this question, there is little added to the precedents previously discussed. That court has had occasion to hold that espionage and sabotage are war crimes.[20] Giving information to the Japanese after the surrender by Germany was considered to be a war

[13] *Ex parte Quirin; U. S. ex parte Quirin v. Cox*, 317 U. S. 1, 63 S. Ct. 1 at p. 2, 87 L. Ed. 3; *Application of Yamashita v. Styer*, 327 U. S. 1, 66 S. Ct. 340 at pp. 345-346, 90 L. Ed. 499.

[14] *Application of Yamashita; Yamashita v. Styer*, 327 U. S. 1, 66 S. Ct. 340 at p. 355, 90 L. Ed. 499.

[15] *Application of Yamashita; Yamashita v. Styer*, 327 U. S. 1, 66 S. Ct. 340 at pp. 361-362, 90 L. Ed. 499.

[16] *Application of Yamashita; Yamashita v. Styer*, 327 U. S. 1, 66 S. Ct. 340 at p. 344, 90 L. Ed. 499; *Johnson v. Eisentrager*, 339 U. S. 763, 70 S. Ct. 936 at p. 948, 94 L. Ed. 1255.

[17] *Johnson v. Eisentrager*, 339 U. S. 763, 70 S. Ct. 936 at p. 942, 94 L. Ed. 1255. But see Justice Black's comment upon this question at pp. 951-952.

[18] *Application of Yamashita; Yamashita v. Styer*, 327 U. S. 1, 66 S. Ct. 340 at p. 344, 90 L. Ed. 499; *Johnson v. Eisentrager*, 339 U. S. 763, 70 S. Ct. 936 at p. 948, 94 L. Ed. 1255.

[19] *Application of Yamashita; Yamashita v. Styer*, 327 U. S. 1, 66 S. Ct. 340 at p. 346, 90 L. Ed. 499.

[20] *Ex parte Quirin; U. S. ex parte Quirin v. Cox*, 317 U. S. 1, 63 S. Ct. 1 at p. 2, 87 L. Ed. 3.

[21] *Johnson v. Eisentrager*, 339 U. S. 763, 70 S. Ct. 936 at p. 948, 94 L. Ed. 1255. Justice Black, to the contrary, at p. 951, felt differently

crime.[21] And failure to take steps to control troops under one's command so as to permit them to commit atrocities and acts of terrorism constitutes a war crime.[22] Of course the question is then to be determined as to what right the Supreme Court would have to examine into the evidence at all, or to weigh the facts. This will be discussed at greater length subsequently.

The Geneva Convention was involved in two ways. One provision requires notice to be given to the protecting Power of a prisoner charged with crime, prior to his trial. Another provision of that Convention provides that in the trial itself there shall be employed the "same procedure as . . . . (for the) armed forces of the detaining power." The Supreme Court in considering these two matters found that neither of them was applicable. It held primarily that such provisions of the Geneva Convention referred only to the trials of a prisoner of war for offenses committed by him while a prisoner and did not refer to war crimes committed by him prior to capture.[23] This is consistent with the rulings of all of the military commissions upon this subject, including the tribunals conducted by other nations; and an examination of the historical origin of the Convention seems to support this view.[24] However, Justice Rutledge made a powerful argument against this view in analyzing the logical construction of such provisions,[25] and further pointed out that the prosecutor in the *Yamashita* case had charged General Yamashita with these same violations as war crimes. While this demonstrates a grave inconsistency, the error of the

---

about this subject and spoke at great length concerning patriotic French, Norwegians, and others who continued to battle after their nations had surrendered. One may admire Justice Black's patriotism, but he is incorrect in his construction of international law. A citizen of a conquered nation who continues to resist acts illegally and is subject to specific punishment. This was even held by a Norwegian court in passing upon the liability of a German officer who tried and executed a Norwegian found guilty of such illegal resistance (U. N. 34).

[22] *Application of Yamashita; Yamashita v. Styer*, 327 U. S. 1, 66 S. Ct. 340 at pp. 347-349, 90 L. Ed. 499. This is in line with the results observed earlier (infra, pp. 259, 303-305). Even Justice Murphy, who dissented in the *Yamashita* case, felt that such a crime of omission could constitute a war crime under a proper showing. He felt, however (pp. 354, 357), that under the particular circumstances of this case, when General Yamashita was acting under extremely difficult circumstances, that a different result should have followed.

[23] *Application of Yamashita; Yamashita v. Styer*, 327 U. S. 1, 66 S. Ct. 340 at pp. 350-352, 90 L. Ed. 499; *Johnson v. Eisentrager*, 339 U. S. 763, 70 S. Ct. 936 at pp. 949-950, 94 L. Ed. 1255.

[24] *Infra*, p. 310.

[25] *Application of Yamashita; Yamashita v. Styer*, 327 U. S. 1, 66 S. Ct. 340 at pp. 374-377, 90 L. Ed. 499.

prosecutor could hardly change the scope and extent of international law.

One of the other leading contentions asserted by defendants was that they were not tried in accordance with the American Articles of War. Neither the reasons given by the majority nor the minority of the court carry much conviction. Both seem to have lost sight of the fact that war crimes are violations of international law controlled by international convention. The tribunal to be created for such hearings is to be appointed by the commander in the field, who designates the tribunal and the manner of trial. It is necessary, of course, that the requirements of a fair trial be observed. This would not necessarily require the same type of procedure as is employed in American criminal courts. The procedure, as nearly as possible, should accord with that felt to be equitable under a system of justice common to all nations. In other words, an American captive would not have an arbitrary right to be tried under American law, but he might feel a trial to be wholly unfair which followed Japanese or Russian legal principles. It was for this reason that the international military tribunals adopted provisions which most nearly represented the concepts common to the nations conducting those trials, as well as to those nations represented in the dock.

In addition to the powers conferred by the Hague Rules, Article 38 of the Articles of War gives the president, as commander-in-chief, the power to "prescribe the procedure, including modes of proof" to be employed in such hearings, although this article goes on to prescribe that such procedure should not be inconsistent with that described elsewhere in the articles. The Articles also attempt to make the procedure applying in more usual courts carry over to such hearings. Both the majority and minority opinions point to Article 15, which was a later addition to the Articles of War, the majority of the court feeling that such provision was the only one applying to the trials of war crimes, and that the restriction found in other articles applied only to the trial of American military personnel.[26] Justice Rutledge severely criticized this view, taking the position that the Articles of War were sufficiently broad to include all types of hearings before military commissions and that it was most illogical to apply one standard of justice to American personnel and a wholly different standard of justice to enemy captives.[27]

---

[26] *Application of Yamashita; Yamashita v. Styer*, 327 U. S. 1, 66 S. Ct. 340 at pp. 350-351, 90 L. Ed. 499.

[27] *Application of Yamashita; Yamashita v. Styer*, 327 U. S. 1, 66 S. Ct. 340 at pp. 369-374, 90 L. Ed. 499.

There is much merit to this position, if the distinction is made solely upon the terminology used in the Articles of War and not upon the distinction between crimes recognized under international law and violations of our own Articles by members of the American armed forces or other disciplinary actions.

The extension of constitutional protections to enemy aliens was one of the more troublesome problems. The majority of the court in the Yamashita decision felt it was unnecessary to deal with this question.[28] Justice Murphy attacked this view bitterly, claiming that the requirement of due process applied to "any person" accused of crime by the Federal Government.[29] Justice Rutledge also adhered to this view.[30] In the *Homma* case, as well, Justice Murphy's dissenting opinion was based partially on this ground.[31] Apparently the majority of the court had conceded in the *Quirin* case that constitutional limitations might apply in some charges of war crimes, although they took the view that this did not require indictment by a grand jury or jury trial of such offenses.[32] It is felt, however, that the best answer to this argument was pointed out by Justice Jackson in the *Eisentrager* case, where he pointed out that a complete extension of such constitutional provisions would lead to a manifest absurdity and would, in addition, give enemies greater rights than members of our own armed forces. He stated:

> "When we analyze the claim prisoners are asserting and the court below sustained, it amounts to a right not to be tried at all for an offense against our armed forces. If the Fifth Amendment protects them from military trial, the Sixth Amendment as clearly prohibits their trial by civil courts. The latter requires in all criminal prosecution that 'the accused' be tried 'by an impartial jury of the State and district wherein the crime shall have been committed, which district shall have been previously ascertained by law.' And if the Fifth be held to embrace these prisoners because it uses the inclusive term 'no person,' the Sixth must, for it applies to all 'accused.' No suggestion is advanced by the court below or by prisoners of any constitutional method by which any violations of the laws of war endangering the

---

28 *Application of Yamashita; Yamashita v. Styer*, 327 U. S. 1, 66 S. Ct. 340 at p. 351, 90 L. Ed. 499.

29 *Application of Yamashita; Yamashita v. Styer*, 327 U. S. 1, 66 S. Ct. 340 at p. 353, 90 L. Ed. 499.

30 *Application of Yamashita; Yamashita v. Styer*, 327 U. S. 1, 66 S. Ct. 340 at pp. 361, 377-379, 90 L. Ed. 499.

31 *Application of Homma; Homma v. Styer*, 327 U. S. 759, 66 S. Ct. 515 at p. 515, 90 L. Ed. 992.

32 *Ex parte Quirin; U. S. ex parte Quirin v. Cox*, 317 U. S. 1, 63 S. Ct. 1 at pp. 11, 16, 17, 87 L. Ed. 3.

United States forces could be reached or punished, if it were not by a Military Commission in the theatre where the offense was committed.

* * * * *

"If this Amendment invests enemy aliens in unlawful hostile action against us with immunity from military trial, it puts them in a more protected position than our own soldiers. American citizens conscripted into the military service are thereby stripped of their Fifth Amendment rights and as members of the military establishment are subject to its discipline, including military trials for offenses against aliens or Americans. Cf. Humphrey v. Smith, 336 U.S. 695, 69 Sup. Ct. 830, 93 L. ed. 986; Wade v. Hunter, 336 U.S. 684, 69 Sup. Ct. 834, 93 L. ed. 974. Can there be any doubt that our foes would also have been excepted, but for the assumption 'any person' would never be read to include those in arms against us? It would be a paradox indeed if what the Amendment denied to Americans it guaranteed to enemies. And, of course, it cannot be claimed that such shelter is due them as a matter of comity for any reciprocal rights conferred by enemy governments on American soldiers.

"The decision below would extend coverage of our Constitution to nonresident alien enemies denied to resident alien enemies. The latter are entitled only to judicial hearing to determine what the petition of these prisoners admits: that they are really alien enemies. When that appears, those resident here may be deprived of liberty by Executive action without hearing. Ludecke v. Watkins, 335 U.S. 160, 68 Sup. Ct. 1429, 92 L. ed. 1881. While this is preventive rather than punitive detention, no reason is apparent why an alien enemy charged with having committed a crime should have greater immunities from Executive action than one whom it is only feared might at some future time commit a hostile act.

"If the Fifth Amendment confers its rights on all the world except Americans engaged in defending it, the same must be true of the companion civil-rights Amendments, for none of them is limited by its express terms, territorially or as to persons. Such a construction would mean that during military occupation irreconcilable enemy elements, guerilla fighters, and 'werewolves' could require the American Judiciary to assure them freedoms of speech, press, and assembly as in the First Amendment, right to bear arms as in the Second, security against 'unreasonable' searches and seizures as in the Fourth, as well as rights to jury trial as in the Fifth and Sixth Amendments.

* * * * *

"We hold that the Constitution does not confer a right of personal security or an immunity from military trial and punishment upon an alien enemy engaged in the hostile service of a government at war with the United States."[33]

As indicated, it was claimed by defense counsel in the *Quirin* case that under constitutional limitations one may not be indicted except upon presentment by a grand jury. The court held that such provision did not apply as the Constitution did not contemplate military commissions nor the trial of war crimes as included within its restrictions.[34] The language previously quoted from *Johnson v. Eisentrager* would seem to dispose completely of this contention.

As to other defenses or criticisms noted by dissenting members of the court, Justice Rutledge was the only one who touched upon the doctrine of *ex post facto,* and this was not expanded in his discussion.[35] The same justice also criticized the charges presented in one such case upon the basis of their inadequacy to state a charge,[36] but the majority of the court pointed out that such charges need not be stated with the precision of a common law indictment.[37] The dissenting justice apparently considered that the time given in some of these cases for the defense to prepare to meet such charges was inadequate and felt that such haste amounted to deprivation of a fair trial, which would ordinarily be considered a lack of due process.[38] Criticism was also made of the use of affidavit evidence, hearsay evidence, and abandonment of the best evidence rule and like departures from more familiar concepts of American practice.[39] Justice Rutledge even felt that such departures vitiated the trials completely and went to the competency of the tribunal to act.

It will be seen from these decisions that the determinations by the majority of the court are primarily in accord with the results reached by other tribunals of allied nations conducting or sitting in review upon similar proceedings. It would seem that a revision of the Articles of War should be made in view

---

[33] *Johnson v. Eisentrager,* 339 U. S. 763, 70 S. Ct. 936 at pp. 946-947, 94 L. Ed. 1255.

[34] *Ex parte Quirin; U. S. ex parte Quirin v. Cox,* 317 U. S. 1, 63 S. Ct. 1 at pp. 16, 17, 87 L. Ed. 3.

[35] *Application of Yamashita; Yamashita v. Styer,* 327 U. S. 1, 66 S. Ct. 340 at p. 360, 90 L. Ed. 499.

[36] *Application of Yamashita; Yamashita v. Styer,* 327 U. S. 1, 66 S. Ct. 340 at pp. 360-361, 90 L. Ed. 499.

[37] *Application of Yamashita; Yamashita v. Styer,* 327 U. S. 1, 66 S. Ct. 340 at p. 349, 90 L. Ed. 499.

[38] *Application of Yamashita; Yamashita v. Styer,* 327 U. S. 1, 66 S. Ct. 340 at pp. 353, 354, 359, 361, 367-369; *Application of Homma; Homma v. Styer,* 327 U. S. 759, 66 S. Ct. 515 at pp. 515-517, 90 L. Ed. 992.

[39] *Application of Yamashita; Yamashita v. Styer,* 327 U. S. 1, 66 S. Ct. 340 at pp. 361, 363-367, 90 L. Ed. 499.

of the fact that some members of the court have felt that an ambiguity exists therein. The constitutional questions raised by the minority members do not seem to be well taken. However, considering the fact that those objections are based primarily upon what such members felt amounted to deprivation of a fair trial, it should be most strongly urged that the procedure in future hearings suggested elsewhere in this work be followed, without deviation for the sake of expediency.[40]

[40] *Infra*, p. 344.

XL

SPECIAL COURTS AND NATIONAL COURTS

It early became apparent that the International Military Tribunal at Nuremberg could not do more than to try a few persons charged with crime. The object of that trial was to try those persons representative of the major factors in Nazi aggression or in the commission of crimes against war, peace, and humanity; and in so doing to establish the controlling law and procedure. It was likewise obvious that special tribunals of American judges, or even of military officers, could not try the tens of thousands of persons constituting the sub-leaders and followers of the Nazi movement. As an undercurrent, also, it was felt that the German people should have a hand in trying those who had sinned principally against Germany as a nation, and who had brought impoverishment, servitude, and death to multitudes of its citizens. Perhaps it was felt that the German people would thereby become more familiar with the details of these very offenses.

These factors dictated, as a policy of expediency, that courts be created which should be administered by Germans for the trials of members of the organizations which had been decreed by the International Military Tribunal at Nuremberg to be criminal organizations. The personnel of these courts was to be selected largely from the ranks of anti-Nazis or Germans friendly to the Allied cause, imbued with the general concept of democracy. By virtue of the Council Control laws, Spruckhammer, or denazification courts, were created in principal cities. It was their task to try the many offenders who were members of the Nazi party, and particularly its leaders—a sort of judicial purge of those of political leanings not attuned to the sensitivities of the victors. What was hoped to be accomplished thereby in a sense of reconstruction is not clearly understood, in view of the fact that the power of the courts to punish was limited to a maximum of ten years. It is difficult to believe that an ardent Nazi would alter his belief because of a few years' imprisonment, or that others would be so fear inspired that they would become sincerely democratic. The concept of democracy is not grasped through fear, but through the patient practice of liberty.

When, for example, Schacht was freed by the International Military Tribunal, he was promptly arrested and retried by a denazification court. Other persons charged with offenses rolled through these judicial processes by the hundreds, by the thousands.

There was no consistency in the results reached. They varied widely, depending upon the caliber of the court, its location, and various influences brought to bear. In the beginning the Allies kept close watch over the proceedings; as time went on, many persons in the A.M.G. and in the Department of the Army grew tired and less observant.[1] It became apparent that Nazism was not a matter imposed upon a people by the dictates of one man—but a militaristic spirit alive in Germany at its roots and all too often affecting the men in charge of such denazification tribunals or in positions of political power.[2] And even outright bribery became so common that many Nazi leaders either were not brought to trial or were speedily acquitted or readily pardoned.[3] Of course, pardoning or reduction of sentences was not limited to such proceedings, as even fairly major war criminals were released considerably before their sentences had run.[4]

In other words, what had occurred following the First World War has happened again, the very thing pointed out by Justice Jackson in his opening address before the International Military Tribunal—one cannot leave the punishment of the culprits of a defeated nation to its nationals. Too many factors alter the picture when viewed from the standpoint of victor and vanquished. Basic philosophies may differ. He who is a murderer and rabid executioner from the point of view of a democratic nation may be a realistic scientist or national hero from the point of view of a nation steeped in different concepts. Then, too, those placed in a position to pass upon such crimes are all too often sympathizers at heart with the accused; or they may be influenced by pressure brought upon them by those still powerful in their native land. They may be affected by fear of

---

[1] See, for example, former Secretary Royall's testimony before the House of Representatives' Sub-committee on Appropriations, March 2, 1948. However, it is believed that Secretary Royall never had any great sympathy for any of the post-war trials.

[2] Reinhold Maier, Minister-President, for example, pardoned or reduced the sentences of many thousands of Nazis. Evidence of the current wide prevalence of Nazi theories may be found in German newspapers, magazines, and speeches over the period of the last five years.

[3] 34 *Prevent World War III*, page 40.

[4] For example, Georg von Schnitzler, Joseph Alstoetter, Karl Holdt, Emil Puhl, Ernest Wilhelm Bohle. The reason for the premature releases was not improper certainly, as these persons were released for good behavior. However, it was a bit unusual in view of the fact that the sentencing Tribunals made no provision for earlier termination of the sentences, and such probably had not been taken into consideration in passing judgment. While provision had been made for reduction of excessive sentences, these sentences had not initially been regarded as excessive.

reprisal, or by contemplation of the effect their actions will have upon their own futures. Perhaps, they feel, another Hitler will arise and they will be condemned as traitors, not inconceivably by one of those upon whom they are passing sentence today. Bribery, of one form or another, has its effect. In short, the impulses toward abstract justice which may have stirred the German judges initially became more and more dulled. As the proceedings dragged out over periods of years, people wanted to forget and did forget the brutal nature of the offenses. They wanted to stop the mockery and the trials degenerated into a shadow tilt, the mere pretense of a formality.[5]

This may sound like a brutal denunciation of these trials, but experience has not shown them to be successful. That which was bred into the youth of Germany has not been distilled from their spirits by these proceedings. The older men, chauvinistic in their views, have not changed. The German people have not been swung from anti-Semitism to a love, or even a tolerance, for Jewry. There have been incidents of efforts to secure materials for rearmament; little fuehrers are coming to the fore; again the questions of German unification and power are being discussed openly. Once again even the Allied nations talk, as they did after the last war, of strengthening Germany as a threat against Russia—the inevitable discussion of balance of power. There, again, speaks the thought of avoiding wars through the balance of military might, a precarious and dangerous philosophy, as opposed to the philosophy of international political cooperation and judicial sanctions to avoid the crises leading to future wars. And yet, these steps are under way and will come into fruition within a very few years, under the benevolent and frightened direction of our statesmen and military leaders.

Schacht is a particularly interesting example of German mode of thought. An international financier, his business acumen and personable manner brought him high esteem in Germany and abroad. His convincing defense brought him acquittal by the International Military Tribunal. He was later tried by a German denazification board, found guilty, and sentenced to eight years' imprisonment. He appealed and again won acquittal. Finally, the Minister of Denazification of Wuerttemberg-Baden overruled the Appeals Court and ordered a new trial. An effort was made to arrest him for retrial. Schacht refused to appear before a German Court of Ludwigsburg, in the American zone, because he lived in the British zone. At last reports, he was still at liberty.

Schacht then offered his services to the American economic planners in Germany. Certainly, one would say, a man with

---

5 For example, Saturday Evening Post, January 21, 1950, p. 28.

Schacht's financial background would be invaluable. There was also discussion of his appointment as an official of the West German Government. After all, he was a free man—he had been cleared of crime, a loyal German. Thus, he stood for everything which was sane and best in Germany . But, there is just one more little incident to add.

In a prominent American newspaper in 1948,[6] our Dr. Schacht went into the economic ills of Germany, placing them squarely upon the shoulders of the victors. Reminiscent of 1919 and the period after Versailles? Since then, however, Schacht has not confined his publications to America. His "Settlement with Hitler" (Abrechung mit Hitler) became a best seller in Germany. Hundreds of thousands of copies were purchased avidly as they came off the press. The book, it is true, takes as its thesis the fact that the German people did not, in the main, agree with Naziism, embrace its ideology, or desire war. Apparently the author considered all governments of Germany since the first war "stupid." But, the true purpose of the book seems designed to lead the Allies to reconstruct Germany financially—a goal which may be well worthwhile, and which may be perfectly sincere on the part of the author. However, one is led to question his repudiation of Hitlerian philosophy when he speaks of Mein Kampf in the following vein: "A brilliant mind dealt expertly with social and political problems and gave well-founded opinions about them." One is inclined to question Herr Schacht's often repeated protestations of lack of sympathy for the Nazi regime.

There is yet another chapter in the judicial aftermath of the war. Nationals of Allied countries had become indoctrinated with the views of the aggressor nations and collaborated actively with them. There were, of course, private reprisals such as the shaven heads of French maidens who consorted too freely with their robust captors. There was some measure of popular disapproval of those who had spoken over the radio upon isolated occasions at Nazi request—such as P. G. Wodehouse. The more serious offenses, involving charges of treason, were far too lengthy in character to discuss here—but involved such persons as Lord Haw Haw, Tokyo Rose, and the much mooted case of Ezra Pound. However, the trials conducted on such grounds were handled by domestic courts of the nation admitting citizenship of that particular individual, sitting in judgment upon its own national for a crime against the government. The procedure, therefore, was not unique and contributed nothing of outstanding interest to the realm of international jurisprudence.

---

[6] See, Letters to the Editor, Chicago Tribune, February 15, 1948.

PART VI

DEVELOPMENTS SINCE NUREMBERG

XLI

DEVELOPMENTS SINCE NUREMBERG

Strangely enough, even though many people have disrespect for the legal profession, they have an abiding faith in courts of justice. They seem to feel that if a wrong is threatened or committed, redress can be secured. This is largely true. In one respect, only, are they wrong. Lawyers themselves are deeply imbued with this concept of justice. They will fight bitterly, savagely, to right a wrong—spend hours, months, years, if necessary, battling an almost hopeless cause to accomplish this result, even if they are not wholly in sympathy with their clients. When American defense attorneys were appointed in the Fukuda, Yamashita, and Malmedy Massacres cases, for example, the trials were not Gaston and Alphonse affairs. The attorneys laid aside all obligations except those to their clients and fought viciously every step of the way. The daily friendships of attorneys for prosecution and defense ceased abruptly—the attorneys became bitter foes during the trial and some retained this bitterness after the close of their cases. It is this adversary method of trial procedure which has brought Anglo-Saxon justice to a point of great respect, by bringing out all of the facts, efficiently and vividly, for the determination of a court or jury.

When a man takes the oath of office as a judge of a court of record, or of a higher court, a strange mutation occurs. With but few exceptions, the role of adversary is forgotten; former friendships, alliances, and influences terminate. He weighs the facts, law, and arguments of counsel dispassionately—and each party can expect to receive, and almost without exception does receive, the honest judgment of the court. True, such judgment is of necessity affected by the background, education, personality, and experiences which go into the shaping of that judge's thought processes—his analysis may be governed by the mores of that stratum of society from which he comes. But, accepting the fact that all jurists are human beings with ordinary frailties and prejudices, the litigant may still expect, and does expect, to receive a result reached by fair, deliberate meditation. There are no mechanical devices contrived into which one may drop the facts upon each side of the case and have an automatic decision ejected. Perhaps that would not be desirable, when equities must be evaluated—when human beings are affected by the result.

Nor is this ability of jurists confined to the Anglo-Saxon nations. Strangely enough, it matters little whether a judge be selected from the United States, Spain, China, or Brazil. Moral men tend to think along parallel lines when confronted with the problem of justice, irrespective of race or nationality. Jurists of high caliber who hold the principles of justice dear are even more similar in their reactions. Given a certain set of facts creating an international controversy, they are almost without exception able to disregard the identities of the nations concerned, national self-interest, and render a decision which is legally accurate and equitably just. That capacity is well demonstrated by an examination of the decisions rendered by the Permanent Court of International Justice. To a large degree, it is also demonstrated by a reading of the record of the subsequent Nuremberg trials where jurists from many different states and with very diversified backgrounds presided.

For a court to operate with efficiency, however, it is necessary that it have more than the capacity to render competent decisions. This is particularly true when controversies of an international character are involved, and the issues are such as could easily lead to war. Political bodies have likewise been hampered in this regard. The League of Nations, founded for a noble purpose, accomplished much but was hampered greatly by lack of power and by coalitions along political lines. The so-called World Court was hampered primarily by one thing —a lack of cases to adjudicate. Each case brought to its attention, either for advisory opinion or decision, was of great importance, frequently involving some controversy which could easily have been used as an excuse for hostilities. Its decisions were learned and dispassionate, settling the disputed issue with no loss of dignity to the parties and leaving no need for a recourse to arms. Boundary lines were settled, citizenship questions determined, water rights adjusted, decisions as to reparations were accepted by the contesting parties. More and more treaties came to provide for construction or settlement by the court. But, since jurisdiction was not compulsory in the great majority of instances, the volume of litigation tended to dwindle rather than to increase.

The present court is, to all intents and purposes, the same as that preceding it, and should operate with equal efficiency, but the questions arising are, first, how can nations be compelled to submit problems for judicial determination instead of resorting to arms, and second, how can a decision of such a court be enforced? If these problems could be answered satisfactorily, world peace would not be too distant.

Let us look at our own nation to see how we proceed in cases of controversy. If parties have a legal controversy which it is necessary to settle, one party may sue the other before some detrimental action has occurred and secure what is called a "declaratory judgment," fixing the rights and liabilities of each party. If Smith burns down Jones' house, he will be prosecuted by the State for arson, and Jones can recover damages from Smith in a civil suit. The court, if it finds Smith guilty of the crime, may fine him and put him in the penitentiary. If Jones recovers a civil verdict, he can levy on Smith's bank account, house, car, furniture, and other assets to collect his damages. In other words, our courts not only give opinions as to what should be done, but actually punish the transgressor and see that redress is awarded.

If Brown, standing in the court room, threatens the judge or another with a gun, the court's bailiff may knock him down. If a witness refuses to appear when subpoenaed, or a man refuses to pay alimony awarded his wife, the court may sentence him to jail and have its officers physically place him behind the bars. If a serious riot rages, and the parties refuse to desist under an order of court at a time when the court's officers are insufficient to stop the disorder, the court may request the governor to send in troops to restore order. In other words, while our courts may render a decision declaratory of the rights of parties before any wrong has occurred, or render an opinion or judgment after one has suffered injury, it may go further and physically enforce its decrees.

If two states in this nation have a dispute over boundary lines, diversion of water, or other problems, they do not resort to force for settlement of their differences. The controversy is heard and determined by our Supreme Court. When Canada felt that the City of Chicago was improperly wasting water in Lake Michigan and lowering the water level to Canada's detriment, it did not call out its troops. The matter was settled by legal means. Arbitration, determination by special commissions, and judicial decision are the peaceable methods of settling international as well as private controversies, which all too many statesmen and political figures have forgotten. War solves no problems. It does not determine who is the wronged and who is the wrongdoer. It determines only who is the better prepared, the more powerful—and this may be the culprit rather than the victim.

The International Court has no bailiffs under its control to enforce its decrees. It has, first, public opinion, which means little to persons of totalitarian impulses. It, or the wronged nation, has, second, the right to appeal to the Security Council of the United Nations. But that body, in itself, splits into two pretty distinct groups—one headed by the United States and Great Britain with their camp followers, the other headed by Russia with its satellites. Any decision to enforce a decree by force against a nation would split along those lines. In addition, the Security Council itself has no world police force it could dispatch against the offender. The member nations desiring to enforce the decree would themselves, as individual states, or cooperatively, have to resort to economic pressure or to war against the wrongdoer, as has been done in the Korean affair.

Thus, by comparison with our national courts, we find something gravely lacking in the International Court. It has personnel, judicial experience, and integrity. But it cannot force parties to resort to its processes nor can it directly enforce its decrees. It is a mastiff chained in a very small yard, powerless to stop the burglar invading the house next door—an efficient dog with a resounding bark but a very small bite.

These are the problems. If we can, through the United Nations organization or treaties, compel universal agreement between nations to submit their differences to the International Court for judicial decision, one marked step toward peace would have been taken. Our mastiff will then no longer be chained in a single yard. If we can, as well, fit him with excellent teeth, the day of marauders will come to an end, except for the occasional lawbreaker, as in our own society, who is punished for his misdeeds. But organized violence, the violence of large nations, the grandiose plans for aggression, the maintenance of huge military establishments can be made to collapse if there is no pretext for war, these problems being resolved by legal means.

If these problems are met and resolved squarely, we would not need to discuss the punishment of individuals. Without war, actions in violation of the Rules of Land Warfare and crimes against peace would not be committed. True, there still might be crimes against humanity. But if nations cannot modify their stiff-necked nationalism into a yoke of obedience to law, international in scope, what then can be done to mitigate offenses by individuals?

The post-war trials demonstrated the possibility of punishing persons for crimes incident to war committed against their own nationals and those of other lands. Would this fear of punishment deter others from like offenses? Possibly, but not likely. The small fry might be apprehensive, but they do not shape the policies for war. Those are determined by persons in power, whether we call them presidents, prime ministers, or dictators. The lust for power is usually greater than the fear of death. Thus, the fact that one might be punished if he loses would be no deterrent, as these persons do not undertake a war expecting to lose. We have already seen from the Nuremberg and other trials that victors are not punished. Any war criminals of this nation, Britain, Russia, and other lands have never been placed upon trial. All received absolution by being upon the side of the victors. But if a man can expect punishment even if he wins, then there might be some deterent effect. This premise might be carried a step further. There usually is no method in Anglo-Saxon law of punishing a man for crime prior to its commission, so we have made threats to kill and similar pre-crime acts offenses in themselves. If threats to wage war and the taking of steps toward aggression are now recognized international crimes, then we can conceivably hale the malefactors into a court prior to the outbreak of war and by their punishment prevent the commencement of hostilities.

It will be pointed out, of course, first, that this is visionary and impractical and that, second, there is no international court which could take cognizance of such crimes. As to the first objection, the suggestion is admittedly visionary. So, too, were the International Red Cross, the League of Nations, the United Nations organization, the Permanent Court of International Justice, and its present successor. Each step toward world cooperation is the visionary outgrowth of some idea which has been classified as impractical, but nations are constantly coming closer toward the ideal of world cooperation. It has been said also that nations will not surrender their leaders for trial, but in national law a family has no option as to the surrender of a son or brother to the law for trial. A nation will probably surrender a leader for trial and submit to a judgment of court as readily as it will agree to submit its international controversies to a tribunal and to abide by its determination. Its independence is no more sacred in the one instance than in the other. But, securing any such submission to international judicial authority will take time. It cannot be done this year or next. The machinery must be created, steps taken in the right direction, and gradually over periods of years and decades, the new will cease to be new, and such practices will be established and accepted as a part of international conduct.

The second objection is the lack of machinery—the absence of an international court of criminal justice. Proposals have been made in this direction at intervals over the last thirty years. It was embarrassing to decide to try war criminals at Nuremberg and then be required to create a new court for this purpose, lacking all other judicial machinery. If the Nuremberg and like trials served any valid purpose, that purpose should be perpetuated by the creation of a permanent Tribunal—one preferably constituted of neutrals, with the judges of the interested nations disqualified from service—where victor may charge the vanquished with violations of international law, but where the vanquished may likewise bring charges against the victor. Whether such a court would be called upon to act this year or next would be immaterial. If the Tribunal is in existence with qualified personnel, established rules of procedure, and the ability to proceed as an accepted reality, then it will be ready to act when any charge is filed and evidence offered, and to create such auxiliary tribunals as may be necessary in an emergency. Then, no nation could be accused of creating a Tribunal to administer its individual whims and desires. It will be a court of all nations, a truly international court for administering questions of penal responsibility as distinguished from the contractual and tortious matters handled by the International Court. Individuals would no longer be able to require their nation, as an entity, to answer for their personal misdeeds —but, having violated rules recognized by the present or future laws of international society, would be subject to personal punishment.

The Commission established after the First World War had recommended the establishment of a penal tribunal, but without specifying the nature of its composition.[1] A draft statute was prepared by the International Law Association in 1927,[2] suggesting definite provisions. Professor Pella drafted a detailed plan subsequently adopted by the International Association for Penal Law at Paris in 1928, and which plan was revised by Professor Pella in 1946.[3] In 1937 a Convention was actually signed for the establishment of such a court by nations participating in the League of Nations, but the convention was never brought into force.[4] The London National Assembly, June 21, 1943, concluded that an International Criminal Court should be created, and a draft convention was prepared for this purpose.[5] And a draft convention was submitted by the United Nations War Crimes Commission upon September 30, 1944, for the establishment of a United Nations War Crimes Court.

This indicates that interest in the proposition of an International Criminal Court with broad powers has not been lacking and is constantly growing more intense. Other steps have also

1 United Nations, A/CN.4/7/Rev. 1, pp. 47-52.

2 International Law Association, 34th Report, Vienna, 1927, pp. 113-125.

3 Pella, La Guerre-Crime et les Criminels de Guerre, Geneva, 1946, p. 129.

4 United Nations, A/CN.4/7/Rev. 1, pp. 3, 4, 88-97.

5 United Nations A/CN.4/7/Rev. 1, pp. 97-112.

been taken to codify certain principles which would form a jurisdictional basis for the principles to be enforced by such court. Upon December 11, 1946, the General Assembly of the United Nations created a Committee on the Progressive Development of International Law and Its Codification, with one of its tasks that of the codification of the Nuremberg principles.[6] Although strictly speaking, it was outside of the scope of the Committee's responsibility, it adopted a French recommendation to report to the Assembly that an International Criminal Court should be established.[7] This recommendation was over the specific opposition of Great Britain, Egypt, the U.S.S.R., Poland, Yugoslavia, and, in part, the United States. The Yugoslavian representative stated that the creation of a criminal chamber would violate the statute of the International Court, which provided that only states could be parties to any proceeding. However, despite varied objections, the majority of the Committee supported the French view and so reported to the Assembly.[8]

The General Assembly thereupon, by resolution, took two successive steps. It referred the work of codifying the Nuremberg principles to the International Law Commission elected by the Assembly.[9] The Secretary General submitted a memorandum prepared pursuant to earlier Resolution 175 (II) to the members of that body, containing a survey of the international proceedings and the deliberations concerning those principles in the United Nations.[10] As a result of later discussions in the Assembly concerning genocide, the General Assembly then took the final step (by a vote of 43 to 6, with 3 abstentions) of referring to the International Law Commission the question of international criminal jurisdiction.[11] General Assembly Resolution 260 (III) B is somewhat broader than the general concept of genocide and requests the study of the "desirability and possibility of establishing an international jurisdictional organization for the trial of persons charged with genocide *or other crimes* over which jurisdiction will be conferred upon that organization by international conventions," and referred specifically to the "possibility of establishing a criminal chamber of the International Court of Justice." (Italics author's.)

It will be observed that this is not as sweeping a direction as should be made, since it refers to matters "over which jurisdiction will be conferred . . . . by international conventions,"

6 Resolution 94 I.
7 United Nations, A/CN.4/7/Rev. 1, p. 25 *et seq.*
8 United Nations, A/CN.4/7/Rev. 1, pp. 29, 30.
9 Resolution 177 (II), Nov. 21, 1947.
10 United Nations, A/CN.4/5.
11 United Nations, A/PV. 179, pp. 56-60, 68-70, 71.

not referring either to customary law or to conventions of past years. It is not believed by this author that the Commission will limit its conclusions or recommendations so narrowly. If it does, it will be a simple matter to extend and to expand such jurisdiction in the future. A start will at least have been made in the right direction.[11A]

The International Law Commission has not been idle upon the tasks assigned to it. A report of the principles embraced at Nuremberg has now been made and accepted as of December 12, 1950, which includes the following:

> "Any person who commits or is an accomplice in the commission of an act which constitutes a crime under international law is responsible therefor and liable to punishment.
>
> "The fact that domestic law does not punish an act which is an international crime does not free the perpetrator of such crime from responsibility under international law.
>
> "The fact that a person who committed an international crime acted as Head of State or public official does not free him from responsibility under international law or mitigate punishment.
>
> "The fact that a person acted pursuant to order of his Government or of a superior does not free him from responsibility under international law. It may, however, be considered in mitigation of punishment, if justice so requires.
>
> "Any person charged with a crime under international law has the right to a fair trial on the facts and law.
>
> "Crimes against peace: (i) Planning, preparation, initiation or waging of a war of aggression, or a war in violation of international treaties, agreements or assurances; (ii) Participation in a common plan or conspiracy for the accomplishment of any of the acts mentioned under (i).
>
> "War Crimes: namely violations of the laws or customs of war. Such violations shall include, but not be limited to murder, ill-treatment or deportation to slave labour or for any other purpose of civilian population of or in occupied territory, murder or ill-treatment of prisoners of war or persons on the seas, killing of hostages, plunder of public or private property, wanton destruction of cities, towns or villages, or devastation not justified by military necessity.
>
> "Crimes against humanity: namely murder, extermination, enslavement, deportation and other inhuman acts done against a civilian population, or persecutions on political,

[11A] Since the above comment was originally written, very definite progress has been made. See, for example, the very comprehensive report of the committee on International Criminal Jurisdiction to the General Assembly in August, 1951, including a draft statute for this purpose. United Nations, A/AC. 48/4, Sept. 5, 1951. See also further deliberations of the legal committee which are found largely under later documents classified under the heading of A/C. 6/——.

racial or religious grounds, when such acts are done or such persecutions are carried on in execution of or in connection with any crime against peace or any war crime."[12]

A Universal Declaration on Human Rights was passed and proclaimed by the General Assembly of the United Nations upon December 10, 1948.[13] It embodies fundamentally the principles contained in our Bill of Rights. Prior to that time, upon December 11, 1946, the Assembly requested the Economic and Social Council to prepare a draft convention on genocide.[14] This organization upon March 28, 1947, passed this responsibility over to the Secretary General. The Secretary General undertook this study, such a convention was prepared, various discussions and transmittals followed,[16] and the resulting Convention on the Prevention and Punishment of the Crime of Genocide[17] was unanimously approved by the General Assembly on December 9, 1948.[18] Requiring the ratification of twenty member Nations to become effective, it came into force as between the ratifying or acceding nations upon January 12, 1951. A total of 31 governments had recognized it by November 12, 1951, but, as yet, not the United States.

These treaties have met with determined objection from lawyers in this country in their present form.[19] These objections are principally of two opposing types: (1) The conventions are too broad; (2) They are not broad enough. To understand how these objections can be levelled simultaneously, it is necessary to consider some of the language in these instruments. If adopted, it has been said that they will become part of the organic law of the United States upon an equal basis with the Constitution and paramount to state constitutions and state legislation.[20] Naturally, then, lawyers are as cautious about imposing new treaty obligations as they would be to add new provisions to our Federal Constitution. The provisions are sufficiently general in character to be construable as referring

---

[12] 36 American Bar Association Journal, pp. 505-507; United Nations, Doc. A/1706, Dec. 13, 1950; Committee Report in the Official Records of the General Assembly, Fifth Session, Supp. No. 12.

[13] Doc. A/810 (Third Session of General Assembly); U. N. Pubs., Sales No. 1949. I. 3.

[14] Resolution 96 (I).

[15] Resolution 47 (IV).

[16] United Nations, A/CN.4/6/Rev. 1, pp. 30-32.

[17] See particularly, United Nations Doc. No. ST/DPI/SER.A/68, Nov. 12, 1951.

[18] Resolution 260 III.

[19] See Report of Special Committee on Peace and Law through United Nations, American Bar Association, Sept. 1, 1949; Carlston, The Genocide Convention, 36 American Bar Association Journal, pp. 206 *et seq.*

[20] Constitution of the United States, Article VI, Section 1.

to prejudiced news articles or radio addresses, employment practices, and other acts pertaining to civil liberties which are now in general deemed to be a part of our right of liberty, free speech, and free control of property. The term "genocide" literally means "killing of a type or race." Broadly construed, it could mean suppression, oppression, segregation, or discrimination of any type. While few would contend that the right of free speech implies the right to incite others to kill, they do maintain that a democracy implies the right to think and act as one will in non-violent ways, to hire and fire whom he will, to hold biases and prejudices, to tell Jewish and Irish stories, or to refuse to sit next to a negro. Whether these be admirable traits or not, it seems that in a democracy a native Indian should have the right to look down upon pale-faces as newcomers and to bar them from attending tribal dances, that negroes should have the right to refuse to admit whites to their organizations, or to bar them from attendance at social functions; that one should have the right to be gregarious or a snob, as he will, a philosopher or a fool. The first question is, then, to define "genocide" precisely.

This considers primarily the sweeping terminology employed by the Convention. On the other hand, the Convention fails to extend to its proper scope in other respects. It seems to require proof of a specific intent in order to establish guilt, which would often be difficult to establish. Of even greater importance is the fact that it excludes oppression of political and economic groups, thereby failing to check Russian subjection and elimination of opposing factions. Inclusion of such added provisions would prevent the United States from discriminating against or attempting to eradicate Communists; but if Russia were wholly prevented from discriminating against advocates of democracy in that country, then Communism elsewhere would hardly continue to be a menace. Again, if the only power to enforce such provisions against genocide is placed in the hands of the Security Council, use of the veto by Russia or any other nation in that body would render the Convention largely worthless.

It is apparent from these few comments that all international Conventions must be carefully studied, the terminology properly defined, and effective provisions adopted. To enforce such provisions effectively international machinery must be created in line with the suggestions advanced. If a proper International Criminal Court is created, with adequate machinery for the disposition of cases and the enforcement of its judgments, not only may conflicts be reduced and the rights of individuals protected, but many causes underlying conflicts between nations which would otherwise lead to war may be eliminated.

BIBLIOGRAPHY

Allen, "Human Rights and the International Court," 35 *American Bar Association Journal,* 713-716, Sept., 1949.

Allen, "Nuremberg Trial Implements World Law," 34 *Women Lawyers Journal,* 6-8, 26-28 (1948).

Alexander, *Justice at Nuremberg, a Pictorial Record of the Trials of Nazi War Criminals,* Marvel Press (1946).

American Bar Association, "Report of Special Committee on Peace and Law Through United Nations," Sept. 1, 1949.

April, "The Nuremberg War Crimes Trial—An Inquiry Into the Judicial Basis for," 30 *Minnesota Law Review,* 313-331 (1946).

Basu, "Tokio Trials," 3 *Indian Law Review* 25-30 (1949).

Baty & Morgan, *War, Its Conduct and Legal Results,* Dutton & Co. (1915).

Belgion, *Victors' Justice,* Regnery Co. (1949).

Bennett, "Notes on the German Legal and Penal System," 37 *Journal of Criminal Law and Criminology,* 368 *et seq.,* Jan.-Feb., 1947.

Bernays, "Nuremberg; Its Justification and Lessons" (Address), 62 *West Virginia Bar Association,* 68-83 (1946).

Bernstein, *Final Judgment, the Story of Nuremberg,* Boni & Geer (1947).

Bial, "The Nurnberg Judgment and International Law," 13 *Brooklyn Law Review,* 34-49 (1947).

Biddle, "The Nurnberg Trial," 33 *Virginia Law Review,* 679 *et seq.,* Nov. 1947.

Black Book of Poland, The, G. P. Putnam's Sons (1942).

Bogoslovsky, "The Nuremberg Trials" (Address), *New Jersey State Bar Association Year Book,* 72-85 (1946).

Bordwell, *The Law of War Between Belligerents,* Callaghan & Co. (1908).

Brand, "Crimes Against Humanity and the Nuernberg Trials," 28, 2 *Oregon Law Review* 93-119 (1949).

British War Blue Book, The, Farrar & Rinehart (1939).

Brunet, *La Garantie Internationale Des Droits de L'Homme,* Grasset (1947).

Bull, "Nurnberg Trial—Value to Civilization," (Address) 7 *Federal Rules Decisions* 175-182 (1947).

Calvacoressi, *Nuremberg, The Facts, The Law, And The Consequences,* MacMillan Co. (1948).

Caming, "Nuremberg Trial: Partisans, Hostages, and Reprisals," 4 *The Judge Advocate Journal* 16-22, January 1950.

Carlston, "The Genocide Convention," 36 *American Bar Association Journal* 206 *et seq.*, March 1950.

Carnegie Foundation, *International Law of the Future,* 1944.

Chicago Tribune, "Letters to the Editor," Feb. 15, 1948.

Clay, "Decision in Germany," excerpt in *New York Herald Tribune,* page 1, Jan. 24, 1950.

Commission on the Responsibility of the Authors of the War and on Enforcement of Penalties, "Report," 14 *American Journal of International Law* 95 *et seq.* (1920).

Constitution of the United States, Article I, Sec. 8.

Cowles, "Trial of War Criminals by Military Tribunals," 30 *American Bar Association Journal* 330-333, 362 (1944).

Cowles, "Trials of War Criminals (Non-Nuremberg)," 42 *American Journal of International Law* 299 *et seq.*, April, 1948.

Cowles, "Universality of Jurisdiction Over War Crimes," 33 *California Law Review* 177 *et seq.*, April 1949.

Creel, *War Criminals and Punishment,* Robert McBride Co. (1944).

Dantricourt, "Crimes Against Humanity—European Views on Its Conception and Its Future," 40 *Journal of Criminal Law* 170-175, July-Aug. 1949.

Department of the Army, *Compilation of Statistics on U. S. War Crimes Programs as of 1 October 1949.*

Department of the Army, *List of Defense Counsel, List of Prosecution Staff, Statistics of Nuremberg Trials, Lists of defendants, Cumulative Records of Nuremberg Trials.*

Department of State, *International Conference on Military Trials,* London (1945) Publication 2783, *Occupation of Germany, Policy & Progress,* U. S. Govt. Printing Office (1945-1946).

Department of State Publication 2420, *Trial of War Criminals,* U. S. Govt. Printing Office (1945).

"Draft First International Covenant on Human Rights," 36 *American Bar Association Journal* 579, July 1950.

Dulles, "International Law & Individuals—a Comment on Enforcing Peace," 35 *American Bar Association Journal* 912 *et seq.*, Nov. 1949.

Ehard, "The Nuremberg Trial Against the Major War Criminals and International Law," 43 *American Journal of International Law* 223 *et seq.*, April 1949.

Fairman, "Some New Problems of the Constitution Following the Flag," 1 *Stanford Law Review* 587, June 1949.

Feller, "Tribunal of the Nations," *The Rotarian,* p. 20, Aug. 1950.

Ferencz, "Nuremberg Trial Procedure and the Rights of the Accused," 39 *Journal of Criminal Law and Criminology* 144-151, Northwestern University (1948).

Finch, "Genocide Convention" 43 *American Journal of International Law* 732-738, Oct. 1949.

Finch, "The Nuremberg Trial and International Law," 41 *American Journal of International Law* 20 *et seq.*, Jan. 1947.

Finch, "The Nuremberg Trials—Significance" (Address), 71 *Report of American Bar Association* 22-28 (1946).

Forbes, "Legal Aspects of the Trial Major War Criminals at Nuremberg" (Address), 24 *Canadian Bar Review,* 584-599.

Franklin, "Sources of International Law Relating to Sanctions Against War Criminals," 36 *Journal of Criminal Law and Criminology* 153-179 (1945).

Fratcher, "American Organization for Prosecution of German War Criminals," 13 *Missouri Law Review* 45-75 (1948).

Freeman, "War Crimes by Enemy Nationals Administering Justice in Occupied Territory," 41 *American Journal of International Law* 579 *et seq.*, July 1947.

French Yellow Book, The, Reynal & Hitchcock (1940).

Garner, *International Law and the World War,* Longman, Green & Co., I and II (1920).

Garner, "Punishment of Offenders Against the Laws and Customs of War," 14 *American Journal of International Law* 70 *et seq.* (1920).

Gault, "Prosecution of War Criminals," 37 *Journal of Criminal Law and Criminology* 180-183 (1945).

Gilbert, *Nuremberg Diary,* Farrar and Straus (1947).

Glueck, "By What Tribunal Shall War Offenders Be Tried?", 24 *Nebraska Law Review* 143-181 (1945).

Glueck, "The Nuremberg Trial and Aggressive War," 59 *Harvard Law Review* 396-456 (1946).

Glueck, *The Nuremberg Trial and Aggressive War,* Knopf & Son (1946).

Glueck, *War Criminals—Their Prosecution and Punishment,* Knopf & Son (1944).

Glueck, "War Criminals—Their Prosecution and Punishment—The Record and History," 5 *Law Guild Review* 1-10 (1945).

Goodhart, "Nuremberg Trials—the Legality of," 58 *Judicial Review* 1-19 (1946).

Goodhart, "Questions and Answers Concerning the Nuremberg Trials," 1 *International Quarterly* 525-531 (1947).

Green, "The Military Commission," 42 *American Journal of International Law*, 832 *et seq.*, Oct. 1948.

Gregory, *"The Nuremberg Trial,"* 21 *Connecticut Bar Journal* 2-20 (1947).

Gregory, "The Nuremberg Trial" (Address), 1946 *Wisconsin State Bar Association* 94-109 (1946).

Hale, "Nurenberg War Crimes Tribunals," 21 *Tennessee Law Review* 8-19, Dec. 1949.

Harris, "The Nuremberg Trial," 22 *State Bar Journal of California* 97-117, 120-121 (1947).

Heiden, *Readers Digest,* Sept. 1949—"Why They Confess" (condensed from *Life,* June 20, 1949), p. 22 *et seq.*

Herbert, "Nurnberg Subsequent Trials," 16 *Insurance Counsel Journal* 226-232, July 1949.

Hobbs, "Nurnberg's Indecent Burial," 169 *Nation* 534-535, Dec. 3, 1949.

Holborn, *War & Peace Aims of the United Nations,* World Peace Foundation (1948).

Holland, *The Laws and Customs of War on Land,* Clarendon Press (1908).

Hubbert, "Nuremberg—Justice or Vengeance?", *Military Government Journal,* pp. 11-14, March 1948, The Military Government Association., Washington, D. C.

Hudson, *Permanent Court of International Justice,* 1920-1942.

"International Human Rights—A symposium," 14 *Law & Con. Problems* 411-536, 545-646, Summer-Autumn 1949.

International Military Tribunal for the Far East, *Trial of Japanese War Criminals,* Transcript and Documents.

International Military Tribunal, Nuremberg, *Trial of the Major War Criminals, Proceedings,* I-XLII.

Ireland, "Ex Post Facto from Rome to Tokyo," 21 *Temple Law Quarterly* 27 *et seq.,* July 1947.

Jackson, "International Conference on Military Trials," State Dept. Publication 3080 (1949), Government Printing Office.

Jackson, "Nuremberg in Retrospect," 35 *American Bar Association Journal* 813 *et seq.,* Oct. 1949.

Jackson, "Memorandum for the President on American Participation in Further International Trials of Nazi War Criminals."

Jackson, "Nuremberg Trial of the Major Nazi Leaders" (Address) 70 *New York State Bar Association Bulletin* 147-158 (1947).

Jackson, *The Case Against the Nazi War Criminals,* Knopf (1946).

Jackson, "War & War Crimes Trials" (Address & Recording delivered to U. S. Naval officials).

Jaffe, "Natural Law and the Nurnberg Trials," 26 *Nebraska Law Review* 90-95 (1946).

Jaspers, "Significance of the Nurnberg Trials for Germany and the World." Translated from the German by William B. Ball, *Notre Dame Law* 150-160 (1947).

"Judgment of the International Military Tribunal Against Major Nazi War Criminals and Criminal Organizations," 22 *Philippine Law Journal* 175-204 (1947).

Keenan, "Observations & Lessons from International Criminal Trials," 17 *University of Kansas City Law Review* 117-128, Apr.-June 1949.

Kelley, 22 *Cells in Nuremberg; A Psychiatrist Examines the Nazi Criminals,* Greenberg & Co. (1947).

Kelsen, *Peace Through Law,* University of North Carolina (1944).

Kelsen, "Punishment of War Criminals—Collective and Individual Responsibility in International Law with Particular Regard To," 31 *California Law Review* 530-571 (1943).

Kelsen, "The Draft Declaration on Rights & Duties of States," 44 *American Journal of International Law* (No. 2) 259-276, April 1950.

Kelsen, "Will the Judgment in the Nuremberg Trial Constitute a Precedent in International Law?", I *International Law Quarterly* 153 *et seq.,* Summer 1947.

Kuhn, "International Criminal Jurisdiction" (Editorial comment), 41 *American Journal of International Law* 430-433 (1947).

Kuntz, "United Nations Convention on Genocide," 43 *American Journal of International Law* 738-746, Oct. 1949.

Lachs, *War Crimes, an Attempt to Define the Issues,* Stevens & Sons (1945).

LaFollette, "Justice Case at Nuremberg," 138-139 *OMGUS Information Bulletin* (1948).

Lauer, "International War Criminal Trials (Nuremberg) and the Common Law of War," 20 *St. John's Law Review* 18-24 (1945).

Letters and correspondence with Telford Taylor, Rawlings Ragland, Robert H. Jackson, Edward H. Young, and others.

Letters and documents from Ellis, Hayett, Senator Baldwin, and others.

Leventhal and others, "The Nuremberg Verdict," 60 *Harvard Law Review* 857 *et seq.,* July 1947.

Lipstein, "The Doctrine of Precedent in Continental Law with Special Reference to French and German Law," 28 *Journal of Society of Comparative Legislation* (3rd Series) 34 *et seq.*, Nov. 1946.

Lowenstein, "Law and the Legislative Process in Germany," 57 *Yale Law Journal* 724 *et seq.* (1947).

Lund, "Legal Procedure at the Nuremberg Trials," 16 *Fortnightly Law Journal* 41-43 (1946).

Marsh, "Some Aspects of the German Legal System under National Socialism," 62 *Law Quarterly Review* 366-374 Oct. 1946.

McConnell, "Trial of War Criminals at Nuremberg" (Address), 1 *Wyoming Law Journal* 3-12 (1946).

McNarney and others, Control Council Law No. 10, Berlin, Dec. 20, 1945.

Meltzer, "Nuremberg Trials, a Note on Some Aspects of the Nuremberg Debate," 14 *University of Chicago Law Review* 455-469 (1947).

Merignhac, *Les Lois et Coutumes de la Guerre sur Terre,* Chevalier-Marescq & Cie (1903).

Mignone, "After Nuremberg, Tokyo," 25 *Texas Law Review* 475 *et seq.*, May 1947.

Military Government, Germany, U. S. Zone, Ordinance No. 7, Oct. 18, 1946. Military Government, Germany, Ordinance No. 11, amending Ordinance No. 7, Feb. 17, 1947.

Miller, "War Crimes Trials at Yokohama," 15 *Brooklyn Law Review* 191-208. Apr. 1949; 20 *Oklahoma Bar Association Journal* 1212-1223, August 27, 1949.

Mitscherlich and Mielke, *Doctors of Infamy, the Story of the Nazi Medical Crimes,* H. Schuman (1949).

Morgenstern, "Asylum for War Criminals, Quislings, and Traitors," 25 *British Year Book International Law* 382-386 (1948).

Multer, "The Malmedy Case," Congressional Record 845702-30738.

Munro, "Trial of War Criminals, Plans for the," 95 *Law Journal* 5-7 (1945).

Myerson, *Germany's War Crimes and Punishment. The Problem of Individual and Collective Responsibility,* MacMillan (1949).

Nartatez, "Right of Military Occupant to Establish Courts in Occupied Territory," 24 *Philippine Law Journal* 182-185, June 1949.

Nazi Conspiracy and Aggression—8 Vols., 2 Supps., Government Printing Office (1947).

Neumann, "German Democracy 1950," *International Conciliation,* No. 461, May 1950, Carnegie Endowment.

Newspaper Reports on Malmedy Proceedings (including Detroit-Free Press, April 22, 1949).

Nubergall, *Final Report upon Disposition of Materials Used in Post-War Trials,* July 10, 1949, Neurnberg.

"Nuremberg Trials, The," 110 *Justice of the Peace* 464 (1946).

"Nuremberg Trials, The," 62 *Law Quarterly Review* 229-233 (1946).

"Nurnberg Trial Symposium," 19 *Temple Law Quarterly* 133-235, 371-389; 20 *Temple Law Quarterly* 85-107, 167-338 (1946).

O'Donnell, "How Many Germans Are Buying Democracy," *Saturday Evening Post,* Jan. 21, 1950, p. 28 *et seq.*

Parker, "The Nuremberg Trial" (Address), 30 *Journal of the American Judicature Society* 109-115 (1946).

Parker, "The Nuremberg Trial," 11 *Kentucky State Bar Journal* 157-165, 185 (1947).

Perlman, "Habeas Corpus and Extra-territoriality," 36 *American Bar Association Journal* 187, Mar. 1950.

Phleger, "The Nuremberg Trials" (Address), 1946 *State Bar Journal of California* 72-80.

Prevent World War III, Vols. 25 *et seq.,* Society for the Prevention of World War III, Inc.

Quentin-Baxter, "Task of the International Military Tribunal at Tokyo," 25 *New Zealand Law Journal* 133-138, June 7, 1949.

Radin, "International Crimes," 32 *Iowa Law Review* 33 *et seq.,* Nov. 1946.

Reel, *The Case of General Yamashita,* University of Chicago Press (1949).

Renault, "De l' Application du Droit Penal aux fait de Guerre," 25 *Revue Generale de Droit International Publique* 22 *et seq.* (1917).

Reuter, "Nurnberg 1946—the Trial," 23 *Notre Dame Law* 76-97 (1947).

Rheinstein, "The Legal Status of Occupied Germany," 47 *Michigan Law Review* 23 *et seq.,* Nov. 1948.

Richman, "Highlights of the Nuremberg Trials," 7 *Federal Rules Decisions* 581-584 (1948).

Rix, "Genocide Convention and the U. S. Constitution," 16 *Living Speeches* 369-372, Apr. 1, 1950.

Rix, "Human Rights and International Law; Effect of the Covenant under our Constitution," 35 *American Bar Association Journal* 551-554, 618-620, July 1949.

Schick, "Crimes Against Peace," 38 *Journal of Criminal Law and Criminology* 445 *et seq.*, Jan.-Feb. 1948.

Schick, "International Criminal Law, Facts and Illusions," II *Modern Law Review* 290 *et seq.*, July 1948.

Schick, "The Nuremberg Trial and the International Law of the Future," 41 *American Journal of International Law* 770 *et seq.*, Oct. 1947.

Schulberg, "Nuernberg—Symbol of the People's Rights Against International Lawlessness," 164 *OMGUS Information Bulletin* 9-12, June 1949.

Schwarzenberger, "The Judgment of Nuremberg," 21 *Tulane Law Review* 329-361 (1947).

Sevenaer, *L'Occupation Allemande Pendant La Derniere Guerre Mondiale,* Martinius Nyhoff (1946).

Shawcross, Letter to Mr. Justice Jackson, July 25, 1946.

Simpson, Van Roden, Lawrence, *Survey of the Trials of War Crimes Held at Dachau.*

Smith, "The Nuremberg Trials," 32 *American Bar Association Journal* 390-396 (1946).

Snyder, "It's Not Law-War Guilt Trials," 38 *Kentucky Law Journal* 8-104, Nov. 1949.

Sohn, "American Redraft of the Covenant on Human Rights," 36 *American Bar Association Journal* 233, March 1950.

Spaight, *Air Power and War Rights,* 3rd Ed., Longman (1947).

Spiropoulos, "Report on the Nuremberg Principles," 36 *American Bar Association Journal* 505, June 1950.

Spurlock, "The Yokohama War Crimes Trial," 36 *American Bar Association Journal* 387, May 1950.

Stephens, "The Nuremberg Trial, Aspect of," 8 *Georgia Bar Journal* 375-383; 9 *Georgia Bar Journal* 57-65 (1946).

Stimson, "The Nuremberg Trial: Landmark in Law," *Foreign Affairs Quarterly* (1947).

Storey, "The Nuremberg Trials" (Address), 19 *Tennessee Law Review* 517-525 (1946).

Sutton, "The Trial of Tojo," 36 *American Bar Association Journal* 93, Feb. 1950.

Swearingen, "Nuremberg War Crimes Trials," 12 *Kentucky State Bar Journal* 11-20 (1947).

Szilard, "My Trial as a War Criminal," 17 *University of Chicago Law Review* 79-86, Autumn 1949.

Tatge, "The Nuremberg Trials 'Victors' Justice?' ", *American Bar Association Journal* 247-248, March 1950.

Taylor, *Final Report to the Secretary of the Army,* U. S. Govt. Printing Office, Aug. 15, 1949.

Taylor, Memorandum for Mr. Benjamin Cohen, June 18, 1946.

Taylor, Memorandum for Mr. Justice Jackson, June 27, 1946.

Taylor, "Nuremberg Trials—Synthesis and Projection," 162 *OMGUS Information Bulletin* 3, 6, 21-24 (1949).

Taylor, "The Nuremberg Trials," 450 *International Conciliation* 262 *et seq.*, April 1949.

Taylor, "The Nuremberg War Trials; An Appraisal," 23 *Proceedings of the Academy of Political Science* 239 *et seq.*, May 1949.

"Trial of Japanese War Criminals," 20 *U. S. Dept. State Bulletin* 596-571, May 1, 1949.

Truman, Executive Order No. 9547, May 2, 1945.

Truman, Executive Order No. 9679.

Tushins, "Notes on International Law, the Nuremberg Trial of World War II Criminals," 12 *Law Society Journal* 321-326 (1946).

"United Nations Convention on Genocide," III *International Organization* 206-209, Feb. 1949.

United Nations, *Historical Survey of the Question of International Criminal Jurisdiction,* Document A/CN.4/7/Rev. (1949).

United Nations Organization Information Office, *Punishment for War Crimes* (1943).

United Nations, *Report of the International Law Commission,* A/CN.4/5.

United Nations War Crimes Commission, *History of the United Nations War Crimes Commission & the Development of the Laws of War,* His Majesty's Stationery Office, London (1948). (Contains an extensive bibliography on war crimes at pp. 557-573).

United Nations War Crimes Commission, *Law Reports of Trials of War Criminals,* His Majesty's Stationery Office, London (10 vols.) (1947-1949).

United States Senate Malmedy Massacre Investigation, *Hearings Before a Subcommittee of the Committee on Armed Forces,* 2 Vols., Government Printing Office (1949).

United States Senate Malmedy Massacre Investigation, *Report of a Subcommittee of the Committee on Armed Forces,* I Vol., Government Printing Office (1949).

United States v. Hans Altfuldisch and others (Mauthausen Concentration Case), Dachau, Mar. 29-May 13, 1946, Transcript of Proceedings.

United States v. Josef Altstoetter et al., Nuremberg Subsequent Proceedings, Case No. 3, Transcript of Proceedings.

United States v. Karl Brandt et al., Nuremberg Subsequent Proceedings, Case No. 1, Transcript of Proceedings.

United States v. Friedrich Flick et al., Nuremberg Subsequent Proceedings, Case No. 5, Transcript of Proceedings.

United States v. Kurt Goebbel and others (Borkum Island Case), Official Transcript.

United States v. Ulrich Greifelt et al., Nuremberg Subsequent Proceedings, Case No. 8, Transcript of Proceedings.

United States v. Alphonse Klein and 6 others (Hadamar Case), Dachau, Oct. 8-15, 1945, Official Transcript.

United States v. Carl Krauch et al., Nuremberg Subsequent Proceedings, Case No. 6, Transcript of Proceedings.

United States v. Alfried Krupp von Bohlen und Halbach et al., Nuremberg Subsequent Proceedings, Case No. 10, Transcript of Proceedings.

United States v. Wilhelm von Leeb et al., Nuremberg Subsequent Proceedings, Case No. 12, Transcript of Proceedings.

United States v. Wilhelm List et al., Nuremberg Subsequent Proceedings, Case No. 7, Transcript of Proceedings.

United States v. Erhard Milch, Nuremberg Subsequent Proceedings, Case No. 2, Transcript of Proceedings.

United States v. Nichizawa and 6 others, Yokohama, Transcript of Proceedings.

United States v. Otto Ohlendorf et al., Nuremberg Subsequent Proceedings, Case No. 9, Transcript of Proceedings.

United States v. Oswald Pohl et al., Nuremberg Subsequent Proceedings, Case No. 4, Transcript of Proceedings.

United States v. Jurgen Stroop and 21 others, Dachau, Jan. 10-Mar. 2, 1947, Official Transcript.

United States v. Josias Prince Zu Waldeck et al., Transcript of Proceedings.

United States v. Ernst Weizaecker et al., Nuremberg Subsequent Proceedings, Case No. 11, Transcript of Proceedings.

United States v. Tomoyuki Yamashita, Manila, Oct. 8-Dec. 7, 1945, Transcript of Proceedings.

"Universal Declaration on Human Rights," III *International Organization* 202-206, Feb. 1949.

Walkinshaw, "The Nuremberg and Tokyo Trials: Another Step Toward International Justice," 35 *American Bar Association Journal* 299, 302, 362, 363 (1949).

War in Outline, The, The Infantry Journal (1939-1944).

Wechsler, "Issues of the Nuremberg Trial," 62 *Political Science Quarterly* 11-26 (1947).

Wolf, "The Trial at Nuremberg," 51 *Case and Comment* 23-26 (1946).

World Organization, American Council on Public Affairs, 1942.

Wright, *A Study of War,* University of Chicago Press, Vol. I.

Wright, "International Law & Guilt by Association," 43 *American Journal of International Law* 746-755, Oct. 1949.

Wright, "Killing of Hostages as a War Crime," 25 *British Year Book International Law* 296-310 (1948).

Wright, "Law of the Nuremberg Trial," 41 *American Journal of International Law* 38-72 (1947).

Wright, "The Nuremberg Trial," 37 *Journal of Criminal Law and Criminology* 477-478 (1947).

Zeck, "Nuremberg: Proceedings Subsequent to Goering et al.," 26 *North Carolina Law Review* 350-389 (1948).

INDEX

References are to pages.

A

References are to pages.

References are to pages.

References are to pages.

References are to pages.

References are to pages.

References are to pages.

References are to pages.

References are to pages.

References are to pages.

References are to pages.

References are to pages.

References are to pages.

References are to pages.

References are to pages.

References are to pages.

References are to pages.

References are to pages.

J

K

References are to pages.

References are to pages.

References are to pages.

References are to pages.

References are to pages.

References are to pages.

References are to pages.

References are to pages.

References are to pages.

References are to pages.

References are to pages.

References are to pages.

References are to pages.

References are to pages.

References are to pages.

References are to pages.

References are to pages.

W

References are to pages.